D0141512

Greg Richards, PhD
Editor

Cultural Tourism
Global and Local Perspectives

More pre-publication
REVIEWS, COMMENTARIES, EVALUATIONS . . .

"Through the case studies the ideas presented make the perspectives of the contributors readily accessible. As such, there is much here for students and practitioners to reflect upon through comparison of the different perspectives offered. The book is part of the emergent tradition of challenging the propensity of academics to demean tourists as passive and uncritical clones trying to escape their otherwise lived experiences."

Richard Prentice, BA, PhD
Professor of Heritage Interpretation
and Cultural Tourism,
University of Sunderland,
United Kingdom

"This book presents the latest installment in what has been the prime 'cultural tourism observatory' project over the past 15 years. The case studies are supported by survey data and useful signposts to more sustainable cultural tourism practice (and pitfalls), however the value of this book is its avoidance of the quantitative, quasi-scientific tendency to explain and compare tourism flows and impacts, but instead concentrating on the everyday and cultural exchanges which make up the cultural tourism experience. This latest addition to the cultural tourism canon will serve policymakers, planners, lecturers, and students of culture and tourism well, and provide practical insights to the cultural tourism phenomenon from geographical, social, and longitudinal perspectives."

Professor Graeme Evans, PhD, MA
Director, Cities Institute,
London Metropolitan University

"This book provides a sound review of some of the most salient issues facing cultural heritage tourism and its management in the contemporary world, including power, identity, and sustainability. It provides a balanced mix of empirical case studies and conceptual discourse on cultural heritage from both the developed and developing world perspectives and within urban and rural settings."

Dallen J. Timothy, PhD
Professor, School of Community
Resources and Development,
Arizona State University

"Greg Richards is the master of cultural tourism studies, the authority we all need to pay attention to. *Cultural Tourism: Global and Local Perspectives* contains enough solid material to thoroughly inform the student, stimulate the researcher and theorist, and positively assist the cultural tourism practitioner. A major strength of this book is the provision of research data from various ATLAS surveys, giving many of the chapters a solid research basis. Another is the multitude of specific examples and case studies to illustrate strategies as well as the challenges of cultural tourism development. Although nominally 'transnational' in scope, this edited compilation arises from an ATLAS project and is very Eurocentric. I was nevertheless impressed by the topical range of the contributions, which included several from South Africa."

Donald Getz, PhD
Professor, Haskayne School of Business,
University of Calgary, Calgary;
Author, *Event Management
and Event Tourism* (2005, second ed.)

Cultural Tourism
Global and Local Perspectives

Cultural Tourism
Global and Local Perspectives

Greg Richards, PhD
Editor

THHP

The Haworth Hospitality Press®
An Imprint of The Haworth Press, Inc.
New York • London • Oxford

For more information on this book or to order, visit
http://www.haworthpress.com/store/product.asp?sku=5749

or call 1-800-HAWORTH (800-429-6784) in the United States and Canada
or (607) 722-5857 outside the United States and Canada

or contact orders@HaworthPress.com

Published by

The Haworth Hospitality Press®, an imprint of The Haworth Press, Inc., 10 Alice Street, Binghamton, NY 13904-1580.

PUBLISHER'S NOTE
The development, preparation, and publication of this work has been undertaken with great care. However, the Publisher, employees, editors, and agents of The Haworth Press are not responsible for any errors contained herein or for consequences that may ensue from use of materials or information contained in this work. The Haworth Press is committed to the dissemination of ideas and information according to the highest standards of intellectual freedom and the free exchange of ideas. Statements made and opinions expressed in this publication do not necessarily reflect the views of the Publisher, Directors, management, or staff of The Haworth Press, Inc., or an endorsement by them.

Identities and circumstances of individuals discussed in this book have been changed to protect confidentiality.

Cover design by Jennifer M. Gaska.

Front cover photographs of Barcelona (Catalunya, Spain) by Greg Richards.

Library of Congress Cataloging-in-Publication Data

Cultural tourism : global and local perspectives / Greg Richards, editor.
    p. cm.
    Includes bibliographical references and index.
    ISBN-13: 978-0-7890-3116-7 (case : alk. paper)
    ISBN-10: 0-7890-3116-7 (case : alk. paper)
    ISBN-13: 978-0-7890-3117-4 (soft : alk. paper)
    ISBN-10: 0-7890-3117-5 (soft : alk. paper)
    1. Heritage tourism. I. Richards, Greg.

    G156.5.H47C855 2007
    338.4'791—dc22
                                                                            2006023764

DEDICATION

This book is dedicated to the memory of Eduard Delgado i Clavera (1949-2004), Director and founder of Interarts, without whom this project would not have been possible.

Eduard dedicated much of his life to the study and development of cultural policies, and in recent years he had become particularly interested in the effects of globalization and the developing relationship between culture and tourism. A graduate of Modern History and Anthropology from the London School of Economics and Political Science, he worked as a journalist for the BBC World Service before returning to his beloved Barcelona in 1980 to direct the cultural decentralization of the city, initiating a network of local community centers. He also created the Centre for Cultural Studies and Resources (CERC) and initiated the forum "Interacció," a meeting point for cultural officers from local authorities. His vision and innovative drive helped the development of many local cultural policies and gave rise to the organization of education and training modules for cultural management, the first of their kind in Spain.

Between 1992 and 1994, he worked at the Cultural Policies Division of the Council of Europe, researching and advising on cultural policymaking at European and international levels. In 1995 he established the Interarts Foundation as a European Observatory of Urban and Regional Cultural Policies, and became its director. The Interarts Foundation is a nonprofit body dedicated to applied research on cultural policies and to the promotion of international cultural cooperation. Among recent projects initiated by Eduard are a study on Cultural Cooperation in Europe for the European Commission in 2003, and the Congress on Cultural Rights and Human Development in the framework of the Universal Forum of Cultures 2004.

Eduard's vision of the international dimension of working in the cultural domain has been influential in the creation of some of the most important international cultural networks, such as CIRCLE (Cultural Information and Research Centres Liaison in Europe) and ENCATC (European Network of Cultural Administration Training

Centres); and he also became president of the Forum of European Cultural Networks. His dedication to cooperation also led him to work closely with ATLAS on a number of cultural tourism projects in recent years, including a European Union project on cultural events in Catalunya. His interest in the issue of cultural tourism was central to the staging of the ATLAS Expert Meeting "Cultural Tourism: Globalising the Local—Localising the Global" in October 2003. Unfortunately he was unable to attend the meeting in person, but the spirit of cooperation he engendered was a major factor in the success of the event. We hope that the publication of this book will help to carry on the debate that Eduard had such a large role in creating.

CONTENTS

PART II: CULTURAL TOURISM DEVELOPMENT
IN A GLOBALIZING WORLD

PART IV: CULTURAL EVENTS AND FESTIVALIZATION

ABOUT THE EDITOR

Greg Richards has over 20 years of experience in the fields of tourism education, research, and consultancy. As a partner in Tourism Research and Marketing (United Kingdom and Spain) he has directed numerous projects in the fields of tourism marketing, tourism development, cultural tourism, and special events. He is a European Executive Member of the Association for Tourism and Leisure Education (ATLAS) and has directed a number of ATLAS projects for the European Commission on topics including cultural tourism, crafts tourism, sustainable tourism, tourism education, and labor mobility in the tourism industry. His publications include *Cultural Tourism in Europe, Cultural Attractions and European Tourism, Tourism and Gastronomy,* and *The Global Nomad.* He is currently undertaking research on the creative industries and creative tourism.

Cultural Tourism: Global and Local Perspectives
© 2007 by The Haworth Press, Inc. All rights reserved.
doi:10.1300/5749_a

xiii

CONTRIBUTORS

María José del Barrio Tellado is Professor of Accounting at the University of Valladolid (Spain). Her research interests are linked to financial instruments and performance indicators for cultural institutions.

Ana Bedate Centeno is Professor of Statistics at the University of Valladolid (Spain). Her major research is associated with the economic valuation of cultural goods and heritage and the economy of museums.

Jenny Briedenhann is Project Leader for the Local Alchemy program, which is a new, bottom-up way of approaching local economic development in deprived communities, by building on the passions and energy that reside with local people. This project builds on her previous work in tourism development. Her research interests include cultural tourism; community-based tourism; tourism policy and planning; rural tourism; evaluation of tourism projects and programs; the public sector role in tourism development; and the impacts of tourism development.

Patricia de Camargo is Professor of Culture Tourism and Heritage with Unicenp/Brazil and ULPGC/Spain. She is a PhD student in the ULPGC Doctorate Program of Tourism and Sustainable Development and a Research Assistant on the EuroMed Heritage II Project, Mediterranean Voices. She is Vice President of the Superior Institute of Sustainable Tourism (ISTS/Brazil). Her major research interests include museums and tourism, education, and cross-cultural modelling in tourism marketing.

Miguel Cervantes Blanco is Professor of Marketing at the University of León and is the author of a number of papers and contributions to publications dealing with market research and marketing. He also advises commercial enterprises and institutions. His research interests include marketing, brands, and city marketing.

Cultural Tourism: Global and Local Perspectives
© 2007 by The Haworth Press, Inc. All rights reserved.
doi:10.1300/5749_b

María Devesa Fernández is Teaching Assistant of Applied Economics at the University of Valladolid (Spain). Her research is related to the economy of cultural festivals and economic impact studies.

Carlos Fernandes is Adjunct Professor in Tourism and Head of the Laboratory of Tourism at the Polytechnic Institute of Viana do Castelo in Portugal. He is also a PhD candidate in tourism at Bournemouth University (United Kingdom). His research interests include tourism as a strategy for rural development and heritage and cultural tourism.

Jaume Franquesa obtained his PhD in 2006 at the University of Barcelona with a study of the relationship between collective neighborhood action, the real estate market, and urban regeneration in the historic center of Palma de Mallorca. He has been a researcher in the Universitat de Barcelona and in the Universitat de les Illes Balears (Spain), where he took part in the EU-financed Mediterranean Voices Project on cultural heritage.

Ana González Fernández is Professor of Marketing at the University of León. She is the author of a number of papers and contributions to international and national publications specializing in marketing. She has worked on many international (FEDER, ATLAS) and national research projects. Her research interests include marketing, consumer behavior, market segmentation, and lifestyles.

Luis César Herrero Prieto is Senior Professor of Applied Economics at the University of Valladolid (Spain). His main research fields are cultural economics, heritage and economic development, and economy of museums.

Erik Hitters is Assistant Professor of Media and Cultural Industries at Erasmus University Rotterdam. He publishes on aspects of urban development, creative industries, (urban) cultural policy, and cultural participation. He is also Coordinator of the Erasmus Arts and Culture Research Centre.

Robert Maitland is Director of the Centre for Tourism at the University of Westminster. His research focuses on urban and cultural tourism in major cities, tourism policy, and regeneration. He has written extensively on these themes, and also advised several U.K. Government Departments and the National Audit Office.

Mauro R. Miranda Barreto is a PhD candidate in Marketing. His research areas include the behavior of aged consumers and cognitive age. He has made many contributions to the area of marketing and research on markets at the University of León.

Marc Morell, a social anthropologist and historian, is Researcher in the Policy, Work and Sustainability Research Group at the Universitat de les Illes Balears (Spain) and is the local coordinator of the Mediterranean Voices Project (EU) in Ciutat de Mallorca. He is currently writing his PhD thesis on the rebuilding of Sa Gerreria, a historic neighborhood in Ciutat de Mallorca.

Norberto Muñiz Martínez is Professor at the University of León, Spain, where he teaches and researches in the areas of distribution and marketing. In addition to his PhD from the University of León (cum laude, 1995) he also obtained an MSc in Transport and Distribution Management in the United Kingdom.

Xerardo Pereiro Pérez is an anthropologist at the University of Trás-os-Montes e Alto Douro in Portugal. He teaches cultural tourism and anthropology. His research interests include urban anthropology, museums, cultural heritage, and tourism in Galiza, Portugal and Kuna Yala (Panamá).

László Puczkó is Consultant (President of the Association of Tourism Consultants, Hungary) and Professor at Heller Farkas College (Budapest). His main areas of expertise are visitor management, health and heritage tourism, and themed attractions. He is a co-author of books on impacts of tourism, visitor management, and tourism management in historic cities.

Pranill Ramchander is Senior Lecturer in Tourism Development at the University of South Africa. He completed his PhD thesis, "Towards the Responsible Management of the Socio-Cultural Impact of Township Tourism," in 2004.

Tamara Rátz is Professor at the Tourism Department of the Kodolányi János University College, Hungary, and Visiting Lecturer at Häme Polytechnic, Finland. Her recent research interests include cultural tourism management and the socioeconomic aspects of tourism development.

Mª Carmen Rodríguez Santos is Assistant Professor at the University of León. Her research interests include consumer behavior, advertising, strategy, and brand image. She has worked on a number of research projects with ATLAS, and with the Castille and León Regional Government. She has contributed to numerous national and international publications and congresses.

José Ángel Sanz Lara is Professor of Statistics at the University of Valladolid (Spain). His principal research concerns the economic valuation of cultural goods and heritage as well as the economy of museums.

Frans Schouten is Associate Professor of Visitor Management at the NHTV International University, Breda, The Netherlands. He is interested in the relationship between tangible and intangible cultural heritage and tourism and is currently working on the process of authentication of souvenirs and researching the application of GIS in the monitoring of tourism development.

Melanie Smith is Senior Lecturer in Cultural Tourism Management at the University of Greenwich and a Visiting Lecturer in Budapest, Hungary. She is also Chair of ATLAS (Association for Tourism and Leisure Education). She is currently researching in the fields of cultural tourism, heritage management, urban regeneration, ethnic festivals, and holistic tourism.

Eugenia Wickens is Reader in Tourism at the Faculty of Leisure and Tourism, Buckinghamshire Chilterns University College, United Kingdom. She has a special interest in tourists' experiences and travel motivation. Eugenia has published extensively on cultural tourism, tourist typologies, tourism and health, and, more recently, on rural tourism development. Her current research is on understanding undergraduate students' learning experiences and student retention.

Preface

This book is one of the products of a transnational research project developed by the Association for Tourism and Leisure Education (ATLAS). The Cultural Tourism Research Project was initiated in 1991 and was the first major research initiative developed by ATLAS. The project was originally funded by the European Commission, but the network of researchers has gradually grown well beyond the original European focus.

At present there are eighty-five collaborators spread across thirty countries on five continents. Over the years, the members of the group have carried out cultural tourism surveys and other research activities, which have led to a wide range of publications (see www.atlas-euro.org for more details). However, apart from the initial meeting of the group, held in Germany in 1991, there have been very few occasions on which members of the group have been able to meet and discuss their research activities.

The expert meeting organized by ATLAS and Interarts in Barcelona in October 2003 was therefore a valuable opportunity to add an important reflective dimension to the largely quantitative research conducted up to that point. The meeting was attended by twenty-five members of the group, largely from Europe. The decision to discuss cultural tourism from a more global perspective was made in recognition of the expansion of the group as well as the increasing integration and convergence of issues in cultural tourism in different parts of the world. The chapters collected in the present volume are based largely on the contributions made to that meeting by members of ATLAS.

The activities of the group would not be possible without the unflagging support of a wide range of individuals and organizations, only a few of whom can be mentioned here. In particular we would like to recognize the contribution made by long-standing members of the group to the research program and its development, including Carlos Fernandes, Florence Ian, Brian King, David Leslie, Ian McDonnell, Frances McGettigan, Wil Munsters, Lazló Puczkó, Tamara Rátz, and Timo Toivonen. The 2004 research program has been managed by Célia Queirós, and Julie Wilson helped with the organization of the Barcelona event. As always, the activities of the cultural tourism group have been managed professionally by Leontine Onderwater from ATLAS headquarters in Arnhem.

Chapter 1

Introduction: Global Trends in Cultural Tourism

Greg Richards

Today, cultural tourism seems to be omnipresent, and in the eyes of many it also seems to have become omnipotent. It is the holy grail of quality tourism that cares for the culture it consumes while culturing the consumer. Cultural tourism has therefore been embraced globally by local, national, and transnational bodies. UNESCO promotes cultural tourism as a means of preserving world heritage, the European Commission supports cultural tourism as a major industry, and the newly emerging nation-states of Africa and Central Europe see it as a support for national identity. In many parts of the world it has become a vital means of economic support for traditional activities and local creativity.

The globalization of cultural tourism arguably coincides with a number of fundamental cultural and social changes, as well as changes in the structure of tourism itself. The culturization of society has led to more and more areas of consumption being viewed as "cultural." This has shifted the focus of cultural tourism away from the "shining prizes" of the European Grand Tour toward a broader range of heritage, popular culture, and living cultural attractions (Richards, 2001). The extension of education has democratized travel and cultural consumption, turning cultural tourism from an elite pursuit into a mass market. At the same time, growing competition in traditional tourism markets has caused a search for alternatives on the part of destinations worldwide.

Cultural Tourism: Global and Local Perspectives
© 2007 by The Haworth Press, Inc. All rights reserved.
doi:10.1300/5749_01

The tendency to alight on cultural tourism as the primary alternative for such a large number of different places in different regions of the world is mainly driven by supply-side logic. Cultural tourism is arguably a "good" form of tourism for the destination, which avoids many of the pitfalls of conventional tourism while offering additional benefits in the form of high-spending tourists who are keen to support culture (Richards, 2001). Cultural tourism is also available as a development option to all destinations, because all places have culture. As the demand for culture grows in society, there is also growing pressure on the public sector to support more and more cultural facilities. Tourism becomes one means of finding external sources of income to achieve this.

Growth in cultural tourism has also been stimulated by rising demand, although research indicates that cultural tourism is growing no faster than global tourism as a whole (de Haan, 1998). Rising education levels enable more people to access culture, while the effects of globalization create more interest in distant cultures as well as local heritage. Surveys in the United States, for example, indicate that 46 percent of domestic tourists visit cultural attractions (TIA, 2003).

Cultural tourism has therefore become a global common currency. In fact, as Richards (2001) has argued, it may have become such a common form of tourism that it is beginning to lose all meaning as a distinct category. Many argue, as the World Tourism Organization (1985:2) does in its "wide" definition of cultural tourism, that all tourism trips can be considered as cultural tourism, because they "satisfy the human need for diversity, tending to raise the cultural level of the individual and giving rise to new knowledge, experience, and encounters."

The problem is that as cultural tourism has expanded, so have the meanings attached to it. In the past, cultural tourism was largely associated with high culture and with "cultured" people. Today, cultural tourism includes many popular cultural attractions (McKercher et al., 2004), sport, living heritage, recent nostalgia, and the "everyday life" of "local" communities (Howie, 2000). The resources associated with cultural tourism have expanded from the largely fixed, tangible heritage of the past toward the mobile, intangible products of contemporary culture (Richards, 2000).

Many of these changes are linked to issues of globalization. If globalization is viewed in terms of an increasing integration of economic, social, and cultural systems, then tourism can be seen both as a cause and an effect of globalization processes. Tourism becomes one of the flows through which economic, social, and cultural exchange takes place, and the increasing scale of such exchanges in turn becomes a stimulus to tourism. Although studies of globalization have tended to concentrate on its economic aspects, there is increasing attention for "cultural globalization," which Nijman (1999:148) defines as "acceleration in the exchange of cultural symbols among people around the world, to such an extent that it leads to changes in local popular cultures and identities." This definition implies that changes in the global flows of culture will also impact on localities everywhere. At a global level, for example, cultural forms have become globalized and therefore accessible to tourists worldwide through the growth of personal mobility, the travel industry, the Internet, and the media. Not only do tourists travel to consume cultural resources in every corner of the globe, but those resources are themselves becoming more mobile, as art exhibitions embark on global tours, musicals are replicated on different continents, and the process of "McGuggenheimization" develops globally branded museums. Nijman further argues that this process is dependent on the global extension of a culture of consumption, and that economic globalization is therefore in many ways dependent on cultural globalization.

The fact that globalization has deep cultural consequences is also evident in the countervailing process of localization. Arguably, the processes of homogenization and disembedding that accompany globalization have stimulated localization, as local communities work to establish new identities and reclaim their heritage. In the tourist industry there has also been a growing realization that local identities and distinctiveness can also provide the basis for tourist products. For example, the *Sense of Place Toolkit* produced by the Wales Tourist Board (2002:2) advises on the creation of tourism products based on the "sense of place" or "authentic essence of place." This practical guide also contains a strong recognition of the role of quotidian culture in cultural tourism, reminding users that "our everyday life is someone else's adventure" (p. 2).

The idea that "local" identities are somehow more "authentic" is deeply rooted in the analysis of tourism as well as in the practice of tourism product development.

Authenticity is seen as being important for all tourism, as Taylor (2001:7) has argued:

> Authenticity has become the philosopher's stone for an industry that generally seeks to procure other peoples' "realities." In tourism, authenticity poses as objectivism. It holds the special powers both of distance and of "truth."

But authenticity has been particularly important in the study of cultural tourism, as Schouten argues in Chapter 2 of this volume. A number of studies of cultural tourism have argued that cultural tourists are seeking more "authentic" or "deeper" experiences than other types of tourists (McKercher and du Cros, 2002). These authentic experiences were also usually seen as encompassing high culture, or traditional local culture, while specifically avoiding popular and contemporary culture. MacCannell (1976) was one of the first analysts to problematize this relationship, by showing how "authentic" cultural attractions were created as contemporary cultural productions. By marking something as "authentic" and therefore worthy of the tourist gaze, destinations could assure themselves a steady flow of tourists engaged in sightseeing or "the ritual performed to the differentiations of society" (p. 13).

Cultural tourism, because of its supposed connections with a search for authenticity and meaning, is also usually seen as a more serious form of tourism. For example, Meethan (2001:128) argues:

> Rather than the simple aimless pleasures of mass tourism, the cultural tourists are those who go about their leisure in a more serious frame of mind. To be a cultural tourist is to attempt, I would suggest, to go beyond idle leisure and to return enriched with knowledge of other places and other people even if this involves gazing at, or collecting in some way, the commodified essences of otherness.

However, such dichotomies between idle and active, or authentic and inauthentic, do not generally stand up to empirical scrutiny, as May

(1996) has indicated. Package tourists in beach destinations often see themselves as seekers of authenticity as well. The concept of authenticity may well differ between tourists, but it is a widely sought-after experience (Lengkeek, 1996).

The problem seems to have become the growing realization among many tourists that authenticity is in the eye of the beholder. Why bother queuing to view "authentic" historic monuments when there are equally authentic bits of local culture to be found everywhere? Where McCannell (1976) identified the process of "marking" attractions as something special and worthy of attention, current trends in society and in tourism in particular seem to have shifted toward a logic of "reverse marking." As Brekhus explains in the context of social science:

> reverse marking is an explicit strategy whereby one consciously ignores what is typically marked as though it were mundane and focuses on the unmarked as though it were *"exotic"* and *"unusual."* Rather than gravitating to what already stands out as exceptional, reverse marking tries to find the exceptional in what is ordinarily taken-for-granted as unexceptional. (Brekhus, 1998)

This also seems to be a strategy that is gaining ground with tourists. For example, Ramchander examines the growth of "township tourism" in South Africa in Chapter 3 of this volume. The townships, the cruel physical manifestations of the policy of apartheid, have now become tourist attractions as tourists visiting the new South Africa seek a glimpse of what everyday life is like for people marginalized by the system. The attraction of the everyday is also to be found outlined in travel guides, as the Lonely Planet for Singapore shows:

> In the crowded streets of Chinatown, fortune tellers, calligraphers, and temple worshippers are still a part of everyday life. In Little India, you can buy the best sari material, freshly ground spices, or a picture of your favourite Hindu god. In the small shops of Arab St, the cry of the imam can be heard from the nearby Sultan Mosque. (Lonely Planet, 2004)

There is a growing awareness that the exotic, the surprising, and the challenging are to be found in the everyday lives of others: "India jolts your senses awake like no other country. And it happens through its people and everyday life" (Lonely Planet, 2004). Places increasingly situate themselves as windows onto everyday life, from Norway to New Zealand:

> Lillesand (pop. 3,000) presents an opportunity to experience what daily life is like in a traditional Norwegian coastal village. (iexplore, 2004)

> Dunedin offers all the facilities you would expect within a modern, thriving city, without the traffic jams and parking problems! Daily life is vibrant, and bars compete for space with a fabulous mix of shops and entertainment venues. (Tourism.net.nz, 2004)

Experiencing everyday life is also positioned as a sign that you have arrived, because the other tourists are still only scratching the surface:

> Joy's House is not for backpackers or for standard tourists, rather for people who want to allow the daily life and the people in Thailand into their lives, who have possibly been in other countries without really arriving there. (Joy's House, 2004)

The emergence of the everyday or the mundane as a source of authentic experience in tourism has much to do with the development of consumption in modern societies. In his study of the "Joyless Economy," Scitovsky (1976) focused attention on the way in which people learn. The processing of information during the learning process is essentially a process of creating redundancy in information. As we develop skills, certain actions become automatic, and we cease to process large amounts of information that are taken for granted. Such redundancy is also necessary if we are not to be overwhelmed with the rising tide of data generated by the information society. Redundancy is what enables us to move on and learn new things, which is arguably the basis of cultural consumption in general, and cultural tourism in particular (Richards, 2001).

The learning process, therefore, consists in making new things visible, while at the same time making invisible what we have already learned and can take for granted. Because everyday life is so full of already-learned facts, our own everyday lives essentially become invisible, which is one reason why travel to other places is so pleasurable. It is not just a discovery of the new, but a rediscovery of the quotidian, which is revealed by our newfound perspective. It is this aspect of travel that has come to be used as a new attraction and a new form of exoticism in tourism.

This perspective also problematizes the concept of "placelessness," which is discussed at length by Melanie Smith in Chapter 5. The tendency for globalization to produce similar landscapes and spaces in different parts of the world has been a concern for a long time. Some authors have also posed the question of whether it will make sense to travel in the future, if everywhere begins to look the same. However, as Robert Maitland suggests in Chapter 6, it is possible to develop "placefulness" in "new tourism areas" which have previously been overlooked by tourists. This line of argument is essentially one that Alain de Botton (2002) makes much more prosaically in *The Art of Travel*. He examines the way in which we tend to ignore everyday details that can make our home environments just as exciting, engaging, and exotic as distant destinations.

The idea that we can find just as much cultural diversion at home as by going on holiday is not as far removed from the current practice of cultural tourism as it may seem. For example, Thrane (2000) found that the cultural consumption of cultural tourists is actually very like their consumption at home. Cultural tourism, he concludes, is not so much a process of reversal, but is in fact an extension of everyday life. This argument also finds echoes in the ATLAS research, which has uncovered a strong relationship between people's work and their cultural tourism experiences. Those who work in museums, for example, are also particularly likely to visit museums on holiday. People with a high level of cultural consumption at home are also those most likely to visit cultural attractions on holiday (Richards, 2001). The consumption of the familiar is made interesting not by the content, but by the context. In some ways, cultural tourism may be seen as a form of "suspension," in which the tourist travels within a cultural frame of reference that is an extension of home, while seeking an experience of the "Other" that does not produce culture shock or go as far as a reversal of the home culture (Richards and Wilson, 2004).

As Nijman (1999) suggests, our ability to extend our consumption culture to other locations is heavily dependent on the extension of new technology, and particularly the Internet. Cultural tourists are increasingly finding information about cultural attractions over the Internet, particularly before they leave home. The 2004 ATLAS surveys indicate that a third of cultural tourists used the Internet to search for information about attractions before leaving home, and more than a quarter of all international tourists booked travel and/or accommodation products via the Web.

Not surprisingly, dedicated sites are now springing up to meet the needs of this growing market for information. What many of these sites have in common is that they allow travelers to construct their own cultural tourism products by combining travel, accommodation, and attraction products into tailor-made packages (or part-packages). In the past, this would have been a function of specialist cultural tourism tour operators (Richards et al., 2001).

Information in the destination is also being revolutionized, so that tourists now have more access to information about arts performances and festivals, and can book tickets from the comfort of their armchairs. On arrival they can be guided around major sites using portable information systems, or view reconstructions of archaeological sites in virtual reality. As Sigala (2003) indicates, there is an increasing integration of the "bricks and mortar" world of tangible heritage and the virtual world of cultural tourism and heritage information, animation, and interpretation.

These technological developments are also creating new modes of tourism consumption. Cultural sites that at one time were experienced collectively as part of a crowd of authenticity seekers (Mac-Cannell, 1976) are now experienced individually through the earpiece of an audio guide or the viewfinder of a camcorder. These aids effectively remove the need to discuss cultural artifacts with fellow travelers, creating as they do a surrogate personalization of space, in which each tourist creates and consumes his or her own museum.

New technology and the ability to consume intangible culture in the form of images and sounds almost anywhere also pose problems for the cultural and creative production systems of specific locations. The reproduction of culture and the disembedding of culture from its everyday context makes it more difficult for the regions that originate those cultural forms to control and exploit them. While specific productions, such as musicals or TV programs, can be protected by copyright, much of the intellectual property embodied in creative products is highly mobile and difficult to protect.

There is therefore a growing need to invent new forms of delivery to embody such intellectual property and tie it to a specific location. In Barcelona, for example, music festivals such as Sonar and Primavera Sound have become very successful cultural tourism products, attracting visitors from across Europe and beyond. These festivals have received support from the City of Barcelona, which now wants to capitalize on its investment by exporting the formula to other countries. The question will be if this exportation will lead to a diminution of visitors to the "originals" in Barcelona, or if it will lead to more people wanting to experience the product in its original context (Avui, 2004).

EMERGING STYLES OF CULTURAL TOURISM

Cultural tourism is spreading to all corners of the globe, and the study of the cultural tourism phenomenon with it. This has begun to create awareness of different regional styles of cultural tourism, which relate not only to the culture being consumed, but also to the organization and management of that consumption.

The classic image of cultural tourism still seems strongly tied to the European model of passive consumption of historic sites and museums. But in other areas of the world, particularly those in which built heritage is more sparse, different models are evident. In Africa, for example, the recent review undertaken by ATLAS Africa (Akama and Sterry, 2002) has underlined the current concentration of the product on traditional village life and natural attractions, particularly wildlife. As Briedenhann and Wickens show in Chapter 4 of this volume, this is beginning to change in the case of South Africa, where the increasing urban focus of cultural life is beginning to produce a wide range of new cultural products for tourism consumption.

In Australia and New Zealand the search for distinctiveness and identity in a globalizing world has led to an emphasis on creativity. The Keating government's "Creative Nation" policy launched in

Australia in 1994 specifically identified cultural tourism as a policy area, distinct from "heritage" (Commonwealth of Australia, 1994). In New Zealand, the definition of "cultural tourism" by Creative New Zealand (the rebranded Arts Council) specifically identifies Maori culture as a strategic priority in cultural tourism:

> The (cultural tourism) strategy will aim to tap and support the development of those cultural dimensions that enable more depth of interaction with, and understanding of, our people, place, and cultural identity. An important part of this is recognising that Maori culture is indigenous and unique to Aotearoa/ New Zealand. (Creative New Zealand, 2004:1)

However, the development of tourism with indigenous peoples in Australasia has raised many issues about the interpretation of their culture, as McIntosh (2004) discusses. Tourists demand an "authentic" experience of indigenous communities by meeting their members directly; however, they often preferred brief encounters rather than immersion in the culture. Maori culture is not usually seen as a primary motive for visiting New Zealand, for example, but is usually just one of many experiences that the visitor will try to cram into a relatively short trip. As a result, visitor knowledge of the culture tends to remain superficial and stereotypical.

New Zealand has also been taking a leading role in developing creative tourism, a logical extension of the positioning of the country as a "creative nation." The creative image of New Zealand, as well as the attractions of the physical landscape, are being promoted globally through the *Lord of the Rings* films. Creativity is also being used as the basis for new tourism products. For example, Creative Tourism New Zealand (2004) now provides a wide range of creative tourism courses in the Nelson area, which has long been famous as a region rich in artistic talent. This may be one indication that globalization is helping to spread the concept of the "creative class" (Florida, 2002) beyond the urban environment.

Cultural tourism has always been important in North America, but until recently has not been recognized as a distinct market segment. A growing number of communities are now recognizing cultural tourism as a means of supporting culture and generating income. Research by the Travel Industry Association of America (TIA, 2003) has indicated that domestic cultural tourism (defined as the number of travelers visiting cultural attractions) grew by 13 percent between 1996 and 2002. Almost 217 million person-trips were taken in 2002, and these cultural tourists spent more and stayed longer at the destination than other visitors.

Destinations which have traditionally relied on other forms of tourism, such as leisure travel or conventions, are now trying to add cultural tourism to their portfolio, often for economic reasons. For example, a recent study by Florida Arts (2004) indicated:

> Tourists who enjoy Florida's arts and cultural programming (cultural tourists) have a larger economic impact than do tourists in general. These cultural tourists spent an average of $348.84 each while visiting Florida, compared to $291.16 spent by other individual tourists. Cultural tourists spent more than other tourists because they stayed for a longer period of time.

In order to capture these high-spending visitors, many destinations are now developing specific marketing programs, or developing new cultural attractions. For example, the new Niagara Experience Center is "a cultural tourism attraction focused on historical and cultural elements of the Niagara region and designed to boost tourism and attract visitors" and represents "a 'brand extension' of the successful Niagara Falls State Park" (USA Niagara Development Corporation, 2004).

In Latin America, cultural tourism is already crucial to the development of international tourism. A recent study by the World Tourism Organization (2004), for example, indicated that Peru classifies 93 percent of its visitors as cultural tourists. Many Latin American countries have developed cultural routes, often linking cultural and archaeological features with rural and natural environments, such as the Inca Trail in Peru, or the Mayan Route, which links Mexico, Belize, Guatemala, and Honduras (Evans, 2004). There is also emerging interest in gastronomic tourism, centering on the wealth of indigenous food products and the fusion of local and imported cooking techniques (CONACULTA, 2002). Some countries here are also beginning to discover the potential of indigenous culture for cultural tourism, as in Paraguay, where the National Tourism Plan emphasizes indigenous Guaraní language, folklore, dance, and gastronomy (World Tourism Organization, 2004).

In many Latin American countries, the domestic cultural tourism market is also emerging as an important source of development. As de Camargo shows in Chapter 12 of this volume, cultural tourism has become an important means of learning about history and local identity. This has led to a revalorization of cultural heritage in many cities, and increased attention for the preservation of historic city centers and archaeological and architectural heritage. This has also arguably led to the development of specialized historic "tourist cities," such as Parati in Brazil, which offers colonial heritage as a leisure product to the nearby inhabitants of São Paolo and Rio de Janeiro (Lanci da Silva, 2004).

In the Middle East and the Arab nations of North Africa, the development of tourism was strongly affected by the events of September 11, 2001, although the decline in European visitors has been compensated to some extent by a resurgence of intraregional travel. Berriane (1999) illustrates that there are three groups of countries in the region with respect to cultural tourism. In countries such as Syria, Jordan, and Yemen there is a low intensity of international tourism and the product is largely based on cultural tours. In Tunisia, the development of beach tourism has followed a pattern much more like that of the Spanish costas, with the development of large resorts with a low cultural content. Finally, in countries such as Morocco and Egypt there is a mixture of cultural tours and fixed point resorts (including inland destinations based on culture, such as Luxor and Aswan).

In Asia, culture has long been at the forefront of the tourism product in many countries. In the face of globalization and modernization, however, many of the major cities in Asia are being rapidly transformed by economic development. Cities like Singapore have therefore belatedly begun to preserve (or even re-create) their historic centers as tourism attractions. In other countries, cultural attractions may be the primary generator of tourism. In Cambodia, for example, the World Heritage Site of Angkor Wat serves as a major tourist draw and as a national icon. Recent research indicates that for 28 percent of tourists visiting Angkor Wat this was their only reason to visit the country (Ravinder and Phuong, 2004).

As in Latin America, the emergence of domestic or regional cultural tourism markets in Asia means that national identity functions of cultural heritage are being supplemented by popular culture attractions as well. As McKercher and du Cros (2002) show in the case of China, new "cultural theme parks" are opening to cater to the growing demand for domestic leisure tourism. The expansion of some of these Asian parks into other areas of the world, such as the Splendid China theme park in Florida, also show that the process of "Disneyfication" is not simply one-way, but may be accompanied by countervailing processes of creolization as well.

Another aspect of cultural tourism that has been studied more extensively in Asia than elsewhere has been the emergence of a specific group of informal cultural intermediaries, who guide tourists around cities and cultural sites and who introduce them to "local" culture (Dahles and Bras, 1999). These unofficial guides are often in conflict with their official counterparts at major tourist sites and with government agencies attempting to police access to the guiding profession. The unofficial guides create narratives about local culture that the tourists are unlikely to hear from official sources. They also contribute directly to global flows of culture, sometimes following their guests back to the home country, or persuading them to stay and finance a joint business in the destination.

In Europe cultural tourism is one of the oldest and most well-entrenched forms of tourism in most countries (Richards, 1996). Although cultural tourism has historically been related heavily to Europe's incredibly rich stock of cultural heritage, particularly in terms of monument and museums, there is growing evidence of a shift toward popular culture and other forms of intangible heritage to diversify the basic cultural tourism product. Even here there are significant regional differences, which are currently particularly evident in the newly emerging nations of Central and Southeastern Europe. Whereas the established destinations in Western Europe are keen to promote cultural diversity as a source of cultural tourism development, in the newly emerging nation-states there is much more emphasis on developing cultural heritage as a source of national identity. As Hughes and Allen (2005) show, cultural tourism is seen as a particularly important market in these countries, which also tend to have a relatively uncritical view of the relationship between tourism and culture.

Cultural tourism is even reaching the least accessible corners of the globe, such as the polar regions. With 22,000 tourists visiting the Antarctic every summer, tourism has now become the main human activity in the region (Guardian, 2003). Many of the Antarctic tours are sold on the idea that visitors can retrace the footsteps of explorers such as Shackleton and Scott. Their expedition huts have now become cultural attractions alongside the natural wonders of the continent. Lack of connection with global systems may impede the development of large-scale cultural tourism. But on the other hand, some aspects of "peripherality" are now being developed as a cultural advantage in some areas. In the Yukon region of Northern Canada, for example, the idea of "isolation" is actively sold to potential visitors as a virtue (de la Barre, 2004), even though the isolation of the region is increasingly more cultural than physical.

THE GLOBAL CULTURAL TOURISM MARKET

In order to provide more empirical grounding for the global analysis of cultural tourism, ATLAS and Interarts collaborated to organize a further phase of the Cultural Tourism Research Project in 2004. This included visitor surveys at cultural attractions and events around the world. Some fifty institutions from twenty-five countries participated in this project, which examines the relationship between culture and tourism in a range of different contexts around the world. More details of this research program can be found at www.atlas-euro.org or on the project home page (www.tram-research.com/atlas). Only preliminary results were available at the time of writing, but the ATLAS Cultural Tourism Research Group intends to publish more-detailed results in the near future. The initial results reported on here include the first 6,000 visitor surveys from twelve countries in Europe, Africa, Asia, and Australasia.

Who Are the Cultural Tourists?

One of the most important points to make about cultural tourism is that not all visitors to cultural sites are tourists. About 40 percent of the 2004 ATLAS survey respondents lived in the local area. Less than

20 percent were foreign tourists. This emphasizes the point that apart from a select few sites or events where the majority of visitors come from abroad, the domestic market is of vital importance for most cultural tourism attractions.

In contrast with the traditional view of cultural tourism, younger people are a very important segment of the total audience. The single largest age group is between 20 and 29, and almost 40 percent of visitors are under 30. This matches the findings of other research, such as a recent study by the AFIT (2002) in France, which indicated that 40 percent of visitors to historic sites were under 35. In addition, research conducted on the youth tourism market by ATLAS and the International Student Travel Confederation (ISTC), indicated that "discovering other cultures" was the single most important motivation for young travelers. The youth market is important for cultural tourism not only because people visit cultural attractions when they are young (and many use youth discount cards to do so), but also because the cultural experiences they have in their youth may influence their future tourism behavior as well.

One of the reasons that youth travelers, and particularly students, are important for cultural tourism is because of the strong link between cultural consumption and education. Highly educated people tend to consume more culture—not just high culture, but popular culture as well. One of the major reasons for the growth of cultural tourism in recent decades has therefore been increased participation rates in higher education. The visitors in general and the cultural tourists in particular are very highly educated. Over half have had some form of higher education, compared with about one-third of the EU population.

Higher education levels tend to lead to better jobs and higher incomes. It is not surprising, therefore, that cultural tourists tend to have professional (32 percent) or managerial occupations (15 percent) and have relatively high salaries.

One of the seemingly contradictory aspects of cultural tourism is the fact that people working in jobs connected to the cultural sector tend to engage in cultural tourism more frequently. Twenty-seven percent of cultural tourists have an occupation connected with culture, compared with about 3 percent of the EU population. It seems that people who work in museums also visit other museums when they are on holiday.

Why Do They Come?

One of the most important questions from the point of view of cultural tourism marketing and management is the motivation of cultural tourists. About half of the visitors surveyed in 2004 were on holiday. Other important purposes for visiting were visiting friends and relatives (15 percent) and cultural events (13 percent). Asked about more specific aspects of their motives for visiting the location, the most important aspect was experiencing the atmosphere of the place. This underlines the importance of the discussions in Chapters 5 and 6 about the nature of place and distinctiveness, as well as the increasing search for experiences on the part of tourists (Richards and Wilson, 2004).

In terms of the type of holiday that the tourists considered they were taking, the most common label chosen was "cultural holiday" (39 percent), followed by "touring holiday" (25 percent) and "city trip" (19 percent). This underlines the findings of previous ATLAS research, which has consistently pointed to the fact that a minority of cultural visitors are in fact "cultural tourists." This appears to be true not just for Europe, but for most other parts of the world as well.

When we look in more detail at the reasons why cultural tourists go to a particular place, it is clear that the main motivation is a combination of atmosphere, local culture, and history. People want to learn something during their visit, particularly about the unique character of the place they are visiting. The basic motivations for visiting cultural sites have changed little over the years. The most important motivation has tended to be "learning new things." However, in 2004 "experiencing the atmosphere" of the attraction was more important for foreign visitors. It seems that cultural tourism is becoming an experiential product, in which the visit is judged in terms of all attributes of the attraction, and not just its cultural value.

Where Do They Go?

The "traditional" attractions, such as museums, galleries, and monuments, are still the most important sites visited by tourists. In

2004, almost 60 percent of the ATLAS respondents had visited a museum (other than the site they were interviewed at), while 30 percent had visited a monument and 29 percent a gallery. However, there is evidence of a trend toward greater dispersion of visitors among different cultural attraction types in the destination, and in particular a shift from "heritage" attractions toward "arts" attractions. The figures for 2004 show museums consistently being most important since 1997 and monuments losing share. On the other hand art galleries, performing arts attractions, and festivals have all increased their share of visitors in recent years.

Another area of cultural tourist choice we have studied over the course of the survey is the cities that people consider to be most attractive as cultural destinations. In terms of the cities that cultural tourists consider being attractive cultural destinations, there have been few changes in the major destinations in recent years. Paris, Rome, and London are always present in the top three, in the case of London and Paris probably because of their undisputed position as "world cities" and in the case of Rome because of the depth of history and richness of modern culture of the Italian capital. A fairly consistent group of cities contests the second rung on the ladder, including Athens, Florence, Barcelona, and Vienna. These cities in fact compete more fiercely with one another than they do with London or Paris.

One of the major strategies now being used by cities to position themselves in cultural tourism markets is the staging of major cultural events. In Europe, the hosting of the annual European City of Culture (ECOC) event has become a hotly contested prize. A recent review of the ECOC program published by the EU (Palmer/Rae, 2004) shows that the program has been relatively successful in attracting cultural visitors to the host cities, with an average increase of 12 percent in overnights in each city. Graz was particularly successful in this regard, attracting 25 percent more visitors in 2003. However, as competition to attract events becomes stiffer, cities must be innovative to maintain their competitive edge.

How Do They Gather Information?

The main source of information for cultural tourists is personal recommendation from friends or family (45 percent). Guidebooks are the most important source of published information (24 percent), but the Internet is rapidly becoming a major factor, already being consulted by 33 percent of tourists, compared with 17 percent of tourists in 2002. Far fewer use tour operator brochures (6 percent) or tourist board information (6 percent). More people are also booking their travel or accommodation via the Internet (15 percent in 2004, compared with 8 percent in 2002).

Cultural tourists (high incomes, access to the Internet) were significantly more likely than other tourists (45 versus 32 percent, respectively) to use the Internet to find information about the destination prior to their visit. They are also more likely to use guidebooks and tour operator brochures as a source of information, which may reflect the high information content of cultural tour operator brochures. Altogether, 17 percent of cultural tourists surveyed were on a package tour, although this proportion increases to almost a quarter for foreign tourists.

An important aspect of information gathering is the stage at which cultural tourists make the decision to visit a site or event. The ATLAS surveys indicate that almost half the tourists decide to visit a cultural attraction before leaving home, while about a quarter make the decision during the journey to a region and a quarter only decide once they have arrived at the destination (Richards, 2002). This indicates the importance of attracting the attention of the tourists before they arrive in the destination. Because it is unlikely that individual cultural attractions will have the resources necessary to market themselves abroad, there is an important role for collaborative destination marketing in developing cultural tourism.

How Much Do They Spend?

The attractiveness of cultural tourists for most tourist destinations lies in their high overall spending. The image of cultural tourists as relatively rich tourists is partially confirmed by the research. The average total spending in the destination for cultural tourist groups in 2004 was over €1500 ($1920), which is higher than visitors on a rural holiday (€1030/$1320), at the beach (€1425/$1825), and on city trips (€1200/$1535).

Summing up the results of the research, it seems that today's cultural tourists are generally well-educated people with high-status occupations and good incomes. These elements fit the stereotype of cultural tourists that has persuaded so many destinations to pursue them. What is often overlooked, however, is that not all cultural visitors are cultural tourists, and the level of cultural motivation varies greatly from one tourist to the next. They are often looking for a mixture of culture, entertainment, and relaxation, not just traditional "high-culture" products. It is also clear that younger tourists are much more important than has previously been recognized, and the youth market will be particularly important in creating repeat visitors for the future.

STRUCTURE OF THE BOOK

The contributions presented in this book include both general considerations of the consequences of cultural tourism, as well as more-specific studies of the local impacts of global flows of cultural tourists. The chapters are organized into four major sections. Part I deals with the tensions caused by globalization, and particularly the issue of authenticity. Part II concentrates on cultural tourism demand, profiling the motivations and behavior of cultural tourists in urban, coastal, and inland destinations. Part III looks at the relationship between tourists and local communities, and concentrates on how the "local" culture can be interpreted not only for visitors but also for residents. Part IV looks at cultural events and their use as a tool to develop tourism, and the final chapter presents some general conclusions.

As Schouten points out in Chapter 2, the concept of authenticity that emerged in the context of modernity is a relative one. The "authentic" culture expected by tourists is often far removed from what locals may regard as being authentic, or even "cultural." In the light of differing interpretations of the supposed object of tourism (MacCannell, 1976) and of cultural tourism in particular, it is not surprising that debates also emerge about "whose" culture is being presented, and what impacts this presentation will have on local identities and sense of place.

Pranill Ramchander (Chapter 3) analyzes the growth of "township tourism," which represents a form of "local culture" previously considered to be dangerous and inaccessible. In South Africa the townships represent a specific example of how human suffering (and ultimately the triumph of the human spirit) have become a focus of tourist attention. This type of tourism is now developing as an "alternative" form of adventure to the wildlife tourism traditionally promoted by South Africa. However, one of the main problems with this type of tourism, as in many tourism projects in developing areas, is how the "locals" maintain control of the product and the way it is presented to tourists. The creation of grass roots cultural tourism projects has often been seen as one way forward, but as Jenny Briedenhann and Eugenia Wickens illustrate in South Africa (Chapter 4), idealistic community-based projects often fail for lack of commercial realism.

The effects of tourism as a carrier (as well as a result) of globalization have also led to concerns that tourism is degrading local culture, removing local distinctions and replacing them with the differentiations of modernity. This debate has recently shifted into the arena of "placelessness," as Melanie Smith discusses in Chapter 5. She reviews the wide range of theoretical debates surrounding the impact of globalization on the distinctiveness of place, and the implications this has for tourism. The idea that the world is becoming increasingly "placeless" as a result of globalization also finds echoes in the search for "new" areas for tourism consumption. These now include the peripheral areas of major cities, as Robert Maitland shows in Chapter 6. He examines the development of tourism in two Inner London areas that are now developing tourism based on both new cultural attractions and the ethnic diversity inherent in such areas.

In urban and rural areas alike, attempts are being made to link localities to global themes through the construction of cultural routes, as László Puczkó and Tamara Rátz discuss in Chapter 7. They outline the basic steps that need to be taken to establish, manage, and market such routes, and examine the case of a new type of "cultural avenue" being developed in Budapest.

Ana González, Miguel Cervantes, Mauro Miranda, Norberto Muñiz, and Carmen Rodríguez (Chapter 8) analyze the case of Castilla y León in Spain, which is trying to develop new markets for cultural tourism in order to be able to compete more effectively with coastal areas. They show that the market has remained relatively stable in recent years, with an upmarket, highly educated clientele reminiscent of the profile highlighted by the ATLAS surveys.

One consequence of the resurgence of locality and distinction is that the "local" is increasingly being interpreted, not only to tourists but also to "locals." As Jaume Franquesa and Marc Morell (Chapter 9) show in their study of heritage tourism in a Mallorquin context, destinations are now increasingly looking for new ways of presenting their narratives to a broad audience. Particularly in major destinations such as Spain, the question of "whose culture" or "whose heritage" is being complicated by the dissolving boundaries between "tourists" and "locals." Although their cultural references may be different, their consumption and spatial connections within cities and at attractions are increasingly similar. This problematizes the search for "distinction" still further, since not only do locations in different countries and regions become similar, but their strategies for distinction also tend to converge.

Xerardo Pereiro Pérez also examines the way in which new types of cultural attractions such as "ecomuseums" are playing an increasingly important role in the cultural tourism market in Chapter 10. If the original wave of open-air museums in Europe at the turn of the nineteenth century marked a concern to preserve artifacts of rural culture threatened by industrialization, the current trend in developing ecomuseums seems to be a reaction to the much wider threat to rural lifestyles posed by globalization. New niches are also springing up in the wider cultural tourism market, such as religious tourism (Greg Richards and Carlos Fernandes, Chapter 11). Although religious tourism has long been important for many major religious and pilgrimage sites, more active efforts are now being made by many of these destinations to attract tourists without a specific religious motive, especially cultural tourists.

As Patricia de Camargo argues in Chapter 12, heritage can be a tool for teaching in a formal sense as well as in more informal settings. She presents empirical evidence from Brazil to back up the general concept long utilized by ATLAS of cultural tourism as a process of informal learning (Richards, 2001). Greg Richards (Chapter 13) discusses the much smaller local cultural events staged in Catalunya, which seem to be employed more readily as tools of socialization than festivalization.

This convergence is also evident in the staging of major events, and the growing tendency to see cities or regions as "stages" or "backdrops" for a stream of festivals aimed at local and global consumers. The final section of this volume presents case studies of the relationship between cultural events and tourism. Erik Hitters (Chapter 14) discusses the impact of the European Cultural Capitals in Rotterdam and Porto (2001), and emphasizes the process of "festivalization" taking place in these cities. Luis César Herrero, José Ángel Sanz, María Devesa, Ana Bedate, and María José del Barrio (Chapter 15) analyze the economic impact of the European Cultural Capital in Salamanca (2002). These studies show that the aims and outcomes of such events can be very different, and they are by no means a guarantee of tourism success. The concluding chapter attempts to pull together some of the varied strands of the arguments presented in the different areas of research presented in the foregoing chapters.

REFERENCES

AFIT (2002) *Etude des comportements des clienteles de visiteurs europeens sur les sites de patrimoine FranÇais*. Paris: AFIT.

Akama, J. and Sterry, P. (2002) *Cultural Tourism in Africa: Strategies for the New Millennium*. Arnhem: ATLAS.

Avui (2004) Interview with Carles Sala, Director of Music Promotion and Diffusion, City of Barcelona, 15 September. http://db.avui.com/avui/rc/04/set/15/ie/8a.htm

Barre, S. de la (2004) Selling "Isolation": Place-based values and tourism in Canada's Yukon. Paper presented at the International Geographical Union Pre-Congress Meeting on Tourism and Leisure. Loch Lomond, August.

Berriane, M. (1999) *Tourism, Culture and Development in the Arab Region*. Paris: UNESCO.

Botton de, A. (2002) *The Art of Travel*. London: Hamish Hamilton.

Brekhus, W. (1998) A sociology of the unmarked: Redirecting our focus. *Sociological Theory* 16: 34-51.

Commonwealth of Australia (1994) Creative Nation: Commonwealth Cultural Policy, October 1994. http://www.nla.gov.au/creative.nation/contents.html

CONACULTA (2002) *Patrimonio cultural y Turismo*. México D.F.: CONACULTA.

Creative New Zealand (2004) Cultural tourism. www.creativenz.govt.nz/resources/tourism.rtf

Creative Tourism New Zealand (2004) www.creativetourism.co.nz

Dahles, H. and Bras, K. (1999) Entrepreneurs in romance: Tourism in Indonesia. *Annals of Tourism Research* 26: 267-293.

Evans, G. (2004) Mundo Maya: From Cancun to city of culture. World heritage in post-colonial Mesoamerica. *Current Issues in Tourism* 7: 315-329.

Florida, R. (2002) *The Rise of the Creative Class: And How It's Transforming Work, Leisure, Community, and Everyday Life.* New York: Basic Books.

Florida Arts (2004) www.florida-arts.org/resources/culturaltourism.htm

Guardian (2003) summer holiday Shackletons but Antartica in peril. The Guardian, 17th June.

Haan, J. de (1997) *Het Gedeelde Erfgoed.* Rijswijk, SCP.

Howie, F. (2000) Establishing the common ground: Tourism, ordinary places, grey-areas and environmental quality in Edinburgh, Scotland. In Richards, G. and Hall, D. (eds) *Tourism and Sustainable Community Development.* London: Routledge, pp. 101-118.

Hughes, H. and Allen, D. (2005) Cultural tourism in Central and Eastern Europe: The views of "induced image formation agents." *Tourism Management* 26: 173-183.

Iexplore (2004) www.iexplore.com/dmap/Norway/Where+to+Go

Joy's House (2004) www.joyshouse.net/recommen.htm

Lanci da Silva, M. (2004) *Cidades Turísticas: Identidades e cenários de lazer.* São Paolo: Aleph.

Lengkeek, J. (1996) *Vakantie van het leven. Over het belang van recreatie en toerisme.* Boom, Amsterdam.

Lonely Planet (2004) www.lonelyplanet.com

MacCannell, D. (1976) *The Tourist: A New Theory of the Leisure Class.* New York: Schocken Books.

May, J. (1996) In search of authenticity off and on the beaten track. *Society and Space* 14: 709-736.

McIntosh, A.J. (2004) Tourist's appreciation of Maori culture in New Zealand. *Tourism Management* 25, 1-15.

McKercher, B. and du Cros, H. (2002) *Cultural Tourism: The Partnership Between Tourism and Cultural Heritage Management.* New York: Haworth Press.

McKercher, B., Ho, P.S.Y. and du Cros, H. (2004) Attributes of popular cultural attractions in Hong Kong. *Annals of Tourism Research* 31: 393-407.

Meethan, K. (2001) *Tourism in Global Society: Place, Culture, Consumption.* Basingstoke: Palgrave.

Nijman, J. (1999) Cultural globalization and the identity of place: The reconstruction of Amsterdam. *Ecumene* 6: 146-164.

Palmer/Rae (2004) *European Cities and Capitals of Culture.* Brussels: Palmer/Rae Associates.

Ravinder, R, and Phuong, S. (2004) Cultural tourism and tourism generation: The case of Angkor Wat. Paper presented at the Third ATLAS Asia Pacific Conference, Beppu, Japan, November.

Richards, G. (1996) *Cultural Tourism in Europe.* Wallingford: CAB International.

Richards, G. (2000) World Culture and Heritage and Tourism. *Tourism Recreation Research* 25(1): 9-18.

Richards, G. (2001) *Cultural Attractions and European Tourism.* Wallingford: CAB International.

Richards, G. (2002) Tourism attraction systems: Exploring cultural behaviour. *Annals of Tourism Research* 29(4): 1048-1064.

Richards, G., Goedhart, S. and Herrijgers, C. (2001) The cultural attraction distribution system. In Richards, G. (ed.) *Cultural Attractions and European Tourism.* Wallingford: CAB International, 71-89.

Richards, G. and Wilson, J. (2004) *The Global Nomad: Backpacker Travel in Theory and Practice.* Clevedon: Channel View Publications.

Scitovsky, T. (1976) *The Joyless Economy.* New York: Basic Books.

Sigala, M. (2003) Internet heritage and cultural tourism under virtual construction: implications for online visitors' experiences and interpretation management. *Tourism Today* 3(3): 51-67.

Taylor, J. (2001) Authenticity and sincerity in tourism. *Annals of Tourism Research* 28, 7-26.

Thrane, C. (2000) Everyday life and cultural tourism in Scandinavia: Examining the spillover hypothesis. *Society and Leisure* 23: 217-234.

TIA (2003) *The Historic/Cultural Traveler, 2003 edition.* Washington: TIA.

Tourism.net.nz (2004) tourism.net.nz/new-zealand/about-new-zealand/regions/dunedin.html

USA Niagara Development Corporation (2004) http://www.usaniagara.com/press_releases_display.asp?id=78

Wales Tourist Board (2002) *Sense of Place Toolkit.* Cardiff, Wales Tourist Board.

World Tourism Organization (1985) *The State's Role in Protecting and Promoting Culture as a Factor of Tourism Development and the Proper Use and Exploitation of the National Cultural Heritage of Sites and Monuments for Tourism.* Madrid: WTO.

World Tourism Organization (2004) *Tourism Market Trends 2003 Edition.* Madrid: WTO.

PART I:
TOURISM, GLOBALIZATION, AND AUTHENTICITY

Chapter 2

Cultural Tourism:
Between Authenticity and Globalization

Frans Schouten

The globalization process has reawakened the longstanding debate about the advantages and disadvantages of tourism for local cultures. On the positive side there is the revival through tourism of local crafts, traditions, music, and dance. The negative side is concerned with the erosion of the same phenomena through tourism and emphasizes the danger of staging for the tourist gaze, producing crafts solely for tourists, and the detrimental results of the "demonstration effect." This chapter concentrates on a discussion of the concept of "authenticity" as a vital element of cultural expressions and the way it shapes cultural identities.

Cultural Tourism: Global and Local Perspectives
© 2007 by The Haworth Press, Inc. All rights reserved.
doi:10.1300/5749_02

CULTURAL TOURISM

There are two misconceptions concerning cultural tourism that we should discuss at the outset. First, the idea that cultural tourism will bring a destination more income with fewer visitors. There is very little evidence of significantly higher spending by cultural tourists, who probably only have slightly different spending patterns from other tourists. In the ATLAS surveys in 2004, for example, spending by "cultural tourists" only averaged just over 10 percent more than that by other leisure visitors. In any case, as with all holidaymakers much of the money for vacation is spent in the home country and not in the country visited.

Second, there is the idea that cultural tourism is the fastest growing market in global tourism (e.g., World Tourism Organization, 2004). This statement may be correct, but it is nevertheless meaningless. If growth occurs in a niche market at the same time as growth occurs in the main market, the difference will only increase, even if the niche market is growing faster. If cultural tourism accounts for 20 percent of the market and it increases by 100 percent in five years, and traditional forms of tourism (80 percent) increase by 50 percent in the same period, there will be a bigger demand in volume for traditional forms of tourism in five years' time than for cultural tourism. Besides, cultural tourism is difficult to define, and it is not a single market. It looks more like a continuum from incidental encounters with cultural phenomena to intentional decisionmaking based on cultural preferences.

Cultural Tourists

Visitors are not a homogeneous group; their interest and involvement differs greatly. McKercher and du Cros (2002) did research in Hong Kong on the different types of cultural tourists, of which they identified five distinct types (see also Figure 2.1):

1. The *purposeful cultural tourist* (high centrality/deep experience), for whom learning about and experiencing other cultures is the major concern, chooses a destination.
2. The *sightseeing cultural tourist* (high centrality/shallow experience) is less concerned with experiencing the other culture and more interested in visiting the cultural highlights.

3. The *casual cultural tourist* (modest centrality/shallow experience) sees culture as a less important element in the decision-making process for the destination and does not get deeply involved while there.
4. The *incidental cultural tourist* (low centrality/shallow experience) does not choose a destination based upon culture, and once there will only superficially be involved.
5. The *serendipitous cultural tourist* (low centrality/deep experience) did not seek cultural involvement in the choice of the destination, but while there gets really involved and has a deep experience.

McKercher and du Cros found that for Hong Kong the *purposeful cultural tourist* accounted for 11.8 percent of total visitors. For American visitors it was 20 percent, however for the UK market only 6.8 percent and for Australia 9.8 percent. Probably the farther tourists travel and the less the destination reminds them of home (or the more exotic the destination), the higher the proportion of tourists who deliberately seek a genuine cultural experience.

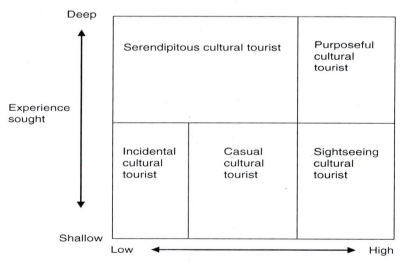

FIGURE 2.1. Types of cultural tourists. *Source:* McKercher and du Cros, 2002:32. © 2002 The Haworth Press, Inc. Reprinted by permission.

The *sightseeing cultural tourist* segment accounts for an average of 30.7 percent of Hong Kong visitors, with high scores for the U.K. market (44.8 percent) and the U.S. market (38 percent). Chinese visitors to Hong Kong only scored 8.5 percent. This segment chooses the destination for its cultural offer, but does not seek deep involvement in it. The *casual cultural tourist* accounted for 23.5 percent of the market in Hong Kong, and the *incidental cultural tourist* for 27.9 percent. So more than 50 percent of the visitors do not seek involvement in the culture visited and the cultural offer plays only a secondary role in their choice of destination.

The *serendipitous cultural tourist* in Hong Kong represents 6.2 percent of visitors on average. Chinese visitors from Taipei (12.5 percent) and visitors from Singapore (11.8 percent) were particularly important in this segment. It is probable that visitors who expect a culture they are familiar with are taken by surprise if they get really involved, while not seeking involvement. These kinds of encounters are based upon individual reactions and subsequently are rather difficult to predict. It would be interesting to repeat the research of McKercher and du Cros in other destinations, to see if the same characteristics appear in other places as well and to investigate the divisions of the different types of cultural consumption in other places of tourism interest.

The question, however, is also if tourists consider themselves to be cultural tourists. Probably only a few tourists have a self-perception as cultural tourists, and maybe the whole concept is something that derives primarily from the drawing board of scientists looking for labels to categorize phenomena. A small survey was done in the Dutch historic town of Haarlem through interviewing tourists and day-trippers. None of the interviewees considered themselves cultural tourists. However, when asked in what kind of activities they were involved, the answers were these, looking at these cute old houses, shopping, drinking coffee, or having lunch in a cozy old-fashioned inn. They visited the church and sat listening to someone playing the organ (which was considered quite an experience), and most of them planned to visit a museum in the afternoon. However, they did not view themselves as cultural tourists.

AUTHENTICITY

We have to make a distinction between "authenticity" in the eye of the beholder (the "guest" perspective) and as a form of self-perception at the destination (the "host" perspective). These two can be quite distinct, although Franquesa and Morell argue that the host and guest are becoming increasingly difficult to distinguish (Chapter 9). First we will explore the "guest" perspective, then we will proceed to self-perception of authenticity at the destination level. The basic assumption of this exercise is the idea that tourism is all about selling dreams. The core of the tourism industry is the commodification of escapism, the commercial answer to the longing of humankind for another reality beyond the dull and gray of the everyday experience.

Authenticity from the "Guest" Perspective

People going to historic places are primarily seeking an image of the past, rather than an authentic historical experience. Visitors to a reconstructed peat cutters' village in the eastern part of Holland have a particular interpretation of the "historical evidence" presented to them. Although the presenters tried to convey a message about the hardship of making a living in such conditions, most of the visitors do not see the poverty, but only their own poetic projections. It reminds them of times when life was simple and easy, for which they have a longing, living quietly "in the country," far away from the frustration, responsibilities, and a hectic life. Likewise their reactions as noted in field observations are: "Look how cute" and "Isn't it funny?" Visitor reactions can be even more awkward. The Dutch art historian Pierre Jansen once told a group in front of Van Gogh's painting the *Aardappel eters* (Potato eaters) about the poor living conditions in those days. One of them reacted, "It cannot have been so hard, look, they even had an antique oil lamp above the table!"

The past is perceived as very distant, as David Lowenthal (1985) puts it in the title of his famous book: *The Past Is a Foreign Country.* As foreign countries are not dissimilar to historic places from the point of view of the visitor, in most cases the shallow experience prevails.

In his article "The Ethnographer/Tourist in Indonesia," Edward Brunner (1995) describes his experiences as a tour guide of a group of highly educated American tourists who were on an explicitly cultural tour in Indonesia, accompanied by academics to introduce them to the culture visited. While visiting Bali he as an anthropologist noticed that in a certain temple a ritual was performed only once a year. The timing of such an *odalan* festival is unpredictable and it is a performance that the Balinese keep for themselves. He decided to go there with the group for a genuine authentic experience. I quote from his description what happened at the site:

> Shortly after noon, the festival started, and it was spectacular. Elderly Balinese women began dancing in a line around the temple courtyard. Their faces intense, as if in trance, their finger and body movements slow and delicate. Other women arrived with offerings to the temple gods. Priests were sprinkling holy water . . . incense was burning, the gamelan playing, the odours, sounds, and colours were coming from everywhere, it was all happening at once, an ethnographer's paradise. At that point, just as the festival was beginning, around 12:30 p.m., the tour director announced that we had to go back for lunch and that everyone should go back to the tour bus. I protested, and explained . . . that this was a rare opportunity. Stay, I said, to see this dazzling ceremony. "But we have seen it," replied one tourist as the group followed the tour leader back to the air-conditioned bus. (Brunner, 1995:233)

This is not a unique example and many more could be added. In this respect Mason (1994) rightly stated that the core of the tourism product is to "mystify the mundane, to amplify the exotic, minimize the misery, rationalize the disquietude, and romanticize the strange."

Staged Authenticity

At a conference in Africa someone involved in a cultural tourism development project in a tribal community announced that he had included in the tour to the village a visit to a ritual circumcision of a boy. Such an announcement raises many questions, such as, Might they run out of boys in the peak season, or how many times can you circumcise someone? More seriously, Are there any limits to the exposure of foreign eyes? But most important of all: Who is demanding such a "product"? The underlying assumption is that tourists are looking for an "authentic" experience.

MacCannell's (1973) classic work on staged authenticity and his concept of front stage and back stage areas have led some in our profession to the idea that staging is degrading the original cultures and in time will diminish the cultural values attached to them. The same applies to allowing strangers into someone's most private and sacred space, as in the example of the circumcision mentioned earlier. But there are many different shades of gray in this area and where the line is drawn between the public and the private space is different in many cultures. And is all staging really that bad?

Why do we call "Williamsburg" an attraction, and why is an arranged "surprise" visit of tourists to a Moroccan wedding in Marrakech a fake? Are we measuring with two different standards? Yes, we are, because although leisure and recreation are firmly considered in the Western countries to be an enterprise, tourism is still haunted by the myth of the host and the guest, a concept that largely ignores the economic exchange that is at the basis of the tourist's experience. Staging can also be seen as the way in which people at a destination guarantee the value of the tourism product, while at the same time safeguarding their private lives.

It is a misconception of the nature of the "authentic experience" that leads to the example given previously. To witness such a personal event as a circumcision is for both the tourist and the host community embarrassing. Many tourists wish therefore to experience what they are happy to believe to be the authenticity of a place, but not necessarily its reality (McKercher and du Cros, 2002).

Authenticity As Self-Perception

When working in Indonesia I asked an Indonesian colleague why so few of his compatriots were attending the rehearsals of the court dances at the sultan's palace. His answer was simple and revealing: "Are you regularly going in Europe to 18th-century court dances in royal palaces?" Obviously the answer was "No," and his response was that Indonesians are the same. He did not consider these dances as representative of his own culture, but of the upper-class culture of the past.

When indigenous dances, music, and ceremonies are performed in a staged setting it is suggested that they lose their original meaning and value for the cultures involved. But folklore in Western countries shows that performance, enjoyment, and feeling of local pride can go hand in hand. Besides, no one knows if these performances would not change due to other social developments. Michel Picard (1983) observed that the dances performed on Bali are dances that were staged specifically for tourists in the early days of tourism on the island. This saved the authentic dances for the indigenous religious ceremonies, and kept them away from the profane visitors, who would anyway have no clue as to their "true significance." The Balinese now see these dances themselves as their genuine heritage, but the original "sacred" and "forbidden" dances are no longer remembered. Is this the effect of staging for the tourists, or would the Balinese have lost their knowledge of their dances anyway, who can say for sure? Cultures obviously are strong enough to survive such a loss, and even maintain an "authentic" atmosphere, as the case of Bali proves.

The island of Bali offers another interesting example of self-perception. I quote from article by Michel Maas (Maas, 2002):

> Wayan Sutedja sells his own sculptures. He has a workshop in Ubud where his employees carve sculptures that are for sale all over Bali. There are cats with long necks, "African" masks, Egyptian figurines, "Swiss" dollhouses, and characters from "Tintin." He calls them "unique designs" and has a thriving business. Critics however say this has nothing to do with Balinese culture. They say "Bali has sold itself to tourism, and loses its identity." Balinese like Sutedja think differently. Sutedja is not ashamed about his sculptures, this is woodcutting and it is a craft. It is what Balinese are good at and have done for many centuries.

His response makes clear that he considers the act of sculpting more essential for his cultural identity as a Balinese than the forms that he created in the process.

A last example from Bali. During the Balinese new year effigies in the form of huge monsters are made in every village and neighborhood to drive out the evil spirits from the island. There is a traditional design for these monsters, but increasingly other images are used as well to frighten the spirits. We noticed during our stay enormous Hells Angels on motorbikes and Westerners depicted as drunkards with a beer bottle. You can view these as derivations of the original design, but also as proof of the vitality of the underlying belief system which uses new images of what locally is perceived as horror to frighten off the evil spirits even more effectively.

Change will occur in any society, and probably tourism is only one of the factors in this process. Modern communication systems have certainly a much bigger impact. These processes of cultural exchange are, however, as old as culture itself. Any culture in the world has shaped itself in an endless process of giving and taking. Culture is a phenomenon constantly in development, a living identity. Culture is a dynamic pattern and when it is forced into a static pattern it will cease to be a source of inspiration. When conservation of culture turns into conservatism, the treatment will be worse than the disease and will eventually kill the "patient."

THE SHAPING OF CULTURAL IDENTITY

Before we can judge the deterioration of traditional cultures in developing cultures, we have to look at the evolution of our own traditions in the Western countries. The leading Dutch ethnographer Gerard Rooijakkers mentions that in the first half of the twentieth century there was the strong idea that the processes of modernization and urbanization where gradually undermining all kinds of old customs, traditions, songs, stories, and rituals. Researchers saw it as their task to safeguard as much of the "authentic" culture of farmers and fishermen as possible. They did so by meticulously describing the phenomena they encountered. The next generation of ethnographers grew up with the idea that this kind of work was finite; at a certain stage everything traditional would have vanished. But they were in for a surprise, because in the 1960s they discovered that popular traditions were ever-changing. They became critical of their own research and discovered that some of the old traditions were not as old as believed. They discovered that some traditions did not date back to the Middle Ages but only some fifty years, or they were the result of a romantic and nationalistic upheaval in the nineteenth century, such as the kilts in Scotland. They made a distinction between real folklore and fake-lore, the new ersatz-folklore. But Rooijakkers is specifically interested in these new phenomena. He is not so much concerned with the past as such, but how it is mobilized for all kinds of purposes.

He emphasizes that there is an enormous need for what he calls "social fiction": the "mythomania" around traditions, rituals, and customs, in short the cult of heritage. With that we give meaning to our time and space and shape our emotions. A perfect example is the hype around the death of Lady Diana, which is increasingly copied on many occasions to give grief a voice. The process by which people nourish and design their illusions is a reflection of the way they perceive the world around them. Rooijakkers states: "Folklore is never innocent." He researches the process of "folklorization and musealization." He observes that when the local elite notices a particular custom or traditional building is about to disappear, they form a committee to preserve it. The bright side is highlighted and the negative aspects—fighting at the annual festival, suppression of the rural poor by landlords—are forgotten. At the end of the process the custom or the object is transformed and fundamentally has changed both functionally and in signification. It has become a tourist attraction or a museum piece (Rooijakkers, 2002).

Not only do cultures change, but also the appreciation of cultures changes over time. Heritage is reevaluated by each generation anew; some aspects are added to it and others may be fading away. The rise in Western Europe of visitor centers dealing with the life of ordinary people at the turn of the nineteenth and twentieth centuries is a measure of the shift of attention to other forms of heritage than the more traditional upper-class expressions. This also applies to the increasing popularity of industrial archaeology and the growing demand for so-called rural tourism in Western Europe. It is interesting to notice that these developments are not spread out over time in the different European countries. In the United Kingdom, The Netherlands, and in Germany these phenomena arose much earlier than in the Mediterranean countries. In the northern part of Europe the Industrial Revolution started earlier, so the desire for nostalgia came about earlier than in the south of Europe. A time gap of some generations seems to be needed in order to appeal to nostalgia. When a society still has the personal memory of the hardship of industrial labor, there seems to be no wish to encounter it again in leisure time. It is also interesting to note that the phenomenon of rural tourism is very much an urban European trend, which has no equivalent in Asia, Africa, or Latin America. Even for the urban elite outside Europe, not enough time has elapsed to look back at the countryside with the same romantic longing, as is currently the trend in Europe. It was, however, also interesting to observe my own reaction to an anthropologic presentation of a folkloristic event in Macedonia. As I looked, fascinated at the film, I realized that if these images had been taken in Holland, I would have dismissed them as another backwater tradition. It is obvious that distance in time and space is needed to appreciate phenomena and to trigger either nostalgia or the search for authenticity as a driving force in tourism.

Cultural identity is the expression of one's place in the world. In tourism both the "host" (provider) and the "guest" (client) carry their awareness of identity with them and from the encounter of the two something new always emerges. From one perspective it can renew the bonds with one's own roots, both for the provider as well as for the visitor. It can make one curious about what was lost in the process and interested in trying to revive it. It can also lead to further deterioration of local cultures, resulting in cultural uniformity described as processes of Disneyfication and McDonaldization (see also Chapter 5).

This is true and untrue at the same time. Tourism can indeed lead to imitation of Western behavior, but be honest, who would not prefer to go to work on a motorcycle instead of going all the way on foot or on a bicycle, or would not prefer a cool drink from a fridge over a warm one? But cultural identity is a living force, and will eventually prove itself as a powerful countertrend against the global cultural domination of the West and the cultural uniformity it brings with it. Cultural identity represents the wish to protect the uniqueness of one's own culture, language, and identity—and their attached value systems—from foreign influence. Our roots are becoming increasingly important, to quote Naisbitt and Aburdene (1990):

> The more homogeneous our lifestyles become, the more steadfastly we cling to deeper values, we all seek to preserve our identities, be they religious, cultural, national, linguistic, or racial, the more worlds grow more similar, we shall increasingly treasure the traditions that spring from within.

This is arguably one of the driving forces of localization in society, and the production and reproduction of the "local" for cultural tourism.

The more the world turns into the global village, the bigger the need is to identify with what is at hand. The revival of regional idioms, the renewed interest in regional and local history, folklore, etc., are an expression of this development. The enormous growth of museums in Europe over the last twenty years is not particularly in prestigious national institutions, but in modest developments at the local level (English Tourist Board, 1991). Bringing together a collection and building a museum, being proud of one's own history and achievements is the expression of trying to find a solid base for one's identity in a world becoming so complex, abstract, and obscure that it no longer provides the foundation that is needed.

Within many Western countries there is a growing interest in the regions, the dialects and regional languages, the past, and nature. It is a move away from a political culture dominated by economics. In tourism, the regions try to build a distinct profile, based on the different atmosphere, different people, different culture, different language, different heritage, different food, and different customs. Tourism takes an active part in these developments, where cultural expressions are used to create unique selling points that make the distinction between destinations. But it is more than being competitive in a tough market; it is also the rediscovery of identity.

CONCLUSIONS

Obviously a balance is needed between the tourist, the experience of the culture visited, and the host community. The tourist, the culture, and the community are dependent upon one another. The tourists need, for their authentic experience, the living culture and the maintenance and improvement of the resources, which in their turn depend on the spiritual and economic development of the local community.

Cultural tourism can give incentives to training and education. Improvement of local skills, traditions, arts, and crafts are of mutual benefit to the population, the tourists, and the government. In this respect modernization in a society is not always an improvement. Originally, in the Dutch colonial period, the Sonobudoyo Museum in Yogyakarta on Java had a crafts-school annex to the museum. The students used the collections as examples to learn different styles and techniques. That has all been abandoned, but I assure you our ancestors often had better ideas of cultural continuity than we have today. Museums and heritage centers could also develop into focus points of quality souvenirs and handicrafts; they have the original models and the expertise, and increasingly the sophisticated tourist is bored with the junk for sale on the streets and on the tourist markets. They want a genuine piece to take home. In order to succeed, cultural heritage attractions must be actualized, commoditized, or somehow commercialized to facilitate consumption of the experience (McKercher and du Cros, 2002).

REFERENCES

Brunner, Edward (1995) The Ethnographer/Tourist in Indonesia. In: Lanfant, M.F. Allcock, J.B. and Brunner, E.M. (eds) *International Tourism, Identity and Change*, London: Sage, pp. 224-241.

Dann, Graham (1994) Tourism and Nostalgia: Looking forward to going back. *Vrijetijd en Samenleving*, 1-2: 75-94.

Dann, Graham (1996) *The Language of Tourism. A Sociolinguistic Perspective*. Wallingford: CAB International.

English Tourist Board (1991) *English Heritage Monitor*. London: ETB.

Lowenthal, David (1985) *The Past Is a Foreign Country*. Cambridge: Cambridge University Press.

Maas, Michel (2002) U komt toch zeker ook nooit meer naar Bali? *Volkskrant* 19/10/2002.

MacCannell, Dean (1973) Staged authenticity: Arrangements of social space in tourist settings. *American Journal of Sociology* 79 (3): 589-603.

Mason, G. (1994) The "Fakelore of Hawaii," manufactured myths. *The Eye* 11(4): 56-61.

McKercher, B. and du Cros, H. (2002) *Cultural Tourism: The Partnership Between Tourism and Cultural Heritage Management*. New York: Haworth Press.

Naisbitt, J. and Aburdene, P. (1990) *Megatrends 2000*, New York: Avon.

Picard, Michel (1983) *Community Participation in Tourist Activity on the Island of Bali: Environment, Ideologies and Practices*. Paris: UNESCO/URESTI-CNRS.

Picard, Michel (1995) Cultural heritage and tourist capital: Cultural tourism in Bali. In: Lanfant, M.F. Allcock, J.B. and Brunner, E.M. (eds), *International Tourism, Identity and Change*, London: Sage, pp. 44-66.

Picard, Michel (1996) *Bali, Cultural Tourism and Tourism Culture*. Singapore: Archipelo Press.

Rooijakkers, G. (2002) Quoted from an interview in the *Volkskrant*, 19/10/2002.

Schouten, Frans (1995) History as historical reality. In Herbert, David (ed.), *Heritage, Tourism and Society*. London: Mansell, pp. 21-31.

World Tourism Organization (2004) *Tourism Market Trends 2003 Edition*. Madrid: WTO.

Chapter 3

Township Tourism—Blessing or Blight? The Case of Soweto in South Africa

Pranill Ramchander

INTRODUCTION

South Africa's Cultural Resources

Traditionally, in terms of tourism, South Africa's unique selling points have been scenic beauty, wildlife, and climate. Before the first democratic elections in 1994, 30 percent of visitors came to South Africa for its scenic beauty, while 26 percent were drawn by its wildlife (Lubbe, 2003; Gauteng Tourism Authority, 2002). Yet, in the words of Goudie et al. (1999:24), with the demise of apartheid, "increasing emphasis has been placed on the role of township tourism as a catalyst for social change and healing in South Africa by the state, the private sector, and community organizations." In similar vein, Lubbe (2003:96) notes that "[a]fter 1994, 27 percent came to see the 'new South Africa,' while 21 percent came to view our cultural attractions. That is 48 percent of tourists coming to South Africa with a cultural motivation." In a more recent survey, the number of tourists whose motivation for visiting South Africa was cultural or socio cultural had risen to 46 percent (Lubbe, 2003).

South Africa consists of a remarkable mix of cultures, with African, European, and Asian influences intermingled to create a unique South African multi cultural society. The many-faceted heritage bequeathed by this mixture of exotic and indigenous culture is inextricably bound up with the social and political history of the country (Parker, 1997). Although cultural tourism in South Africa is still in its infancy, the political changes of 1994 have stimulated increased interest in the fascinating mix of cultures found in townships. In this melting pot, some things have remained unchanged, while other new and unique cultural expressions have evolved. Many forms of dance, music, song, theater, and cuisine, both traditional and modern, from every cultural group, may be encountered. Festivals, concerts, and performances reflecting lifestyles and regional interests are numerous. History and heritage are preserved in existing and newly developing museums and monuments in townships, living cultural villages, and places where the freedom struggle took place (Damer, 1997). There is also the wealth of arts and crafts produced by talented South Africans for sale in craft centers and open-air markets in townships (Soweto Tours, 2003a; Gold Reef Guides, 2003).

TOWNSHIP TOURISM

The urban black townships in South Africa differ from other deprived areas in the world largely as a result of the circumstances which prevailed under the ruling white minority during apartheid (Ramchander, 2003). To achieve social segregation, the National Party implemented a broad range of acts and ordinances ensuring that different races could not come into contact with each other, even in their free time (Soweto Tours, 2003a; Soweto SA, 2003). The segregation of housing, education, and health and leisure facilities such as beaches, hotels, restaurants, libraries, cinemas, camping sites, and national parks was an elaborate and humiliating system often entrenched with force, and which extended to the development of the townships as dormitory towns, as a means of segregating black labor. Townships were established far away from the central business districts, and from the white urban areas, and were not allowed to develop as an integral part of the white city (Mabogane and Callaghan, 2002; Ramchander, 2003). Many black townships, in particular, have suffered as a result of the perception that they are places of violence and squalor.

Over the past decade tourists have exercised a preference for travel that involves broadening the mind and learning, as opposed to the mass tourism culture of relaxation in the sun. The 1990s saw the emergence of various types of popular tourism, such as green, alternative, sustainable, cultural, adventure, health, and ecotourism, with each destination marketing its own unique offering (Poon, 1993). In South Africa cultural tourism, which is a component of special-interest tourism, has primarily taken the form of township tourism and cultural village tourism (Dondolo, 2001; Ramchander, 2004). Township tours present themselves primarily as offering insights into post-apartheid progress and development, and cite attractions such as beer makers, traditional healers, traditional dancing, arts and craft centers, taverns, bed and breakfast establishments, crèches, political landmarks, and shanty towns (Wolf, 2002; Chapman, 2003; Ramchander, 2003). Township tourism is growing rapidly as international tourists are eager to see how South Africa has progressed since 1994 (Sithole, 2003; Ramchander, 2004). Tourists are interested in townships that reflect past and present human experiences; they want to see the "real" people and witness their daily life, their present developments, and their cultural heritage (South Africa Online Travel Guide, 2002). As township tourism involves tourists motivated by interests in other people's cultures and a search for the different, it falls incontrovertibly within the body of cultural tourism.

Township tourism involves traveling for the purpose of observing the cultural expression and lifestyles of black South Africans, and offers firsthand experience of the practices of another culture (Mabogane and Callaghan, 2002; Ramchander, 2004). Tourists are typically transported in a microbus accommodating no more than fifteen people at a time. Many tourists visit South Africa's most famous townships because they symbolize political freedom and because visits to the sprawling townships fit in perfectly with the new paradigm of special-interest tourism. Political violence may have made black townships no-go areas for foreign tourists in the days of apartheid, but the 1976 uprising and the political strife of the 1980s subsequently made townships such as Soweto world-famous (Mabogane and Callaghan, 2002; Ramchander, 2004), and it is not surprising that township tourism has increased significantly since the first democratic elections in South Africa in 1994. Their legacy of violence and pain has made townships unlikely tourist destinations, yet busloads of visitors arrive every day to sample the renewed vitality of township life (Joburg Gateway to Africa, 2001; Sithole, 2003). Most leave with a very different impression from the one with which they arrived, having gained new insights following tours led by local entrepreneurs, and discovering that townships are not depraved areas of violent crime, but vibrant centers populated by friendly people with inspirational stories to tell (City of Johannesburg, 2003; Chapman, 2003). Tourists are given a glimpse of local residents' daily lives and living conditions. There is the mandatory visit to a few carefully selected people in their homes, which range from a small tin-and-wood house to a room in a hostel (Ian, 1999; Latherwick, 1999). A day-care center is chosen to put on a daily performance for the tourists. A short walk through a series of designated streets, under the watchful eye of the guide, is intended to impart the "feel" of the townships (Ramchander, 2004). At a craft center tourists are able to satisfy their expectation of encountering work and development, and at the same time feel they have made a contribution by purchasing what appears to be a handmade memento of Africa. Finally there is the social experience, set up in a "safe" shebeen, where the tourists will be able to partake of township life without being harassed by drunken and disorderly clientele (Chapman, 2003).

Despite urbanization, displacement, and modernization, people in the townships hold their customs and traditions dear (CNN-Travel-Guide, 2003), and township tours also include visits to traditional healers. Traditional healers are a source of health care to which Africans have turned throughout the ages, and even with the expansion of modern medicine, healers are still popular (Wolf, 2002).

Like other forms of community tourism development in the rest of the world, township tourism is increasingly being seen as an important economic activity with the potential to enhance the local economy. The term "tourism impact" has become increasingly prominent in the tourism literature (Allen, Long, and Kieselbach, 1988; Pearce, 1989; Ap, 1990; Brunt and Courtney, 1999; Brown, 2000; Ratz, 2003), as the literature has demonstrated, at least to some, that tourism development has both negative and positive outcomes at the local level. Tourism development is usually justified on the basis of economic benefit, and challenged on the grounds of social, cultural, or environmental destruction.

The actual contribution made by tourism in a development program has come increasingly into question because of an alleged meagerness of actual benefits, an inequality of benefit distribution, and the high social costs exacted by tourism (Ashley and Roe, 1998). Further, economic benefits traditionally associated with tourism development are now being measured against its potential for social disruption. Some governments are now starting to realize that the welfare of the public should be considered along with the needs of tourists and investors.

Although the South African White Paper on Responsible Tourism (South Africa, 1996) addresses the development, management, and promotion style of tourism development in the country, there is nevertheless a lack of information on the potential sociocultural impacts that township tourism may have on the host destination. This very lack opens the way to the research problem to which this study will attempt to provide a solution.

FORMULATION OF THE RESEARCH PROBLEM

Political violence may have made townships no-go areas for foreign tourists in the days of apartheid, but since South Africa's first democratic elections in 1994, township tourism has been growing rapidly as international tourists are eager to see how the country has progressed. Communities living in and around townships are thus affected by township tourism, either positively or negatively. Township tourism is a new and unique tourism product that is rapidly gaining currency in South Africa, with little or no research on its development, planning, and impacts.

Research in this domain would be particularly enriched by the debates concerning the way in which the culture and lifestyle of people in townships are marketed and commodified through cultural tourism in post-apartheid South Africa. There is a clear need to look beyond the obvious economic networks associated with the tourism industry to a deeper understanding of the issues of power, access, empowerment, and participation. Focusing on residents' perceptions of the sociocultural impacts of township tourism, the researcher in this study assesses some of the challenges associated with the development of more responsible and socially sensitive township tourism in South Africa. Using Soweto as a case study, this chapter examines the opportunities for and constraints on tourism development and the influences of these factors on township residents, questioning how tourism can be practiced in these areas in a way that ensures that benefits reach locals without being detrimental to their social and cultural heritage.

In the past, few black South Africans were allowed access to the tourism industry, either as tourists, operators, or managers. At worst, black cultures were ignored or repressed; at best they became stereotyped and trivialized commodities (Beavon, 1982; Ian, 1999; Goudie et al., 1999). An analysis of the township tourism market should therefore necessarily be extended to include the perceptions of the host community towards this new form of tourism that has engulfed their communities. As already mentioned, tourism research reveals increased attention to the social impacts of tourism on local communities, particularly marginalized indigenous groups. Urry (2001) contends that the process of creating a commercial tourism product from local cultures involves the careful selection, as well as screening, of cultural elements; these products are never simple mirror images of reality. A constant struggle, he argues, has emerged between market viability and authentic representations of local cultures, frequently resulting in a commercial (and political) screening and packaging of reality (see Chapter 2). Urry suggests that what tourists are guided through are more often than not profitable "pseudo-events" that are reflective of neither past nor present realities.

This raises important questions in South Africa about the social and cultural representation of township residents, and makes an examination of township tourism in South Africa particularly relevant. Black alienation and exclusion from mainstream tourism in the past has meant that most black South Africans have lacked control over the way in which their diverse cultures have been portrayed (Wolf, 2002). Yet the extent to which South Africa, like other developing countries, is benefiting by showcasing indigenous or marginalized communities as part of a cultural tourism strategy must be interrogated. Are the desired side effects of cultural tourism, such as job creation, the uplifting of communities, and the preservation of cultural lifestyles and expressions truly being realized, or have cultural expressions in fact changed and adapted to suit the demand and needs of the consumer tourist? Further subjects for debate are whether the ownership of cultural products should lie in the hands of the community or the developer, and whether the township community is exploited in the practice of cultural tourism as a result of its need for consumer goods and financial gain.

Many authors stress that cultural tourism brings about the gradual demise of traditional forms of art, craft, and design, or its replacement with reproductions (Nash and Smith, 1991; Fladmark, 1994; Pearce, 1995). The deterioration and commercialization of non material forms of culture has been a matter of major research concern, and the marketing of culture appears to be most prevalent in developing countries. The staging of contrived experience to compensate for the lack of real cultural experiences is another development that has become an accepted outgrowth of contemporary tourism (MacCannell, 1973; Pearce and Moscardo, 1986; Robinson and Boniface, 1998). Communities living in and around townships and cultural villages fall within the category of host populations, and so are included among those affected by cultural tourism. Sociocultural impacts in these areas, however, are less well documented.

AIM AND OBJECTIVES OF THE STUDY

The purpose of this study is to document township tourism and to investigate the sociocultural impacts of township tourism in Soweto as perceived by the host population and to examine the extent to which these coincide with the classifications in the literature. The study aims specifically to examine local residents' perceptions of and attitudes toward tourism, without measuring the actual social effects of tourism development on the area. Results from the study may provide the basis for formulating responsible tourism guidelines that will shape appropriate policies and measures intended to prevent negative tourism impacts and reinforce positive ones.

Soweto (originally an acronym for South Western Townships) is an urban area near Johannesburg, South Africa (see Figure 3.1). Dur-

FIGURE 3.1. The study area.

ing the apartheid regime, Soweto was constructed for the specific purpose of housing African people who were then living in areas designated by the government for white settlement. Today it remains an overwhelmingly black-dominated city.

Soweto gained the world's attention when it became the center of the antiapartheid movement. With a population of over two million, the township is the biggest black urban settlement in Africa with a rich political history. Soweto was the center of political campaigns aimed at the overthrow of the apartheid state. The 1976 student uprising, also known as the Soweto uprising, started in Soweto and spread to the rest of the country. Black students protested against the introduction of Afrikaans as medium of instruction at black high schools. Onto this legacy of repression and resistance Soweto tourism has grafted a sense of cultural Africanness.

Although reports of crime in the townships have caused many travelers to bypass them, more adventurous visitors are now taking tours. Many visitors take driving tours that let them see the world of the township from a van window, while others prefer the opportunity to get out and interact with the locals.

REASONS FOR SELECTING SOWETO
AS THE STUDY AREA

Townships throughout South Africa are in many ways similar in terms of their historical, geographical, and socioeconomic arrangement. Having originally been established as dormitory towns as a means of enforcing segregation, townships in South Africa are perceived as being inhabited by poor and crime-ridden communities in which high levels of political strife are prevalent. Consequently, there has been a deep-rooted perception among many South Africans and foreigners that townships are not a place to visit because of the threat they pose to personal safety.

There are townships located on the outskirts of all major cities in all nine provinces of the country, and in selecting a study area the researcher recognized that an investigation of the sociocultural impacts of cultural tourism spanning all townships in South Africa would have proved excessive in scope. Since the researcher is situated in Johannesburg, Soweto constituted the most practical and accessible choice of site for a study of this kind. The researcher was further led to select Soweto as the site for the present study because it is representative of South African black townships, while simultaneously being an icon:

> Soweto has developed from a mere geographical concept into an international symbol of victory over oppression. Throughout the world there are monuments condemning fascism, tyranny, and abuse of human rights, with the implicit message: let this never happen again. Soweto, like townships around South Africa, represents living proof that, with determination, spirit, and a just cause, an ordinary community can make a difference. (City of Johannesburg, 2003)

This sentiment was reiterated by Mrs. M. J. Woods, director of the City of Johannesburg's Tourism and Marketing (personal communication, August 21, 2003); in her view, Soweto is internationally known and is South Africa's most famous township because it symbolizes political freedom to people around the world. As a result, with little or no marketing, and despite a great deal of adverse publicity, it has established itself as a major destination for foreign tourists in

South Africa. Thus, because of both Soweto's representativeness and what it represents, the researcher considered that findings and conclusions reached from this study could be applicable to other townships in South Africa.

Woods describes Soweto as an unusual tourist destination because the events for which it is famous took place within recent living memory and the people responsible for these events are ordinary Sowetans. In this sense, Soweto is not an artifact or a museum, but a living place. It is not just another tourist destination; it is in part a memorial to those who died for freedom and in part a celebration of what human beings can achieve (Soweto SA, 2003). Soweto boasts special attractions as it is home to people who resisted the apartheid system. Tourists visit sites that were the frontiers of antiapartheid battles and today hold memories of that struggle (Mabogane and Callaghan, 2002). Cultural tourism is therefore an integral element of all tourism in Soweto.

A final compelling reason for selecting Soweto as the site for this study is its popularity as a tourist destination. Soweto has drawn innumerable visitors because international tourism trends for South Africa have also moved to cultural tourism patterns, and the sprawling township satisfies the new paradigm. Despite a scarcity of precise data on tourism markets and marketing relating to Soweto, evidence suggests that the majority of tourists originate from Europe. The perception is that they want to make contact with local people and experience the Sowetan way of life. National tourism statistics suggest that 8 percent of all visitors who visit South Africa's main attractions visit Soweto. Soweto holds joint fourteenth position on the list of the most popular attractions in South Africa, and is one of only eight attractions to have drawn an increased number of tourists over the past year (SA Tourism, 2003a,b).

According to a report from the Gauteng Tourism Authority (2002), the number of visitors who pay to enter the Hector Peterson Memorial site is an indication that an average of 1,498 tourists visit Soweto each month. However, as not all tours visit the memorial square, this figure is likely to be conservative. Mr. W. Radebe, a tour guide employed by Jimmy's Face to Face Tours, the largest tour operator in Soweto, explained that the enterprise takes approximately 3,000 tourists to Soweto per month. Three smaller operators take in the region of 1,000 visitors to Soweto per month between them (Radebe, personal communication, June 12, 2003).

Mr. K. Sithole, research manager of the Gauteng Tourism Authority (personal communication, September 15, 2003), estimated the total number of foreign and domestic tourists entering Soweto daily at 800. This figure does not take into account those not participating in official tours.

THE SOWETO TOWNSHIP TOURISM TRAIL

Township tours are currently gaining enormous popularity, as international tourists are eager to see how the country has progressed since its first democratic elections in 1994 (Masland et al., 2002; Soweto Tours, 2003a). A small but growing number of foreigners are overnighting in the homes of middle-class and working-class families in Soweto, seeing the rhythms and routines of the new era firsthand. Most tourists come from Europe, and some from the United States (South Africa Online Travel Guide, 2002). The most infrequent visitors, tour operators say, are white South Africans (Chapman, 2003).

Mabogane and Callaghan (2002) describe Soweto as containing lively hubs of humanity. It is not merely a place for squatters, criminals, and the poverty-stricken—amidst the apparently grim living circumstances, there is hospitality and hope, and even beauty. Soweto has always had a small and thriving middle class. The professionals—the teachers, doctors, shopkeepers, and civil servants—have taken pains to build comfortable double-story houses with roses in the gardens, satellite dishes on the roofs, and, in some instances, luxury cars parked in the driveway (Ramchander, 2003).

Local tour operators are of the opinion that at present tourists are generally not interested in cultural villages, as they are beginning to realize that cultural villages offer no more than staged authenticity (Ramchander, 2003); these villages commercialize the culture(s) of the people who are on display and have no spiritual links with the real culture of the people whatsoever, as they have been established expressly for the purposes of tourism (Dondolo, 2001; Witz, 2001). By contrast, however, the number of tourists visiting the townships is increasing, as tourists want to see the "real" people. They are more interested in townships as reflections of past and present human experience, and in people's daily lives as an amalgam of current developments and their cultural heritage (Witz, 2001; Ramchander, 2003).

Mrs. J. Briscoe, CEO of Gold Reef Guides (personal communication, 2003), cited the fact that a number of entrepreneurs from Soweto have established tour operations or shuttle services. The relatively high start-up costs, as well as the difficulties involved in obtaining tour operators' licenses and competition from large players in the field have meant that only the most determined have endured. They are now well organized: Tours are conducted in air-conditioned vehicles with cell-phone contact, by trained guides and staff.

Popular stops during tours include the huge mansion built by Winnie Mandela for her estranged husband; the tomb of Hector Peterson, the first victim of the 1976 riots; and the recently constructed Hector Peterson Museum, which offers visitors a detailed account of the events of 1976, including visuals and eyewitness accounts. Further stops are the Regina Mundi Catholic Parish Church, formerly the venue of protest meetings; the street on which stands the house that former President Nelson Mandela occupied prior to his imprisonment, and the home formerly occupied by Dr. Desmond Tutu (Soweto Tours, 2003a). Tourists also have the opportunity to peek into old hostels, visit Freedom Square, which commemorates the struggle for liberty, pay a call on merchants selling traditional African medicines, and savor typical African dishes (Gold Reef Guides, 2003). The Credo Mutwa Cultural Village, built by Credo Mutwa, herbalist, author, diviner, and sangoma (traditional healer), features a number of impressive mythical statues within its grounds, and provides the ideal setting to learn about the different dimensions of Soweto's cultural heritage (Farrow, 1999; Joburg Gateway to Africa, 2001; Soweto Tours, 2003b).

TOWNSHIP TOURISM: A MIXED BLESSING

Township residents say tourism has been a mixed blessing—some see it as an intrusion, while others are benefiting from the financial and cultural exchanges the tours offer. Because cultural tourists are presumably motivated by a desire to experience local cultures when choosing to visit a particular location, they are perceived as both a blessing and a blight in terms of their social and cultural impact. Some authors suggest that culturally motivated tourists are desirable because they tend to be relatively few in number and are also more sympathetic in their approach to the local population and its culture than other tourists (Smith, 1989). Others have suggested that it is precisely this cultural motivation that makes cultural tourists less desirable in some areas. "Alternative" tourists seeking authentic cultural experiences can open up culturally fragile areas, clearing the way for more potentially damaging mass tourism (Burns and Holden, 1995). Cultural tourists can also severely damage (in terms of sociocultural impact) local communities. Those in search of active contact with the local population are likely to cause far more disturbance by seeking out "local" places where their presence may cause friction with the local population. Local culture may become commercialized, and the youth may begin to copy the behavior and styles of foreign tourists. An increasing presence of tourists may lead to inflated prices.

Townships are the new tourist trend in South Africa, where the emphasis is on cultural tourism. Townships are meant to provide a more authentic and nonperformative experience, depicting "real" history, "real" people, and the "real" South Africa (Witz et al., 1999:17). Township tours are presented as an alternative to cultural village performances where tourists are invited to see the local residents in the townships as more authentic and in a nonperformative environment. Despite the claim that township tours are nonperformative, the local people do perform for tourists in different ways, for instance in preschools that are visited by tourists, shebeens, and open-air meat markets; some cultural groups also perform for visitors. This is the experience of a township tour package provided by many township tour operators (Dondolo, 2001).

During the researcher's fieldwork, local entrepreneur Lekau had this to say about the tours: "What you have to understand is that that township people do not always like the tours that now pass regularly through this place. Some of these give them the feeling that they are living in a zoo." Lekau has therefore been "educating" her neighbors to make sure they welcome her guests, ensuring that they know that the more visitors she receives, the more they—as local suppliers—will benefit. Some feel that tour operators and guides who live in the township should interact more with the local people.

On the downside, tour guides say too many companies run safari-style drive-through tours, where tourists snap photos and peer at the surrounding poverty from air-conditioned buses. After snapping up their postcards and African masks, most tourists leave with only the most fleeting of contacts with the local people. An unnamed resident says she saw one guide stop his bus in the township and allow tourists to throw money at the people below. Another guide was embarrassed by two guests who demanded that local children dance for their cameras.

Many township residents are still alarmed by visitors in their neighborhood. According to a tourism development officer working in the area, the tours have had some negative impact. There has been an invasion of privacy: For example, people barging into homes, which is not taken to kindly by the community. But guides insist the tours are not an attempt to make a voyeuristic theme park out of poverty, saying they brief tourists on acceptable behavior and offer them an opportunity to interact with residents.

There are the more enlightened tour operators, however, who allow tourists to meet locals in the township taverns, jazz clubs, and restaurants, and encourage them to support local artists and community projects. Some residents say they are being exposed to the world through these tourists.

A local bed and breakfast entrepreneur says: "Some days, I have two buses full of people. There's no room to sit down, so I have people in my kitchen and everywhere, just talking about everything. They come from Germany, Ireland, Florida, Michigan, Denver, Denmark. Because of apartheid, we never had the opportunity to share our cultures before."

Robinson and Boniface (1998) argue that the positive and negative consequences of contact fostered by tourism have been closely linked to debates about authenticity. It is well documented that the concept of authenticity in tourism studies has been shaped by the work of MacCannell (1973, 1976), who first made the connection between a formal concept of authenticity and tourist motivation, suggesting that tourists seek authentic experiences that they can no longer find in their everyday lives. MacCannell proposes that, for Western tourists, the primary motivation for travel lies in a quest for authenticity.

MacCannell (1973, 1976) notes that although tourists demand authenticity, it may be difficult to distinguish between true authenticity and what he terms "staged" authenticity, where a situation has been contrived so as to seem authentic. MacCannell argues that attractions vary in terms of the degree to which they are staged, and suggests that tourists today seek "backstage" (genuine or noncontrived) experiences, since modern tourists demand true authenticity (MacCannell, 1988). MacCannell further argues that "backstage" is where the real life of the community is carried out and authentic culture is maintained. The front stage, by contrast, is where commercial and modified performances and displays are offered to the mass of the visitors, and it is this area that tourists try to get beyond in their search for authenticity (Richards, 1996). Ramchander (2003) comments that in South Africa, both front-stage and backstage authenticity are evident, for instance in cultural villages, where locals "perform" culture for the tourist in the front-stage area, returning to the backstage area when they return to their real homes at the end of the day and carry out their normal cultural activities.

Townships as destinations are intended to reflect what in MacCannell's terms is the backstage. In the South African context, a visit backstage reveals the effects of racially discriminatory laws on the past and present human experiences, while front stage experiences involve purely favorable images. However, Dondolo (2001) argues that not all of the township tour package is authentically based. Rather, part of the package is carefully constructed, structured, and well planned.

The link between the issue of authenticity in tourism and township tourism is a topic of active debate, and has a direct bearing on the manner in which residents perceive tourism in townships. It is necessary to distinguish, however, between township tourism situations that involve a purely visual display of arts, crafts, and political landmarks and those that involve visitors in a genuine context, such as visits to people's homes, traditional healers, and active dance (Ramchander, 2003). While the country often benefits by showcasing township communities, it is important to understand how tourists and the host community feel about such cultural experiences.

METHODS OF DATA COLLECTION
USED IN THE STUDY

In selecting a suitable methodology for this study, the benefits and shortcomings of various methodologies were considered and a decision made to employ methodological triangulation, which combines elements of both qualitative and quantitative techniques, making a convergence of results possible. In-depth semistructured personal interviews, participant observation, and a Likert scale questionnaire were used to assess residents' perceptions of township tourism development in Soweto. A sample of 350 residents of Soweto living around the fourteen main tourism hubs of Soweto was obtained, at least 143 of whom earned income from tourism. On the basis of the literature review fifty-seven sociocultural impact variables were selected and used to formulate item statements designed to determine respondents' perceptions of township tourism in Soweto. A 5-point Likert scale was used to measure the levels of agreement and disagreement with each statement, with 1 = strongly disagree and 5 = strongly agree. This scale was selected as reflecting a better conceptual framework with regard to perceived tourism impact. Content validity of the scale was first secured through a pre-test and evaluation by academic staff members and students resident in Soweto.

Social exchange theory provided the theoretical background for this study. In the tourism context Ap (1990) incorporates social exchange theory into a conceptual framework using the social exchange processing model as a theoretical basis to assist scholars in understanding why residents have positive and negative perceptions of tourism. Social exchange theory suggests that residents will be inclined to exchange their resources with tourists if they can acquire benefits without incurring unacceptable costs. This theory articulates further that those who perceive the benefits of tourism to be greater than the costs may be more amenable to participating in the exchange and giving full-fledged support for tourism development—in other words, if residents perceive themselves as receiving more benefits through the exchange process, they will tend to more loyally support their community tourism business.

PROFILE OF RESPONDENTS

For both quantitative and qualitative data collection methodologies, the sample was selected from the following categories:

Type 1: Residents who are in constant and direct contact with township tourists; because they depend on township tourism and would perhaps be unemployed without it, they welcome visitors.

Type 2: Township residents who have no contact with tourists or see them only in passing and whose household income is not derived from township tourism.

Analysis

Quantitative data collected was initially coded into numerical representations so that statistical analysis using the software package called SAS version 8 could be performed. Analysis techniques used included single frequency distributions and means, standard deviations (central tendencies) as tools for descriptive analysis, univariate analysis and correlations as instruments of bivariate analysis, and factor analysis as means of multivariate data analysis techniques. Section C of the survey questionnaire as well as qualitative data collected through interview schedules were coded and repeated themes (responses) recorded and then sorted into categories as they emerged. The above analysis assisted the researcher to describe trends in the data and also determine whether there were relationships between variables.

DISCUSSION OF PRINCIPAL FINDINGS

The Most Positively Perceived Sociocultural Impacts

Frequency distribution and measurements in the form of means and standard deviations (SD) for the most positively perceived impact variables are reflected in Tables 3.1 and 3.2. A higher mean indicates a stronger level of agreement with the statement. Table 3.1 re-

TABLE 3.1. A selection of the most positively perceived attitude statements.

Positive Attitude Statements	Respondents with Income from Tourism		Respondents with No Income from Tourism	
	Mean	Std Dev	Mean	Std Dev
Township tourism has resulted in a greater demand for female labor.	3.56	1.20	3.30	1.32
Tourism development increases the development of recreational facilities and amenities for residents.	4.01	0.79	3.89	0.94
Township tourism has made residents more conscious of the need to maintain and improve the appearance of the area.	3.93	0.94	3.58	1.15
The development of township tourism has generally improved the appearance of Soweto.	3.75	0.99	3.46	1.29
Tourist interest in culture has resulted in a strengthening of traditional activities and cultural pride.	4.07	0.81	3.99	0.94
Township tourism has stimulated the locals' interest in participating in traditional art forms.	3.86	0.76	3.92	0.90
Local culture is being renewed as a result of township tourism.	3.67	0.98	3.64	1.18
Township tourists show respect for the cultural lifestyle of the local people.	4.14	0.82	3.82	1.03
Tourism encourages a variety of cultural activities by the local population.	4.00	0.59	3.90	0.86
Township tourism helps to conserve the cultural identity and heritage of the host population.	4.08	0.73	3.85	1.05
Meeting tourists promotes cross-cultural exchange (greater mutual understanding and respect for one another's culture).	3.90	0.98	3.84	1.15
By creating jobs and generating income, township tourism promotes an increase in the social well-being of residents.	4.02	0.72	3.72	1.11
Township tourism has led to more people leaving their former jobs for new opportunities in tourism.	3.10	1.15	2.68	1.22
Township tourism provides many worthwhile employment opportunities for Soweto residents.	3.79	0.88	3.28	1.25
Township tourism holds great promise for Soweto's economic future.	4.08	0.71	3.65	1.14

Source: This table appears by kind permission of Channel View Publications and was previously published in *Cultural Tourism in a Changing World: Politics, Participation and (Re)presentation,* edited by Melanie Smith and Mike Robinson (Clevedon: Channel View, 2006, ISBN 1845410432).

1 = Strongly Disagree 2 = Disagree 3 = Undecided   4 = Agree   5 = Strongly Agree.

TABLE 3.2. A selection of the most negatively perceived attitude statements.

Negative Attitude Statements	Respondents with Income from Tourism		Respondents with No Income from Tourism	
	Mean	Std Dev	Mean	Std Dev
Township tourism will gradually result in an increase in municipal rates and taxes.	3.10	1.01	3.26	1.25
Traditional African culture in Soweto is being commercialized (sold) for the sake of tourists.	3.29	1.02	3.35	1.36
Locals often respond to tourist needs by adapting traditional practices to enhance their commercial value.	3.79	0.72	3.84	0.94
Township tourism causes changes in the traditional culture of local residents.	2.82	0.98	3.30	1.25
Only a small minority of Soweto residents benefit economically from tourism.	3.59	1.04	4.16	0.96
The development of township tourism in Soweto benefits the visitors more than the locals.	2.99	1.13	3.54	1.21
Township tourism in Soweto is in the hands of a few operators only.	3.83	1.01	4.04	1.07

Source: This table appears by kind permission of Channel View Publications and was previously published in *Cultural Tourism in a Changing World: Politics, Participation and (Re)presentation,* edited by Melanie Smith and Mike Robinson (Clevedon: Channel View, 2006, ISBN 1845410432).

1 = Strongly Disagree 2 = Disagree 3 = Undecided 4 = Agree 5 = Strongly Agree.

flects higher mean values for both groups of respondents (type 1 and type 2), indicating an overall strong agreement with the positive impact statements.

The Most Negatively Perceived Sociocultural Impacts

Frequency distribution and measurements in the form of means and standard deviations for the most negatively perceived impact variables are reflected in Table 3.2. A higher mean indicates a stronger level of agreement with the statement. In Table 3.2, there are higher mean values for both groups of respondents (type 1 and type 2), showing an overall strong agreement with the negative impact statements.

It was found that the Soweto community's perceptions of township tourism and tourists fluctuate continuously between the negative and the positive. Findings revealed that the host community's support for township tourism was affected by three factors: socioeconomic, cultural and physical, and participation in benefits. One of the most important theoretical contributions of this study is the confirmation by the findings of the usefulness of exchange theory principles in explaining residents' perceptions of tourism. The factors thought to directly influence support for tourism actually influence the perceptions of its costs and benefits. Perceptions and expectations of township tourism in Soweto can therefore be very different depending on which group of residents is being considered. Those respondents in continuous contact with tourists and who depend on tourism viewed tourism favorably, and those who have no contact with tourists or see them only in passing exhibited a range of attitudes.

Respondents demonstrated a predominantly positive attitude toward a number of sociocultural impacts and agreed strongly that township tourism in Soweto is dismantling the stereotypical perceptions of townships as dangerous and a haven for criminals and hijackers; increases the development of recreational facilities and amenities for residents; has increased their awareness of tourism and hospitality and the need to maintain and improve the appearance of the area; has fostered a renewed interest in local arts, craft, and traditions; has instilled a sense of pride in locals concerning their heritage and culture; broadens their knowledge about international tourism, foreign places, and people due to the cross-cultural exchange of learning taking place; and leads to the conservation of cultural practices and political landmarks.

Appreciation was shown for the employment benefits generated by tourism, which has resulted in a greater demand for female labor and offered new career opportunities for locals to enter the industry as tour guides, tour operators, and entrepreneurs. Respondents further believed that the creation of employment through tourism holds a great promise for Soweto's economic future.

Although township residents demonstrated a predominantly positive attitude towards tourists and township tourism, they were also able to point out some specific sociocultural costs. Not all residents were of the opinion that tourism had a positive influence on local culture. Older respondents in particular voiced the concern that traditional African culture was being commercialized and claimed that certain locals sell or trivialize their culture to make a profit.

Residents argued that certain tourists and tour operators do not show acceptable standards of behavior, and cited intrusion as a significant problem. Some residents expressed concern about the escalation of crime in tourism hubs. Residents further cited inadequate consultation about township tourism development and planning as a negative aspect. Moreover, the benefits of township tourism appeared to accrue to only a small elite within the Soweto community. Respondents were in strong agreement that township tourism benefits only a small minority of Soweto residents, with those with the most power, education, and language skills or those who happen to live in the right place being most likely to get new jobs, set up enterprises, make deals with outsiders, or control collective income earned by the community. Increasing disparities in income can exacerbate conflicts within a community and has led to resentment between local people who have started tourism businesses and those who have not, as well as antipathy between residents not benefiting from tourism and tourists.

A broad conclusion drawn from this study is that township residents who benefit economically from township tourism are supportive of it, and this support is associated with a belief that township tourism causes mostly positive benefits. As a corollary, those without a commercial interest in township tourism tend to regard its impacts in a negative light. In keeping with this argument, Soweto residents who expressed the view that township tourism attracts organized crime and causes traffic congestion, for example, would almost automatically be opposed to tourism.

The identification of Soweto as a tourism destination has undoubtedly affected the quality of life of local residents. Effects of township tourism include an increased number of people, increased use of roads, and various economic and employment-based effects. Because Soweto is in the early stages of its life cycle as a tourism destination, Soweto residents seem to do and accept everything that is demanded by outsiders, ranging from the tourist trade and tourism promoters to their own government and entrepreneurs. They believe the promises when they are told that tourism is their big chance, and that it is of vital importance for the region, and, indeed, for the whole country. Yet no one has taken the trouble of asking Soweto residents whether township tourism clashes with their own values and ideas. No one mentions the negative sociocultural aspects. Tourism development in

Soweto appears to take place over the heads of the majority of residents, and few Soweto residents participate in tourism development as equal partners with tourism developers. Sadly, once township tourism takes hold of Soweto completely the locals will begin to realize what they have got themselves into. As the literature reveals, in such circumstances disillusionment and more realistic attitudes tend to replace the initial euphoria. By then it is usually too late and the locals soon lose control over their own destiny.

While success in this industry depends upon attractions and services, it requires the hospitality of local residents. If the tensions as mentioned by the respondents in this study are not adequately addressed, and the host community gradually reaches the stage of antagonism as identified in Doxey's Irridex model, tourists to Soweto will cease to be perceived by residents as individuals on holiday who may be talked to or who may be interesting. Instead, tourists will be seen simply as unidentifiable components within the mass. In a sense they will then be dehumanized, and as such become fair game for anyone who wishes to cheat, ridicule, or even rob them. The hosts' anger, antipathy, or mistrust will ultimately be conveyed to the tourists, and is likely to make them reluctant to visit places where they feel unwelcome.

CONCLUSION

The tourism industry in postapartheid South Africa has placed the responsibility for constructing, packaging, and transmitting images and representations of the "new" South African society and its past in the hands of a limited number of stakeholders within the public and private sector. The alienation and exclusion of black people from mainstream tourism both in the past and currently has meant that most township residents have lacked control over the way in which their diverse cultures are portrayed. While the tourism industry has been recognized both locally and internationally as a substantial and attractive source of economic benefits, problems such as those relating to the representation of and participation by the township community experienced by Soweto residents have been identified.

If we accept that township tourism in South Africa is going to increase, then we face the challenge of finding the balance between consumption and conservation, in other words, the challenge of achieving sustainable township tourism. The present study reveals that township tourism has become a complex phenomenon of unprecedented proportions, which can constitute either an opportunity or a threat with regard to culture, depending on how tourism is managed. Planning and managing township tourism requires that a number of issues be dealt with. For those involved in the preservation of culture, the challenge lies in understanding and working effectively with the tourism industry. For those in the tourism sector, there is a need to understand the needs of host communities as well as the principles and concerns that are a part of cultural heritage preservation (McKercher and du Cros, 2002). Township tourism as a phenomenon is not about to disappear, and poorly managed township destinations will have a negative effect on both local communities and the tourism industry if cultural resources and values are degraded. The challenge is not to stop township tourism, but rather for stakeholders to work together in achieving sustainable planning and responsible management.

Responsible township tourism development presents many challenges, and policymakers and communities will have to meet these challenges if they are to achieve comprehensive and sustainable township tourism development (Bramwell and Sharman, 1999; Bramwell and Lane, 2000). Tourism development is dependent on destination area resources and the goodwill of the communities involved. In utilizing cultural and natural resources, the tourism industry has a responsibility toward the community in that these resources are being exposed and sold as by-products; these actions affect the lives of everyone involved in such activities (Mann, 2000; Smith, 2003). It is therefore important that at the local level, township tourism planning should be based on the development goals, priorities, participation, and capacities as identified by, and to the mutual benefit of, its residents (Mann, 2000). Community-based planning is a local area planning approach that involves full participation by the local community, drawing on local skills and expertise, and providing for empowerment of the local community through the development and implementation of the resultant plan (Mann, 2000; Singh et al., 2003). This is essentially a bottom-up approach to planning, the objective of which is to build effective communities where residents or neighboring communities have a high quality of life, and to contribute to community well-being and cultural development.

If township tourism is to be encouraged as a new basis for cultural tourism development, the active collaboration of local cultures is required. The literature is clear on the fact that collaboration should address issues such as the redistribution of tourism revenue and the need to involve host cultures in ownership and management roles in the community. Unfortunately the reality for most communities is that outside forces usually determine the speed and direction of tourism development, and local people are seldom consulted. False expectations are often raised among the people when they are promised that the arrival of tourists will bring new wealth to the community. They soon discover that the real economic gain from tourism goes to the organizers and entrepreneurs.

Nongovernmental organizations, governments, and private initiatives therefore need to work more closely with the townships to develop sustainable cultural tourism that will benefit the community as a whole, and not just the handful of residents who live around tourism hubs or political landmarks. Empowering the locals and giving them the means to develop their culture in their own way must be seen as the key to solving the township tourism problem. It should be up to the local people to decide the limits of tourism. In general it can be said that the more the local community is able to participate in the decisions affecting their own tourist development, the less they will be socially affected by the rapid changes.

Even though South Africa celebrated a decade of democracy in 2004, South African society continues to face enormous social, cultural, and economic challenges in its attempts to confront the legacies of previous generations. For cultural tourism, this challenge lies not only in product development, but also in the issues relating to the impact of culture that are central to development, education, training, marketing, and management. Cultural tourism presents a very good opportunity to generate economic growth and development that can be sustainable in the long term. For the previously marginalized groups this constitutes a much-yearned-for injection of development infrastructure and brings the hope of real economic development, job creation, education, and training.

Township tourists need information to enable them to behave in a responsible and sensitive way, both before they depart for their destination and at the destination itself. The tourism industry has the responsibility to provide township tourists with accurate information about local cultures and appropriate behavior. Host communities need to understand why township tourism is important, how tourism works, its benefits and costs, and how they can participate. Important questions to be asked regarding township tourism in South Africa are: "Who should control township tourism?" and "What should be controlled?"

Resident perceptions are undoubtedly a key component in the identification, measurement, and analysis of township tourism impacts. However, investigation of community perceptions of township tourism is not just an academic exercise. These perceptions are also important in terms of the determination of local policy, planning, and responsible management responses to township tourism development and in establishing the extent to which public support exists for township tourism.

Cultural diversity and authenticity are central aspects to the township tourism experience. Township tourism requires a higher level of community involvement than most other forms of tourism and offers greater opportunities for local communities. Supporting services and products can be equally rewarding and add local flavor to the experience through the showcasing of local goods and customs. Support for the revival and maintenance of traditional cultural skills and practices, as well as new cultural products, is an integral part of the development of cultural tourism. At the same time, awareness of the various economic, social, and cultural opportunities associated with township tourism should be created among locals.

Township tourism ventures need to involve local communities, through a community tourism approach, and should be developed through a process of consultation and negotiation, ensuring opportunities for locals to participate in and determine decisions about the nature of their involvement. Prior to any township tourism development, assessment of both future as well as present needs and expectations of the community should be undertaken. Proper development for township tourism should be informed by both market requirements and societal needs and development objectives. Socially, environmentally, and economically beneficial responsible township tourism development requires achieving a balance between commercial success, the maintenance of cultural integrity and social cohesion, and the maintenance of the physical environment.

REFERENCES

Allen, L., Long, P.R. and Kieselbach, S. (1988) The impacts of tourism development on residents' perceptions of community life. *Journal of Travel Research* 27(1):16-21.
Ap, J. (1990) Residents' perceptions: Research on the social impacts of tourism. *Annals of Tourism Research* 17:610-616.
Ap, J. and Crompton, J.L. (1993) Residents' strategies for responding to tourism impacts. *Journal of Travel Research* 32(1):47-50.
Ashley, C. and Roe, D. (1998) *Enhancing Community Involvement in Wildlife Tourism: Issues and Challenges*. London: International Institute for Environment and Development.
Beavon, K.S.O. (1982) Black townships in South Africa: Terra incognita for urban geographers. *South African Geographical Journal* 64(1):2-20.
Blanche, M.T. and Durrheim, K. (1999) *Research in Practice: Applied Methods for the Social Sciences*. Cape Town: University of Cape Town Press.
Boniface, P. (1995) *Managing Quality Cultural Tourism*. London: Routledge.
Bowen, K.A. (2003) An argument for integration of qualitative and quantitative research methods to strengthen internal validity. Trochim.human.cornell.edu//gallery/bowen/hass691.htm [Accessed: 2003-06-22].
Bramwell, B. and Lane, B. (Eds) (2000) *Tourism Colloboration and Partnerships: Politics, Practice and Sustainability*. Clevdon: Channel View.
Bramwell, B. and Sharman, A. (1999) Collaboration in local tourism policymaking. *Annals of Tourism Research* 26: 392-415.
Brown, F. (2000) *Tourism Reassessed: Blight or Blessing?* Oxford: Butterworth Heinemann.
Brunt, P. and Courtney, P. (1999) Host perceptions and sociocultural impacts. *Annals of Tourism Research* 26(3):493-515.
Burns, P. and Holden, A. (1995) *Tourism: A New Perspective*. Englewood Cliffs, NJ: Prentice Hall.
Chapman, K. (2003) Township tours offer glimpse of "Mandela's country." www.cnn.com/SPECIALS/1999/safrican.elections/stories/township.tours/ [Accessed: 2003-03-15].
City of Johannesburg (2003) Soweto. www/joburg.org.za/soweto/index.stm [Accessed: 2003-08-23].
CNN-TravelGuide. 2003. Experiencing Soweto. Poverty lingers but things are changing in Mandela's birthplace. [Online] Available from: www.cnn.com/TRAVEL/DESTINATIONS/9810/safrica.2/soweto.html [Accessed: 2003-04-13].

Damer, B. (1997) *Soweto Township, South Africa.* Johannesburg: South African Picture Gallery.

Dann, Graham (1996) *The Language of Tourism: A Sociolinguistic Perspective.* Wallingford: CAB International.

Dawie, L. (2001) Hector Peterson gets his memorial. www.goafrica.co.za/joburg/ october/hector.stm [Accessed: 2003-04-12].

Dondolo, L. (2001) Depicting history at Sivuyile Township Tourism Center. Paper presented at the Mapping Alternatives: Debating New Heritage Practices Conference, University of Cape Town, 26-27 September.

Farrow, P. (1999) *Soweto: The Complete Township Guide.* Houghton: Soweto Spaza CC.

Fladmark, F.M. (Ed) (1994) *Cultural Tourism.* London: Donhead.

Gauteng Tourism Authority (2002) *Soweto Tourism Strategy Implementation Plan.* Johannesburg: Heritage Agency CC.

Gold Reef Guides (2003) Township tour—memorable in every way. www.gold reefguides.co.za/TownshipTour.htm [Accessed: 2003-05-04].

Goudie, S.S., Khan, F. and Killian, D. (1999) Transforming tourism: black empowerment, heritage and identity beyond apartheid. *South African Geographical Journal* 81(1):23-31.

Ian, F. (1999) Where apartheid ruled, tourists are swarming. *New York Times,* 149:4-8.

Joburg Gateway to Africa (2001) A tourist guide to visiting Soweto. www.goafrica. co.za/joburg/november/soweto.stm [Accessed: 2003-07-06].

Latherwick, P. (1999) Soweto Township Picture Gallery. www.damer.com/ pictures/travels/southafrica/phils-pix/index.html [Accessed: 2003-07-23].

Lubbe, B.A. (2003) *Tourism Management in Southern Africa.* Cape Town: Pearson Education South Africa.

Mabogane, M. and Callaghan, R. (2002) Swinging safaris in Soweto. www.mg.co. za/mg/africa/soweto.html [Accessed: 2002-11-19].

MacCannell, D. (1973) Staged authenticity: Arrangements of social space in tourist settings. *American Journal of Sociology* 79:589-603.

MacCannell, D. (1976) *The Tourist: A New Theory of the Leisure Class.* New York: Schocken Books.

MacCannell, D. (1988) *The Tourist: A New Theory of the Leisure Class* (2nd ed). Berkeley: University of California Press.

Mann, M. (2000) *The Community Tourism Guide.* London: Earthscan Publications.

Masland, T., Esther, P. and Mike, C. (2002) Turning history into tourism. *Newsweek* (Atlantic edition), 140(16):42-48.

McKercher, B. and du Cros, H. (2002) *Cultural Tourism: The Partnership Between Tourism and Cultural Heritage Management.* New York: Haworth Press.

Nash, D. and Smith, V. (1991) Anthropology and tourism. *Annals of Tourism Research* 18(1):12-25.

Parker, S. (1997) *Culture and Heritage Tourism and their Potential Impact on Local Communities: The Challenges of Ownership, Developments and Other Requirements.* Discussion paper, Department of Arts, Culture, Science and Technology. Pretoria: Government Press.

Pearce, P.L. (1989) Social impacts of tourism. *The Social, Cultural and Environmental Impacts of Tourism.* Australia: New South Wales Tourism Commission.

Pearce, P.L. (1995) From culture shock and cultural arrogance to culture exchange: ideas towards sustainable socio-cultural tourism. *Journal of Sustainable Tourism* 3(3):143-154.

Pearce, P.L. and Moscardo, G.M. (1986) The concept of authenticity in tourists' experiences. *Australian and New Zealand Journal of Sociology* 22:121-132.

Poon, A. (1993) *Tourism, Technology and Competitive Strategies.* Wallingford: CAB International.

Ramchander, P. (2003) Township tourism—blessing or blight: The case of Soweto. Paper presented at the ATLAS Cultural Tourism Group Expert Meeting on Cultural Tourism: Globalising the Local—Localising the Global, Barcelona, 1 November.

Ramchander, P. (2004) Soweto set to lure tourists. In: Bennett, A. and George, R. (eds.) 2004. *South African Travel and Tourism Cases.* Pretoria: Van Schaik.

Ratz, T. (2003) The socio-cultural impacts of tourism. Case of Lake Balaton, Hungary. www.ratztamara.com/balimp.html [Accessed 2003-01-06].

Richards, G. (1996) *Cultural Tourism in Europe.* Wallingford: CAB International.

Robinson, M. and Boniface, P. (Eds) (1998) *Tourism and Cultural Conflicts.* Wallingford: CAB International.

SA Tourism (2003a) Monthly arrival reports—November 2003. www.southafrica.net/index.cfm?SitepageID=223 [Accessed: 2004-01-12].

SA Tourism (2003b) Quarterly reports—quarter two 2003. www.southafrica.net/index.cfm?SitepageID=223 [Accessed: 2004-01-12].

Singh, S., Timothy, D.J. and Dowling, R.K. (2003) *Tourism in Destination Communities.* Wallingford: CABI.

Smith, M.D. and Krannich, R.S. (1998) Tourism dependence and resident attitude. *Annals of Tourism Research* 25 (4):783-802.

Smith, M.K. (2003) *Issues in Cultural Tourism Studies.* London: Routledge.

Smith, V.L. (1989) *Hosts and Guests: The Anthropology of Tourism.* Philadelphia: University of Pennsylvania Press.

South Africa Department of Environmental Affairs and Tourism (1996) *White Paper on the Development and Promotion of Tourism in South Africa.* Pretoria: Government Printer.

South Africa Online Travel Guide (2002) Soweto Johannesburg. Southafrica-travel.net/north/aljohb06.htm [Accessed: 2003-04-16].

Soweto SA (2003) Soweto: South African history. www.sowetosa.co.za/soweto.history.html [Accessed: 2003-04-11].

Soweto Tours (2003a) Soweto, an overview. www.soweto.co.za/html/history.htm [Accessed: 2003-09-16].

Soweto Tours (2003b) Soweto tours and picture gallery. www.soweto.co.za/html/gallery.htm [Accessed: 2003-09-16].

Urry, J. (2001) *The Tourist Gaze: Leisure and Travel in Contemporary Sciences* (Second Edition. London: Sage.

Witz, L. (2001) Repackaging the past for S.A. tourism. Proceedings of the American Academy of Arts and Science. *Daedalus* 130(1):277.

Witz, L., Rassool, C. and Minkley, G. (1999) Tourism in African Renaissance. Paper presented at the conference entitled Public History, Forgotten History, University of Namibia, August 22-23.

Wolf, L. (2002) Beyond the shacks: The vibrant world of the townships. HYPER-LINK "http://www.travel.iafrica.com/activities/townships/212881.htm" www.travel.iafrica.com/activities/townships/212881.htm [Accessed: 2002-09-12]

Chapter 4

Developing Cultural Tourism in South Africa: Potential and Pitfalls

Jenny Briedenhann
Eugenia Wickens

INTRODUCTION

In South Africa, tourism development and its practice have been confined to one small sector of the population and have been only vaguely understood concepts, considered predominantly as a "white man's thing." The new South African government, struggling to deal with the ravages of skewed development among its multiethnic population, envisages tourism as the tool through which to bring about the alleviation of poverty and the mitigation of unemployment, rampant in rural and "township" communities. The danger of creating unrealistic expectations of tourism as a potential panacea and remedy for the socioeconomic maladies that beset the country's marginalized communities, however, poses an inherent danger to which those espousing its benefits frequently fall prey.

For the most part South Africa's marginal communities are bereft of a sense of pride. Brainwashed by years of struggle, many accept their lot as a lost cause and in so doing make the prediction of failure self-fulfilling, thus further undermining their self-belief. In many areas people are so desperate that they will accept any proposal with little or no consideration of future impacts. The reality for most communities is that what counts is today, with scant thought for tomorrow. Over the past eight years the face of tourism in the country has slowly changed. Recognition has dawned that the population of the "rainbow nation" has a wealth of cultural resources, which are of great interest to the tourist. A tourism industry traditionally focused on the wealth of its wildlife is gradually diversifying to include the cultural wealth of its people. As a result of historical isolation from the tourism sector many communities do not realize either their potential or the value of their rich cultural resources as tourist attractions. The gradual acceptance by rural African people of the legitimacy of charging for accommodation and food, things that historically were freely given, heralds a major breakthrough.

Small tourism projects are slowly becoming sought-after attractions for tourists seeking to experience what they perceive as the authentic lifestyles and traditions of the country's indigenous people. This chapter presents a comparative case study of two rural community cultural tourism projects. It critically examines the approach adopted by the "champion" of each project and considers the factors, which have contributed to their success or failure. Finally, it determines the essential criteria in ensuring the sustainability of cultural tourism projects developed as agents of poverty alleviation in South Africa's marginalized rural communities.

BACKGROUND TO THE STUDY

As already discussed in Chapter 3, the advent of democracy in 1994 brought to an end centuries of political oppression for the vast majority of South Africa's multiethnic population. Despite a politically smooth transition the new democratic government was confronted with escalating problems of poverty alleviation and the ravages of historically skewed development. This deprivation was most prevalent in the country's vast rural areas, where minimal provision of health care, education, electricity, or clean drinking water placed growing demands on government to ensure speedy delivery of services to counter the backlog engendered by fifty years of neglect. There were no easy solutions. Many of the country's largest rural communities had, by virtue of forced removal under the old regime, been resettled in areas with scant resources and marginal agricultural land. For example, in the sprawling rural communities bordering the world-renowned Kruger National Park, unemployment is as high as 40 percent (Honey, 1999). Searching for alternatives, the government settled on tourism as one of the few viable options to stimulate the economy in marginalized rural areas and, through its potential to create jobs and entrepreneurial opportunities, uplift the quality of life of rural communities. The White Paper *Development and Promotion of Tourism in South Africa* endorses the role of tourism as perceived by government:

> The population needs to be provided with meaningful employment and entrepreneurial opportunities so as to be able to afford housing, water and sanitation, electricity, transport, and health care. The tourism industry, more than any other industry, can provide sturdy, effective, and sustainable legs for the RDP (Reconstruction and Development Program) to walk on. (Government of South Africa, 1996:14)

Over the last decade phrases such as "transparency" and "community participation" have become an integral part of development rhetoric in South Africa. To a significant extent community inclusion in tourism has, however, remained little more than tokenism. The country has an abundance of cultural tourism resources—the mere fact that there are eleven official languages is indicative of her diversity—yet tourism development has evolved with minimal involvement of either indigenous communities or of their rich cultural heritage. Historical isolation from the tourism sector, as well as years of brainwashing that maligned non-Western culture as uncivilized, deprived communities of their sense of cultural pride and led to an inability to realize either their potential or the value of their rich cultural resources as tourist attractions.

The face of tourism in the country is, however, slowly changing. The "rainbow nation" is now beginning to employ its wealth of cultural resources to diversify its traditional wildlife product and to offer tourists an experience of the lifestyles and traditions of the country's indigenous people.

PERSPECTIVES FROM THE LITERATURE

The national White Paper *Development and Promotion of Tourism in South Africa* asserts that "tourism brings development to rural areas [and] allows rural people to share in the benefits of tourism development" (Government of South Africa, 1996:16). Tourism academics conversely warn that tourism is unlikely to be a sustainable development option on which to base a weak rural economy but is better used as a means of complementing a local economy that is already thriving (Butler and Clark, 1992). The dangers inherent in the promotion of tourism as the panacea to heal the economic ills of rural areas in South Africa are ever prevalent. For example, Fowkes and Jonsson (1994:16) experienced the conflict and frustration that arose when "as a result of national advertising and promotion, communities wanted to move into tourism development . . . expectations were raised that tourism is the way to make money in rural areas"; but the communities were unable to do so due to lack of financial resources. Lack of access to funding is an acute barrier to entry into tourism for economically marginalized indigenous groups who have no means of providing collateral against which to procure loans (Department of Environmental Affairs and Tourism, 1996). In addition, few communities appreciate that the anticipated benefits of tourism projects are not immediate and that it takes time before projects reach fruition and show results (Ashley et al., 2001). Hall and Jenkins (1998) allege that there is a proclivity to regard tourism as the easy option in rural areas and argue that there is a danger that unrealistic economic expectations, together with a lack of understanding and management of its negative aspects, may minimize tourism's potential benefits. Despite such caveats, the reality for many rural communities in South Africa is that there are few viable options. The growth of rural tourism offers the opportunity for the development of small-scale projects catering to tourists who, in visiting less-developed countries, increasingly seek experiences encompassing the traditions, cultures, religions, and events of their host communities (Harrison, 1994).

The literature is awash with arguments about the meaning of culture (e.g. Geertz, 1957; Richards, 1995; de Sola Pool, 1979; Wallerstein, 1990), studies that slate tourism as a cultural commodifier and demeaner (MacCannell, 1976, 1992; Greenwood, 1977) or document community hostility at perceived cultural exploitation (Bossevain, 1993). The role of indigenous people as performers has become a particularly sensitive issue (Butler and Hinch, 1996; Getz and Page, 1997). For example, Hitchcock (1997:98) records that Botswana Bushmen voiced antipathy to conducting their traditional activities for the benefit of tourists, arguing, "We do not want to have to perform for tourists. It is not right that we should be treated like animals in a circus." Researchers argue that tourist exposure to indigenous culture is denigrated as events and performances, packaged to be commercially viable and attractive and comprehensible to tourists, become simplified, abbreviated, and homogenized (Picard, 1995; Stanley, 1998; Hashimoto, 2002). The practical reality, however, is that cultural tourism projects, like any other, are faced with the imperative of "deliverable" products (Getz and Page, 1997:200) that are compatible with tour operator schedules and offer reliable, regular show times and a guaranteed experience (McKercher, 1993). This can be problematic to South African rural communities whose emphasis on time differs radically from that of their visitors. For example, Fowkes and Jonsson (1994:12) found that

> a problem was encountered in creating community understanding of the underlying concepts of time and the relationship between a tourist's needs, limited time, and fixed schedules. This is further complicated by the tourist's desire to see and do everything —a concept that is far from the reality of a rural community.

Despite allegations that tourism can be a distorter, commodifier, and ultimate destroyer of indigenous culture, Hashimoto (2002:215) argues that tourism can "contribute to the protection and enhancement of traditions, customs, and heritage, which would otherwise disappear." Presentation of their culture to tourists can also bring about a renewed source of community pride. For example, there is evidence that amongst the Djabugay, an Australian Aboriginal community, "employees took pride in and enjoyed presenting their culture for others. They saw cross-cultural interaction between themselves and tourists as reducing stereotypical impressions thus enhancing understanding" (Dyer et al., 2003:93). The operator of a South African township "homestay" has similarly highlighted the positive outcomes of cross-cultural interaction. "This is the real reason I opened Vicky's Place: I want people to overcome their prejudices—the whites who think townships are too dangerous, and the blacks who are suspicious of the whites" (Tavner, 2003). The impacts of cultural tourism projects on their host community are thus context-specific, dependant upon the circumstances in which projects are developed, the communities who reap their benefits and bear their costs, and the attitude and approach of the developers. The fundamental principle of any cultural tourism development is that local people must retain ownership of their culture and the power of decision-making with regard to what elements they wish to portray and which they wish to conceal (Crouch, 1994).

Developers of cultural tourism projects in South Africa have, however, found that adhering to the principles of community-based project-planning and decision-making is only the first step in a long journey in which harsh economic realities ultimately dictate project success or failure. This chapter presents a comparative case study of two rural community cultural tourism projects. It critically examines the approach adopted by the "champion" of each project and considers the factors, which have contributed to both success and failure. Finally, it determines the criteria essential in ensuring the sustainability of South Africa's rural cultural tourism projects.

Methodology

Research into tourism in rural areas in South Africa has been ongoing since 1996. Involvement at the coalface of the South African tourism industry provided the opportunity to undertake case studies of projects as a means of improving practice within the researcher's own field of responsibility at that time. In the period between 2000 and 2002, a three round Delphi Study was undertaken as the preliminary stage of data collection toward a PhD thesis pertaining to the evaluation of rural tourism development projects. The Delphi panel comprised thirty South Africans, all with considerable expertise in the rural tourism field. Participation was purposely solicited from tourism academics, consultants, public sector officials representing regional and local tiers of government, public sector tourism agencies, and private sector rural tourism operators. The projects, which serve as case studies for this chapter, are analyzed in terms of the criteria developed by Delphi respondents against which to evaluate rural tourism projects. Direct quotes are included in the text in order to give voice to respondents in their own terms. In order to protect the confidentiality of informants, the projects are referred to merely as Project A and Project B.

INITIATING THE PARTICIPATORY PROCESS

Eighty-two percent of the Delphi panelists agreed that projects should illustrate the principles of community planning through an extended, inclusive, and ongoing consultation process during which the information necessary to facilitate informed decision-making is shared and local concerns taken into account. Despite agreement that this was the ideal situation, caveats were sounded with regard to the difficulties of operationalization. Panelists pointed out that "working with a community is hugely difficult because of all the different interests and agendas" and counseled that "care should be taken of the prevalence of participation paralysis and also of being too naive as to what really drives tourism development." Eighty-five percent of the panelists believed that a transparent process should be followed in selecting participants/stakeholders or partners in projects.

The projects are very different. Project A was located in a typical rural village, situated in a mountainous area with reasonably poor road access. Authority in the village is vested in the traditional chief. The champion (or partner operationally involved in the project) was an altruistic small rural tour operator who embarked on the project believing that she had a moral obligation to play her part in addressing past inequalities and assisting a poor rural community to develop their tourism potential. Project B was driven by commercialism. The developers identified an opportunity to develop a unique cultural tourism project that had the potential to make money. They looked for a return on their investment, at the same time believing that the project could, and striving to ensure that it did, bring genuine benefits to the local community.

Both projects embarked on ongoing processes of consultation and decision-making following Hall's (2002:31) concept of "a bottom-up form of planning, which emphasizes development in the community rather than development of the community." The composition of the members of the "community" who were involved in these processes, however, differed. In the case of Project A it was the chief who gathered the villagers and drew them into the consultation process. The central role played by the chief did not prove to be an inhibiting factor since he was an ardent supporter of the project. Despite the fact that tourism was a foreign concept, he was open to discussion of the potential opportunities that this new idea could hold for his people. The approach in Project B was totally different. The developers believed that trying to deal with the "community" as an entity would be rendered unworkable as a result of conflict engendered by contradictory agendas and opinions. Their mode of approach was a much more business-oriented "work with individuals and incentivize them to want to make money." Notices were widely distributed and anyone who was interested in participation was invited to attend meetings and subsequently to participate in mass interviews for employment.

PLANNING THE PROJECT

Clarity and realism with regard to the aims, goals, rewards, and impacts of a project was perceived as crucial by 96 percent of the Delphi panel. The ability of communities to sustain their belief in projects during the long development period was also highly rated (89 percent). An academic respondent pointed out that one of the complications encountered in undertaking a process of consultation was the "great difficulty of a community to visualize" a project and gain an understanding of both its potential benefits and its negative impacts. Respondents cautioned that "there is always the danger of creating unrealistic expectations of tourism being a potential poverty and socioeconomic remedy for all communities and individuals. Communities that are desperate for economic development and jobs could easily latch on to tourism as the savior if it is not communicated properly and realistically." A respondent with many years' experience at the development coalface captured the problems succinctly:

> The trick is to get people to see what you see, but to see it in a realistic way. I think where we make a mistake is to envisage what the project could be ten years hence, but poor rural people

are going to have a faster expectation. So, lighting a fire in somebody, you've got to be very careful that the fire doesn't burn you and them at the same time. So it's a question of igniting a little glowing ember rather than this fierce fire.

From the outset Project A was problematic. Neither chief nor champion could speak each other's language. The inability of the project champion to communicate directly with either the chief or his villagers was a significant constraint, exacerbated by the fact that the interpreter also did not fully understand the tourism concept. Fowkes and Jonsson (1994:5) highlight the difficulties of using an interpreter, pointing out that the potential opportunities and threats of tourism development are, in any event, not easily understood: "The concept of travel to distant places with leisure as an objective is foreign to most rural communities." Equally foreign is the concept of charging for hospitality, an anathema in the African culture of "ubuntu." The gradual acceptance by rural African people of the legitimacy of charging for things that historically should be freely given heralds a breakthrough in the realization of their tourism potential.

Planning the project became a long, drawn-out process. Through the medium of the interpreter, the chief and his villagers expressed their vision for the little community and outlined those aspects of their daily lives that they were willing to share with tourists.

The approach in Project B was significantly different. Mass interviews took place for people interested in becoming involved in the project, and employees were selected on the basis of language and communication skills. Every employee is, however, a member of the local community: "We only employ local people. They stay longer and are more comfortable within their own social network." A musician from the local community, who was also a playwright, was appointed as the consultant to develop the tourism product. The choir employed was an existing collective. The cultural presentation, which tells the history of the tribe through song, dance, and local interpretation, was choreographed on a consultative basis between the consultant, the selected employees, and the project developers. The champion asserts that "those employed for the presentation then came up with their own great ideas. This consultative process stimulated self-thinking and creativity."

PROJECT IMPLEMENTATION

Ninety-six percent of the Delphi panel were in agreement that projects should contribute to host community confidence and pride in their culture. This principle was affirmed by the belief that the "script should be developed by key stakeholders, everyone involved in and impacted by tourism." It was further contended that all development should be in accordance with the "image, values, theme, character, and philosophy of the community." Respondents further supported the incorporation of local flavor into all aspects of a project and contended that the community should take the lead in its design and construction. This, they argued, "helps build community respect, and they take ownership." Respondents emphasized that perceptions of community ownership were imperative in securing the cooperation and commitment needed to ensure project success.

Project A can be lauded on the basis of its "authenticity." The project, built on legendary Swazi hospitality and charisma, was no custom-built "cultural village." It was the people's home. The tourist experience included a visit to the village, entertainment in the form of traditional song and dance, and the enjoyment of a meal prepared by the village women. The project champion was adamant that the community should agree to the type of tourism envisaged for their village. All decisions with regard to the type of entertainment, the mode of dress, the meal provided, and the time of day most convenient to receive visitors were thus left to the villagers. The fact that their day-to-day lifestyle could hold a unique appeal to tourists visiting the area was a very new and exciting concept for this little community.

A group of traditional Shangaan villages provides the backdrop to Project B. Although the vernacular architecture of the tribespeople is found in scattered communities in very rural locations, it is steadily being replaced by Western construction. The skills required for traditional construction are similarly being lost. The buildings at the project have been designed and built by rural people using natural materials and traditional techniques. This has regenerated interest in the value of traditional architecture in surrounding communities. Participants in the project live at the site, making these living villages. A guide accompanies all visitors and explains to them how to behave in a respectful manner. The tourism product includes tours of the villages, traditional lunches hosted and served by resident families, and an evening festival of choirs, acting, dancing, and a traditional meal. The people themselves decide what and how to present their culture so that it is done with pride and enthusiasm and earns the respect of visitors. All decision-making is done through consultation, and staff members are encouraged to voice their own ideas and concerns. Employees thus feel that they "own" the project in terms of joint decision-making, active participation in its day-to-day operation, and the ability to influence its future direction. This sense of ownership was considered crucial to securing the commitment elemental to project success. As pointed out by a Delphi panelist, "once the community has taken ownership of the project it will make every effort to ensure that it survives and so will nurture it."

CAPACITY BUILDING, EMPOWERMENT, AND SELF-RELIANCE

Ninety-three percent of the Delphi panel agreed that projects should lead to community empowerment through participation in the construction, management, operational supply systems, and contribution to the tourism product. There was also emphasis that community role-players should be encouraged to stand on their own feet as soon as possible. Respondents, however, perceived the lack of tourism awareness and understanding among rural communities as a significant constraint to effective participation, communication, and decision-making. There was an emphasis on the need for pragmatism and the necessity of educating communities to understand tourism so that they would be able to take informed decisions. Caution was voiced against the dangers of patronization: "Work in a facilitatory manner to get those skills through without being condescending. Beware of being condescending in rural community projects. Communities dislike being patronized." Recognition was afforded to the fact that there was a "need for people to be tourists themselves in order to understand tourism and tourists."

Sen (1984) argues that meaningful development does not entail an increase in commodities but rather the enhancement of people's capabilities. Kinsley and Lovins (2000) agree, asserting that people should be viewed as the instruments of their own upliftment rather than detachedly objectified as something to be developed. Unless the development of tourism projects in South Africa's marginalized communities includes the transfer of skills as a prime component of the development process, a continued state of disillusionment and dependency on external assistance will be perpetuated. The exigency of tourism education and awareness was highlighted by a public sector panelist who levied the accusation that unscrupulous developers are able to take advantage of naive rural communities: "We have experienced so many 'fly-by-night' developers coming in and destroying all economic opportunities for ground-level communities."

In both projects training in the practical aspects of product delivery was essential. Because Project A was located off the main tourist route, previous contact with tourists had been negligible. It was very difficult for the community to understand that tour operators worked on fixed schedules and that products had to be "delivered" on time. It was equally complicated for them to grasp what sort of experience would represent value for money to tourists. Several years into the project, problems still existed, with the community not being ready when tourists arrived or not having a meal prepared on time. Although most visitors appreciated the simplicity and genuineness of the experience, occasionally cultural differences would be starkly highlighted. For example, on one occasion an American guest asked the interpreter to invite the community to join them in their meal. At the invitation the villagers, accustomed to communal eating, delightedly flocked around the food. The Americans stood nervously to one side, hugging their empty plates. By the time they approached the table the meal was depleted.

The "champion" of Project B agrees that a lot of capacity building was necessary to establish a tourism culture. In the start-up phase of the project, two white hotel/game lodge managers were employed to manage the project and build capacity among the local staff. After three years, the entire management structure, including the position of general manager, was comprised of local people whose capacity had been built to fulfill these roles. The "champion" reports that a very strong culture of ownership was built with employees from the outset. This had resulted in a "strong sense of pride now felt in management and in doing things properly." In his opinion, the most important questions to ask when evaluating a project would be: "Is it developing people? Is it maximizing employment? Is it making a proud contribution to people's lives?"

NETWORKING AND SUPPORT

Ninety-six percent of Delphi panelists recognized the need for strong working relationships between projects and existing tourism enterprises, enabling projects to become an integral part of existing provisions and activities in the wider locality. Public-sector inter-viewees and project operators alike emphasized the necessity and dif-ficulty of securing tour operator support. A panelist with extensive experience as a facilitator in the development of rural community projects alleges "the operators who are facilitating land arrangements to get into rural areas are by a long way not anywhere near comfort-able with it yet, so the new product has a heck of a time to survive." The importance of strong working relationships and networking are articulated by a Delphi panelist:

> Nothing in tourism lives in a vacuum. If you really want to lever-age the project, you've got to link it. Whether it be to the tour operator, whether it be a follow-up project that links with your project, whether it be the agents who book this. There would be a need for the outer plant to be interested in this project, or it would be in the interest of this project for the outer plant to know about this and to link into this. If you didn't originally plan the project with that in mind and how you were going to create those linkages you're stuffed before you started.

Both projects report having experienced great difficulty in dealing with tour operators. The champion of Project A, herself a tour opera-tor, is critical of the private sector, claiming that they are exceedingly negative about community-based projects. She claims that "without exception there is no support" and that ongoing approaches to tour operators inevitably elicited a negative response. Despite the fact that many never bothered to visit the project, operators argued that it could not offer the standards tourists demanded; did not represent value for money; and was situated too far off the main routes for tour operators to divert their vehicles. To a degree these allegations were valid. There were no toilet facilities in the village and no clean water. Road access was poor, and the diversion of coaches would have involved a significant amount of "lost time" in operator schedules. This is one of the dichotomies of tourism development in South Africa. On the one hand, tourism is perceived as the vehicle that will bring the necessary development, including that of infrastructure, to rural communities. On the other hand, operators want the infrastructure in place before they will support projects. The "champion" tried to compensate for the difficulties experienced in accessing the project by identifying minibus taxi owners and training them as tourist taxis. Despite the reservations expressed by others, local taxis were vetted for their roadworthiness and cleanliness and drivers for their safety and capability. In a country with minimal rural public transport for independent travelers, training taxis and other small transport operators to furnish transport for tourists presents a significant opportunity, but one which has to date been little capitalized upon.

The "champion" of Project B is adamant that it is "vital to fit the product into tour operator schedules." He reports that the project's day product has never been a success, since most tours are not in the vicinity during daylight hours but overnight in the nearest town. "Our nighttime product is absolutely fantastic as it provides entertainment for all the operators' clients staying over in the vicinity. We are going to have to enlarge our 'boma' (enclosed camp). It is currently built to take 100 people and we have on numerous occasions lately squeezed in 150 where there have been groups." He also points out that projects have to be put clearly on the agenda for tour operators and believes that they should be forced to use at least one community project. It had, he reports, "taken three years to get into itineraries—we had to drag operators kicking and screaming to the project."

Establishing good relationships with tour operators was not the only difficulty. The champion reports that the "existing accommodation establishments are anti-us because they see our evening show and meal as taking away their dinner money. They do not see the contribution the project makes to the area, the addition to the diversity of product resulting in potentially longer stays in the area." He is equally adamant that projects cannot work without the correct infrastructure.

Although traditional in style, these villages have been equipped with toilet facilities and clean running water—a factor that is also of immense benefit to the villagers whose home this is. The project, located close to a major tourist route, is easily accessible.

Both champions report difficulties in securing public sector support. Project A made numerous appeals to the provincial tourism department for assistance. Despite verbal commitment to the project and expressed appreciation for the initiative of the champion, no assistance, either financial or otherwise, was ever forthcoming. The altruistic champion thus funded all aspects of the development of the project herself. The partners in the development of Project B contributed 60 percent of the financial requirements. The remaining 40 percent was procured as a loan. The champion reports that there was initially little public-sector support for the project. Once its success had been proven, marketing grants were made available. Nonetheless, he reports, "We get an offish feeling from government because of our ownership structure. What they don't realize is that it has taken three and a half years for the project to become profitable. A project needs someone with money to support it and keep it going that long." Repayment of the loan still presents a significant challenge to the developers.

PROJECT MARKETING

Delphi panelists were united in their belief that a well-resourced, robust, and appropriate strategic marketing plan, based on up-to-date market research, was imperative to project success. Eighty-one percent of the panel were also of the opinion that projects should strive to broaden their customer base, avoiding overdependence on single products or markets. They argued that two essential questions should be answered prior to embarking on a project: "What evidence is there that the proponents have identified and understand the market?" and "Is there evidence for a sufficient flow of visitors to make it financially viable?"

Since the champion of Project A had an established target market for her tours, a visit to the chief's village was built into her itineraries. This provided a client base for the chief's cultural project and a new and unusual experience for the tourists. No preimplementation research was undertaken to ascertain potential tour operator support or to establish whether a market base, other than the operator's own clients, could be established to ensure the viability of the project. The "village experience" proved to be extremely popular with the champion's clients. Numerous tourists, appreciating its genuineness and simplicity, were heard to proclaim it as the highlight of their visit to South Africa. In view of project dependence on the tour operator for its source of clients, opportunities for further growth were, however, severely constrained.

The champion of Project B, who develops the market plans and undertakes the related activities, conversely argues that speaking to potential visitors and clients (including tour operators) and listening to what they say is critical. He also believes that project proponents should not put too much emphasis on advice from consultants and other outside bodies. "In theory, all their input is valuable, but they can also talk rubbish, so it can be difficult to prioritize and choose what is most valuable and appropriate. The visitors/clients are the ones who really will make the project sink or swim, so theirs should be the overall guide." Extensive marketing campaigns are waged on an ongoing basis. The fact that tour operators now support the project means that they are, to a significant extent, undertaking marketing on its behalf.

WIDER ECONOMIC BENEFITS

Ninety-three percent of the Delphi panel agreed that projects should contribute to local money flows, create markets for local products, and retain the benefits of tourism spending in the local area. The generation of employment for local residents was seen as a primary criterion against which projects should be evaluated: "If locals benefit from employment they will support the project all the way."

Both projects successfully contributed to wider community benefits. In the case of Project A, the visit was extended to include the local shop, the community school, and the "sangoma" (traditional healer) training school. Payment for the village visit was made to the chief, who deposited it in a communal banking account opened by the champion on his behalf. As soon as enough money had been accumulated, the entire community sat down for a village "indaba" (round-table discussion) and by mutual consent decided how it was to be spent. Projects undertaken included the building of a shop in which the village women could complete and sell their handicrafts. Another project entailed the building of a library at the local school. Visitors to the village pledged their support to the library project, and on their return to America a group of tourists raised funds and purchased the books to stock its shelves. The chief and his people had expectations that tourism would increase, a prospect welcomed by the villagers who had ambitions to build a traditional "hotel" to house their visitors. The question of employment was not an issue in this project, which belonged to the entire village and in which everyone participated. The village shop and local market also benefited in that supplies for the refreshments provided to visitors were locally purchased. Visiting this village was a humbling experience. People's pride in their culture and their village had been rekindled, and the warmth of their welcome was indicative of their pleasure in welcoming tourists and their appreciation of the benefits the tourists were bringing to the little community. On one visit the chief articulated the feelings of the villagers through the interpreter: "We love tourists in this village."

Ownership of Project B was not vested in the community. Nonetheless, the project developers were committed to spreading the economic benefits of their undertaking as widely as possible. Thirty-four permanent and 100 part-time jobs were created. Twenty small entrepreneurs from local communities were contracted to supply products and services, providing employment for 100 additional people. The village was extended to include a craft market, which provides access for tourists to fifteen local crafters and curio makers. Sixty-three percent of the project's total monthly expenditure flows to businesses wholly or partly owned by members of previously disadvantaged communities. The project, which currently hosts some 22,000 tourists annually, also provides access, tours, and information to other local people planning to start tourism businesses and assists a range of community tourism developments with advice, training, planning, and building services. Local dance groups formed by teachers to raise funds for school uniforms and textbooks are supported by inclusion in the cultural presentations. Performance times for these groups are scheduled outside school hours so that teaching is not affected.

THE CURRENT SITUATION

Project A does not have a happy ending. Over a period of eight years, the champion's clients increasingly became repeat visitors, and ongoing inclusion of the project could not routinely be sustained as a standard feature of the itineraries. The lack of support from other tour operators and the local tourism industry meant that there was no other source of a steady and secure market and the champion was unable to carry the burden of sustaining the project alone. A Delphi panelist with in-depth experience of tourism development in marginalized communities was unsurprised by this turn of events. "When the community are totally dependent on the energy of one particular person, [the project] has a three- to five-year life span, because that is the life span of somebody's energy and somebody's focus, and if they are burnt-out the project falls apart." The champion is angry and disillusioned. She feels that the villagers have been let down both by myopic tourism operators who are unwilling to adopt socially responsible practices in spreading the benefits of tourism to small cultural projects, and by the government, who she believes are not doing enough to support these ventures. She argues that inasmuch as tourism awareness needs to be developed in communities, so too does an awareness of what communities have to offer the tourist in the way of unique cultural experiences need to be fostered in the existing tourism industry. The onus, she believes, is on government to educate operators by taking them into rural communities and giving them the opportunity to get to know the local people.

The champion of Project B believes that their project is evidence that cross-cultural development can work if support is carefully earned. The market for the project continues to grow. An environmental management program has been introduced that works to conserve energy and water and recycles 77 percent of the project's waste. Alien trees have been removed from the property and over 100 indigenous trees replanted. The past year has been marked by two important developments. The first has been the Land Claims Commission's restoration of the land and buildings to the community. The project developers now lease these from the community. A new company is being established to operate the village. Shareholding will include both the private investors and the community and staff of the village. According to the champion, "We hope that this will create a balance between the developers of the village, the people who run it, and the community that surrounds us."

CONCLUDING REMARKS

Although cultural tourism undoubtedly has great potential in the new South Africa, there are some stark realities that must be faced if projects are to fulfill the expectations of those communities in which they are being developed. Many cultural tourism projects come under attack by virtue of their perceived demeaning of the culture on which they are built. This is not the case in either of the projects examined. In both instances decision-making, with regard to how and which elements of their culture they wished to portray to visitors, was left in the hands of the people involved. Both projects served as a source of renewed cultural pride, and both projects undoubtedly delivered benefits to the wider community.

The comparative case studies, however, hold a salutary lesson for communities and champions embarking on the development of cultural tourism projects. Unless potential developments are approached from a business as opposed to a social perspective, they are doomed to ultimate failure. Tourism is a highly competitive industry in which any project that does not have a reliable, deliverable product that offers value for money cannot survive. In the words of a Delphi panelist, "You need to stand back from your altruism to say, how do I make this work? Stand back and become really hard-nosed, work out a really good project plan. There is a very limited market in appealing to people's conscience. Very few people will visit a project from altruistic values if it doesn't have what interests them."

The great danger facing South Africa is a proliferation of small cultural tourism projects that do not offer sufficient differentiation and will thus be in fierce competition with one another for the tourism market. In a desperate attempt to spread the benefits of tourism to marginalized rural communities, falling prey to the dangers of ad hoc, random, supply-led development is an ever-present threat. Though questions hang over the development of cultural tourism projects by private investors who, it is perceived, will manipulate the culture of the host community into a saleable, profitable product, this need not necessarily be the case. Government has at its disposal the means to regulate cultural tourism developments and could, for example, legislate that projects have at least 50 percent local community ownership. Other stipulations such as empowerment and progressive capacity-building of local people into management positions could also be included. This implies that cultural tourism projects should be regularly monitored and evaluated to ensure that outside investors are delivering on their promises. Evaluation would also be a valuable means of assessing the sustainability of a project from a holistic perspective.

The risk of failed cultural tourism projects perpetuating communities' sense of hopelessness and lack of self-esteem is significant. Do the villagers involved in Project A understand that tourists no longer visit them because of market failure and a lack of proper planning? Or do they perceive that their culture is not interesting, unique, and important enough to be of value as a tourist product? Is their disillusionment with tourism or is it their self-pride, which has again suffered a battering? Project A is not unique. A Delphi panelist located at considerable distance from the project in question claims: "I work in a rural area where any development will be welcomed [51 percent unemployment]. I have, however, seen the detrimental effects of bad planning, no research, and raising expectations with locals who wish to better their economic environment." If South Africa is to realize the potential of her cultural diversity as a tourist attraction, it is imperative that project champions adhere to the principles of meticulous planning and informed decision-making. Failure to do this will leave in its wake a swath of cultural projects suffering the consequences of crushed expectations, frustration, and a degeneration of cultural pride and self-esteem, resulting from the broken promises of economically unviable cultural tourism project development.

REFERENCES

Ashley, C. and Roe, D. (1998) *Enhancing Community Involvement in Wildlife Tourism: Issues and Challenges*. London: International Institute for Environment and Development.

Ashley, C., Roe, D., and Goodwin, H. (2001) *Pro-Poor Tourism Strategies: Making Tourism work for the Poor. A Review of Experience*. London: Overseas Development Institute.

Bossevain, J. (1993) "Some Problems with Cultural Tourism in Malta." Paper presented to the International Conference on Sustainable Tourism in Islands and Small States, Malta, Foundation for International Studies.

Butler, R.W. and Clark, G. (1992) Tourism in Rural Areas: Canada and the United Kingdom. In Bowler, I.R., Bryant, C.R. and Nellis, M.D. (eds) *Contemporary Rural Systems in Transition, Vol. 2: Economy and Society,* Wallingford, Oxon: CAB International, pp. 166-186.

Butler, R.W. and Hinch, T. (eds) (1996) *Tourism and Indigenous Peoples.* London: International Thompson Business Press.

Crouch, D. (1994) Home, Escape and Identity: Rural Cultures and Sustainable Tourism. In Bramwell, B. and Lane, B. (eds.) *Rural Tourism and Sustainable Rural Development.* Clevedon: Channel View Publications, pp. 93-101.

Department of Environmental Affairs and Tourism (1996) An Assessment of Market-Based Instruments: Suitability for Environmental Management in South Africa. Project: *The Use of Environmental Resource Economics in Environmental Impact Management.* Pretoria: DEAT.

de Sola Pool, I. (1979) Direct Broadcast Satellites and the Integrity of National Cultures. In Nordenstreng, K. and Schiller, H.I. (eds.) *National Sovereignty and International Communication.* New Jersey: Ablex, p. 139.

Dyer, P., Aberdeen, L. and Schuler, S. (2003) Tourism Impacts on an Australian Indigenous Community: A Djabugay Case Study, *Tourism Management* 24(1): 83-95.

Fowkes, J. and Jonsson, P. (1994) *Lessons Learned During a Pilot Project to Introduce a Tourism Development Programme to Rural Communities in Kwazulu, South Africa,* Unpublished Paper, October 1994.

Geertz, Clifford. (1957) Ethos, World View, and the Analysis of Sacred Symbols, *Antiach Review* 17, 4.

Getz, D. and Page, S.J. (1997) Conclusions and Implications for Rural Business Development. In Page, S.J. and Getz, D. (eds) *The Business of Rural Tourism.* London: International Thomson Business Press, pp. 191-205.

Government of South Africa (1996) White Paper: *The Development and Promotion of Tourism in South Africa.* Pretoria: Government Printer.

Greenwood, D. J. (1977) Culture by the Pound: An Anthropological Perspective on Tourism and Cultural Commoditization. In Smith, V. L. (ed.) *Hosts and Guests: The Anthropology of Tourism.* Pennsylvania: University of Pennsylvania Press, pp.129-138.

Hall, C.M. (2002) *Tourism Planning: Policies, Processes and Relationships.* Harlow: Prentice Hall.

Hall, C.M. and Jenkins, J.M. (1998) The Policy Dimensions of Rural Tourism and Recreation. In Butler, R., Hall, C.M. and Jenkins, J. (eds) *Rural Tourism and Recreation.* Chichester: John Wiley, pp. 19-42.

Harrison, D. (1994) Tourism, Capitalism and Development in Less Developed Countries. In Sklair, Leslie (ed) *Capital and Development.* New York: Routledge, pp. 232-257.

Hashimoto, A. (2002) Tourism and Sociocultural Development Issues. In Sharpley, R. and Telfer, D. (eds) *Tourism and Development, Concepts and Issues.* Clevedon: Channel View Publications, pp. 202-230.

Hitchcock, R.K. (1997) Cultural, Economic and Environmental Impacts of Tourism Among Kalahari Bushmen. In Chambers, E. (ed.) *Tourism and Culture: An Applied Perspective.* Albany: State University of New York Press, pp. 31-57.

Kinsley, M.J. and Lovins, L.H. (2000) *Paying for Growth, Prospering from Development.* Snowmass, Colorado: Rocky Mountain Institute: 1-9.

MacCannell, D. (1976) *The Tourist: A New Theory of the Leisure Class.* New York: Schocken Books.

MacCannell, D. (1992) *Empty Meeting Grounds.* London: Routledge.

McKercher, B. (1993) Some Fundamental Truths About Tourism: Understanding Tourism's Social and Environmental Impacts, *Journal of Sustainable Tourism* 1: 6-16.

McNamee, P.B. (1985) *Tools and Techniques for Strategic Management.* Oxford: Pergamon Press.

Page, S.J. and Getz, D. (1997) The Business of Rural Tourism: International Perspectives. In Page, S.J. and Getz, D. (eds) *The Business of Rural Tourism: International Perspectives.* New York: International Thomson Business Press, pp. 3-37.

Picard, Michel (1995) Cultural Heritage and Tourist Capital: Cultural Tourism in Bali. In: Lanfant, M.F. Allcock, J.B. and Brunner, E.M. (eds), *International Tourism, Identity and Change.* London: Sage, pp. 44-66.

Richards, H. (1995) For the Use of Healers: Education for Constructive Development. *Second Nehru Lecture,* Gujarat, India: University of Baroda, pp. 1-15.

Sen, A.K. (1984) *Resources, Values and Development.* Oxford: Blackwell.

Stanley, N. (1998) *Being Ourselves for You: The Global Display of Cultures.* London: Middlesex University Press.

Tavner, T. (2003) A Life in the Day. *The Sunday Times Magazine* London, 19 January 2003, p. 86.

Wallerstein, Immanuel. (1990) Culture as the Ideological Battleground of the Modern World System. In Featherstone, Mike (ed.) *Global Culture.* London: Sage, pp. 31-55.

PART II:
CULTURAL TOURISM DEVELOPMENT IN A GLOBALIZING WORLD

Chapter 5

Space, Place, and Placelessness in the Culturally Regenerated City

Melanie Smith

INTRODUCTION

The aim of this chapter is to examine the way in which urban spaces are being transformed through cultural regeneration, often resulting in the creation of international tourism arenas for mass consumption. This has arguably led to an encroaching standardization or "placelessness," manifesting itself in the kind of "could-be-any-where" feeling experienced by tourists in many global cities. Although the enclavic bubble of standardized attractions like theme parks or shopping malls has typically provided the post-tourist with a predictable, safe, and comfortable experience, it has also led to the over-writing of heritage (Hughes, 1998), the "heritagization" of space

(Walsh, 1992), and the erosion of a sense of place (Relph, 1976). In an increasingly competitive tourism environment, many cities are clamoring to promote their cultural distinctiveness, yet the concomitant destruction of a specific place identity is threatening their future development and promotion potential.

This chapter will look at the spatial transformation of cities, focusing on a number of key developments, such as themed tourist spaces (Edensor, 2001), waterfront developments, shopping malls, and cultural quarters. Questions will be asked about their economic, social, and cultural contribution to urban environments, focusing in particular on local perceptions and usage. Clearly, many global urban developments serve to alienate or exclude local communities because of gentrification and other barriers to access. However, it could also be argued that they sometimes represent a powerful means of drawing local people into a global arena, from which they may previously have been marginalized.

Bauman (2001) has suggested that the "global elite" are generally less concerned than their counterparts with a sense of place, living as they do in a state of "exterritoriality." However, it is ironic to note that it is often the educated, mobile, cosmopolitan elite who are most concerned about the loss of local cultures, traditions, and heritage. Local communities may be more interested in frequenting standardized spaces of mass consumption such as entertainment zones or "hyperreal" themed environments focusing on new media and technology. Nevertheless, care must be taken to conserve the urban fabric where appropriate, especially in cases where there is a strong local attachment to the history and heritage of place.

The latter part of the chapter will consider how far it is possible to plan for place in the context of cultural regeneration, for example through "discursive" planning (Ploger, 2001) or cultural planning (Bianchini, 1999; Evans, 2001). Planners and developers should take into consideration both the needs of local people and those of global tourists when undertaking spatial reconfiguration. Clearly, a reconciliation of global and local tensions in urban planning is not always viable, especially where economic and financial imperatives drive regeneration strategies. However, cities need the cultural diversity of their local communities and their distinctive heritage and place identities in order to maintain competitive advantage in the tourism marketplace. If everywhere starts to look the same, then why travel? Placelessness is arguably the end of cities; therefore, we must rethink the way in which urban spaces are transformed and regenerated through culture.

WHEN SPACE BECOMES PLACE

Entrikin (1991) suggests that place has always played a peripheral role in scientific discourse (even more so than space). However, both phenomena are inextricably linked, as stated by Rotenberg and Mc-Donogh (1993:xiv): "State actions on space and peoples' understandings of place form a dialectic, that is, each contributes to the other in a constantly changing pattern of influence." However, the relationship between the definitions and concepts of space and place is a complex and contested one. Lefebvre (1974) rarely used the term "place" in his writings, focusing instead on the notion of "lived space" and "everyday life." Soja (1996) suggests that the tendency in cultural geography to separate the concepts of space and place is both unnecessary and misleading. However, a distinction can and should be made if we are to reemphasize the importance of place in debates about urban development and regeneration. The work of Relph (1976) is pivotal to this discussion, as his work provides us with some meaningful definitions and distinctions with regards to space, place, and placelessness.

Relph (1976:8) describes space as "amorphous and intangible and not an entity that can be directly described and analysed." Similarly, he argues that the study of place cannot easily be confined by the boundaries of any formally defined discipline and does not lend itself easily to scientific analysis. Although the framework for this chapter is derived mainly from the field of postmodern cultural geography, it advocates multidisciplinarity as an approach to understanding this complex phenomenon. Thus the works of sociologists, anthropologists, and urban theorists have also been consulted. For example, Augé (1995) provides an interesting analysis of the anthropology of "non-place." He describes space as being more abstract than place, and discusses de Certeau's (1984) contention that space is a frequentation of places. This notion is, of course, entirely relevant to travel and tourism, and will thus be returned to later in the chapter.

Lefebvre (1974) argued that space always embodies a meaning, and that social or cultural practices generally determine that meaning.

However, it is clear that meanings are never constant, but perpetually in flux. Space provides a context for places and arguably derives its diversity of meaning from those places. "Places in existential space can [therefore] be understood as centres of meaning, or focuses of intention and purpose" (Relph, 1976:22). However, Entrikin (1991) states that place should not be reduced to a mere location in space, because of the human identity component that is inherent within it: "Place serves as an important component of our sense of identity as subjects" (p.13). Rotenberg and McDonogh (1993:xiii) describe how "peoples' understandings transform space into place." Lippard (1997) suggests that space combined with memory defines place, and that place is a result of the union between space and lived culture. Therefore, place becomes based on a combination of heritage and contemporary lifestyles. She also argues that although place and community are not the same thing, they tend to coexist, living out a common history. In urban environments where diasporic, dispersed, and fragmented "communities" abound, this may be a slightly more tenuous argument, and the convergence of contemporary lifestyles may create stronger bonds than past traditions.

The concept of place embodies the geographies of our everyday experiences. It could be argued that places are constructed within a collective consciousness, building on both past and present cultural associations and memories. Inherent within this mental and perceptual construction is the idea of personal geographies, which may be variously complementary or conflictual. Places are perhaps ultimately "constructed" through a process of consensus in which the majority of inhabitants relate to common practices, activities, and associations. Entrikin (1991) describes how places are also significant not because of their inherent value, but because of the value that is assigned to them. Value can be assigned to a place by various user groups at different times, and value systems tend to be multiple and contested, especially in relation to territoriality. Values may be assigned to place by local inhabitants who will feel varying degrees of affinity with that place. Tourists entering a place are likely to have all kinds of psychological preconceptions as a result of being fed media representations, myths, and fantasies. Their response might be one of fulfilled expectation, pleasant surprise, or alternatively one of disappointment and dissatisfaction. The difference is that they can easily leave, moving on to another place that affords them greater satisfaction. The complexities of the impacts of tourist visitation of place have been extensively researched, often coming to dire conclusions. It is worth noting, however, that the tourist gaze can also reinforce local perceptions of, and pride in, place and local identity. Tourism can put relatively unknown places on the map, and although they may be irrecoverably altered as a result, it is not always for the worse.

A phenomenological understanding of the concept of place is derived from the analysis of existential or "lived" space. Each individual occupies an egocentric space, of which he or she will have a certain perceptual awareness: "Through particular encounters and experiences perceptual space is richly differentiated into places, or centres of special personal significance" (Relph, 1976:11). Our lived geographies consist of an intricately woven network of personal and social/collective perceptual spaces and places. We may feel at home in one particular location, where we have always lived, and fear displacement from it. We may have a collective relationship to that location—for example, many tribal peoples have an intangible or spiritual relationship to certain landscapes, which are deemed sacred, but whose meaning may not be apparent to outsiders. Such places are often exposed to tourism development before any efforts are made to engage in appropriate local interpretation, therefore a sense of place can be compromised, commercialized, or even eroded.

Increasingly, global mobility and travel are leading to the fragmentation and displacement of communities, therefore a sense of place may not always be dependent on a permanent physical location. It may be based on a collective sense of cultural continuity or cohesion. For example, many immigrant groups and diaspora have been forced to relocate, but manage to re-create their cultural traditions in whichever environment they find themselves. Thus, the creation of a "China Town," an "Arab Quarter," or a "Little Italy" is not uncommon within a decontextualized environment. This is how spaces are transformed and new places are constructed. This may happen as a result of structured planning or it may develop organically. Within the context of urban regeneration or tourism development, it is more likely that spaces will be built for entertainment, leisure, or recreation. A certain degree of sensitivity, control, and regulation is therefore needed if development is to be appropriate and engaging.

Global, virtual spaces are being created endlessly in the form of new media, technology, and communications. These can be accessed from a remote portal almost anywhere in the world. In addition, many citizens (mainly urban "cosmopolitans") are increasingly travelling more than ever before, and appear not to be defined by any particular location or community. Bauman (2001) suggests that place is becoming irrelevant to such citizens, and that they are merely seeking standardized enclavic bubbles. Global tourism, especially business and conference tourism, is arguably instrumental in this process. The quest for speed, convenience, and familiarity is leading to a proliferation of standardized facilities. Augé (1995) describes spaces of transit, such as airport lounges, service stations, even supermarkets as being archetypal "non-places." They do not contain any organic society, anonymity prevails (except where proof of identity is suddenly required), and they are essentially transitory.

It is interesting to consider how far the naming of spaces transforms them into places (e.g., Paris, the Sahara, the Mediterranean). These are evocative tools in destination marketing, but they clearly have more serious political overtones. Jordan and Weedon (1995) suggest that the power to name and rename is one of the most contentious issues in the history of cultural politics. Of course, boundaries and borders have been endlessly redrawn over the course of history, and space (like time) is artificially divided according to human direction and power. Some of the boundaries that contain space are politically defined—such as counties, boroughs, or wards—therefore they may seem somewhat artificial to their inhabitants. A sense of place is largely derived from the perceptions of those that are located within a given area, and those perceptions may transcend given boundaries. And although nationality, regionality, or locality are often major determinants of collective and individual identity construction and community cohesion, numerous intangible factors also play a role. Tourists may be oblivious to the political significance of the places that they visit, but increasingly they are becoming victims of political manipulation, often linked to the assertion of place identity.

How far we can talk of an "essence" or "spirit" of place is debatable, especially when physical locations can so easily be destroyed or appropriated, and their inhabitants displaced or dispersed. Entrikin (1991) suggests that a place has no essence that can be threatened.

A place can surely only be defined by the people for whom it is still home? Individuals are not distinct from place—they are that place: "The essence of place lies in the largely unselfconscious intentionality that defines places as profound centres of human experiences" (Relph, 1976:43). Of course, numerous artists, writers, poets, and photographers have attempted to capture the essence or spirit of place in their work. Although their efforts are largely subjective, we recognize our own perceptions and emotions in some of the best representations. However, Lippard (1997:278) is critical of the way in which "too much art 'about place' [. . .] is more about art than about the actual place where artists and viewers find themselves. Places, even contexts, become absences rather than presences." She argues that a "place ethic" needs to be about more than just an aesthetic version of the tourist gaze. Of course, the travel industry produces numerous idyllic and idealized (mis)representations of place, which frequently lead to disappointment on the part of the first-time visitor. De Botton (2002) deals humorously with the inevitable disillusionment that regularly plagues travellers who have been overpromised and undersold. However, he suggests that there should also be a certain onus on the tourist to enhance his or her experience. Rather than relying wholly on guidebooks and attempting to capture scenes and moments through a camera, tourists can train themselves to really *see* the world anew.

A fundamental question for this chapter is whether place actually matters. It almost certainly does in the context of tourism development, as places need to retain some kind of distinctive place identity to differentiate themselves from other places and to be worth visiting. But tourists also come from somewhere and will assess their perceptions of other places in relation to home. Bauman (2001) argues that even the globe-trotting elite need a familiar and secure home to come back to. However, existentialists would argue that modern life is essentially a "homeless," alienated existence. This has been exacerbated by the fragmentation of communities and the family, and the secularization of Western societies. Relph (1976) describes this as a form of existential "outsideness," which is characteristic of the nineteenth and twentieth centuries. People are increasingly being separated from places.

The following is a summary of Relph's (1976) analysis of *insideness* and *outsideness:*

Existential outsideness: Alienation, homelessness, sense of not belonging. All places have the same meaningless identity.

Objective outsideness: Deliberate adoption of dispassionate attitude toward places (e.g., planners and geographers), allowing logic, reason, efficiency.

Incidental outsideness: Largely unselfconscious attitude, with places experienced as little more than background (e.g., global business premises, conference centers).

Vicarious insideness: Experiencing places in a secondhand or vicarious way without actually visiting them (e.g., through art, poetry, music, travel accounts, media).

Behavioral insideness: Being in a place and engaging with it; awareness of distinctiveness of place.

Empathetic insideness: Open to and respectful of significance of place (e.g., sacred or spiritual) but not necessarily involved directly in that meaning.

Existential insideness: Inside a place and belonging to it; feeling its significance; deep and complete identity.

It is interesting to consider how far planners and developers adopt an "objective outsideness" in their approach to urban regeneration and tourism development, and how far they are receptive to planning for place. Some tourists (e.g., post-tourists) are increasingly engaging in a kind of "vicarious insideness," whereby media and new technology are used to view or simulate travel experiences. Others (e.g., cultural tourists) are keen to adopt a sense of "behavioral" or "empathetic insideness," which frequently involves interaction with local people. Globe-trotting business tourists may alternatively be confronted with "incidental outsideness" as they are shunted from one enclavic bubble to another. A sense of "existential insideness" may be a feeling only really experienced by local residents in a place, or tourists involved in some kind of longitudinal, anthropological research.

WHEN PLACE BECOMES PLACELESSNESS

Can "placelessness" be said to exist in the context of cultural regeneration? The terminology is contentious in that it would be possible to argue that there is no such thing as "placelessness," especially in the context of cultural geography. Every space perhaps has some kind of perceived or attributed collective or individual meaning, which transforms it into a "place." Perhaps the term "anonymity" or "standardization" captures the notion better. Lippard (1997:9) refers to a "geography of nowhere," where place is ignored, unseen, or unknown, buried beneath the asphalt of monoculture. Augé (1995) talks about "non-places" as anonymous, transitory environments lacking distinctiveness and identity. Placelessness is arguably more of an emotion or a feeling, an intangible response to one's immediate environment. Most people have surely experienced the feeling that they are in a "placeless" environment. This term encapsulates the "could be anywhere" feeling that we may experience in a shopping mall, leisure center, theme park, or certain waterfront development. It may even apply to a foreign resort, which combines familiar elements to make the tourist feel "at home." Of course, these elements are displaced or misplaced, local heritage has often been eroded to make way for them, and the result is a kind of nowhere land, home to no one.

Entrikin (1991:57) describes "placelessness" as the "creation of standardised landscapes that diminish the differences among places," and Relph (1976:6) describes it as "the weakening of distinct and diverse experiences and identities of places." Of course, like globalization, the concept of placelessness is nothing new. Both of these phenomena may have altered in their various manifestations over time, but they have always existed in some form or other. Standardization of culture was a common characteristic of imperial or colonial rule, as indigenous and local cultures were suppressed, diluted, or even destroyed. Cultural and geographical uniformity was widespread. For example, the legacy of Greek influence or the Roman Empire has resulted in Europe being littered with (now displaced) temples and remains from a past era. However, it is interesting to note how much interest such sites now attract from both the perspective of tourism and conservation. This suggests that the current values attached to contemporary developments may not be indicative of their future value, especially if only a few examples of such constructions remain.

Mumford (1961) suggested that modern architecture was being increasingly dictated by mass, global fashions, and had shifted from being largely humanistic to being an expression of prestige, wealth, and power. Norberg-Schulz (1965) expressed his concern about the number of varied places being replaced by "flatscapes"—that is, standardized landscapes of a similar nature. International monopolies and oligopolies clearly characterize the postmodern era of global capitalism, therefore the standardization of culture and consumption is perhaps inevitable. Nevertheless, it is worth noting that there has more recently been a concomitant development of unique arcitectural features that serve as landmarks for branding and place marketing. The tradition of "Grands Projets" in Paris led to the construction of several interesting and (initially) controversial buildings, such as the Pompidou Centre, the Pyramid at the Louvre, and the Grande Arche at La Defense. Other cities have since followed suit. More recent examples might include the Millennium Dome in Greenwich, London, and the Guggenheim Museum in Bilbao. Both are unique landmarks, "flagship" cultural projects, and were designed as catalysts for regeneration. Interestingly, both have also been subject to the criticism that they represent typical postmodern examples of "style over content." It is also true that they could technically be anywhere and represent little of local culture.

Architecture undeniably makes a significant contribution to both urban regeneration and tourism development. Blazwick (2001:10) notes:

> Twentieth-century Modernism offered a symbolic means for erasing not only the monuments but the memories of the recent past, offering a model for a new, forward-looking identity— coupled with the resurgence of suppressed cultures. Concrete, skyscrapers, flyovers, radio towers—these were the public signifiers of progress given an intellectual and cultural agenda by the avant-gardes of art, cinema, dance, music, and literature.

Cities can thereby offer an exciting juxtaposition of globally standardized architecture, which is often inhabited by culturally diverse groups and their creative projects. However, there have also been major criticisms of postwar architecture, which was deemed to lack humanism. For example, the Austrian architect Hundertwasser was intensely critical of urban archicture that put up "torture chambers for the soul" (Rand, 1991). He set about developing ecological housing projects and beautifying factories and disused incinerators as part of his vision of architectural urban regeneration. Harvey (1990:40) also comments on such soul-crushing architecture:

> The glass towers, concrete blocks, and steel slabs that seemed set fair to steamroller over every urban landscape from Paris to Tokyo and from Rio to Montreal, denouncing all ornament as crime, all individualism as sentimentality, all romanticism as kitsch.

He is even more critical of what has replaced it, however, suggesting that the postmodern era of regeneration has largely engaged in pastiche and incoherent eclecticism in a vain attempt to create more "satisfying" urban environments. Evidence of such iniatiatives are widespread, and have been criticized for overwriting heritage (Hughes, 1998) and creating a "heritagization" of space (Walsh, 1992). Architectural enhancement or aestheticization is all well and good so long as it does not compromize a sense of place, identity, and "authenticity."

Some theorists have argued that the postmodern urban landscape can accommodate a diversity of global and local features. Doel (2000:124) suggests, "Place and placelessness are no longer opposed, as the humanistic geographers believed. Hereinafter, a place is NowHere and NoWhere." This is an interesting statement, in that it implies that place and placelessness can coexist in harmony. Augé (1995:79) states, "Place and nonplace are rather like opposed polarities: The first is never completely erased, the second never totally completed; they are like palimpsests on which the scrambled game of identity and relations is ceaselessly rewritten." Relph (1976:140) similarly states, "There is a geography of places characterised by variety and meaning, and there is a placeless geography, a labyrinth of endless similarities." Soja's (1996) concept of "Thirdspace" implies that there is indeed room for a multilayering of space, interpretations and representations of space, and spatial identities. This sedimentation is perhaps inevitable, but he himself urges that each cross-section should contain representations of the past as well as contexts for the next round of restructuring (Soja, 1989). Regeneration is not just about bulldozing the past to make way for contemporary developments, it requires a coherent intertwining of past, present, and future.

Relph (1976) is critical of planners and developers, who have been instrumental in perpetuating both placelessness and inauthenticity in urban environments: "Planning appears not only to be based on an inauthentic sense of place but generally to involve no sense of place at all" (p. 89). He criticizes planners for their inability to differentiate between space and place, and to see beyond development potential. The concept of authenticity is also a contentious and complex subject. Relph (1976:80) suggests that an " 'inauthentic' attitude of placelessness is now widespread." He goes on to state:

> The everyday landscape is ordinary, lacking in distinction, without high points or surprises. It is largely inauthentic in that it has been designed *for* people and is filled with mass-produced objects. (p. 33)

This perhaps implies that many landscapes have become standardized because that is what people desire and feel comfortable with. It can be no coincidence that global developments (e.g., shopping malls, leisure centers, conference centers) of a similar nature have proliferated in recent years. There are arguably few dissenting voices among the general public. Critiques of the post-Fordist era of global reproduction, such as Adorno and Horkheimer (1947), would no doubt have much to say about the manipulation of public taste and consumption, and the hegemonic forces that have shaped such developments. However, it is interesting to note that those who are most likely to be concerned about issues of globalization, reproduction, and authenticity are the global elite. It is those who travel frequently to the world's unique attractions who are most likely to be chagrined by their replication elsewhere. To the nontraveling masses, the existence of a new attraction, whether it is unique to that location or not, is usually going to be a source of interest and entertainment.

The concept of authenticity is certainly largely a subjective attribution. Cohen (1988) argues that authenticity is a "socially constructed concept" and that the meaning is negotiable. It is also a relative concept, as stated by Moore (2002:55): "One person's absolute fake is another's meaningful experience." Getz (1994:425) states, "Although some believe that authenticity is an absolute, determined by a complete absence of commoditization, many other theorists believe it is transitory, evolving, and open to negotiation." Similarly, Jamal and Hill (2002:103) suggest:

> "Authenticity" is neither a unified static construct nor an essential property of objects and events. It is better to approach it more holistically as a concept whose objective, constructed, and/ or experiential dimensions are in dialectical engagement with each other.

The relationship between authenticity and placelessness is thus a complex one, if authenticity is largely determined by the beholder as a subjective attribution. A sense of place need not be dependent on "authentic" surroundings. They may be contrived or artificial, for example, in the case of new developments that pastiche old ones. How people relate to and engage with that place will arguably be the determining factors in place identity construction. There is a need for some kind of social or cultural continuity, but as stated earlier, communities can grow organically around a particular location, or around specific traditions, which are more intangible and less location-based.

Clearly, globalization, mass communication and technology have been instrumental in creating a more "placeless" world. Certain corporations monopolize the global economy, their ubiquitous outlets dominating and standardizing the urban landscape.

The availability and accessibility of their products has lead to a proliferation of signs and symbols that are recognizable in even the remotest locations (not that the products are always affordable for locals). Urban architecture can be unique and exciting, but it can also be banal and standardized. Numerous "copycat" schemes exist globally for housing, retail, or leisure developments, including iconic structures like the Guggenheim in Bilbao. The "could be anywhere" experience discussed earlier in the chapter is largely engendered by architectural developments and the omnipresence of global corporations and products. This is very much in evidence in many new developments, such as business parks, retail centers and waterfronts. A uniformity is created, which may have overwritten the original significance of the landscape. A financial or economic imperative will usually have dictated the nature of development, often at the expense of aesthetics or social and cultural significance.

Tourism development also plays a key role in the standardization of urban landscape. The previous debate about authenticity is frequently raised in the context of tourism, where there are concerns that contrived and artificial attractions, spectacles, and events are being developed at the expense of local traditions and meanings. Boorstin (1964) argued that tourists deliberately go in search of inauthentic experiences or "pseudo-events," and that tourism has become responsible for rendering most events superficial or "pseudo." Rojek (1993) has suggested more recently that the so-called "post-tourist" is not at all concerned about authenticity, and Boniface and Fowler (1993:7) state that, "We want extra-authenticity, that which is better than reality." Hence, the development of fantastical tourist attractions like Disneyland, which Relph (1976:97) describes as offering "the best of imagined and plastic history and adventure from the world over, and combine this either implicitly or explicitly with a vision of a technological utopia." Some forms of tourism are clearly very much about escapism into fantasy worlds. Other forms of tourism are about escapism from the banal and monotonous reality of everyday life. The standard "sun-sea-sand" package tour offers just that. The place in which we do this is often largely irrelevant, so long as it is sunnier than home! We may even want a few reminders of home there to reassure us (e.g., fish and chip shops, English beer). It is a common characteristic of mass tourism that participants like the reassurance of familiarity. Hence, standardized, placeless, enclavic bubbles becoming instantly appealing.

Some tourists (e.g., cultural tourists) conversely seek difference, authenticity, and cultural diversity (Smith, 2003). However, this experience is constantly being threatened by the appropriation of indigenous lands, the dilution of culture and traditions, and the standardization of urban landscapes. Although many tourists appear to be ticking off a mental checklist of diverse "must-see-before-I-die" sights, disappointment and deception are common within the tourism industry, as tourists are frequently sold a dream or a myth (Rojek, 1997; Tresidder, 1999). Their hopes of experiencing something new, different, or unique are increasingly being thwarted by global developments and encroachments. They are therefore becoming victims rather than perpetrators of standardization and placelessness.

Relph (1976) usefully categorized some of these manifestations of placelessness:

> *Other-directedness in places:* Landscapes for tourists, entertainment districts, commercial shops, Disneyfied, museumified, futurist places (synthetic and pseudo-places).
>
> *Uniformity and standardization in places:* New towns, roads, airports, international designs in architecture—industrial and commercial developments.
>
> *Formlessness and lack of human scale and order in places:* Subtopias, skyscrapers, megalopolises—gigantic, individual features, inappropriate to or out-of-scale with cultural or physical setting.
>
> *Place destruction:* For example, war, excavation, urban expansion, expropriation.
>
> *Impermanence and instability of place:* Redevelopment (e.g., waterfronts, derelict buildings, brownfield sites).

Relph's idea of "other-directedness in places" appeals to those who enjoy entertainment, fantasy, and escapism. It is the ultimate realm of the "post-tourist," who enjoys commercialism, no longer values authenticity, and sees tourism as a game. The uniformity and standardization of places corresponds to Augé's (1995) notion of "non-place," as discussed earlier. These are generally international hubs developed for transit, convenience, and security. Formless developments abound in cities where architects have free reign and there are too few planning regulations. Injections of capital coupled with power-hunger and phallic obsession often drive such developments forward. Place destruction is inevitable without proper protection, such as conservation laws or government intervention. The loss of unique heritage is something that should be preventable except in extreme cases (e.g., the destruction of the Bnayan Buddhas by the Taliban in Afghanistan). The final category of impermanence of place is an interesting one, as it could be argued that all places are continuously in flux. However, the decline of industry in many urban environments has led to total dereliction and a need to restore, revive, or rebuild. Brownfield sites can thereby host "flagship" projects (e.g., the Millennium Dome), derelict buildings can house art collections (e.g., Musee d'Orsay, Tate Modern), and waterfront developments can become sophisticated retail centers for residential and tourist usage. There can be uniqueness in such developments, but on the whole they have been criticized for being essentially placeless.

The postmodern urban landscape tends to afford visitors a combination of all of these forms of placelessness, an eclectic mixture of attractions and architectural features. Ironically, it could be argued that the most popular venues in many cities (at least with local residents) are increasingly those that are replicas or reproductions of similar developments elsewhere. This is particularly true of retail parks, leisure centers, and other multiplex complexes incorporating various entertainment facilities. Maybe this is because they have broad appeal, they are convenient, and like fast food, they provide instant satisfaction. Whether such developments have enough uniqueness to attract tourists is subject to further research. Interestingly, it seems that the success of some cultural developments such as art museums (e.g., the Guggenheim, Tate Modern) cannot be reproduced everywhere. Jones (2000) suggests that a number of projects have failed because they are largely inappropriate for the local community and cultural infrastructure. He cites the example of the failed Centre for Visual Art in Cardiff, which he attributes to a local lack of interest in modern art, suggesting that popular culture and sport generally tend to strike more of a chord with local audiences than high arts. This phenomenon is not unique to Cardiff. Postmodern urban developments that focus on popular culture often seem to draw local people into the global arena of new media, technology, and communications far more easily than small-scale arts, heritage, or museum-based projects.

Ultimately, placelessness is based on numerous factors, some of which involve destruction or dereliction, and others which are based on redevelopment. The nature of that redevelopment perhaps determines the degree of subsequent "placelessness." The way in which planners or developers have approached the design, content, or layout becomes crucial. For example, does it reflect the original significance or heritage of place? Have the original occupants been displaced? Do the new or existing occupants have a strong sense of belonging or engagement with place? How standardized, anonymous, or souless is the landscape? Do visitors feel as if they could be anywhere or are they gaining a unique experience?

PLANNING FOR PLACE AND PLACE IDENTITY

The conclusion to Relph's (1976) work suggests that we can and should plan for place in order to transcend placelessness. Planning must take into consideration local structures of meaning and experience. Philo (2000) suggests that we should emphasize the particular, the local, and the specific over the general, the universal, and the eternal. In terms of the planning process, it has been suggested by Lefebvre (1974) that planners typically produce "representations of space." Relph (1976:23) describes how the "space of modern urban planning is principally the two-dimensional, cognitive space of maps and plans." An idea is conceived for the production, construction or creation of a certain type of environment (e.g., a housing development, a business district, a cultural quarter). Space then becomes inhabited by physical structures, streets, and maybe green spaces, which will then be variously used by different groups over time, until the area is redeveloped or demolished. However, different models of planning are being developed, such as cultural planning, which takes into consideration peoples' lifestyles, cultural associations, and identity so that projects have resonance with local communities (Bianchini, 1999; Evans, 2001), and discursive planning, which "produces a sense of place, place-identity, and common cultural schemes" (Ploger, 2001:64).

One of the problems for urban planners is surely that place is such a subjective, intangible concept, and one which may not be easily defined, let alone captured, preserved, or enhanced. The relationship between the inner and outer landscape is one that greatly influences an individual's response to his or her environment and sense of belonging. Place therefore has a multiplicity of interrelated meanings:

> In our everyday lives places are not experienced as independent, clearly defined entities that can be described simply in terms of their location or appearance. Rather, they are sensed in a chiaroscuro of setting, landscape, ritual, routine, other people, personal experiences, care and concern for home, and in the context of other places. (Relph, 1976:29)

This is particularly significant for the tourist, who may have experienced numerous places. If a distinctive and unique experience is to be offered, then planners need to counteract rather than perpetuate standardized, anonymous development. This is particularly important for those attempting to sell places and to create a unique brand identity.

As mentioned earlier in the chapter, de Certeau (1984) suggested that place was essentially about movement, and Augé (1995) echoed this in his definition of anthropological place. Journeys are often hurried and consequently disorienting, therefore tourists are frequently not fully in a place psychologically, even if they are there physically. So, travel can become a simultaneous accumulation of places, as well as a negation of place. However, it may partly be the responsibility of tourists to see better as advocated by de Botton (2002), but destinations arguably also have to give them something worthwhile to see. Maitland, in Chapter 6 of this volume, suggests some ways in which this can be done.

CONCLUSION

Entrikin (1991:7) states that the debate about place and placelessness is predominantly an academic one:

> A large intellectual gap exists between our sense of being actors in the world, of always being in place, and the "placelessness" that characterises our attempts to theorise about human actions and events.

However, it has been suggested in this chapter that place also matters in a very practical sense, not just to the residents for whom a place is home, but also to those who are visiting that place, and to those who are marketing and selling it. The current lack of planning regulations and control that allow placeless environments to proliferate indicates that there is perhaps a need for place to be given some priority on government agendas. Interestingly, a recent report in Britain has expressed concern about the standardization and loss of character of the countryside (see Campaign for the Protection of Rural England, 2003). The same concerns could be applied to urban environments, especially where tourism has potential as a growth industry and re-generation initiatives are being developed.

History (especially colonial history) has shown us that standard-ization and reproduction of common cultural and architectural features is nothing new, however measures should be taken to ensure that place destruction and the erosion of heritage is not an inevitable consequence of this process. Equally, some attention should be paid to rendering architectural and regeneration schemes more humanistic, producing aesthetic, engaging structures, but not allowing form to override content and substance. Individual and collective alienation should be avoided at all costs, particularly in an age of uncertainty, where secularization and fragmentation of communities is becoming rife.

In terms of tourism, few places can afford to eschew the potential economic benefits of this lucrative industry. However, global competition means that there is little room for complacency, and destinations must work hard to create a unique place identity and differentiate themselves in the marketplace. Unique features are needed within urban environments, and although comfort, security, and familiarity are also important elements of the tourist experience, these can be replicated anywhere. They will not be the deciding factors in the tourist decision-making process.

Identifying what people really want within urban environments is a difficult challenge, and supplying it is another issue altogether. Destination perception surveys can help us to determine and improve tourist perceptions of place. However, few reliable methods seem to exist that inform us of local peoples' perceptions of place. Yet this is arguably the most important determinant of social animation, the creation of ambience and other intangible factors that are pivotal to the creation of livable cities. Place arguably matters even more than theorists and academics have given it credit for, and it may be responsible for the death or life of cities as we know them today.

REFERENCES

Adorno, T. and Horkheimer, M. (1979) *Dialectic of Enlightenment.* London: Verso (first published in 1947).

AlSayyad, N. (2001) Global Norms and Urban Forms in the Age of Tourism: Manufacturing Heritage, Consuming Tradition. In AlSayyad, N. (ed.) *Consuming Tradition, Manufacturing Heritage: Global Norms and Urban Forms in the Age of Tourism.* London: Routledge, pp. 1-33.

Augé, M. (1995) *Non-Places: Introduction to an Anthropology of Supermodernity.* London: Verso.

Bauman, Z. (2001) *Community: Seeking Safety in an Insecure World.* Cambridge: Polity.

Bianchini, F. (1999) Cultural Planning for Urban Sustainability. In Nystrom, L. (ed.) *City and Culture: Cultural Processes and Urban Sustainability.* Kalmar: The Swedish Urban Environment Council, pp. 34-51.

Blazwick, I. (Ed.) (2001) *Century City: Art and Culture in the Modern Metropolis.* London: Tate Publishing.

Boniface, P. and Fowler, P. J. (1993) *Heritage and Tourism in "The Global Village."* London: Routledge.

Boorstin, D. (1964) *The Image: A Guide to Pseudo-Events in America.* New York: Harper and Row.

Botton de, A. (2002) *The Art of Travel.* London: Hamish Hamilton.

Certeau, Michel de (1984) *The Practice of Everyday Life.* Berkeley: University of California Press.

Cohen, E. (1988) Authenticity and Commoditization in Tourism. *Annals of Tourism Research* 15: 371-86.

Campaign for the Protection of Rural England (2003) *Lie of the Land.* London: CPRE.

Doel, M. A. (2000) Unglunking Geography: Spatial Science After Dr Seuss and Gilles Deleuze. In Crang, M. and Thrift, N. (eds) *Thinking Space.* London: Routledge, pp. 117-135.

Edensor, T. (1998) *Tourists at the Taj: Performance and Meaning at a Symbolic Site.* London: Routledge.

Edensor, T. (2001) Performing Tourism, Staging Tourism: (Re)producing Tourist Space and Practice, *Tourist Studies* 1 (1): 59-81.

Edwards, J. A. (1996) Waterfronts, Tourism and Economic Sustainability: the United Kingdom Experience. In Priestley, G. K., Edwards, J. A., and Coccossis, H. (eds.) *Sustainable Tourism? European Experiences.* Wallingford: CAB International, pp. 86-98.

Entrikin, J. N. (1991) *The Betweenness of Place: Towards a Geography of Modernity.* Basingstoke: Macmillan.

Evans, G. (2001) *Cultural Planning: An Urban Renaissance?* London: Routledge.

Gates, R. J. and Stout, F. (eds.) (1996) *City Reader.* London: Routledge.

Getz, D. (1994) Event Tourism and the Authenticity Dilemma. In Theobald, W. F. (ed.) *Global Tourism.* Oxford: Butterworth Heinemann, pp. 409-427.

Graham, B., Ashworth, G. J. and Tunbridge, J. E. (2000) *A Geography of Heritage: Power, Culture and Economy.* London: Arnold.

Harvey, D. (1990) *The Condition of Postmodernity: An Enquiry into the Origins of Cultural Change.* Oxford: Blackwell.

Hughes, G. (1998) Tourism and the Semiological Realization of Space. In Ringer, G. (ed.) *Destinations: Cultural Landscapes of Tourism.* London: Routledge, pp. 17-33.

Jamal, T. and Hill, S. (2002) The Home and the World: (Post)touristic Spaces of (In)authenticity. In Dann, G. M. S. (ed.) *The Tourist as a Metaphor of the Social World.* Wallingford: CABI, pp. 77-108.

Jones, J. (2000) The Regeneration Game. *Guardian Unlimited*, October 16 (www. guardian.co.uk).

Jordan, G. and Weedon, C. (1995) *Cultural Politics: Class, Gender, Race and the Postmodern World.* Oxford: Blackwell.

Lefebvre, H. (1974) *The Production of Space.* Oxford: Blackwell.

Lippard, L. R. (1997) *The Lure of the Local: Senses of Place in a Multicentred Society.* New York: The New Press.

Middleton, M. (1987) *Man Made the Town.* London: The Bodley Head.

Miles, M. (1997) *Arts, Space and the City: Public Arts and Urban Futures.* London: Routledge.

Moore, K. (2002) The Discursive Tourist. In Dann, G. M. S. (ed.) *The Tourist as a Metaphor of the Social World*, Wallingford: CABI, pp. 41-60.

Mumford, L. (1961) *The City in History: Its Origins, Its Transformations and Its Prospect.* New York: Harcourt, Brace & World.

Mumford, L. (1968) *The Urban Prospect.* London: Martin Secker and Warburg Ltd.

Norberg-Schulz, C. (1965) *Intentions in Architecture.* Cambridge: M.I.T.

Philo, C. (2000) Foucault's Geography. In Crang, M. and Thrift, N. (eds) *Thinking Space.* London: Routledge, pp. 205-238.

Ploger, J. (2001) Millennium Urbanism—Discursive Planning, *European Urban and Regional Studies*, 8 (1): 63-72.

Rand, H. (1991) *Hundertwasser.* Cologne: Taschen.

Relph, E. (1976) *Place and Placelessness.* London: Pion.

Rojek, C. (1993) *Ways of Escape: Modern Transformations in Leisure and Travel.* London: Macmillan Press Ltd.

Rojek, C. (1997) Indexing, Dragging and the Social Construction of Tourist Sights. In Rojek, C. and Urry, J. (eds) *Touring Cultures: Transformations of Travel and Theory.* London: Routledge, pp. 52-74.

Rotenburg, R. and McDonogh, G. (eds) (1993) *The Cultural Meaning of Urban Space.* Westport: Bergin and Garvey.

Smith, M. K. (2003) *Issues in Cultural Tourism Studies.* London: Routledge.

Soja, E. W. (1989) *Postmodern Geographies: The Reassertion of Space in Critical Social Theory.* London: Verso Press.

Soja, E. W. (1996) *Thirdspace: Journeys to Los Angeles and Other Real-and-Imagined Places.* Oxford: Blackwell.

Sudjic, D. (1992) *The 100 Mile City.* London: Flamingo.

Sudjic, D. (1999) Between the Metropolitan and the Provincial. In Nystrom, L. (ed) *City and Culture: Cultural Processes and Urban Sustainability.* Kalmar: The Swedish Urban Environment Council, pp. 178-185.

Tresidder, R. (1999) Tourism and Sacred Landscapes. In Crouch, D. (ed) *Leisure/tourism Geographies: Practices and Geographical Knowledge.* London: Routledge, pp. 137-148.

Walsh, K. (1992) *The Representation of the Past: Museums and Heritage in the Post-modern World.* London: Routledge.

Chapter 6

Cultural Tourism and the Development of New Tourism Areas in London

Robert Maitland

INTRODUCTION

Much cultural tourism depends upon the distinctiveness of place, but as Smith outlines in Chapter 5, there is increasing concern that distinctiveness is being lost through processes of globalization, and that destinations are becoming more and more similar. This process of homogenization can affect established and more recently developed destinations. It relates to the rapid growth of tourism and higher volumes of visitors in more destinations, as well as to the impact of broader processes of globalization. It can be seen as part of a more general process of change that results in standardized environments that are "placeless."

Concerns about these supply-side changes are being raised at a time when some commentators have identified the increasing importance of visitors who are more experienced, independent, and discriminating in what they seek from destinations. These visitors have been variously categorized as "new tourists" (Poon, 1993) or "posttourists" (Urry, 2001). It is argued that this group of visitors is particularly seeking an "authentic" or nonhomogenized experience when

This chapter is based on research on NTAs in London that is being carried out with Dr. Peter Newman, School of Architecture and the Built Environment, University of Westminster.

they choose a destination. They might be expected to be drawn to destinations that retain distinctiveness.

This chapter reports research that explores the importance of local distinctiveness and the qualities of place to overseas visitors to London. It is based upon continuing research into the development of what can be termed new tourism areas (NTAs) in London, which includes surveys of visitors to Islington, King's Cross, and the South Bank (Bankside, Southwark). These are NTAs, but the process of development has been significantly different in each case. The chapter explores the characteristics of visitors to the areas, what attracts them to the areas and what elements of the place and its culture they see as having particular value. It argues that there are alternatives to the standardized "tourist bubble" approach to developing NTAs, and that these can build upon some of the distinct qualities of the area. For at least some visitors, it seems that these distinct qualities of place are the main attraction—they are attracted by what we might call "placefulness."

TOURISM DEVELOPMENT IN CITIES

Urban tourism has grown rapidly over the last 20 years, and moved beyond traditional tourism places. Heritage and culture cities have grown in popularity, but there has been an increased interest in non-traditional urban destinations such as former industrial cities. Early pioneers like Baltimore in the United States have been joined by cities such as Birmingham and Bradford in the United Kingdom, Bilbao and Barcelona in Spain. The growth of urban tourism is ascribed to a combination of demand factors and the supply of new attractions (see, for example, Law, 2002). But the way in which this occurs is only partly understood. Fainstein and Judd (1999:5-7) summarize a process that has been common to many cities:

1. More places becoming destinations but, "to appeal to tourists, cities must be consciously molded to create a physical landscape that tourists wish to inhabit."
2. This will require constant change. The tourist is a "moving target" since they "seek distraction from the ordinary experiences of everyday life. Escape may take the form of contrived

diversion and amusement, so families visit Disneyworld. . . . go to the Mall of America, or seek specialized diversions like Planet Hollywood."

3. But tourists also seek the authentic so the tourism industry is concerned with responding to the desire for "carnival-like diversion" and the "yearning for extraordinary but 'real' experience."

4. Tourism thus becomes a series of familiar circuits, and people "know the places they might visit and the sights at which they might look."

5. People expect to experience the heritage architecture and culture that make up a city's essence. A construction of any version of a city's heritage requires large doses of "mythology. Folk memory and popular fantasy" (Graburn and Moore, 1994).

6. Tourist spaces are designed to produce "liminal moments that lift the tourist above ordinary, everyday experience."

Fainstein and Judd argue that this growth has tended to follow a stereotypical model involving investment in the creation of specific tourist spaces or "tourist bubbles," designed to appeal to the visitor, and based around standard components, frequently dependent on funding by large corporations combined with significant public investment. Standard components often include cultural attractions. These range from museums and galleries—the National Museum of Photography, Film and Television in Bradford, the Guggenheim in Bilbao—to popular cultural attractions: Various forms of festival marketplace are common. However, it is argued that the tourist bubble expands to enclose whole areas, which have been developed and reconfigured in a themed way, and are separated from the rest of the city in terms of use, physical form, and image. The area around Piccadilly Circus and Leicester Square in London has developed as a themed tourist or entertainment space, with branded attractions (Rock Circus, Pepsi Trocadero), retail, restaurants (Planet Hollywood and ubiquitous burger chains), and branded bars. Similar reconfiguration has occurred in smaller cities and towns, frequently as part of regeneration initiatives. This reflects the perceived need to attract inward investment and a search for (supposed) predictable and successful outcomes—as well as lack of imagination. The result of tourist devel-

opment is thus wider than the provision of specific attractions—
it affects sense of place. Tourist bubbles seek to increase a destination's
attractions, but do so in a way that is unrelated to specific qualities
of place and locality. In Jansen-Verbeke's familiar terminology, they
affect leisure settings as well as activity places (Jansen-Verbeke,
1986). There is an identified tension between visitors' search for a
"real" or authentic experience and the standardized development of
"tourist bubbles" (Fainstein and Judd, 1999). Equally, it is not clear
that tourist spaces assembled from standardized components can necessarily produce liminal and extraordinary moments.

These changes reflect wider processes of economic change and
globalization. Smith, in Chapter 5 of this volume, discusses spatial
transformation of cities and the idea of placelessness—a sense that
one could be anywhere. She points out that this is not a new phenomenon, and quotes Relph's (1976:6) description of placelessness as "the
weakening of distinct and diverse experiences and identities of place."
In some cases placelessness may be deliberately sought. Kuntsler
(1994) discusses the development of what he terms "the geography of
nowhere" in the United States, which he sees as deriving from mod-
ernism's deliberate rejection of locality—through the International
Style—and also from the search for cheap commercial buildings and
suburban housing, which can be achieved through standardized construction and development.

Tourism development has played a role in these wider processes of
development, but its actual impact is indeterminate. It is not a product
of characteristics of the industry itself, but the way it is structured in a
particular location (Fainstein and Gladstone, 1999). So far as leisure
settings or sense of place are concerned, we might observe that homogenization, contributing to placelessness, has gone further in countries such as the United States and the United Kingdom that have developed more "efficient" retail and leisure industries based on large
corporations offering branded products. Contrasts between the centers of towns and cities in the United States and England with those in
Italy, Spain, or France are noticeable. There is more to this than a loss
of vitality as businesses have moved out of town—the "charity shop
syndrome." Even where town centers survive, the remaining businesses are likely to be chain stores —a Superdrug rather than local
pharmacies—or, increasingly, chain bars. It is rare indeed in the

United States or United Kingdom to find local bakers, patisseries, butchers, or greengrocers selling distinctive local products. As Worpole (1992) pointed out, standardization of the retail offer and lack of identity have been important reasons for the decline of many British town centers.

There is some evidence that concern about loss of destination distinctiveness and its impacts is moving up the research and policy agenda. The European Commission is currently funding the LODIS project to explore local distinctiveness in six European towns; this includes exploration of techniques of place management and interpretation of cultural areas (Grant, 2002). In the United Kingdom, the Council for the Protection of Rural England (CPRE) has just completed a pilot survey of six market towns, designed to assess the way in which they are changing and how far they are retaining distinctiveness. Concerns with local distinctiveness are partly economic: If destinations become more homogenous, will that affect tourist demand? Will visitors be less inclined to visit places that offer a less distinct experience, or one that is perceived as inauthentic? However, there is also concern to maintain local distinctiveness as an inherent value that contributes to residents' sense of place, local pride, and culture. Though tourism can contribute to homogenization, tourism management that maintains the distinctiveness of places could benefit local people and visitors alike.

This account of the development of urban tourism raises some important issues. Fainstein and Judd (1999) see a conflict between standardized tourist bubble development and visitors' search for the "authentic." There is an identified tension between visitors' search for a "real" or authentic experience and the standardized development of tourist bubbles. However, the central concern may not be "authenticity" (a slippery concept, as Schouten points out in Chapter 2) but distinctiveness: tourist cities (increasingly, all cities) becoming more and more alike. This raises obvious questions about whether new urban tourism can develop in ways other than through imposing a template— and questions about changing visitor requirements and motivations.

NEW URBAN TOURISTS

Some commentators have identified the increasing importance of visitors who are more experienced, independent, and discriminating in what they seek from destinations—"post-tourism" or "new tourism." Lash and Urry (1994) argued that standardized, rigidly packaged mass tourism was being replaced by a post-tourism that was characterized by individualized consumption: shorter, more frequent, and more specialized holidays. Similarly, Poon (1993) argues for the emergence of the "new tourist," suggesting that mass tourism is giving way to a new tourism characterized by flexible, independent, experienced travelers. In brief, this group of tourists is independent, discerning, and seeking more authentic experiences. Urry (2001) draws on Ffeifer's (1985) work to argue that the post-tourist wants variety and choice, and is happy to move rapidly between different settings—for example, from high- to low-culture. He also sees the post-tourist as knowing and aware about the experience of being a tourist—"self-conscious, cool, role distanced" (1999:101). Such visitors will continue to search for extraordinary experiences, but may look for ones that are quirkier, less obviously manufactured (although they will be aware of the artifice). "Exotic" (Sassen and Roost, 1999) urban environments are likely to appeal, especially where they can be easily accessed.

These accounts resonate with Clark's work on the city as "entertainment machine" (Clark, 2003). In one of the most comprehensive attempts to link the visitor economy into understanding of broader changes in urban economies, Clark lists several components of change: the volatility of taste, niche markets and a new affluent class, factors such as increased travel and the Internet that facilitate contacts, locational decisions that emphasize taste and quality of life, and the rise of leisure and concern about the arts. This is consistent with some visitors—"new tourists"—seeking urban tourism experiences that are less stereotyped and more distinctive, in new tourism areas. New tourists—experienced, independent, flexible, and seeking the authentic, or at least the distinctive—are the people we might expect to seek out new areas not previously popular with visitors.

NEW TOURISM AREAS IN CITIES

If some tourists are seeking out more distinctive places and areas within London, then we would expect the characteristics of tourists and their preferences to vary systematically between areas. The research reported below was designed to explore this. It did so by interviewing a sample of overseas visitors to King's Cross/Islington and to Bankside, and comparing their responses to overseas visitors to London as a whole. King's Cross/Islington were chosen as plausible but contrasting areas that could be seen as NTAs. Islington is well connected to but separate from the main tourist locations of central London. Although a number of initiatives had sought to develop tourism, there was no comprehensive plan, and no major new tourism attractions were developed. Bankside is adjacent to major tourism areas, and there appears to be a clear policy intention to develop tourism in the area—to promote regeneration and to relieve pressure at existing tourist hotspots. The area includes two new flagship attractions: Tate Modern and Shakespeare's Globe Theatre.

Islington

The build-up of tourism in Islington has been gradual, and change in the area has not been dramatic. Islington was one of the playgrounds of pre-industrial London. This legacy remains in numerous (small) theaters and pubs. New commercial developments have located on Pentonville Road, which climbs from King's Cross to the Angel. Although the road is architecturally uninspiring and traffic relentless, student residences have been refurbished and a site that lay undeveloped for many years now hosts a midrange hotel. Behind the main roads, residential areas divide into either high-value private Georgian and Victorian Streets or mass housing blocks of the 1960s and 1970s. King's Cross and the Angel have a rich mix of land uses. The area has very good public transport connections, to central London in particular. It has been estimated that over four million visitors spent an estimated €105 million in the London Borough of Islington in 1998 (Carpenter, 1999).

There has been considerable investment in renewing cultural assets—including the Scala cinema (refurbished as a nightclub); Sadler's Wells theater (refurbished with a €42 million national lottery grant); and the Almeida Theatre. However, no flagship attraction has been created. There has been substantial private investment in the area, and over the past few years a bustling Islington nightlife has seen the opening of numerous new bars and upscale restaurants. (These included the now-closed Granita, site of an alleged political deal between the U.K. Prime Minister and Chancellor of the Exchequer.) Tourism-related policy in Islington has a broken history. The council financially supported various visitor-related initiatives from the early to mid-1980s and subsequently a Tourism Development Action Plan (TDAP), one result of which was the creation of Discover Islington, an independent not-for-profit organization whose mission was to develop tourism to create economic activity and foster civic pride, which was set up in 1991 and closed in 2001. However, tourist development has not resulted from comprehensive planning by either public or private sectors, in contrast to the process of creating a tourist bubble.

Bankside

The Bankside area stretches along the south bank of the Thames from London Bridge to beyond Blackfriars Bridge, at which point it reaches the long-established South Bank cultural center. Promotions for Bankside describe it as "the new heart of London" where visitors can "enjoy world-class arts and entertainment, riverside eating and drinking, superb views, relaxing walks and millennium architecture" (Bankside welcome page, www.southbanklondon.com). Its best-known attractions are Tate Modern (housed in a converted power station) and Shakespeare's Globe Theatre, but there are other galleries and theaters in the area. For many years, local politicians and community activists strongly resisted tourism and leisure development in the Bankside area. However, attitudes and political control changed in the 1990s and Southwark now sees tourism as a key industry; full-time tourism officers have been employed since 1996.

The area has benefited from public investment through the national lottery (e.g., Tate Modern), charitable trusts (e.g., Shakespeare's Globe), and the private sector (e.g., Vinopolis museum of wine). Public investment in environmental and other improvements has frequently been coordinated and funded by two urban regeneration partnerships—the Pool of London Partnership and the Cross River Partnership. Tourism development in Bankside therefore became part of public policy. Cross River Partnership, which brought together the City of Westminster and City of London with Southwark and Lambeth councils, sought as one of its strategic objectives to spread the benefits and opportunities from congested locations north of the river to the new destinations of Lambeth and Southwark. A key element of the strategy was improving pedestrian links across the river, and a new Hungerford Bridge (from the Embankment to the South Bank Centre) and the new Millennium Bridge (creating a new route from St. Paul's to Tate Modern) were opened in 2002. New culture and new tourism development seems to have been important in Bankside development, but some commentators have argued that this is simply "an opportunist and image-based response to dominant property speculation interests" (Newman and Smith, 2000).

FINDINGS

Understanding of the development of new areas for tourism in London is handicapped by familiar problems of lack of data at the London and particularly the local level (Bull and Church, 2001). There are some data on overseas visitors to London as a whole derived from the International Passenger Survey (IPS) and on domestic visitors from the United Kingdom Tourism Survey. Both are annual samples with sizes large enough to allow accurate estimates of tourist numbers to London. Further information on overseas visitors can be obtained from the Survey of Overseas Visitors to London (SOVL), which is carried out annually on behalf of the London Tourist Board (now called Visit London). The latter provides the most detailed information on the characteristics, actions, and motivations of London's overseas visitors. It is based on a sample of around 1,300 and provides longitudinal data. The major deficiencies, however, are at the more local level. Visitor surveys tend to be sporadic and ad hoc, and do not use consistent methodologies and questions—though inevitably they frequently seek similar information. It is difficult or impossible to define with clarity the areas that tourists visit, especially when one moves away from clearly defined attractions such as the Tower of London. Still less is known about the activities of London workers and residents in the development of tourism areas, in terms of visits to attractions, bars and restaurants, and their role in "discovering" and creating "new" areas. This is despite the fact that there is considerable internal tourism in London: Bull and Church (2001) point out that in 1995, 3.33 million domestic tourist visits (which include an overnight stay) to London were by people whose normal place of residence was in London.

Our research was designed to begin to assemble some information on visitors and their characteristics and perceptions at the local level. We chose initially to focus on overseas visitors because of their perceived importance in London tourism, and because of better data availability at the London level. We wanted to be able to identify the characteristics of visitors in King's Cross/Islington and in Bankside and to compare them with the characteristics of visitors to London as a whole. In order to make this possible, many questions were designed to be compatible with the SOVL, allowing us to read across local and all London characteristics. Though this inevitably restricts what can be explored in the survey, it is necessary in order to determine whether the characteristics of visitors to the NTAs we identified differ from those of visitors to London as a whole. Further, qualitative research will be required to explore visitor characteristics in more detail.

The Islington research questioned people at a series of locations in the King's Cross and Islington areas of London in summer 2001. Interviews took place during the working week and at weekends, and at different times of the day and evening. People who permanently lived or worked in the area were excluded, and a total of 228 usable responses from overseas visitors was achieved. The Bankside research questioned people at a series of locations in the Bankside area in summer 2002. Interviews took place during the working week and at weekends, and at different times of the day and evening. People who permanently lived or worked in the area were excluded. A total of 230 usable responses from overseas visitors was achieved.

The findings discussed below compare characteristics of overseas visitors to London as a whole, derived from the SOVL (2001) overseas visitors to King's Cross/Islington (2001) and to Bankside (2002) derived from the author's surveys.

Country of Origin

There is no systematic variation in the visitors' country of origin, with origins of Islington and Bankside visitors similar to those of all

London visitors as measured by SOVL. However, visitors to the NTAs are older than all London visitors: 45 percent of Islington visitors and 39 percent of Bankside visitors are over forty-five, compared to 30 percent for London.

Purpose and Frequency of Visit

There are some notable differences. Whilst 65 percent of London visitors are on a weekend break or longer holiday, the proportion falls to 56 percent for Bankside, and 48 percent for Islington. Conversely, the proportion of VFR visitors in London is 15 percent, but in Bankside it is 21 percent and in Islington 35 percent. Islington has more business and educational visits.

There are differences too in experience of London. Whilst 55 percent of all overseas visitors to London have been to the city before, 69 percent of Bankside, and 83 percent of Islington visitors are on a repeat visit. Over half (53 percent) of Islington visitors have made three or more previous visits (Bankside 38 percent). When asked about visits to the areas, 51 percent of the Islington visitors said they had been to the area before, and 30 percent were quite frequent visitors, have been there three times or more. Only 32 percent of Bankside visitors were making a repeat visit. There appears to be some variation in length of stay, with more visitors staying over a month in Islington (13 percent) and Bankside (20 percent) than London (7 percent).

Sources of Information Encouraging the Visit

There was variation in the information sources encouraging the visit. The most important sources for London visitors were the Internet (38 percent) and travel agents (22 percent). However, when it came to sources encouraging the visit to the areas of Islington and Bankside, the most important sources were recommendations by a friend or relative (21 percent for Islington, 29 percent for Bankside) and guidebooks (19 percent, 28 percent). The Internet was unimportant (5 percent, 1 percent). And visitors to Islington and Bankside would themselves recommend the areas to family or friends as good places to visit—87 percent for Islington, 97 percent for Bankside.

Visitors' Likes and Dislikes

What did visitors like about the area? Visitors were asked what they most liked, and then asked to rank their responses in order of priority. The responses were analyzed to see whether visitors had come to the area to visit a specific attraction—an activity place—or because of the qualities of the area as a whole—the leisure setting. In Islington 34 percent of visitors identified the element they most liked as an aspect of the leisure setting—either physical (e.g., architecture, trees, canals, river) or sociocultural (e.g., "bohemian," "cosmopolitan," "atmosphere," "quaint"). If a wider definition of leisure setting is taken to include range of bars, restaurants, and shops (rather than a specific bar, restaurant, or shop), the leisure setting is the main priority for 57 percent of Islington visitors. In Bankside, 54 percent ranked leisure setting as their main priority.

Finally, visitors were asked if they would return to the areas, and the responses were very similar. In both Islington and Bankside, 60 percent said they would definitely return and 34 percent (Islington) and 35 percent (Bankside) said they would possibly return. In other words, only some 5 percent said they would not return.

DISCUSSION

The surveys allow us to develop some initial understanding of who is visiting London's NTAs, and what it is about the areas that attracts them.

1. The visitors in our surveys have distinctive qualities. They differ from the SOVL group overall, and in some ways have characteristics that seem to fit well the types of tourist described in the literature about "post-tourism" or "new tourism." They tend to be older, they are considerably more experienced travelers to London, and they make use of friendship networks and guidebooks in deciding which areas to visit.

These qualities are particularly noticeable in Islington, and less prominent in Bankside. This is as one might expect. Bankside is newly well connected to the north bank of the Thames, and sits between the Tower Bridge and the South Bank/London Eye tourist hotspots. A riverside walk from Tower Bridge to Westminster runs through the area, providing easy pedestrian access. This is a new tourist area, but one that is readily accessible—physically and symbolically—from established tourist beats. Islington and King's Cross are less accessible in both respects, and so a higher proportion of its visitors are likely to be exploratory "new tourists."

2. Our visitors have a range of motivations for visiting the area. But in both Islington and Bankside, the area's attractiveness seems to have less to do with major individual attractions and more to do with distinctive built environment and the "leisure setting." In Bankside visitors most like the architecture, river, atmosphere, sense of history, and views. In Islington, physical and cultural elements (e.g., architecture, cosmopolitan) are also important, but the presence of cafés, shops, bars, and restaurants constitute an important component of the leisure setting. It is perhaps particularly notable that although Bankside has two major, new attractions in Tate Modern and Bankside, it is the broader qualities that constitute the sense of place that most appeal to visitors.

Numerous studies of cultural tourism attempt to be more precise about motivations and distinguish "accidental" tourists, "serious leisure" tourists, "purposeful" and "incidental" tourists (see McKercher, 2002, and Chapter 2 of this book) or "arts core" and "arts peripheral" tourists (Hughes, 2000). Whilst visitors to Islington and Bankside identify a number of particular attractions and for some it may be possible to pin down their cultural motivations, the more important finding is that the majority are drawn to more general characteristics of the area. They may come to look, to shop, to stroll, to go to the theater, to eat out, or some combination of these activities—possibly hand in hand with the friends and relations they are visiting. The common factor is that it is the experience of being in the area that is attractive.

Although other areas in London may be seen as becoming more standardized and placeless, Bankside and Islington retain some distinct qualities identified by survey respondents. This raises a range of questions about the importance of authenticity and distinctiveness in attracting visitors. Those of us who watched the transformation of Bankside and saw the timber and plaster (reproduction) Shakespeare's Globe Theatre roofed in shiny, fireproof stainless steel before its thatch was added might see this as a clear example of staged authenticity! Equally, visitors to Islington may well feel it is the "real London" only insofar as London has become entirely middle class and affluent. Yet whether or not they are authentic, both areas are distinctive, and offer an experience that is less standardized or homogenized than tourist bubbles like Piccadilly Circus and Leicester Square or Covent Garden. In terms of our earlier discussion, while the tourist bubbles offer standardized placelessness, Islington and Bankside offer what we might call "placefulness."

Importantly, Londoners and London workers as well as visitors use these areas, and this may contribute to a sense of being in a distinct *place* rather than a tourist bubble or enclave. Some visitors may see cultural tourism as the sense of experiencing "ordinary everyday life" rather than an extraordinary attraction or event that constitutes a "tourism experience" (Maitland, 2000). For them, places where they can mingle with local people will be particularly attractive. It seem reasonable to suppose that this search for distinctiveness and everyday experience will be most likely to be sought after by those who have had the opportunity to visit more conventional tourist sites in London and around the world, and this fits well with the characteristics of our survey respondents—experienced travelers who are repeat visitors to London.

3. The link between visitors and Londoners is important. Bull and Church (2001) point to the importance of VFR in generating more tourist visits to London in the 1990s, but this is even more important in our NTAs. A higher proportion of those who visited Bankside, and many more visitors to Islington, are in London visiting friends and relations. This may well fit with the fact that they are also much more experienced visitors to London. Recommendations by friends and relatives was the most important reason for visiting the area, followed by guidebooks and the visitors' own previous experience of the areas. Recommendations by tourism professionals—BTA/VisitBritain, TIC, travel agents—were of little or no significance. For this segment of the visitor market, and for new tourism areas, development seems to mean word of mouth and recommendations from a few guidebook sources, rather than conventional promotion. This itself raises interesting questions about what visitors are seeking. How much do they

seek familiar landscapes of consumption in a distinct urban setting, and how open are they to the qualities the place has to offer?

4. The role of public policy is ambiguous. In Islington, the development of tourism was not planned (though it was encouraged by TDAP and Discover Islington), and it was comparatively laissez-faire land-use planning that allowed new uses for shopping and entertainment to develop. In Bankside, key elements were property speculation and development pressure on a fringe area of central London, together with social entrepreneurialism of key individuals in pushing forward the Globe and Tate Modern developments with determination and opportunism. Public investment was important in renewing cultural assets, although this was not done primarily with the tourist in mind. Public investment was important in improving the physical environment, and in the case of Bankside, particularly in improving pedestrian links. However, this has so far avoided the sanitization and homogenization characteristic of, for example, Times Square. Indeed, in the case of Bankside, the new bridges add to the area's distinctiveness.

5. The development of Islington and Bankside offer some indications of what NTAs that are distinctive, rather than standardized tourist bubbles, might look like. Though they include some standard components and chain offerings—Starbucks are ubiquitous—they offer a distinctive environment or leisure setting that is the most important attraction to their visitors. They can distinguish themselves from other areas that rely on a standardized, commodity product. In part this is because of the importance of resident and visitor interaction. Visitors are a distinct group, generally more-experienced travelers to London more likely to have family or friendship connections, and more likely to use them in deciding the places they will go. The use of the areas by residents and visitors alike may be a key part of the attraction for many visitors: Londoners help create the bohemian and cosmopolitan atmosphere. This may be equally true for some residents; for Richard Florida (2002) it is amenity that attracts talented workers to cities and thus underpins economic growth, and part of that amenity may derive from the presence of (certain types of) visitors who add to a cosmopolitan atmosphere and help support facilities such as bars and restaurants.

CONCLUSION

This account of NTAs, their visitors, and how they develop remains preliminary and partial. We have shown that there are areas that have developed in ways that attract tourists without following the familiar route of the tourist bubble, and that they appear to attract a particular segment of visitors who have characteristics consistent with being "new" or "post" tourists, and who are drawn by the leisure setting or sense of place, rather than specific attractions. The main attractions of the areas may be their placefulness. There may be lessons here for the development of other NTAs in London and elsewhere, and for the ways in which planning and public policy influences local distinctiveness and placefulness. However, if we are to understand the development of NTAs, considerable additional research is required to explore in detail the motivations of visitors, their perceptions of the areas and how these are formed, as well as the perceptions and motivations of business operators, developers, residents, and workers. But we need to gain that understanding if public policy is to influence tourism development effectively. As the proportion of London's overseas visitors who have previously visited the capital continues to rise; as the distinction between the demands and behavior of tourists, excursionists, and residents continues to blur; and as the interaction between some visitors and some residents becomes more complex, we need a more sophisticated understanding of what constitutes "tourism areas" and how far public policy can influence their creation.

REFERENCES

Bull, P. and Church, A . (2001) Understanding Urban Tourism: London in the Early 1990s. *International Journal of Tourism Research* 3: 141-150.

Carpenter, H. (1999) *Islington: The Economic Impact of Visitors.* London: Discover Islington.

Clark, T. N. (Ed.) (2003) *The City as an Entertainment Machine.* San Diego: Elsevier.

Fainstein, S. and Gladstone, D. (1999) *Evaluating Urban Tourism.* In Fainstein, S. and Judd, D. (eds) *The Tourist City.* Yale: Yale University Press, pp. 21-34.

Fainstein, S. and Judd, D. (1999) *The Tourist City.* Yale: Yale University Press.

Ffeifer, M. (1985) *Going Places.* London: Macmillan.

Florida, R. (2002) *The Rise of the Creative Class: And How It's Transforming Work, Leisure, Community, and Everyday Life*. New York: Basic Books.

Graburn H.H. and Moore R. S. (1994) Anthropological Research in Tourism. In Ritchie, J. and Goeldner, C. (eds) *Travel Tourism and Hospitality Research: A Handbook for Managers and Researchers* (2nd edn). New York: John Wiley, pp. 233-243.

Grant, M., Human, B. and Le Pelley, B. (2002) Destinations and Local Distinctiveness. *Insights* A21-27.

Hughes, H. (2000) *Arts, Entertainment and Tourism*. Oxford: Butterworth Heineman.

Jansen-Verbeke, M. (1986) Inner City Tourism: Resources, Tourists and Promoters. *Annals of Tourism Research* 13: 79-100.

Kunstler, J. (1994) *The Geography of Nowhere*. New York: Touchstone.

Lash, S. and Urry, J. (1994) *Economies of Signs and Space*. London: Sage.

Law, C. (2002) *Urban Tourism*. London: Continuum.

Maitland, R. (2000) "The Development of New Tourism Areas in Cities: Why Is Ordinary Interesting?" Keynote paper given at *Finnish University Network for Tourism Studies Opening Seminar 2000/01:* Managing Local and Regional Tourism in the Global Market, Savonlinna, Finland, 18 September.

McKercher, B. (2002) Towards a Classification of Cultural Tourists. *International Journal of Tourism Research* 4: 29-38.

Newman, P. and Smith, I. (2000) Cultural Production, Place and Politics on the South Bank of the Thames. *International Journal of Urban and Regional Research* 24: 9-24.

Poon, A. (1993) *Tourism, Technology and Competitive Strategies*. Wallingford: CAB International.

Relph, E. (1976) *Place and Placelessness*. London: Pion.

Sassen, S. and Roost, F. (1999) The City: Strategic Site for the Global Entertainment Industry. In Fainstein, S. and Judd, D. (eds) *The Tourist City*. New Haven: Yale University Press, pp. 146-158.

Urry, J. (2001) *The Tourist Gaze: Leisure and Travel in Contemporary Sciences* (2nd ed). London: Sage.

Worpole, K. (1992) *Towns for People—Transforming Urban Life*. Milton Keynes: Open University Press.

Chapter 7

Trailing Goethe, Humbert, and Ulysses: Cultural Routes in Tourism

László Puczkó
Tamara Rátz

INTRODUCTION

Theme-based tourist attractions have enjoyed increasing popularity in the past decade, particularly as a means of diversifying the tourist product and adding distinctiveness to places. An appropriate theme may capture the attention of potential visitors and may become an attraction in its own right if it is presented and interpreted well and is coupled with services that meet visitor requirements. The most well-known theme-based attractions include theme parks (e.g., Legoland, Disneyland, Europapark, or Six Flags), specific theme-based events (e.g., jousting tournaments, reenacted battle scenes, ancient or medieval feasts), and themed routes (e.g., Whisky Trails, wine routes, or the Silk Road [UNESCO, 2004a]).

As tourism products, themed routes (or itineraries or trails) have several features that ensure a unique role for this type of product in the development of tourism, because they can

- be developed with relatively small investment,
- diversify and spread demand for tourism in time and especially in space,
- contribute to the utilization in tourism of unexploited resources, and

doi:10.1300/5749_07

- develop new segments of demand for certain types of tourism— e.g., cultural tourism, heritage tourism, or wine tourism.

The development of tourism has been traditionally related to the development of culture. The tangible (e.g., historic buildings) and intangible cultural heritage (e.g., traditions) of a country will in a broader sense inevitably attract a very wide range of visitors. The unique cultural features of a region serve as a basis for the cultural supply required by the local community, as well as contributing to increased tourism competitiveness.

Cultural routes, or themed routes based on cultural assets, set a good example for merging culture and tourism and creating cooperation between the two sectors. The positive features of themed routes already mentioned, which are obviously also typical of cultural trips, are advantages that could be utilized to the benefit of developing tourism and can have a positive influence on the seasonal and spatial concentration of demand. Cooperation with the domain of culture could serve the interests of both areas, and the development of products based on a properly selected theme could also strengthen the cultural identity of the local community.

Developing a cultural route seems to be an easy job: One just needs to select a theme, assign a few attractions to it, and deliver it all to potential consumers using promotional tools. Nevertheless, there are several stumbling blocks to implementing such a project. This chapter seeks on the one hand to highlight the most important questions one needs to address during the development of a cultural route and on the other hand to illustrate through the Cultural Avenue of Budapest in Hungary the practical challenges that any route organizer might face.

THE CONCEPT AND FEATURES OF THEMED ROUTES

By definition, themed routes are tourism products that associate a selected theme with natural and created attractions that can be reached by a variety of means of transport (Puczkó and Rátz, 2000). Taking the principle of sustainability into account, these routes offer opportunities to gather information, have fun, and relax simultaneously.

A cultural route is a themed route that has a cultural value or an element of cultural heritage as its focus and that assigns a key role to cultural attractions. ICOMOS (2003) has also recently tried to develop a definition of cultural routes, which covers the same basic concepts but emphasizes the cultural dimension:

> A cultural route is a land, water, mixed, or other type of route, which is physically determined and characterized by having its own specific and historic dynamics and functionality; showing interactive movements of people as well as multi-dimensional, continuous, and reciprocal exchanges of goods, ideas, knowledge, and values within or between countries and regions over significant periods of time; and thereby generating a cross-fertilization of the cultures in space and time, which is reflected both in its tangible and intangible heritage.

Cultural routes vary widely because they combine different geographical elements, can be covered with different means of travel, and can combine pre-existing and new cultural elements. In geographic terms a themed route can be

- local (e.g., "Literary Dublin" or the Kumara Festival Route in Katmandu),
- regional (e.g., the Villány-Siklós Wine Route, Hungary, or the Romantische Strasse in Germany),
- national (e.g., the Hungarian Blue Tour or the route "From the Alps to the Baltic Sea" in Germany), and
- international (e.g., Silk Road or the route of Hanseatic Towns).

There may be several ways (means of transport) to complete a route, and individual options may also be combined in several cases:

- Walking trails or routes are mainly located within the confines of settlement or a natural environment (e.g., "A close-up of Porto—Tour of the Tiles").
- Routes that can be completed by means of public transport are mostly typical of large cities (e.g., tram no. 3T in Helsinki, bus no. 100 in Berlin).

- Routes that can be followed by car or motorcycle are especially popular in North America (e.g., the Tennessee Scenic Highway or the Lewis and Clark Trail).
- Routes that one can ride along on bikes normally connect to automobile routes or walking trails, but bikers normally require the development of separate road surface due to the size of traffic along public roads (as illustrated by the bicycle lane around Lake Fertö [or Neusiedler See], Hungary, or the King's Road in Finland).
- Themed riding tours on horseback are still a rarity, but the opportunity to develop them exists (e.g., one can ride down the thermal spring path or the volcano route in Iceland).
- Voyages present marine life on board of a ship with a glass bottom or with diving equipment and stop over specific points on the sea bed (e.g., in Belize).

A classification of themed routes can set apart routes that have been developed along pre-existing routeways, where the development of the tourism product did not involve creating and designing a route. Themed routes of this nature include, for instance:

- Historic pilgrimages (with the most well-known being the network of routes leading to Santiago de Compostela from various corners of Europe)
- Ancient commercial routes (e.g., the Silk Road or the Amber Road)
- Routes delineated by structures marking imperial borders (such as the Great Wall of China or Hadrian's Wall in England)
- Highways that have gained significance for one reason or another (of which the most renowned is Route 66, which cuts across the United States from Chicago to Los Angeles)

The main attraction that these routes offer is normally the journey itself, the "feeling" one gets from covering the route, with the destination and other ancillary attractions along the way being of secondary importance only.

A second group of themed routes are unrelated to an original and existing, geographically identifiable route; the route is a product of tourism and is as such the outcome of connecting artificially certain attractions that have affiliations with and illustrate a selected theme. A good example of this type is what is known as the European Paper Route (2004), which was created by the regions of Capellades in Spain, the Kouvola region in Finland, and Alte Dombach in Germany. Paper mills are the shared heritage of the three locations, represented by Museu Molí Paperer de Capellades in Spain, the Verla mills in Finland, and by Papiermühle Alte Dombach in Germany. There is no real route to connect the three attractions, instead they are linked through the similarity of the heritage of the sites, and are cemented together by an artificially developed themed route and the physical presence of the same visitors at multiple locations. In such a case, the *theme* itself and especially the *attractions* illustrating the theme play a key role in the final product of tourism. Covering a certain distance along a route is not essential; the point is to *visit a specific destination*. The development of these routes underline an important development that has affected routes in all parts of the world, but which seems to be particularly prevalent in Europe at present. Globalization and the attendant shift of power from the nation-state toward the global and regional levels have created a drive to transnational cooperation in route building. This has been supported particularly by European Union programs that require the participation of more than one EU member state to qualify for funding.

The increasing trend toward cross-border cooperation at a variety of geographic scales means that there is a growth of cooperation networks which require:

- uninterrupted communication between the cooperating partners,
- the confrontation of different interests and values,
- the development of common solutions, and
- the development and implementation of joint action plans, all of which will certainly guarantee dynamism.

When themed routes are created, the participants should rely on their own cultural identities to develop a *common cultural image* that is attractive for tourists and that each participant can identify with. This common image is the focal point of a cultural route that serves as a product in tourism. The physical product (including all the attractions and services visitors demand) is organized around this hub; hence, the common cultural identity guarantees the coherence of supply.

The components of a cultural route project can be classified into the following groups:

1. Attractions not created originally to serve the purposes of tourism, which illustrate the particular theme (such as geographical locations, churches, castles, wine cellars)
2. Attractions created to serve the purposes of tourism, which illustrate the particular theme (such as museums, visitor centers, events, animation, and workshops open for the public)
3. Tourist and cultural services (e.g., accommodation, restaurants, shops, bike rentals, open-air theaters)
4. Information services (e.g., information offices, Web sites)
5. State-run and non-governmental tourist organizations (e.g., municipalities, regional tourist organizations, cultural societies)

Partners may be closely or loosely connected to a central theme. For instance, the main attractions of a whisky trail include distilleries and the related visitor centers, but the experience a visitor gets would be incomplete without restaurants offering local cuisine, without fortresses and farms highlighting the historical and social heritage and the present character of the region, or even without the natural environment along the trail.

THE OBJECTIVES OF SETTING UP
A THEMED ROUTE

Those setting up a themed route would typically seek to generate interest directly in a particular theme and the related attractions (Gustke and Hodgson, 1980) and indirectly in the geographical area where these attractions are located. This function may play a pivotal role, especially in the case of routes that present less-popular sights, as routes can convert certain sights into products if they are well suited to the theme, despite their inability to attract visitors independently. Humbert's Route in Northern Ireland, for instance, follows the route of the troops commanded by the French general Humbert, who came to support the 1798 Irish revolt against the English, and directs the visitor to less well-known settlements such as Drumkeeran or Tubbercurry (Humbert's Route, 2004). This creates the option to involve settlements (attractions) that have not featured on tourist maps, which in turn may create further development opportunities for the people living there.

Setting up a themed route can improve the "transparency" of an area, which is especially important for those who are unfamiliar with the territory; the structure the route provides makes a formerly unknown area easy to grasp, visitors can familiarize themselves with thematically (and/or geographically) grouped attractions to the depth and degree of detail that satisfies their individual interests. (For example, "When Was the Last Time You Did Something for the First Time?" route in Guatemala directs visitors' attention to hidden parts of the country where they can still experience living traditions.) As the duration of stay visitors can afford in a particular area is often limited, they normally welcome recommended itineraries.

Diverting (car) traffic from main routes has always been an objective of settlements of the hinterland. A reasonably successful tool to achieve this is the designation of so-called "scenic routes." These routes run through aesthetically picturesque regions, and with the supply of photo-or view-points visitors can explore hidden treasures (several secondary or tertiary routes are relabeled as scenic routes in the United States, but one can find examples in the Black Forest, Germany, too).

Furthermore, using the routes as a tool to manage visitors offers to avoid crowded centers, to become familiar with alternative routes, first of all, because the development of routes works to reduce perceived distance. This is because attractions along a route are identified on tourist maps, which can close the space between locations that used to appear "remote" (Martin Luther's County trail in Saxony-Anhalt, Germany, introduces all those places that played an important role in Luther's life).

"Repackaging" existing attractions, arranging them into complex products, and presenting them in an unusual way can help reach new target groups. The "new look" may relate to the original theme of an attraction, but it may also present a new approach to create additional appeal. The Ulysses Route organized by Italy, Malta, Greece, and Tunisia, for instance, can put the historical and cultural attractions that are related to the story or merely to the time of Ulysses into new perspective and may increase the popularity of prehistoric or ancient Roman values, which are also planned to be incorporated in the route (Ulysses Route, 2004).

Developing new attractions may be necessary when a new route is designed, for instance to present the theme more effectively (such as visitor centers, which serve this express purpose) or to bridge geographic gaps (this is the case in many national parks). Whenever attractions that can be connected through a theme are located too far from one another, ancillary product components may need to be created to ensure that visitors are persuaded to follow the whole route.

Regional (countrywide) or international themed routes may improve cooperation between the participants, as a project of this nature is doomed to fail without common effort. The theme and the development and operation of the route connect both remote and nearby settlements, strengthening the appeal of individual sites integrated into the route, and their collective appeal may grow exponentially (the Glass Route between Neustadt and Passau, Germany, connects plants, museums, galleries, workshops, and festivals related to making glass and crystal along a stretch of 250 kilometers).

Designing a route frequently helps penetrate a new market: The information delivered to local inhabitants can offer access, for instance, to the market of visiting friends and relatives (VFR), which is considered to be hard to reach otherwise (e.g., about the Clerkenwell Historic Trail, Islington, London—see Chapter 6). Tourists with a special interest may take notice of a particular area because of the central theme of a route, and their visits may generate extra income for the providers of tourist services. Initiated by UNESCO (2004b), the Slave Route, which intends first of all to raise global awareness of transatlantic slave-trade, already attracts to Senegal and Ghana many African-American tourists who wish to become intimately familiar with the history of their forefathers.

Besides provoking curiosity, protecting a resource, which forms the central theme of a route, may also be an objective. Preservation through utilization is frequently the only alternative for sustaining tangible heritage, and creating a cultural route is one of the possible ways of utilizing it with beneficial effect. Additionally, when designing a route one needs to bear in mind the vulnerability of the particular resource, and the route that visitors may use should be designed to prevent the increased traffic of tourists from harming the attraction in any way (this concern was a fundamental question when a route along Hadrian's Wall in England was created).

In terms of marketing and management, themed routes tend to be cost-efficient assets, as they require relatively little effort in managing visitors, who guide themselves, which presents opportunities for cutting costs. Self-guidance eliminates the need for employing dedicated staff, as the people working for the attractions incorporated in a route normally attend to the management responsibilities that may arise. Regardless of the more limited direct relationship with visitors, someone must definitely take on the responsibility for coordinating the operation of the components of the route (e.g., the publications about the route, the route signs, the complete marketing of the route) and for managing collaboration. The scarcity of personnel to deliver services (e.g., provision of information or hospitality) may be mentioned as a disadvantage.

CREATING AND OPERATING CULTURAL ROUTES

When selecting the theme of a cultural route, one needs to take several aspects into account to ensure that the project turns into a tourist success and strengthens the cultural identity of the affected communities at the same time. First, the theme should be easy to identify, relatively widely recognized and self-evident, but it should not narrow down too much the scope of attractions that may be incorporated in the route, because that may also limit its appeal. (A "castle route" may attract more visitors than a "route of 15th Century Renaissance castles.")

The themes of cultural routes may vary widely, but the themes are most frequently related to one of the cultural areas listed here:

1. A time period (e.g., Northern Bronze Age Route)
2. A historic event (e.g., UNESCO's aforementioned Slave Route)
3. Religious heritage (e.g., the Route of the Jewish Community in Europe, 2004)
4. Industrial heritage (e.g., German Route of Industrial Heritage, 2004)
5. Social heritage/value (e.g., Freedom Trail, Boston, 2004)

6. Cultural heritage/value (e.g., the Council of Europe Routes of Humanism)
7. A school of art and/or a style of architecture (e.g., the Council of Europe Baroque Route, 2004)
8. Common geographic property/location/identity (e.g., German Alps Route)
9. Local traditions (e.g., the Route of Rural Habitat by the Council of Europe)
10. A product/manufacturing (e.g., the Cheese Route Bregenzerwald)
11. A well-known historic personality or artist (e.g., Goethe Route)

A cultural route will only become a tourist product if visitors are not only familiar with its component attractions, but are also fully aware that the route exists and perceive the experience they get to be superior with it than without it. An important part of this process of raising awareness involves designing the logo that represents the theme of the route and using it permanently, in any marketing communication actions, in physical displays along the route, and in any route-related merchandising.

As a cultural product is really an intangible product made up of tangible components, namely attractions and services, the provision of information, which helps identify and promotes the recognition of the route, should be kept high on the agenda. The most important elements of this activity include the following:

1. Proper application of route signs, needed as a minimum at the two terminal points of the route and at the entrances to all the attractions and service facilities associated with it. Posting route signs is also useful at puzzling junctions. If route signs are posted frequently, they may capture the attention of people who are not trying to find the route right then, which may generate future demand. When posting the signs, one must by all means consider that visitors traveling along the route have less than average knowledge of the territory, so in contrast with local inhabitants (and with the designers of the sign, who are normally quite knowledgeable about the area) they might need more—clearly visible and unambiguous—signs. If passage along the route is possible using different means of transport, the factors associated with the features of

these means (speed, distance from route signs, time required to read a sign) should also be considered.

2. Information boards, which in addition to giving directions to the visitor also offer more detailed information about the values and attractions of the route and the available tourist and cultural services. It is practical to post boards of this nature at the terminal points of a cultural route and at the attractions/settlements along the route. Individual attractions may also have, however, independent boards (presenting information exclusively about the attraction or about the route as a whole).

3. Printed information, such as detailed maps presenting the route along with recommended traveling times, or with itineraries for more complex routes (themed route networks); brochures and catalogs describing the theme, history, values, attractions, services, and events of the route coupled with practical advice, as well as merchandising catalogs or professional publications aimed at tour operators and intermediaries. This information should be made accessible to all participants of a route, at the tourist information offices in settlements along a route—and, depending on the level of the route, also at regional or national information offices—and should also be available over the Internet. (Although video films and CD-ROMs cannot be regarded to constitute printed matter, they can also be grouped in this category in view of their content.)

4. Online information complementing the above (theme, values, attractions, services, events, seasonal features, maps, contact data), with programs to search attraction and service details, with daily updates of weather and traffic information, with online booking of route-related attractions and services, and with an online purchase option for products relevant to the theme of a route (such as cases of wine for a wine trail), or even with a communication forum for future visitors intending to travel along the route or its past visitors and those interested in its theme (e.g., Santiago de Compostela, 2005). Creative interpretation of the route theme provides endless opportunities to create quite unusual experiences, such as the "talking bicycles" in Bordeaux or portable cassettes for car audio devices. These tools provide the visitor with a sound-guided visit as well as a different way of exploring sites and attractions.

In addition to the attractions that stay open year-round, a cultural route marketed as a tourist product can also include cultural events such as festivals, theater performances, music programs, fairs, or games that recall the past. Like attractions, properly selected and organized events will also strengthen the common cultural image of a route and attract a significant number of visitors. It is practical to include both annually recurring events and annual innovations, which should be announced even for individual tourists at least during the autumn of the preceding year. This is an efficient way to appeal to both repeat visitors and newcomers. The distribution of events in time and space will naturally influence the distribution of demand; hence, the development of a calendar of events plays a key role in regulating the demand for a cultural route.

Financial and organizational aspects play a major role in creating and operating a cultural route. During the inception stage, most routes are set up with public funds, which are also regularly used to provide the operating resources, as the contribution of the private sector is insignificant in the majority of cases (Lumsdon, 1998). The costs of developing a cultural route are normally covered by municipal or regional (occasionally national or international) tourist organizations, frequently coupled with earmarked funds offered in support (e.g., in connection with regional cooperation or rural development). Mobilizing private funds is normally mutually beneficial, and the opportunity to do so will only exist if businesses can become directly aware of the benefits of their contribution (and, for instance, if they ascertain that it is a cultural route that attracts most of their guests to the region or that their services are utilized as part of a recommended itinerary).

Experience shows that it is easier to obtain the funds needed to develop a route than to raise the funds required for operating it on a continuous basis (Dartington Amenity Trust, 1978; Dyke et al., 1986). Although a themed route often proves to be a relatively cost-efficient tool, operating the route at the desirable level of quality (e.g., updating publications, maintaining the system of information boards, or coordinating the cooperation of members) requires a continuous flow of funds. The main problem operators face is that they cannot usually collect entrance fees from visitors, which leaves them without any relatively stable source of income.

In addition to funding, organizational and personnel conditions are considered to constitute another critical element in maintaining a themed route. The creation of a route is often initiated by a few people—sometimes even by a single person, who play(s) a key role in designing and operating the route. Individual enthusiasm can naturally work wonders, but the sustainability of a themed route in the long run is normally ensured only in case a compact coordinating body is capable of both marketing the route and the representating the interests of each participant. Also, several countries rely on volunteers to operate routes and their individual attractions and to organize the theme-related events. These volunteers are not driven by the desire to make a profit; rather they are motivated to participate (as tour guides, organizers, or drafters of requests for applications) because of their devotion to the cause or through personal vocation.

CASE STUDY:
CULTURAL AVENUE OF BUDAPEST

Budapest is the most important and most well known international tourist destination in Hungary. Although the Hungarian capital has recently become increasingly popular, it arguably does not introduce its rich cultural and historic assets to visitors in an innovative manner. As previous surveys for the ATLAS Cultural Tourism Research Project have indicated, Budapest still encounters fierce competition from cities such as Prague and Vienna, both of which have been longer established in international tourism markets (Puczkó and Rátz, 2001). In meeting this global competitive threat, Budapest has to develop its local cultural resources more effectively. The current approach lacks clearly identifiable themes, and the physical delivery of these themes is not appealing enough for many visitors. After series of discussions with the representatives of cultural sites, the Cultural Avenue of Budapest project was initiated.

The core theme of the avenue was very well summarized in the project documentation:

> The Cultural Avenue lies on the most significant axis of Budapest between the Buda Castle (which is listed as a World Heritage site [UNESCO, 2004c]) and the City Park. Along this

virtual axis you can find Budapest's most famous cultural institutions, cafés, theatres, confectioneries, and entertaining institutions of the Park Republic (the City Park). Several museums, such as the Museum of Fine Arts, which ranks amongst one of the largest European international museums, and the Hungarian National Gallery represent the very best pieces of Hungarian fine art. The impressive Post Museum and the Museum of Transport attract mainly children and students. There are more than twenty theatres showing a wide range of repertoires, there are the Opera House, the Adventure Park, and the Zoo, all of which guarantee entertainment possibilities for tourists of all kinds. Take a special walk in Budapest, immerse yourselves in the outstandingly rich culture and have a pleasant walk along Europe's most varied Cultural Avenue! Visit the museums offering temporary and permanent exhibitions, have a ride in the Funicular Railway or in the Millennium Underground, walk across the Chain Bridge, watch a play or listen to a concert, taste "Dobos" cake in one of the historical confectioneries, and rest, have fun, enjoy yourselves in the City Park. The Cultural Avenue offers enjoyable cultural and free time activities for people of all age groups. Explore Budapest with the help of this brochure in a little different way and perhaps you will experience something unique, some lasting experience.

Since the basic idea was to create something that is innovative and fashionable, we applied the following guidelines when the project was first communicated to members of the route. The advantages of this route were summarized as follows:

- It supports the image of Budapest and its attractions/sight and introduces less well known sights to visitors.
- It can increase average length of stay of tourists in the country and the city.
- It can decrease seasonality of visitation.
- It can attract new visitor segments.
- It is relatively inexpensive to develop and to run.

The trail, linking the cultural and heritage sites of Budapest, is a city trail. This avenue roughly follows the main axis of the city (i.e., it creates a natural flow for visitors). Although in the title we call this themed route a Cultural Avenue, during the preparation a new approach to the selection of sight was applied. Compared to other routes of its kind, the Cultural Avenue links quite different attractions, all of which have some cultural aspects. Stops along the way introduce the history and heritage of Budapest, and in some cases that of Hungary. This composition of attractions does not follow any standard that might be seen in the case of other city cultural routes. We have applied a wide understanding of culture and heritage, from so-called high culture (e.g., Hungarian State Opera House); to popular or alternative culture (e.g., the Dig Cultural Centre). This approach has included 55 stops along the route, involving the following:

- Museums
- Historic buildings and monuments
- Religious sites
- Means of transport
- Theaters
- Historic cafés and restaurants
- The zoo and the fairgrounds
- The largest spa *(therme)* in Europe

It was quite difficult to find a good name for the project. To date, this virtual product exists in four languages. We wanted to have a name that is easily understandable to foreigners and at the same time fits the content. This is why it has become "avenue" in English and French and not "route." In German, however, the name is different: *Allee der Kultur.* It proved to be even more difficult to select the name for the Web site (www.sugarut.com). Since there were so many options available, the most straightforward was chosen, i.e., the equivalent for avenue in Hungarian, *sugarút.*

Experiences

Although they are relatively easy to establish, international experience proves that without proper preparation, planning, and management trails also tend to disappear quite rapidly. It is presumed that a suitable organization needs to be in charge of the project from the initiation through the development to management. In this case, the organization is a private company. It is planned, however, that the project should be taken over by one of the city's organizations responsible for tourism promotion.

The project was launched in 2002 and took almost eighteen months and much work to bring it into being. The following steps can be identified during the preparation and implementation:

> *Initialization*—Where the idea stems from. The initial idea had been first introduced to decision-makers in the new marketing plan of the Museum of Fine Arts. Then, with the help and financial support of the Cultural Tourism Department of the Ministry of National Cultural Heritage, the actual planning could be started.
>
> *Trademark protection of name*—The product's name, since it is expected to be used during the next steps of product development, was given trademark protection from the beginning.
>
> *Concept fine tuning*—Since the product aimed to appeal to visitors looking for any kind of culture (e.g., traditional partying area of the town, historical spas, etc.), members and potential members were contacted to collect their ideas and expectations.
>
> *Visual design*—Including map preparation, text writing, layout, and Web page design. Initially three quite different variations of layout were designed. After a series of discussions a more elegant than "chic" design was selected, since it was anticipated that its dark-red color scheme and constructivist layout would best fit the content and the intended market positioning.
>
> *Market research*—Both route members and visitors were interviewed concerning their opinions on the route. They could express their comments about the project concept as well as its implementation. A workshop was organized, during which representatives of the fifty-five members could share their experiences and further recommendations. Moreover, foreign tourists were interviewed along the route and their opinions about the project idea, the layout of the brochure, the name, and the color scheme were collected.

Our experiences to date indicate that the route faces some quite interesting challenges for the future. Based on the market research, a new version of the brochure is under preparation. As part of the enhancement of communication, it is planned to install themed plaques at the premises of every member. The financial costs of the second print run of the brochure are partially covered by the National Tourism Office and the Budapest Tourism Office. Since the original principle was that members should not pay for joining the route, further support, preferably from private companies, needs to be collected. In order to provide more practical information, accommodation and catering facilities can also be introduced in future editions of the brochure, but only for a charge. Reflections received to the e-mail account of the Web site and by experiences of colleagues working at the Tourinform points in Budapest and at the representatives of the National Tourism Office abroad have proved that visitors appreciate the effort and they perceive it as an added value to their planned trip to Budapest. We hope that the Cultural Avenue of Budapest will be successful and can become a good example for themed route development in Hungary.

REFERENCES

Alderson, W.T. and Low, S.P. (1996) *Interpretation of Historic Sites* (2nd ed). Walnut Creek, CA: Altamira Press.

Amber Route (2004) amberroad.datenpark.com

Baroque Route (2004) culture.coe.fr/routes/eng/eitin3.4.htm

Campbell, I. (1974) A Practical guide to the Law of Footpaths and Bridgeways, Commons, Henley-on-Thames: Open Spaces & Footpaths Preservation Society.

Cheese Route (2004) www.kaesestrasse.at

Ciste (2004) www.ciste.org

Clerkenwell Historic Trail (2004) www.discover-islington.co.uk

Coleman, A. (1994) The Development of the Hadrian's Wall National Trail. In Harrison, R. (ed) *Manual of Heritage Management.* Oxford: Butterworth-Heinemann and The Association of Independent Museums, pp. 70-71.

The Confraternity of St James (2004) www.csj.org.uk/present.htm

Dartington Amenity Trust (1978) *Self Guided Trails*, CCP 110; Cheltenham: Countryside Commission.

Dyke, J. et al (1986) *Self Guided Trails—A National Survey.* The Centre for Environmental Interpretation, Manchester: Manchester Polytechnic.

European Cultural Routes (2004) culture.coe.fr/routes/

European Route of Paper (2004) www.mmp-capellades.net/watermarkroute/english/pag/culturalroute.htm

European Tourist and Cultural Routes (2004) www.itini.com

Finnish Tourist Board (2004) www.finland-tourism.com

Freedom Trail (2004) www.thefreedomtrail.org

German Alps Route (2004) www.germany-tourism.de/e/12571.html

Germany Tourism (2004) www.germany-tourism.de/e/5334.html

Goethe Route (2004) www.germany-tourism.de/e/5445.html

Gustke, L.D. and Hodgson, R.W. (1980) Rate of Travel Along an Interpretive Trail: The Effect of an Environmental Discontinuity. *Environment and Behaviour* 12(1): 53-63.

Humbert's Route (2004) www.itini.com/route.asp?id=14

ICOMOS (2003) HYPERLINK "http://www.icomos-ciic.org/CIIC/NOTICAS" www.icomos-ciic.org/CIIC/NOTICAS reunionexpertos.htm

Leehey, P.M. (1994) Myths and Realities along Boston's Freedom Trail. *History Today* 44(9):4-8.

Lew, A.A. (1991) Scenic Roads and Rural Development in the US. *Tourism Recreation Research* 16(2):23-30.

Lumsdon, L. (1998) The Mortimer Trail: Marketing of Walking Routes. *Insights* C28-39.

Német kulturális utak (2004) www.germany-tourism.de

Northern Bronze Age Route (2004) www.nsb.norrkoping.se/bronze/eu.htm

On Ulysses's Trail—A Cultural Route www.gogreece.com/learn/ulysses.htm

Puczkó, L. and Rátz, T. (2000): *Az attrakciótól az élményig. A látogatómenedzsment módszerei.* Budapest: Geomédia.

Route of Industrial Heritage (2004) www.route-industriekultur.de

Route of Jewish Heritage in Europe (2004) www.jewisheritage.org/route/index.php/en/

Route of Rural Habitat (2004) culture.coe.fr/routes/eng/eitin3.2.htm

Sarkadi, E., Szabó, G. and Urbán, A. (2000) A borturizmus szervezők kézikönyve I. Pécs: Baranya Megyei Falusi Turizmus Szövetség.

Smith, C. (1980) *New to Britain—A Study of Some New Developments in Tourist Attractions.* London: British Tourist Authority.

Tremblay, D. (2002) The Loire Valley: An Authentic Cultural Landscape. *World Heritage Review* 26:54-65.

Ulysses Route (2004) www.gogreece.com/learn/ulysses.htm (Accessed 17 August 2004).

UNESCO (2004a) Silk Roads. www.unesco.org/culture/silkroads/

UNESCO (2004b) Slave Route. www.unesco.org/culture/dialogue/slave/html_eng/origin.shtml

UNESCO (2004c) World Heritage. www.unesco.org/whc/

Veverka, J.A. (1994) *Interpretive Master Planning.* Helena, Montana, USA: Falcon Press Publishing Co.

Chapter 8

Comparative Analysis of International Tourists in Inland Cultural Destinations: The Case of Castilla y León, Spain

Ana González Fernández
Miguel Cervantes Blanco
Mauro R. Miranda Barreto
Norberto Muñiz
Carmen Rodríguez Santos

INTRODUCTION

The inland regions of a country based on sun, sea, and sand tourism must explore distinctive appeals to tourists, promoting products that strengthen their identity relative to more conventional destinations in the global market. In this sense, cultural characteristics have a greater importance for inland destinations, as culture is often the main motivation for visitors.

Spain is one of the main global destinations, especially for beach tourism; it hosts 75.5 million foreign visitors annually, representing 11 percent of all international travelers. This figure places it in the top three international destinations, alongside the United States and France. Cultural motivations have become one of the most important and dynamic tourism drivers, permitting diversification of the tourism offer, counteracting seasonality, and with great potential for promoting inland destinations. The importance of cultural tourism is evident from

Cultural Tourism: Global and Local Perspectives
© 2007 by The Haworth Press, Inc. All rights reserved.
doi:10.1300/5749_08

the statistical data, which indicate that in the 1990s, 66 percent of the foreign travelers visiting Spain were involved in some form of cultural activity (Cases Méndez and Marchena Gómez, 1999).

CULTURAL ATTRACTIONS IN TOURISM

Given the important role of cultural tourism in international travel, it is necessary to study in depth the possible differences and similarities in behavior according to the nationalities of the travelers who choose cultural destinations, the typology of cultural attractions, and tourist behavior variables (Plog, 1990; Pizam, 1999; Crotts and Erdmann, 2000).

In cultural tourism it is possible to find differences and similarities in demand arising from the membership of cultural groups linked to geographical origins (country, state, or the like). One can also consider the appropriateness of segmenting the tourist market using individual motivations as differentiating variables, leading to alternative forms of cultural tourism. At a deeper level, a further process of segmentation should be undertaken within this format, which may be able to distinguish differentiated products and markets, so targeting more specialized provision. With this in mind, a typology of cultural attractions may be developed as follows (Richards, 2001):

> *Monuments.* The traditional basis for cultural tourism, they are on many occasions key symbols of the image cities use to promote themselves. Cathedrals, mosques, public places, and so forth are in themselves tourist attractions within the cities in which they are located. These elements of a city may also become global icons.
>
> *Museums and Art Galleries.* The most important attraction for cultural tourism, visited by over 50 percent of all cultural tourists, according to the latest ATLAS research.
>
> *Major Cultural Exhibitions.* This is a product normally arising from a combination of the previous two and has burgeoned in Spain, for example in the touring exhibitions taking place in a different locality each year.
>
> *Cultural Landscapes and Nature.* Areas marked out by the appeal of their natural features.

World Heritage Sites. This is a title awarded by UNESCO since 1972, referring at first only to single monuments, later also to urban areas and cities, and nowadays in addition to integrated groupings with an environmental, historic-religious, or archaeological content.

Cultural Routes. As shown in the previous chapter, these are genuine features that enrich the system of cultural tourism. In Spain the Pilgrim Way of St. James stands out, being considered the prime European cultural itinerary, with World Heritage status (1993). However, there is also the Silver Route, whose historical origin lies in the roadways that linked the South-West of the Iberian Peninsula to the North-West for trade in metals.

Language Study. Geographic areas attractive for studying a language in its cultural context.

Cultural Parks. Their aim is the preservation of the rural archaeological heritage. Their roots lie in the landscape where they are located, due both to its archaeological significance and to its natural appearance. They also include a display and study component, in the shape of information centers, guide services, and informative signs. In addition, they are considered Sites of Cultural Interest, having scientific facets, careful conservation, an infrastructure that may be visited, and hence social benefits.

Cultural Legacy. The most striking example of this in Spain is the *Andalusí legacy,* the result of the encounter and coexistence of two cultures, Christian and Muslim, for many centuries in the region of Andalusia. It displays the specific values of each, hence protecting, preserving, and spreading a cultural heritage.

Popular Celebrations. The outcome of religious and civil traditions, these have won such popularity that they have become tourist products. Many could be mentioned in Spain, but the most popular are Easter, the *Feria de Abril,* and Carnival.

Festivals. These are currently thriving, and are characterized by diversity and specialization, there are music, cinema, and theater festivals, among others (see also Chapters 14 and 15).

Ethnographic and Gastronomic Heritage. "Ecomuseums" (see Chapter 10) are intended to preserve the folk heritage of the various regions of Spain: landscapes, houses and other typical buildings, farm equipment, tools, and the like, together with the recuperation of skills and crafts that are in danger of disappearing, such as harvesting crops and features of animal husbandry. It also deals with local crafts, regional costumes, economic activities, and traditional cookery, and thus includes gastronomy. It can be a major attraction differentiating regions within the country. Representative examples would be folk gatherings, with their ethnographic interest, or the way that typical local foodstuffs are on offer almost every where in the country.

Industrial Heritage. This has its source in the locations where the Industrial Revolution took place, areas either providing raw materials or having a concentration of industries. Nowadays, these are becoming important tourist attractions as the result of efforts to restore the traces of early industrial activities as the origin of modern society.

Cities. These are centers for the development of cultural tourism, as they include elements that allow a broadening of the range of cultural and tourist attractions on offer without any need for major intervention (see Chapter 6).

As Table 8.1 shows, in the case of Castilla y León, these individual attractions can be classified into four main groups: artistic and historical sites, human activities of cultural interest, economic activities of cultural interest, and landscapes and nature. This underlines the wide variety of cultural attractions available even at the regional level.

Given the wide variations in the supply of cultural attractions in Spain and other destinations, and the differences in cultural tourist motivation and behavior, it is important to analyze the relationship between supply and demand in order to understand the attractiveness of particular destinations for tourists. This research analyzes the situation in a specific region of inland Spain, providing insights into what drives cultural tourism demand and the utilization of cultural products by tourists.

TABLE 8.1. Cultural tourism resources in Castilla y León.

Dimension	Categories
Artistic, historical, and heritage sites	Monuments: City landmarks, cathedrals, romanic churches, public spaces Museums: Cultural and historic exhibitions and art galleries Cultural exhibitions: Peripetetic exhibitions *Las Edades de Hombre* in different locality each year World heritage sites: Salamanca, Avila, Segovia
Human activity of cultural interest	Popular and religious celebrations: Easter–Semana Santa, Valladolid, Zamora, León Music, cinema, theater, dance: Seminci cinema festival, Valladolid Crafts and popular architecture: Typical villages–La Alberca–farms, rural houses Traditional gastronomy: Typical foods and drink, Ribera de Duero Cultural routes: The Pilgrim Way of St. James *(Camino de Santiago),* the Silver Route *(Ruta de la Plata),* The Spanish/Castilian Language Route *(Ruta de la Lengua Castellana)*
Economic activities of cultural interest	Industrial and mining heritage: Traces of early industrial activities and raw materials *(factory La Granja)* Farming and agricultural heritage: Recuperation of skills and crafts in danger of disappearing Trade exhibitions
Landscapes and nature	Natural parks: National Park *Picos de Europa* Cultural parks: Archaeological heritage and cultural landscapes (*Las Médulas* Roman mining site, Atapuerca archaeological site)

CULTURAL TOURISM IN CASTILLA Y LEÓN, SPAIN

Regional Context

Spain is the second largest international tourist destination, in spite of the development of emergent markets (WTO, 2004). Among the main countries generating tourists to Spain, the United Kingdom occupies first place (28.1 percent of international tourists), followed by Germany (20 percent), France (15.5 percent), and then Holland, Italy, Belgium, and Portugal. These market shares have remained fairly constant in recent years (IET, 2003). In regard to the Spanish tourist destinations preferred by foreign tourists, there is a high degree of concentration in zones that traditionally offer sun and beach products, in which Spain maintains its leading position. However, given the significant changes in consumer behavior in recent years, it seems that the success in the sector will be determined by the capacity, both of the public administrations and of the business environment, for developing a diversified and sustainable tourism model. This model will be based mainly on three parameters: offering new experiences, higher levels of service quality, and differentiated offers.

The main objectives of these actions will be, on the one hand, to reduce the risks of the traditional sun and beach product, whose maturity places it in a state of intense global competition, and on the other hand, to incentivize integrated models of tourist development that increase the degree of tourist loyalty. In this sense, developing "new" tourism destinations in the interior is a high priority. This study is therefore focused on the inland region of Castilla y León (Castile and Leon, in the north of Spain), which has an area of 94,224 square kilometers and 2,500,000 residents. The region has a high tourism potential, offering a diversified tourism product capable of serving different target groups, among which cultural tourism provides one of the most interesting options. This region receives five million tourists per year, one million of them international tourists, and it is visited mainly for cultural reasons. It has heritage cities (Avila, Salamanca, Segovia), cathedrals, monuments, castles, monasteries, historic routes (the Pilgrim's Way of St. James to Compostela, the Silver Route), archaeological sites (Atapuerca, Las Médulas), religious festivals (especially in Holy Week), gastronomy, folklore, and customs (see Figure 8.1 and Table 8.1).

Objectives

The important role of culture in tourism requires study of the characteristics of international travelers who visit destinations in the interior, attracted by cultural features. The main aim of this study is to investigate the relationship between types of tourists of different nationalities and cultural backgrounds and their motives and behavior as tourists in inland destinations. In order to reach this objective, various data sources have been utilized, including secondary data from the

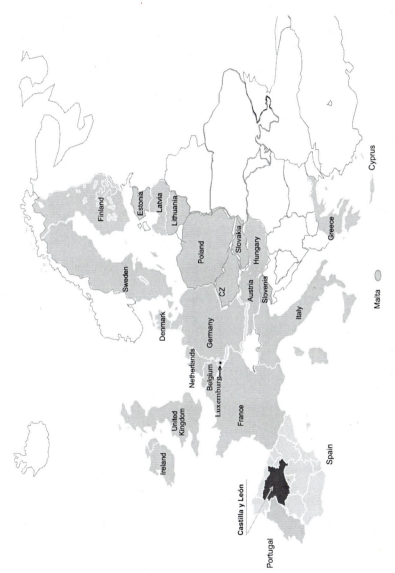

FIGURE 8.1. Castilla y León in Europe.

155

Spanish Institute for Tourism Studies and the National Statistical Institute and primary data collected by the General Tourism Bureau of the Regional Government (Junta de Castilla y León). By comparing these primary and secondary sources we can assess whether the sample of tourists interviewed is representative of visitors to the region as a whole.

DATA ANALYSIS AND DISCUSSION

The General Tourism Bureau of the Junta de Castilla y León has been regularly gathering data on tourists during the months of July, August, and September, through personally administered interviews. In the period 1998 to 2001, 21,126 surveys were conducted with visitors to this region, 2,460 of whom were foreign tourists. In the current study, the information obtained from 1,870 international travelers with leisure motivations has been analyzed.

The aspects included in the survey were as follows:

- Introductory variables, including the province/country of origin.
- Variables related to tourist behavior: length of the journey in the region, accommodation, transport, journey organization, group composition, frequency, expenditure, etc.
- Motivations for the journey.
- Evaluation of aspects of the tourist offer.
- Sociodemographic variables: age, gender, educational level, income level.

The sample included 626 international travelers in 1998, 411 in 1999, 364 in 2000 and 469 in 2001. The Spanish tourists that visited the region of Castilla y León were excluded from this study, because the large number of domestic tourists would not balance the sample of foreign travelers. The random sample of 1,870 foreign visitors gave a sample error of ± 2.2 percent at a 95 percent level of confidence.

The respondent profile indicated that 55.9 percent of visitors were men, and 44.1 percent were women. Visitors were drawn from a wide range of age groups, with 15.8 percent being under twenty-five and 26.2 percent between twenty-six and thirty-five years old. However, the majority were between the ages of thirty-six and fifty-five years old, and 10.8 percent were over fifty-five. Over 70 percent of respondents are employees, with students (12 percent) making up the other significant occupational group. It is notable that the older, retired visitors make up a very small proportion of total visitors (5 percent). The educational level of the sample is high, as 71 percent of the sample had a university degree and 21.5 percent had enjoyed further education.

Finally, while recognizing that the information about the income level of the interviewees has to be treated with caution due to high levels of refusal (28 percent gave no income data) it is clear that respondents have relatively high incomes, as almost half the sample had incomes above €30,000 (Table 8.2).

VISITOR MOTIVATIONS

As shown in Table 8.3, the main reasons for visiting Castilla y León as a tourist destination are related to artistic or historic resources, followed by landscape (understanding the geographical and natural environment in which the region is located). Other motivations tend to be less important, although the interest in pilgrimages in particular seems to be increasing.

Table 8.4 indicates the origin of the international tourists in the period of study. France is the main origin country, accounting for 30.9 percent of the total of international tourists in the year 2001. This is followed by other European markets, such as Germany, Italy, United Kingdom, and Portugal. The most distant regions, such as America or the rest of the world, account for about a quarter of the tourists.

TABLE 8.2. Annual income groups.

Income	%
Less than €12,000	14.5
€12,000-30,000	39.7
More than €54,000	9.1
€30,000-54,000	36.7

TABLE 8.3. Main motivations for visiting Castilla y León (% of respondents; multiple responses).

Motivations	1998	1999	2000	2001
Monuments	67.0	58.0	51.9	55.2
Art/history	55.7	49.5	47.0	49.7
Landscape and nature	37.0	33.7	29.4	25.2
Gastronomy	21.1	18.4	13.5	19.8
Language learning	16.7	6.6	7.1	17.3
Tranquility	10.8	10.9	5.5	15.1
Pilgrimage to Santiago	8.8	3.4	6.0	14.7
Festivals or festivities	7.5	8.3	7.1	4.5
Religious motives	7.8	9.0	6.3	4.5

TABLE 8.4. Countries and regions of origin (% visitors).

Visitor origin	1998	1999	2000	2001
France	23.7	19.5	18.9	30.9
Germany	9.7	9.0	10.2	8.3
Italy	6.1	8.8	10.4	9.2
United Kingdom	7.1	9.0	8.8	7.4
Portugal	3.0	7.2	7.5	6.3
Rest of Europe	16.0	17.6	17.7	16.4
America	26.0	23.5	22.0	17.4
Rest of the world	6.2	5.6	4.5	4.2

With the purpose of analyzing the cultural motivations over the period 1998-2001 and comparing them in terms of tourists from different nationalities, the tourists' cultural motivations, provenance, and year of visit were analyzed jointly, through the use of factor analysis of simple correspondences, which allows the simultaneous representation of individuals and variables in the same space. The statistical data analysis was done with the software SPAD, which, in contrast to other software, such as SPSS, provides a clearer graphic representation and is more flexible in analysis.

From the graphic representation of the results (see Figures 8.2-8.4), the following observations can be made:

1. In Figure 8.2 under dimension 1, the religious and spiritual motivations represent an attraction with regard to the rest of motivations, emphasizing the singularity of the motivation "Pilgrim of the Way of St. James." Since it is distinguished as well from the generic religious motivations (Holy Week, Religious Festivities), appearing in a different quadrant, with regard to dimension 2.

2. In relation to the motivations that appear on the left-hand side of dimension 1, we can see that art and monument motivations are clustered apart from the rest, which means that together they represent an element of tourist attractiveness.

3. In the top left quadrant, festivals and festivity motivations appear as a distinct attraction.

4. In that same quadrant, there is a relationship between peacefulness and language learning, and an association between gastronomy and nature.

5. In Figure 8.3, the "year of visit" is displayed as an illustrative variable, and this shows little difference between the years, since all cluster very close to the origin of the axes.

6. Figure 8.4 also shows that there are no significant differences by country of origin.

The overall picture given by the analysis is that there are significant differences between visitor groups in terms of their cultural motivations for visiting Castilla y León, which have remained stable over the years studied, but there are no differences relating to the origin of the visitors.

TOURIST BEHAVIOR

In regard to the travel habits of the foreign tourists, it is best to look at the most recent data from 2001, since the behavioral patterns are similar to the ones observed in previous years. The majority of the

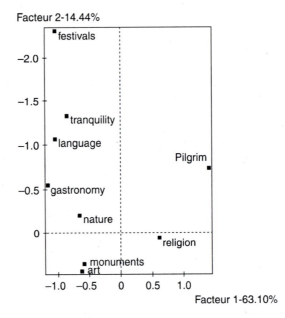

FIGURE 8.2. Relationship between cultural motivations.

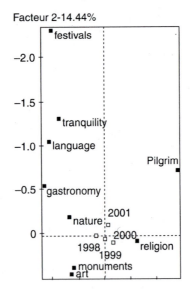

FIGURE 8.3. Cultural motivations by year.

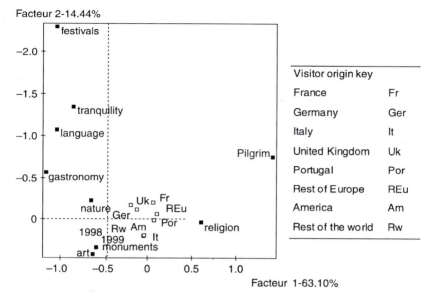

FIGURE 8.4. Cultural motivations by country of origin.

foreign travelers are visiting the region for the first time (70.8 percent), while only 6.5 percent visit several times a year (see Table 8.5).

In relation to the length of the journey in Castilla y León, 58.5 percent are short stays of three nights or less, of which about 23 percent are day-trippers, and the remaining 35.6 percent come to enjoy weekends and long weekends. Almost a quarter of visitors come for four to seven nights, 14 percent between one and two weeks, and very few stay longer than two weeks (see Table 8.6).

It is remarkable, given the characteristics of the region, that 72 percent of the travelers make a tourist trip through various zones of the province. The automobile is the principal means of transport, in most cases their own (40.3 percent) and sometimes a rental car (8.7 percent). The bus is also very well used by tourists (22.1 percent), followed by the train (8.8 percent) (see Table 8.7).

With regard to accommodation, the vast majority choose a regulated form, such as a hotel (70 percent). However, a significant percentage of tourists choose to spend the night in unregulated lodgings. In relation to the regulated establishments, the hotels constitute the form most demanded, as about 40 percent stayed at hotels and 16 percent at hostels or boarding houses (see Table 8.8).

TABLE 8.5. Frequency of visit.

Frequency of visit	%
First visit	70.8
Every now and again	22.7
A few times a year	6.5

TABLE 8.6. Length of trip in Castilla y León.

Nights	%
0	22.9
1-3	35.6
4-7	22.9
8-15	14.2
16-23	2.1
123	2.4

TABLE 8.7. Means of transport.

Transport	%
Own car	40.3
Bus	22.1
Train	8.8
Rental car	8.7
Plane	3.8
Caravan	3.3
Motorcycle	1.3
Others	11.8

Of the foreign tourists that visit Castilla y León, 83.9 percent organize the journey on their own and only 13.6 percent use a travel agency as intermediary. Travel agents tend to be used most frequently by those purchasing packages. This underlines the importance of independent travel in the cultural tourism market, with less than 10 percent of ATLAS international survey respondents buying inclusive packages in 2004, a lower proportion than in previous years (Richards, 2001) (see Table 8.9).

In relation to the travel party, around 50 percent visit the region with family and almost 30 percent with friends. In certain cases, they go accompanied with family and friends simultaneously (15.8 percent), and 15.7 percent visit the region alone (see Table 8.10).

TABLE 8.8. Accommodation.

Accommodation	%
Hotel	39.9
Camping	16.1
Hostel	16.0
Private room	4.7
Rural accommodation	2.7
Rented rooms	1.4
Others	14.1

TABLE 8.9. Organization of travel.

Booking Channel	%
Nontrade prebooking	83.9
Trade prebooking (inclusive holidays)	9.0
Transport only	2.7
Transport and accommodation	1.9
Others	2.4

TABLE 8.10. Travel party.

Travel party	%
Alone	15.7
With family	48.7
With friends	29.7
With family and friends	15.8

The correspondence analysis shows few differences with respect to the cultural motivations of the travelers in terms of country of origin (see Table 8.11). From the behavioral perspective, however, differences are observed. The length of trips to Castilla y León vary substantially according to visitor origin and, curiously, the Portuguese and the Americans display the largest percentages of excursionists, although their motives are different. The geographic proximity of the Portuguese allows them to visit certain areas without the necessity to stay overnight. On the other hand, the Americans, despite the long distance, consider this region to be only a transit region, and not their final destination.

With respect to means of transport, proximity is also a major factor, since visitors from Portugal and France are most likely to use their own car. Regarding accommodation, the Americans and the British tend to stay more often in hotels. The Americans, the French, and the British are the tourists that travel more frequently alone.

CONCLUSIONS

The analysis presented here of visitor surveys from Castilla y León indicates that although Spain is characterized as a "sun and sea" destination, inland regions such as this provide cultural resources that represent a significant attraction factor for international tourists. In particular, monuments, art, gastronomy, the Spanish language, and the Pilgrim's Way of Saint James are the main motives to visit Castilla y León.

The application of correspondence analysis to cultural reasons for choosing Castilla y León does not indicate any significant differences between years (1998-2001) or visitor origin countries, which suggests that the cultural motivations have been stable over time and the motivations for different nationalities are similar. Travel behavior also varies little over time, whether in terms of trip frequency, period of stay, means of transport, accommodation, organization, or travel companions. Nevertheless, there are some differences between origin countries for these variables.

These data seem to suggest that models which emphasize cross-cultural differences in tourism consumption may not apply to the Spanish

TABLE 8.11. Differences among countries in relation to the period of stay, accommodation, transport, and traveling companion.

	Portugal	France	Germany	Italy	United Kingdom	American continent	Rest of Europe	Rest of world
Period of stay (nights in region)	30.6	13.6	13.0	22.2	27.1	32.7	16.2	8.9
Accommodation (% using hotels)	42.5	38.5	31.6	42.2	49.0	53.4	29.8	42.9
Transport (% using own vehicles)	77.7	55.2	30.8	45.6	20.7	21.8	42.5	19.8
Traveling companion (% traveling alone)	6.2	18.8	10.7	9.4	17.7	20.6	14.1	15.7

cultural tourism market. This may reflect the fact that cultural tourism is a niche market that attracts consumers who have a much more homogeneous style of consumption across international borders.

In future investigations, therefore, it will be necessary to analyze in depth the motivations and cultural activities of visitors more specifically, looking not only at differences in motivation, but also relating differences in motivation to differential consumption of tangible and intangible culture (cathedrals, great exhibitions, cities, cultural parks, itineraries). This information would also serve to guide marketing activity more closely.

REFERENCES

Cases Méndez, J.I. and Marchena Gómez, M. (1999) Turismo urbano. In Bayón Marine, F. (ed.) *50 años del turismo español: Un análisis histórico y estructural.* Madrid: Centro de Estudios Ramón Areces, S.A., pp. 653-672.

Crotts, J.C. and Erdmann, R. (2000) Does national culture influence consumers' evaluation of travel services? A test of Hofstede's model of cross-cultural differences. *Marketing Services Quality* 10 (6): 410-419.

Douglas, S. and Craig, C. (1997) The changing dynamic of consumer behavior: implications for cross-cultural research. *International Journal of Research in Marketing* 14: 379-395.

Esteban Talaya, A. (1996) El Marketing turístico: la orientación de la actividad al consumidor. In Monfort Mir. V. (ed.) *Introducción a la economía del turismo en España.* Madrid: Mcivitas, pp. 247-273.

Hudson, S. (2001) Cross-cultural tourist behavior. *Journal of Travel and Tourism Marketing* 10 (2-3): 1-22.

IET (2003) Movimientos turísticos en fronteras (FRONTUR). Madrid: IET.

Mazanec, J.A. (1997) Segmenting city tourists into vacation styles. In Mazanec, J.A. (ed.) *International City Tourism.* London: Pinter, pp. 114-130.

McKercher, B. and du Cros, H. (2003) Testing a cultural tourism typology. *International Journal of Tourism Research* 5: 45-58.

Pizam, A. (1999) Cross-cultural tourist behavior. In Pizam, A. and Y. Mansfeld (eds) *Consumer Behavior in Travel and Tourism.* New York: The Haworth Hospitality Press, pp. 393-411.

Plog, S.C. (1990) A carpenter's tools: An answer to Stephen L. J. Smith's review of psychocentrism/allocentrism. *Journal of Travel Research* 28 (4): 55-58.

Reisinger, Y. and Turner, L. (1998) Cross-cultural differences in tourism: A strategy for tourism marketers. *Journal of Travel and Tourism Marketing* 7 (4): 79-106.

Richards, G. (2001) *Cultural Attractions and European Tourism.* Wallingford: CAB International.

Sussmann, S. and Rashcovsky, C. (1997) A cross-cultural analysis of English and French Canadians' vacation travel patterns. *International Journal of Hospitality Management* 16 (2): 191-208.

Van den Borg, J. and Gotti, G. (1995) *Tourism and Cities of Art.* Geneve: UNESCO.

Vidal-Beneyto, J. (1997) Le Tourisme culturel européen et le développement durable. In *Patrimonio cultural y sus relaciones con el turismo.* Alicante, 7-11 April, pp. 84-86.

Weber, R. (1997) Tourisme culturel et patrimonie. In *Patrimonio cultural y sus relaciones con el turismo.* Alicante. 7-11 April, pp. 82-83.

World Tourism Organization (2004) *World Tourism Barometer,* 2 (2) June. Madrid: WTO.

PART III:
SENSITIZING TOURISTS
AND COMMUNITIES

Chapter 9

Transversal Indicators and Qualitative
Observatories of Heritage Tourism

Jaume B. Franquesa
Marc Morell

INTRODUCTION

In recent times tourism based on cultural and environmental motivations, particularly "heritage tourism" (be it cultural or natural),[1] seems to have become perceived as the remedy to all ills deriving from the evolution of "conventional" tourism. Conventional or "mass" tourism arrived in the Mediterranean islands and *costas* of Spain almost forty years ago, and tends to be based on leisure motivations, rather than the knowledge-based motivations of heritage tourism.

When contrasting desirable and undesirable tourism, it is often evident that those responsible for managing tourism in political and

Cultural Tourism: Global and Local Perspectives
© 2007 by The Haworth Press, Inc. All rights reserved.
doi:10.1300/5749_09

administrative institutions favor the inclusion, in their agendas, of products that can become heritage. Take, for instance, the projects of the Balearic Government's *Fons de Rehabilitació d'Espais Turístics* (Fund for the Rehabilitation of Tourist Spaces) between 2002 and 2003. These projects were financed by the controversial *Impost sobre establiments d'allotjament turístic* (Tax on Tourist Accommodation Establishments), popularly known as the "ecotax." These projects were devoted to palliating the impacts caused by traditional "mass" tourism, as well as making up for apparent deficiencies in the tourism offer, which was perceived as having little respect for environmental and sociocultural issues.[2]

This specific case of the Balearic archipelago shows how important it is to create alternatives to the existing tourism products. In order to develop appropriate alternatives, tools are required for monitoring sustainability and quality. Among these tools, indicators take on a leading role. Nowadays it seems that having a set of indicators is a precondition for any responsible action related to setting up heritage tourism, as well as its management, monitoring, or evaluation. Without denying the usefulness of indicators, this chapter examines the unquestioned status they seem to enjoy, identifying their limitations and disadvantages.

TOURISM, HERITAGE, AND SUSTAINABILITY

Let us consider the following statement: "Heritage includes any natural or manmade place, area, building, or site that is significant to the people (of the District)" (Kapiti Coast District Council, 1999:30). This definition of heritage stresses the importance of social meanings[3] and values. These meanings and values are usually linked with identity and with the (re)construction of memory. According to this definition, anything can be heritage. It only needs to be significant to the people living there. However, obvious as it may seem, not everything is heritage, since not everything becomes heritage. This definition hides the external process of heritage selection, value formation, and attribution of meaning.

Social processes, often conflictive, contribute to the making of heritage products. In these processes, we have to consider a range of groups and social agents who have different political and economic interests and different cultural conceptions, stemming from their distinct positions in social space. Opposed to the discourses that see heritage as something natural and as a product of a consensus, often because of ingenuity as well as dishonest intentions, it is important to stress the dynamic, processual, and conflictive nature of heritage product-making, particularly when it concerns enormously sensitive questions such as identity or memory. That is, heritage-making is inseparable from questions of influence, politics, interests, and authority—in short, power.

On the other hand, this conflictive dimension becomes even worse when we move from heritage to heritage tourism, since the commercial exploitation implied by heritage tourism usually arouses resentment. It is not only the fact that commercial exploitation may be viewed by certain groups as illegitimate when applied to heritage objects of a sacred or inalienable nature,[4] but also the fact that commercial exploitation entails complex political and economic decisions. These issues include the kind of public for which the product is designed (which often does not match with the owners of the ascribed meanings), and the fact that the urban speculation that usually accompanies heritage tourism can lead to a rise in the price of land, to processes of use replacement, gentrification, etc. In fact, these latter issues become especially relevant since heritage tourism is mainly a kind of urban tourism and focuses on the historic centers of cities, which become, as a whole, public spaces made heritage (and therefore not only the meanings become problematic, but also spatial practices and uses of space). This is hardly surprising since historic city centers, besides offering a high concentration of heritage referents, usually characterize themselves by their function of centrality and their symbolic contents, particularly their role in representing the city as a whole. Nevertheless, "touristification/heritagization" is still problematic, and it is in these spaces that most of the conflicts regarding heritage and tourism become visible. These conflicts create social discomfort, hence negatively influencing the political success and the economic viability of heritage tourism; consequently, it seems there is a need to develop common criteria for assessment of the complex factors affecting heritage.

This chapter aims to assess the tools, and particularly the indicators, used to guide the development of products assigned to heritage tourism. The question, though, is which criteria should be used in developing these tools. In order to define these criteria, we have to set a goal to attain. In recent years, the definition of these criteria has been identified with sustainability. Cutting it short: There is a need for tools in order to monitor heritage tourism so that it becomes sustainable.

There are many different ways of understanding sustainable tourism.[5] However, it cannot be anything other than tourism as a part of a strategy towards sustainability. Sustainability, or sustainable development, is (1) an aim to be permanently achieved, and it considers (2) integrating and coordinating (3) the economic development, (4) the conservation of resources, and (5) social and cultural equity (Mega and Pedersen, 1998:13). Here we will briefly explain each of the points that make up the proposed characterization with regards to the idea of heritage tourism.

1. Sustainable development is an aim to achieve, an ideal to reach (which also sounds politically strong), and is therefore useful for establishing policies, principles, criteria, and guidelines against which both the situation at a given moment and the policies adopted may be checked or assessed. Thus, the need for assessment and monitoring indicators takes a leading role, since indicators allow a very visible measurement. On the other hand, the "permanent" achievement of sustainability requires the concept to be understood in a flexible way (allowing change and innovation), and not as a benchmark or a rigid and inflexible method. Sustainability is about achieving a concurrent increase of social, economic, cultural, and environmental benefits in the development process.

2. In the notion of sustainability, the elements it aims to harmonize are probably not as important as the will to harmonize, the strong commitment to achieve a holistic and globalizing scope. It is not only the desire for economic development, the preservation of resources, and social equity arm in arm, but the verification that each of these facets is not a closed compartment, an abstract and segregated sphere, but aspects of the same global process, which maintain between them constant and desirable interrelations. Such verification drives us to the conclusion that any issue requires a transversal approach. If this were to be applied to heritage tourism, it would be convenient for the developed tourist attraction to be profitable while watching over the preservation of heritage, and for it to be alert to the social conse-

quences. Nevertheless, it is more than this. Holism is about more than just taking into account the different factors, since it originates from the idea that they are related from the beginning, that they cannot be understood separately, that in all the steps of the process the object is crossed by a multitude of vectors not only interdependent but insepa- rable. That is to say, the management of sustainable heritage tourism cannot try to remove those fissures it provokes as externalities, but should integrate all these factors from the beginning of the planning and the building processes. Moreover, it should not merely iron out the conflicts, which may happen between the touristification process and the respect to the meanings and their uses, but should include both tension points and pave the way for combining the innovation of the tourist product and social participation from the outset.

In relation to these two points of the definition, and before going on to the others, we should briefly outline an idea. Heritage tourism, or sustainable heritage tourism, has to be fitted into its environmental and sociocultural context, which implies the need to take into account the social structure as a whole, with all its complexity. On the other hand, at least in those places where "conventional" tourism is the main economic sector (as in the Balearic Islands), the complementary statement could be made: Sustainable tourism is one of the best ways to address society (and its sustainable development). Heritage tour- ism, as a kind of alternative tourism, should not be used for de- monizing sun and beach mass tourism and its impacts, but it should rather be seen as an opportunity for society to become aware of itself, not only paving the way for economic development but also for re- thinking itself. That is to say, where tourism is the common denomi- nator of almost everything, the act of thinking about other forms of tourism, originating from the ambition of integrating tourism and society, is an important tool that society has for self-reflecting, for shaping its own destiny, while turning heritage tourism into an arena for debate and civic involvement. In this sense, Hannappi-Egger (2002) proposes we understand cultural heritage as a form of public information.

3. Heritage tourism clears the way for economic development, since it assumes the creation of products with a high benefit. In recent times, it is common for both experts and institutions to attract atten- tion to a change in the tourist profile, increasingly expert and experi-

enced, while demanding more elaborated and differentiated products. These products ought to be environmentally friendly while improving their cultural content.[6] Heritage products would perfectly respond to this change in the tourist profile, and they would place in the avant-garde the destinations owning them. As Scott states: "Places with *unique local characteristics* and *traditional heritage* are modern tourism's latest products" (2001:21).

4. As usually understood, heritage tourism is less damaging than sun and beach tourism, since the heritage tourist is more aware of environmental matters. Leaving aside this idea, which has been criticized from certain sectors as being naive,[7] it does seem unquestionable that heritage tourism supports heritage conservation, given that it is precisely based on the valuing of certain cultural and natural resources a society has and makes use of. Thus, in this sense, heritage tourism is sustainable with regard to heritage; moreover, it is an advanced form of conservation and assessment of these resources. However, it is necessary to bear in mind Mason's (2002) contention that heritage conservation should not be just about resources but also cultural memory and its meanings. What is interesting is that these meanings and cultural memory are not abstract entities, but have owners; that is, conserving cultural memory and its meanings should take into account the social groups which share them, their cultural conceptions, their identity, credo, etc.

5. Social equity and cultural acknowledgement are preconditions, as well as aims of the sustainable development, in a context of dynamic tension between what is local and what is global. This setting favors the development of civil society, the promotion of civic involvement, the assessment of minorities and local cultures, the redistribution of resources, etc.—all of which closely relate to heritage tourism.[8] Shields (1999) states that we are witnessing a tendency towards de-differentiation between culture and economy, of which heritage tourism may well be a paradigmatic case. Heritage tourism poses a double challenge: acknowledgment and redistribution. The making of heritage and its activation as a tourist product implies a choice of certain referents and the fixing of multiple meanings (via interpretation). First, there is the need to consider an extension of the kind of heritage products offered, since these usually center themselves on certain historic periods or certain social groups, specifically

the elites. Because the selection of heritage products also implies exclusion, we need to start considering the right that different social groups have to be subjects capable of signifying their own existence and history. Their meanings ought to be respected, and channels for the expression of these meanings should be offered.[9] The right of citizens to interpret and to conceive their own interpretation should be acknowledged; this is an issue directly linked to civic involvement and the democratization of decision-making with regard to a society's heritage. This concerns not only interpretation and meaningfulness, but also other external issues, such as the uses of space, the frequent collateral urban reforms, the way in which it is commercialized, and so on.

Harvey (1996) suggests that strengthening social place is the best way of meeting the newly emerging challenges of globalization. Without a doubt, heritage tourism can be an adequate form of nurturing local identity and global fluxes (of tourists), providing a means of establishing local pride while allowing people to relate themselves to the whole world. However, it is not always possible to seize this opportunity, and several case studies of tourist destinations[10] show that tourists and locals may experience the same place in totally different ways. This division can increase distrust and apprehension from the locals toward their own heritage, a kind of alienation, which can weaken local networks. This is often due to the commercial development of heritage products as well as a narrow-minded focus on the consumer, that is, the tourist. Such a situation is hardly sustainable because: (1) it is unfair, since it neglects the importance of the locals in the making of meaning and in the use of a place or an object that has become heritage, and (2) it is commercially dubious, especially in the long term, since it can cause conflicts and a fragility of space, which does not favor tourism and does not recognize the potential of the locals to become consumers and users of the product, removing any chance of them benefiting from an important segment of the public and the market. There is the need for a commitment between commercialization and society that does not excessively alter the uses and the meaning of a place.

Therefore, heritage tourism should be generated from mechanisms of civic involvement and vice versa, thus enabling destinations to take advantage of the opportunity heritage tourism offers. This point is probably the most important and delicate issue concerned with heritage tourism as it moves toward sustainable tourism. Up to this point, we have tried to synthesize the main sociocultural challenges confronting heritage tourism in achieving sustainability. The next section will deal with the indicators used for monitoring this process.

WHAT INDICATORS INDICATE

This section reviews and analyzes the indicators used for the assessment and the monitoring of heritage tourism. The existing literature is scarce, so this review focuses on those works which have been considered to be more reflexive while building more accurately their set of indicators (for example: Mega and Pedersen, 1998; Pearson et al., 1998; Farsari and Prastacos, 2000, 2001; Ajuntament de Calvià, 2001; Barioulet, 2001; Martín Vallés, 2001; Blázquez, Murray, and Garau, 2002; Devon County Council, 2003). But first we will consider what an indicator is and the main indicators that are usually used.

An indicator can be defined as a numeric factor, which refers directly or indirectly to a feature of a given situation or action. The use of indicators includes: the measuring of situations, policies, management, impacts, and pressures. Researchers usually distinguish three basic kinds of indicators: condition (or situation), answer, and pressure indicators. However, it is not always possible to clearly detach them from one another. In the words of Martín Vallés, "They [indicators] must be important, numerically measurable, useful, easy to interpret, easy to compare in time and between destinations, objective, directed at improvement, and reliable" (2001:10).

In addition, these characteristics are precisely those that make indicators so popular. Because they are numeric, they are easily visible and useful for graphic communication; on the other hand, their abstract nature makes them especially suitable when comparing different situations and contexts. They are also easy to handle, since radically different issues may be measured in the same way; moreover, they can be added together, achieving in this way set indicators that by amassing very diverse data allow the assessment, quantification, or the judgment of a certain situation, political strategy, or management unity, and the measurement, for instance, of its degree of sustainability performance. Furthermore, indicators link to political aims, and they allow one to foresee the emergence of certain problems and to identify deficiencies. On the other hand, not everything can be expressed numerically, and transforming a feature of a situation into a number is not only an abstraction, but a reduction that can exclude much information.

In addition to specific tourism indicators, more general indicators are increasingly important in providing frame data for analyzing and developing a specific area (e.g., a tourism destination), its people, and their activities. These include data on the labor market, the distribution of wealth, the production of waste, access to housing, demographic data, etc. We should also add those indicators that more precisely focus on environmental questions, such as the pattern of land use, the percentage of urbanized surface, volume of water/energy/concrete per person, recycling data, the ecological footprint of a given territory, and many more. Besides their usefulness, this series of features is very appropriate for quantifying; although in many cases the data, the precariousness of which is a historic problem in several destinations, become tenuous when examined more closely. Likewise, although we might know the water consumption in a given area and therefore the consumption per person, these data are not always available by sector; for instance, the total percentage of water consumption for domestic use, agriculture, industry, tourism, and other services.

In the case of tourist destinations, there is a series of frame data, which are specifically relevant and should be referred to, since they are concerned with tourist activity. These are indicators such as expenditure per tourist, the accommodation carrying capacity of the destination (and the kind of accommodation), the arrival of passengers, the channels they use and how they enter the destination, or the basic indicators of tourist pressures. One of the main problems of these indicators is that they do not consider the influence of tourism on the local population, because instead of measuring per person they measure per tourist (e.g., water consumption per tourist per day). It would also be interesting to add data such as the percentage of the labor force dedicated to tourism, or the percentage of revenue coming from tourism. Other indirect indicators also seem very pertinent but are often forgotten, including the composition of the tourist businesses, the percentage of tourists arriving with major tour operators, the percentage of businesses with local capital, or even the percentage of family businesses and the percentage of capital they represent in relation to the total.

Three kinds of indicators, often combined, are almost unique to tourist destinations: those concerned with seasonality, tourist pressure, and sociocultural impact. In fact, the aim of these indicators is to address the repercussions tourism has on local society, trying to detect possible discomforts and conflicts. The fact is that heritage tourism is perceived as reorientating the dynamic of these three indicators: reducing seasonality, spreading tourist pressure, and mitigating sociocultural impacts. Whether they effectively help to change these dynamics or not is something to yet to be proven. However, we argue that heritage tourism represents an achievable opportunity and not a change in the kind of information these indicators offer, but in what they intend to indicate: a more harmonious development of tourism and society.[11] In order to improve this harmonization, heritage tourism should take a number of factors into account.

First, heritage tourism is not just a way of increasing tourist volume without worsening conflict, but is also an opportunity to solve the already-existing tensions in many tourist destinations. Therefore, heritage tourism is about trying to change the orientation of the destination, as in the case of the Balearic Islands. Second, it is true that heritage tourism creates problems, sometimes new, related to the touristification of cultural resources and their location. In this sense, the case of the historic centers is paradigmatic, a frequent reason for taking them as typical cases. Tensions are often made evident in the way certain touristified spaces become fragile, as well as in the lack of commitment to the practices and social uses traditionally associated with places and in touristification sometimes guided by "malling" criteria,[12] that is to say, adopting a model which is nearer to the shopping mall than to the city. This touristification model is emphasized in the terminology used in certain indicators, which will be analyzed later, and which require us to make certain conceptual adjustments.

Thus, the indicators offered here will be those addressing the problems and challenges heritage tourism encounters. Two points are inseparable from each other: (1) the focus on the distancing problems between locals and tourists and the tourist places, which can lead to a sense of negative impact and to disputes that without a doubt have negative repercussions on the performance of heritage tourism; (2) the approach to the development of the synergies involved in the process of making heritage tourism, as well as of a positive involvement. These indicator issues link to three questions: (1) the management of heritage; (2) the development of the mechanisms of participation and consultation; (3) the social conflicts linked to tourism (or touristification).

THE MANAGEMENT OF HERITAGE

There are several indicators that assess the condition of heritage and its management. Therefore, it is convenient to have a number of indicators at one's disposal, preferably those which are often used, such as those referring to the deterioration or destruction of heritage places, the amount and the distribution of places which have become heritage, and their ownership and management. Let us focus on management: How many cataloged places have been the object of research? Is there a management scheme? Are these places specially protected (classified by the kind of protection they have)? What funding do they receive? What is the profile of the management staff? Are there any training courses for practitioners? Other indicators, as pertinent as the previous ones, focus even more directly on the relationship between heritage and its commercialization or promotion. The data they base themselves on include: the annual number of cultural events and their attendance, the number of sales outlets and exhibitions of typical local products, the number of cultural establishments and number of visitors, the number of publications on local traditions, the budget devoted to cultural infrastructures, and others. However, these indicators do not inform us about how this protection is carried out, what the research sought, what management schemes these places have, whether the locals feel typical local products belong to them, etc. None of these allows the introduction of non-quantitative improvements. These indicators measure policies,[13] and some of them the force of their management, but they do not allow access to the building process of its terms, nor manage to explain if this process addresses people appropriately.

Furthermore, they tend to vaguely assimilate (the action of) a policy with a situation. For instance: an indicator measuring the percentage of resources catalogued as cultural or environmental heritage that have a management scheme. It is a very clear indicator: In principle, the closer to 100 percent you get, the better. But what does this indicator tell us? It only covers the implementation of the management schemes, but it does not allow one to measure whether such schemes are appropriate or not. What happens if these management schemes are not respectful of peoples' opinions and feelings or if they cause them problems? On the one hand, such consequences would mean the questioning of the aim of reaching 100 percent; on the other hand, it would probably imply that people would stop considering such heritage as their own. If this were to happen, would the catalog still be right? Perhaps it would, from the point of view of historians, art historians, or biologists, but not as a present cultural or identity referent. However, the fact is that such an indicator for catalogued heritage never informs us of the criteria used in its selection, or of the scale and form of local involvement.

Similar doubts about current indicators can be found in the work of Pearson et al. (1998), which is the most systematic and in-depth study we have reviewed. Among the complex and polished set of heritage indicators they suggest is the percentage of places of cultural interest receiving protection. However, they then ask, without providing an answer, whether, and if so how, to include noncataloged places of special interest. These questions make the process behind heritage creation evident, given that indicators cannot inform us about the key details of this process and raise further questions about it: How does a certain heritage become cataloged heritage? Who has the power to make decisions about what should be made heritage and how it is allocated to a particular category of heritage? Who interprets, and with what aims and what criteria? An indicator informs us about useful things, but it does not inform us about what should be heritagized and/or touristified, and how. These indicators are incapable of telling us anything outside of their own terms, which are those of the administrative machine that created them, and which are usually set on showing the synchrony, the uniqueness, and the consensus of something that is dynamic, plural, and frequently controversial by nature, and it must not be forgotten that denying or closing our eyes to a conflict is a way of stimulating it.

Therefore, it is necessary to leave the indicators for a while in order to look at specific aspects of their implementation. Nevertheless, indicators quantifying tourist information would help to reveal more about interpretation: Are the local names (that is to say, in the local language) for the places respected in tourist information? Is there a version of this information in the local language?[14] Where do the tourist guides and tourist information staff come from? Let us go on to examine those indicators that could end up compensating to a certain extent for what the indicators analyzed above have neglected, namely measuring the involvement of citizens and stakeholders.

INVOLVEMENT AND CITIZENSHIP

We have to distinguish two types of indicators here. On the one hand, we encounter those that reflect the existence of mechanisms and procedures of citizen awareness and involvement, taking into account the agents involved (which usually measure policies, too). On the other hand, there are those closely linked to the research carried out on people's views and attitudes, that is, indicators that involve mechanisms for reaching people.

The most important indicators of awareness and involvement are the existence of awareness or educational programs addressed to the public; the number of public meetings held before implementing policies; the availability of procedures for the public and stakeholders to involve themselves and suggest changes in policies; the number of studies on the impact of tourism; and, finally, conferences and other activities organized locally, which may attract interest in tourism and sustainable development. Other indicators that may be included are the percentage of people who are members of civic entities, the number of cultural centers, the number of these entities that effectively take part in decision-making, the degree of influence these mechanisms have (e.g., counting the number of changes introduced in the initial proposals).

The information these indicators offer is valuable, and most important, they point out the way forward: the need to establish mechanisms for involving, sensitizing, implicating, and even creating complicity. However, they indicate as much as they do not indicate. They are well-intentioned, since they demand an affirmative answer, but they do not state the success of such mechanisms nor their weight in the process; some, probably very few, encourage the existence of a lot of research, but it is not known whether this will be capable of reaching the meanings, the memory, the everyday life, or the identity of the people. There is another type of indicator, though, which moves in another direction.

These are indicators that try to measure the attitude of the people to certain heritage places or projects.[15] With regards to these indicators, some aspects have to be taken into account: (1) surveys have to be complex and well designed, which is expensive; (2) it ought to be considered beforehand whether or not these surveys will influence the political decisions and to what extent; (3) surveys are interested in people, but do not promote confidence and involvement: Do the surveyed people feel involved in the decision-making processes? Moreover; and (4) these indicators stem from surveys and these are not neutral,[16] like any other method to be used. In fact, the last two points are closely related.

Surveys address individuals, subjects, who are usually classified according to demographic criteria (age, sex, income level, etc.) rather than those internal to the social organization. Individuals own and perform social meanings and values, uses and practices, as members of social groups and not as individuals detachable from the rest and mere units of an aggregate. Identity, which is inseparable from heritage, always refers to a group. On the other hand, the survey already asks about attitudes[17] and seeks to gauge the level of satisfaction with a state of things or concerning a project. Surveys ask individuals about attitudes, perceptions, and views, which are supposed to come from an experience. But individuals are members of social groups, and it is on the basis of this membership that they have values and think in terms of social meanings, with their own logic, which indicates that they express themselves in their practices, uses, and appropriations rather than in their experience (e.g., of space).[18]

Such a survey does not invite participation, because it addresses the communities as if they were clients.[19] It is an approach that has more to do with a market study about potential demand (studies that on the other hand, are convenient to carry out) than with people's values and their logic. At most, these surveys allow the perception of a major or minor discomfort (or satisfaction) concerning the question posed. However, they will not allow us to understand these perceptions or the grammar of the dormant conflicts and, therefore, do not allow us to rethink the situation in better terms.

TOURISTIFICATION AND SOCIAL CONFLICT

Indicators related to touristification and social conflict take two forms. First, surveys directed at locals about the perception they have of tourists, tourism or certain tourist places. There is a subtype of this indicator that asks the same kind of question while trying to see if the locals associate tourists, tourism, or tourist areas with specific problems. Secondly, visitor surveys of the perception of the place they are visiting or the hospitality of the people.

However, undertaking such surveys also raises issues.[20] For example, there are issues of representation, since the perceptions of locals and tourists emanate from a wide range of different groups with different perceptions of the potential for social damage. Surveys can also involuntarily promote conflict and alarm, since they oblige the surveyed individual to think in the terms of the survey, which among other issues takes the perception (and, therefore, its volatility) as a dogma, while also posing tourists and locals in opposition to each other. These surveys objectify and reify the tourist/local dichotomy, as if both groups were compact, cohesive, and homogeneous, with opposed interests and perceptions.

The reification of the tourist/local duality seems delicate, since it tends to create an *us* and an *other,* as well as the very same refusal dynamics this dichotomous thinking implies. Such dichotomous thinking is unlikely to achieve the fruitful cultural contacts heritage and heritage tourism promise, and it is a false dichotomy, or at least not a very neat one. In all cities and particularly tourist cities, different groups coincide when they relate to the city. Following Martinotti's (1993) famous classification, these are: residents, commuters, city users (amongst them the tourists), and international businesspeople (metropolitan businesspeople).

This is not the place for complex sociological digressions, but let us take a hypothetical case. Do the people who live in a middle-class suburb and only go to the (heritagized and touristified) historic center for a walk, a night out, or to process administrative paperwork maintain a relationship with space and mobility patterns closer to those of the lifelong resident, or to the tourist who only spends a week there? They are probably closer to tourists.

There is a kind of indicator that in a subtle, indirect way also focuses on issues related to the involvement of the citizens, the proximity between locals and tourism, and possible conflicts arising from this. These are indicators such as the number of bars and discos per resident in a certain area, the presence of local swimmers and sunbathers on the beaches, the use by the locals of the tourist facilities, etc. These indicators should be exhaustive given the need for a complete topology of the touristified spaces (e.g., a historic center). In order to achieve this, we need to know the frequency of use of a certain area according to the time of day, the day of the week, the month of the year. Moreover, this information can be related to the occupancy and kind of services and businesses on ground floors and mezzanines, as well as the distribution of infrequent or unforeseen uses, such as fights, crime, *botellón* (alcohol consumed by youngsters in public spaces), demonstrations, etc.

In fact, such indicators are relevant because they reveal space and its uses. It often happens that a spiraling gap hides behind conflicts. These conflicts are both caused by and cause the fragility of space. The origin of this fragility of space and what is to be found there is a difficulty of appropriation (this coincides with the thesis Magrinyà Maza and [2001] apply to the case of the Raval district in Barcelona). Residents traditionally appropriate space for themselves.[21] They are the ones who make a daily use of the space, which becomes cumulative over time. Such an appropriation is a form of control and it is cohesive. However, behind this appropriation there are values, meanings, practices, and uses. A space transited by groups that only carry out fragile appropriations is a space at the mercy of conflict.

Why is tourist space usually a space prone to conflict or perceived as conflictive? Because it does not bear in mind the meanings, values, and practices of the residents. Tourist space is often a space designed not to become a place, a social and socialized place merely used according to commercial interests, which have collaborated in its design. A city cannot be a theme park since it becomes conflictive and feeble. This is what usually happens when people are thought of as mere consumers of an experience, or as mere users of a circuit, rather than as citizens.

Tourists find themselves in a recreational context and do not practice heritage tourism as if they were on an MA course on the society and culture of a place. Nevertheless, there may be a consensus between the lived city, signified and soaked with social relations and memory, and the city of recreational experience. The possibility of this consensus depends on giving maximum consideration to the residents (and especially their practices, their memory, etc.) in the planning of the heritagization/touristification of the place. It seems plausible to think that such a form of development will avoid mistrust and conflict. Moreover, the profitability of the product can contribute to the reconciliation of the development of civil society, local culture, and tourism.

It seems as if the indicators currently in use, however valuable they may be, are not able to indicate the key steps of this process, nor how to encourage it, nor allow a holistic way of thinking about it, which would permit one to see its transversal nature. It is not surprising that Mega and Pedersen (1998), after proposing an accurate set of indicators for measuring sustainability and indicating their basic outlines, state that the most valuable indicators are those capable of measuring the interest and hope a certain project awakes among the citizenry, since such hope would guarantee sociocultural sustainability. This project could be heritage tourism, in the case of mature tourist destinations. However, this hypothetical indicator is not capable of generating hope, but capable only of putting it together without knowing what it responds to. Management and research in the heritage tourism field should not only approach the disempowered but should try to empower them.

Having outlined the information that needs to be collected, the following section deals with establishing observatories for heritage tourism. These observatories should be capable of not only gathering values, memory, and meanings, nor only promoting channels for citizen participation and the involvement of the social agents, but should also be capable of generating hope from the fact that people take part in the design of tourist products, through their everyday lives.

A PROPOSAL: QUALITATIVE RESEARCH AND OBSERVATORIES FOR HERITAGE TOURISM

As we have seen, from both the cultural management and the sustainability fields there is a demand for a holistic scope. Anthropology, the academic discipline in the socio cultural field that has insisted more on the convenience of a holistic approach, has shown how this kind of scope requires the use of qualitative research techniques and methods. These techniques are not exclusively anthropological, and their intensive and rigorous use would contribute enormously to the management and development of heritage tourism.[22] These micro techniques allow a holistic understanding of the reality, since they address the origins of meaning from the outset. Overall, they address the assumptions, values, and practices of the huge variety of actors that is always found.

These are techniques such as in-depth and semistructured interviews, life histories (and other techniques connected to history and oral memory), the mapping of practices and the occupation of space, structured observation techniques (be they participative or naturalist ones), cognitive maps, behavior maps, the mapping of physical traces, group interviews, focus groups, guided visits for tourists with the involvement of the locals while collecting their views, commented walks, group follow-ups, document analysis (press, archives, tourist information, etc.), and many more.

This is not the place for explaining in detail each of these techniques. However, they would all coincide in offering a detailed approach, centered on people but also playing down their views. This approach searches for the underlying cultural logic and the understanding of social problems, taking people as the starting point. These techniques could also reveal what indicators failed to indicate. They are usually slow methods, and this has certainly diminished their dissemination. But this slowness is questionable. There are several accelerated qualitative procedures, based on the balanced choice of some of these techniques and adapted to the specific cases, which can produce successful results.[23] Furthermore, if the monitoring and the research are continual, it is possible to produce multiplier effects that help to mitigate problems of speed. The achievement of such continual monitoring will be possible thanks to the implementation of the observatories proposed here.

Indeed, we propose the implementation of heritage tourism observatories that carry out global monitoring, both quantitative and qualitative; focusing on heritage and tourism as complex processes while monitoring them continuously; promoting civic involvement; gathering expert knowledge while generating expertise. One would argue, and not without good reason, that these centralized research management and tourist promotion tools already exist. Thus, what makes this proposal distinctive? Precisely its systemic, although not exclusive, adoption of qualitative techniques and its capability in approaching society, the final reason for privileging them. Moreover, the adoption of qualitative techniques is not only a mere addition to the usual management methods and, therefore, it should involve a reconsideration of the whole machinery. The key to the question is not the techniques, which are nothing other than a tool, but the aim of conciliating social and tourist development.

In fact, the current entities usually keep a watch on the issue of social or cultural impacts, and they even foresee the inclusion of the actors and stakeholders involved at some point in the decision-making process, just as the indicators analyzed here suggest. Nevertheless, the management approach often seems to view these affairs as mere externalities of the main process, while the qualitative techniques are there because there is the need to get to the root of the question. Stakeholders feel obliged to *speak* in the terms of the administration, although neither group understands the language of the other. Qualitative techniques are a tool for understanding people, groups, and spaces on their own terms. Thus, the inclusion of qualitative techniques means a more radical degree of citizen involvement and participation—one that should get rid of the division between the tourist and heritage management, everyday life, and people's memory. If this distance were to disappear from the very start of the process, social impacts and conflicts would stop being externalities or negativities to be patched up.

As we have pointed out throughout the chapter, these observatories should adopt a methodological, conceptual approach. In general, *real people* are only taken into consideration in three roles: as individuals, as stakeholders, and as community. We have already discussed the problems associated with seeing people as mere individuals, detached from one another; then we have the stakeholders, mainly characterized by vested interests; and, finally, the community. But what do we know about community? We argue that the concept of community is used as an excuse to avoid social analysis. The community always appears as a black box, as if it lacks internal structure, cultural negotiations, or power struggles.

Other papers in this volume discuss the distinction between *content* and *context* (see Chapter 16, this volume). The argument is that the suitability of a tourist destination appears more linked to the context than to the content. What is this *context*? We would say it is society and its vitality. Doubtless, we will never fully apprehend the complexity and subtlety of an entire social organization. Nonetheless, categories such as individuals or community become obstacles because they don't let us understand what is social. Thus, we propose a more radical approach through categories such as "residents," giving the opportunity to every resident to become, and to be recognized as, a potential stakeholder. We argue there is a necessity to rethink tourism management and monitoring in the light of its shift toward culture, heritage, and everyday life (see Chapter 2), and this *aggiornamento* requires a change in our practices and methods and a rethinking of our concepts.

Such a drastic change explains the observatories we propose. Without a doubt, these observatories would not end conflict, since the issues we are dealing with are processes with an inherent potential for conflict given the variety and complexity of the actors, aspects, interests, and the points of view at stake. An observatory will never end conflicts, but it will always monitor them without being scared of them, since understanding conflict must be essential to its activities.

Qualitative techniques are a tool for addressing social processes. Therefore, adopting them means acknowledging the subjects of these processes, to recognize their interpretation. Thus, it is possible to create trustworthy, authentic channels for civic participation, which at the same time allow the generation of completely new knowledge and the innovative development of new tools. The creation of channels for organic participation and the generation of expertise should be the most relevant outcomes of the proposed observatories.

The importance of generating expert knowledge is often ignored as a tool for diversifying the economic activities of tourist destinations. In this sense, it is interesting to note what Professor Javier Rey of the Universitat de les Illes Balears recently said in a journalistic interview (Matías Vallés, 2003). When the interviewer asked him what was left of Mallorca besides tourist activity, he answered: "We ought to can our tourist knowledge, sell it, and live from it.' In order to maximize this resource, a tourist destination needs to be at the leading edge, and it must have a huge innovative capability. In fact, heritage tourism can provide this opportunity, and the dynamic of the observatories suggested here should contribute to promoting innovation and creativity.

Turning back to the crux of this chapter, these observatories need to develop general indicators for heritage tourism. Indicators cannot measure everything, and, to a certain extent, this is because they are not based on sufficient knowledge. It may be that qualitative analysis will create subtler indicators. The observatories could resolve the following questions:

1. To identify the meanings and values inscribed in the objects and places under heritagization and touristification processes, through qualitative techniques. Thus, there would be a chance of understanding and treating the root of the problem concerning potential social conflicts.
2. To promote the participation of the citizens while generating confidence and involving them in the research task; all in all, recognizing the portrayers of meanings, values, and practices. Such an involvement should help to end the isolation of people in the planning of tourism.
3. They can help to reduce tensions between hosts and guests as well as understanding them, by questioning the assumption that the tourist should be the object of policy and research. Reducing the rooted dichotomy between "hosts" and "guests" should advance our understanding of social processes as well as promote social sustainability.

There is a need to create heritage tourism observatories largely based on a sound knowledge base and the use of qualitative techniques. Therefore, they should develop *in situ* involvement of researchers and field workers. This should not be an obstacle for these observatories to carry out market and promotion studies together with indicator development and strategic planning, but just the opposite, because the knowledge acquired in the field will contribute to the development of indicators. Proceeding in such a manner will encourage expert knowledge (not only gathering together values and meanings, but also producing them) as well as mechanisms for civic participation. Likewise, these qualitative observatories should reach the citizens, all in all speaking a more intelligible language and supporting the development of civil society from true heritage tourism.

NOTES

1. Throughout the chapter, it is possible to feel that an approach on the environment heritage issue with regards to tourism is missing. Certainly, the authors are social anthropologists and this accounts for the focus on heritage tourism matters. Nevertheless, the fact of focusing on the sociocultural aspects of heritage does not imply concentrating on the cultural heritage and obviating the natural one. In fact, the "meaning" of natural heritage is something cultural by definition, and processes of a social kind grant the value of natural heritage. That is to say, the chapter will not deal with questions of a purely ecological or biological kind (e.g., maintenance of the diversity of fauna or flora) but in no way should this be sensed as an inhibition with regard to natural heritage, since it is heritage and therefore it is something sociocultural by definition.

2. It may be advisable to stress that the case of the Balearic Islands quoted here is an illustrative example and not a case for assessment. However, besides the in depth knowledge the authors may have, it is especially relevant given the Balearic Islands is a first-rate tourism destination in the Mediterranean, one of the biggest tourism centers in the world.

3. In the Catalan original, *significant* refers to ideas such as relevance, significance, meaning, interpretation, and symbolism, and is translated here as "meaning."

4. It is convenient to stress that the sense assigned to the adjective "sacred" is the one social anthropology usually maintains and which stems from Durkheim. Thus, sacred would not (exclusively) refer to what is related to religion or spirituality, but to whatever a group may identify itself with to such a point that it is able to represent it (e.g., a flag), and therefore considered as incapable of being exchanged or commercialized.

5. Coccossis (1996) identifies four meanings for the term: (1) the sustainable economy of tourism; (2) an ecologically sustainable tourism; (3) a sustainable development of tourism; and (4) tourism as a part of the strategy toward sustainable development.

6. Keller (2002: 7) sets out all the topics of this new profile related to what comes to be named economy of experience. According to him, in these destinations the tourist would look for: "Holistic experiences with emotional character; consumption as a meaningful act of self-realisation; authentic and manmade attractions; op-

portunities for intercultural contacts; differentiation by typical local elements; fascination for cultural attractions."

7. One of the entities with such a discourse is the GOB *(Grup Ornitològic Balear)*, which is the most important conservationist association in the Balearic Islands, when stating that activating new tourism formulas increase the number of tourists and, therefore, the pressure on resources.

8. Without a doubt, it is a significant fact that in the *Cumbria's First Sustainability Report* (Charras and McKenzie, 2002) of the ten key aims they deal with, three are (1) to assess and celebrate the diversity and distinctiveness of local people, its culture and landscape, trying to strengthen the local communities and their role in a broader context; (2) to reduce the risk of people's alienation with an accurate design and development of our cities and rural areas; and (3) to grant power to all the sections of the community for them to take part in the decision-making.

9. It is interesting to underline that meaning always depends on the relative position it takes up with regard to other meanings and, in essence, on the political and social position the owners of such meaning occupy with regard to other social groups. This issue becomes especially relevant when dealing with subaltern groups. It is often the case that the mere making of heritage from certain objects bonded to the history and the identity of the subaltern groups results in a radical alteration of the meaning, even if it has maintained itself seemingly intact, because it drastically modifies their position.

10. For instance, the already classic volume of Smith (1989) on hosts and guests, the also well-known monograph of Herzfeld (1991), and his distinction between *social time* and *monumental time,* or the opposition Tucker (2000) finds between *oral memory* and *official memory* in the management of UNESCO's world heritage in Cappadocia.

11. It is important to highlight the fact that this chapter does not directly deal with these three indicators, but with those more directly centered on social aims. However, a specific case of a seasonality indicator quoted by Farsari and Prastacos (2001) about Hersonissos (Crete) is on the scent of very important points. The municipality of Hersonissos designed a series of policies that encouraged the lessening of seasonality, seen as a way toward sustainability. These policies failed and, therefore, the indicator measuring the lessening of seasonality gave negative sustainable results. However, what happened is that the workers of the tourist sector had a long peak season (7-9 months) with long working days although getting good earnings. They preferred to devote the other 3-5 months to their olive trees, relaxing and strengthening their social and family bonds. That is, they devoted themselves to strengthen sustainability, both in their most strictly social aspect and in diversifying the local productive activities. Two conclusions stem from this case: (1) measuring political will or a political action is not the same as measuring the attainment of the root aims; and (2) indicators encounter problems when aiming to reach the language of cultural logic and their social practices because of their performance. That is to say, sustainable indicators are a very useful measure, but they should not reach a credo status. Moreover, we need to see what hides behind a number.

12. Crawford (1992) refers to the science of malling as a new applied discipline created by real estate promoters, with the help of architects and lawyers, when refer-

ring to the design of social spaces that follow the latest market trends and, as already proved, heritage tourism would be one of these trends.

13. The measurement of policies, in spite of its limitations, is much better than certain indicators, which intend to "weigh" culture (often linked to impact issues) without being aware that all culture has more of a network than contents, and that all culture is permeable and open to change.

14. Language and its use, especially those languages considered more or less as belonging to minorities, lack of in-depth studies, although it is said language and its use are elements of great importance in the living heritage.

15. Some indicators simply assess this issue by asking about people's attitude concerning very general matters such as "the conservation of heritage." These indicators are not valid when considering that support for a general principle is not equal to the support given to a particular project or a certain political direction.

16. "... the statistical survey only encounters nothing else but what is homogeneous. It reproduces the system it belongs to and leaves out of its field the proliferation of stories and heterogeneous operations, which make up the *patchworks* of what belongs to everyday life. The force of its calculations is sustained thanks to its capability of dividing, but it is precisely through analytic fragmentation that it loses what it thinks it is looking for and representing" (de Certeau, 2000: xlix).

17. What people do, a notion guided by the everyday practice, is not the same as what people say they do, which rather shows the support given to a normative principle.

18. Here, the term *experience* is taken as it is used in expressions such as "economics of experience." Thus, it must not be confused with the concept of "experience" in authors like Raymond Williams or E. P. Thompson: a process of forming and transforming social relations in the everyday context of production, culture, family environment, etc., being at once an individual process and a social process. On the contrary, this latter notion of experience fits with our claim to consider individuals, belonging to social groups in a social and political order, giving meaning to social relations in real life.

19. This idea is parallel to what Hitters (Chapter 14 of this volume) calls a shift from *cultural planning to cultural programming of cities,* referring to cultural policies of festivalization that measure its success in pure terms of audience.

20. In fact, even Farsari and Prastacos (2000), when proposing them, underline that the most important thing is to inquire into the underlying assumptions the indicators do not indicate.

21. It ought to be stated that the residents are not a homogeneous group because they do not all share identical interests and values. Furthermore, there can be residents who happen to be newcomers and may be closer to the prototype of the city user rather than to the resident one. Nonetheless, we argue that, in the kind of destinations we are dealing with, the resident has to emerge as the main typological category under monitoring. Thus, the differences and cleavages between "different kinds of residents" will be subsumed within the same scope. This conceptual removal will allow the construction of a political arena of citizen involvement, introducing the diversity of actors-residents in a debate more fruitful than the abstract and distant states and perceptions based in the lack of communication.

22. There are also other demands to bring heritage management closer to the owners of the meanings and values, which can benefit from commercial exploitation (de la Torre and Mason, 2002). Other positions demand that client satisfaction be exclusively addressed (Goulding, 2000). This is not surprising, since both aspects should not be in conflict.

23. Low (2002) offers a very successful choice.

REFERENCES

Ajuntament de Calvià (2001) *La sostenibilitat d'un municipi turístic. Calvià Agenda Local 21: Observatori sobre sostenibilitat i qualitat de vida: 1997–2000*, www.calvia.org.

Barioulet, H. (2001) *Matrix for Evaluating Tourism Projects on the Basis of Sustainable Tourism Indicators.* www.islandonline.com (accessed 23 February 2004).

Blázquez, M., Murray, I. and Garau, J.M. (2002) *Tercer Boom. Els indicadors de sostenibilitat del turisme a les Illes Balears*, Ciutat de Mallorca: CITTIB.

Certeau, Michael de (1984) *The Practice of Everyday Life.* Berkley: University of California Press.

Charras, Y. and McKenzie, A. (2002) *Cumbria's First Sustainability Report.* Carlisle: Cumbria County Council.

Coccossis, H. (1996) Tourism and Sustainability: Perspectives and Implications. In Priestley, G.K., Edwards, J.A. and Coccossis, H. (eds.), *Sustainable Tourism? European Experiences.* Wallingford: CAB International, pp. 1-21.

Crawford, M. (1992) The World in a Shopping Mall. In Sorkin, M. (Ed.), *Variations on a Theme Park.* New York: Hill and Way, pp. 3-30.

De la Torre, M. and Mason, R. (2002) Introduction. In de la Torre, M. and Mason, R. (eds) *Assessing the Values of Cultural Heritage: Research Report.* Los Angeles: The Getty Conservation Institute, pp. 3-4.

Devon County Council (2003) *Tourism's Everybody's Business: Devon County Council Role and Action Programme*, www.devon.gov.uk.

Farsari, Y. and Prastacos, P. (2000) *Sustainable Tourism Indicators: Pilot Estimation for the Municipality of Hersonissos, Crete*, Hersonissos: Municipality of Hersonissos.

Farsari, Y. and Prastacos, P. (2001) Sustainable Tourism Indicators for Mediterranean Established Destinations. *Tourism Today* 1: 103-121.

Goulding, C. (2000) The Museum Environment and the Visitor Experience. *European Journal of Marketing* 34(3/4): 261-278.

Hannappi-Egger, E. (2002) Cultural Heritage: The Conflict Between Commercialisation and Public Ownership, www.oeaw.act.at.

Harvey, D. (1996) *Justice, Nature, and the Geography of Difference.* London: Blackwell.

Herzfeld, M. (1991) *Place in History: Social and Monumental Time in a Cretan Town.* Princeton: Princeton UP.

Kapiti Coast District Council (1999) *Kapiti Coast State of Environment Report-Heritage,* Kapiti Coast District Council.

Keller, P. (2002) Management of Cultural Change in Tourism Regions and Communities. *International Colloquium on Regional Governance and Sustainable Development in Tourism-driven Economies,* Cancún. www.unpan.org.

Low, S. M. (2002) Anthropological-Ethnographic Methods for the Asssessment of Cultural Values in Heritage Conservation. In de la Torre, M. and Mason, R. (eds) *Assessing the Values of Cultural Heritage: Research Report.* Los Angeles: The Getty Conservation Institute, pp. 31-50.

Magrinyà, F. and Maza, G. (2001) Inmigración y huecos en el centro histórico de Barcelona (1986-2000). *III Col·loqui Internacional de Geocrítica,* Barcelona: Universitat de Barcelona, www.ub.es/menu.html.

Martín Vallés, D. (ed.) (2001) *Tourism and Employment: Improving the Quality of Tourist Products (final report).* Brussels: European Commission.

Martinotti, G. (1993) *Metropoli: la Nuova morfologia sociale.* Bologna: Il mulino.

Mason, R. (2002) Assessing Values in Conservation Planning: Methodological Issues and Choices. In de la Torre, M. and Mason, R. (eds) *Assessing the Values of Cultural Heritage: Research Report.* Los Angeles: The Getty Conservation Institute, pp. 5-31.

Matías Vallés (2003) Entrevista de a Javier Rey-Maqueira. *Diario de Mallorca* (20-9-2003).

Mega, V. and Pedersen, J. (1998) *Urban Sustainability Indicators.* Dublin: European Foundation for the Improvement of Living and Working Conditions.

Pearson, M., D. Johnston, J. Lennon, I. McBryde, D. Marshall, D. Nash and B. Wellington (1998) *Environment Indicators for National State of the Environment Reporting-Natural and Cultural Heritage.* Canberra: Department of the Environment.

Scott, J. (2001) Traditional Places, Modern Products: A Case Study of Tourist Images from the Mediterranean. In *Culture, Man and Tourism: Report on the Asia-Europe Seminar,* Hanoi. www.ulg.ac.be.

Shields, R. (1999) Culture and the Economy of Cities. *European Urban and Regional Studies* 6(4): 303-311.

Smith, V.L. (1989) *Hosts and Guests. The Anthropology of Tourism.* Philadelphia: University of Pennsylvania Press.

Tucker, H. (2000) Tourism and the Loss of Memory in Zelve, Cappadocia. *Oral History* Autumn: 79-88.

Chapter 10

Ecomuseums, Cultural Heritage, Development, and Cultural Tourism in the North of Portugal

Xerardo Pereiro Pérez

THE DEVELOPMENT ROLE OF MUSEUMS AND CULTURAL HERITAGE

After World War II, "development"[1] dominated world politics, but it was not a completely new concept, since it had its origins in the "idea of progress," according to which the only model of improvement of the quality of peoples' lives was the occidental model. "Development" has replaced the previous imperialist and colonialist model, and created another basic concept with which it formed a dichotomy: "underdevelopment." This dichotomy served to characterize the situation of the "Third World" countries, with fewer capital and technological means to exploit their own resources. This model was inspired initially by the modernization theories of the 1950s and 1960s, which defined development as economic growth oriented to the market, a growth that would be sufficient to support the social distribution of wealth. In addition, this model was based on the nation state, it followed a model of growth from the United States and Europe, and it became a permanent feature of national economies.

In the 1970s, theories of independence changed to some extent the concept of development, emphasizing the structural causes of inequality and the unequal exchange between rich and poor countries,

Cultural Tourism: Global and Local Perspectives
© 2007 by The Haworth Press, Inc. All rights reserved.
doi:10.1300/5749_10

promoting state intervention to end these inequalities. By the 1980s the concept of development had changed definition and scale, becoming endogenous, local, and sustainable.[2] In the 1990s critical views of development increased, due essentially to the failure of many of its programs, and some authors started to talk about "postdevelopment" (Rahnema and Bawtree, 1997), characterized by total resistance to externally driven development and the proposal of cultural alternatives by the community. Other authors state that development is "a new version of the colonial system" (Escobar, 1995), which sees nature as a limited good that therefore has economic value and is susceptible to private possession, which made it necessary to abandon this ethnocentric concept. Development is therefore an ideological discourse that denies the importance of the local and the collective, but which is also a historically anchored statement of power, that flows "to" and not "from" the people and the diversity of human groups.

In Europe, development became more oriented to a rural world that was experiencing deep transformation. We can see how concepts like "community organization"[3] arose in the context of rural European development, to create a distinction with community development in nonoccidental contexts. If "community development" was applicable to the economically dependent and underdeveloped countries included in the "Third World" and to the former colonies of the European countries, it was as part of an effort to make these countries participate in economic and social development plans created in the developed world. On the contrary, "community organization" indicated grassroots efforts to organize and resolve problems locally, and make their needs and demands known to the competent authorities. "Community organization" was wrongly associated with the people of the industrialized and "rich" countries as well as with urban populations.

In this line of community organization, rural development in Europe experienced a very important impulse after 1962, with the creation of the Common Agricultural Policy (CAP), and in 1974 with the establishment of the European Regional Development Fund (ERDF). The purpose of the ERDF was to manage, together with other European institutions, the "regional equilibrium and the development of the economic and social structures" of the member countries, through the so-called Structural and Cohesion Funds, granted initially to Portugal, Spain, and Greece. Policies changed from a productive model, at the time of the birth of the EU, to a "conservation" model, especially with the application of the Leader II Program of rural development (1994-1999), which granted to the rural world and its inhabitants a more environmental program. These narratives of power were elaborated in the hegemonic urban world without taking into account the social actors and the right to diversity, by asking the farmers to stop producing and to dedicate themselves to serving the tourists and to taking care of the new "garden."

The role of museums and cultural heritage in these processes of development was of great importance in Europe, especially after the 1970s. For instance, in England there were 500 local ethnographic museums in the 1980s (Walsh, 1992); these represented a cultural reply to the severe industrial crisis. Another important example was the case of France, where the concept of the "ecomuseum"[4] was developed, connected to the politics of natural parks, to overcome the agrarian crisis of rural regions.

In the Iberian Peninsula the use of cultural heritage as a development strategy took place later than in France and England, and is only now being discussed and debated. Iberian museums and cultural heritage appear increasingly connected to cultural tourism and to an urbanizing agricultural world (see Pereiro Peréz, 2003, 2005). The museums change because of the new requirements and cultural politics, and stop being predominantly places of conservation to turn themselves into "chronotypes" of cultural heritage interpretation, while being a symbolic representation of culture for visitors.

THE ECOMUSEU DO BARROSO
AS A CULTURAL TOURISM PROJECT

The use of culture and cultural heritage as resources, products, and experiences has motivated the growth of cultural tourism (Pereiro Peréz, 2002), so that many cultural resources, such as ecomuseums, end up being converted into manufactured products for cultural tourist consumption. This process, also highlighted by authors such as Richards (1996; 2001) or Craik (1997), has also diversified the types of tourism and of tourists.

From this point of view we can understand the Ecomuseu do Barroso as a process of conversion of the rural space and of rurality into tourist-cultural products. In this new cycle of production what is offered is an anthropological "other" ("native," "exotic," "different". . .), that is, a cultural heritage that represents symbolic identities and an experience of acquiring cultural capital. I believe that this is an old process, but with new means, functions, and structures that enlarge and democratize the educative experience of cultural tourism. In this way cultural tourism grows not only through the tourist search for authenticity in late modernity, but also through the growth of cultural and heritage attractions (Richards, 1996:14; Richards, 2001) built to restructure areas in socialeconomic crisis. Therefore cultural tourism increases and the conservation of the natural and cultural heritage increases at the same time (Zeppel and Hall, 1991).

In what context does the Ecomuseu do Barroso fit? In the 1970s the "environment," the territory, the population, and the cultural heritage started to be part of the museum concept (Iniesta, 1994:95-97), leading to the formulation of the ecomuseum (Riviére, 1993) as a mirror of community identity, a laboratory of inquiry, conservatory, and school. In Portugal this new idea, promoted by the new museology, was disseminated a little later, connected to the development policies of the natural and national parks. It was 1982 before the first ecomuseum, the Ecomuseum do Seixal (Dias, 1997:65-70) was opened in the metropolitan area of Lisbon. Promoted by the autarchy, this ecomuseum represents a fundamental icon of the anthropological museology of the country. Years later the ecomuseum concept began to spread around the country.

The Barroso is situated in the north of Portugal, in the Trás-os-Montes region on the border with Galiza (Galicia, Spain). It is in a micro region that includes the municipalities of Boticas and Montalegre and forms part of the Alto Tâmega, a geographic and cultural territory that incorporates the municipalities of Boticas, Chaves, Montalegre, Ribeira de Pena, Valpaços, and Vila Pouca de Aguiar.

From the point of view of local identity, the Alto Tâmega, a small territory of 2,922 square kilometers, divides itself in two subunits: the Alto Tâmega—Chaves, Valpaços, Vila Pouca de Aguiar, and Ribeira de Pena—and the Barroso—Montalegre and Boticas. This is also the image the tourist promotion of the region offers of the Alto Tâmega and Barroso, which in general matches that of the basin of the Portuguese Alto Tâmega.

The demographic profile of the Alto Tâmega presents a landscape with losses of population in the last 20 years. In particular, the Barroso lost 31.84 percent of its population between 1981 and 2001. It should be pointed out that the pace of this loss has decreased since 1991 and that on the Galician side of the border the demographic losses are greater than on the Portuguese side (Tables 10.1 to 10.4).

TABLE 10.1. Population living in Alto Tâmega (1981-2001).

Municipality	1981	1991	2001	Variation 1981-2001
Boticas	8,773	7,936	6,411	−22,362
Chaves	45,883	40,940	43,558	−22,325
Montalegre	19,403	15,464	12,792	−26,611
Ribeira de Pena	10,796	8,504	7,406	−23,390
Valpaços	26,066	22,586	19,374	−26,692
Vila Pouca de Aguiar	20,121	17,081	14,962	−25,159
Total	131,042	112,511	104,503	−226,539 (−20.25%)

Source: INE (National Statistic Institute).

TABLE 10.2. Territorial distribution of the population in Alto Tâmega.

Municipality	Km^2	No. of parishes	Km^2 per parish	Inhabitants per Km^2 in 2001
Boticas	322	16	20.2	23.7
Chaves	590	50	11.8	68.2
Montalegre	806	35	23	17.8
Ribeira de Pena	218	7	31.1	37.4
Valpaços	553	31	17.8	39.4
Vila Pouca de Aguiar	433	17	25.5	38.2
Total	2,922	156	18.73	35.76

Source: INE (1996).

TABLE 10.3. Territorial distribution of the population in Limia (Galiza).

Municipality	Km²	No. of parishes	Km² per parish	Inhabitants per Km² in 2001
Calvos de Randín	97.97	9	10.88	12.84
Baltar	93.90	7	13.41	13.25
Cualedro	117.50	10	11.75	20.86
Os Blancos	47.40	7	6.77	26.79
Xinzo de Limia	132.30	20	6.61	74.34
Total	489.07	53	9.22	32.83

Source: Galician Statistic Institute (IGE, 2001) and own data.

TABLE 10.4. Population variation in Limia (Galiza).

Municipality	1981	1991	2001	Variation 1981-2001
Calvos de Randín	2,074	2,044	1,258	–2,786
Baltar	4,018	1,867	1,245	–22,773
Cualedro	5,642	2,658	2,452	–23,190
Os Blancos	2,216	1,272	1,270	–2,946
Xinzo de Limia	10,544	9,170	9,836	–2,708
Total	24,494	17,011	16,061	–28,433 (–232.42%)

Source: IGE and own data.

It is in the municipality of Montalegre where the idea of the creation of the Ecomuseu do Barroso was born. Montalegre has the longest border with Galiza (municipalities of Calvos de Randín, Baltar, and Cualedro). There is a considerable body of literature on the Barroso region, including Lourenço Fontes, 1992; Da Cruz, 2000; Rocha, 2001; Dias Guimarães, 2002; Santos Dias, 2002; see also www.cm-montalegre.espigueiro.pt. The idea of creating the Ecomuseu do Barroso arose in the 1980s, but was not effected until the year 2001 (Dr. João Azenha and Dr. David Teixeira, personal communication, 2003):

With an investment of one thousand million escudos—Fernando Rodrigues promises an Ecomuseum.

The Ecomuseu do Barroso, approved in the last meeting of the Town Hall, is a project of "harmonious development" in the areas of environment and heritage, from which comprises several initiatives. This is the way that the Lord Mayor of Montalegre, Fernando Rodrigues, defines it. These initiatives, many of which are still "ideas," are going to cost approximately one thousand million escudos (€5,000,000). However, some units that will be created are already outlined. For example, the thematic park of the Minas da Borralha, which will preserve the heritage of the wolfram mines, as well as all the documents related to the history of the mines, which, according to the mayor, might be used as a basis for investigators and scholars to study the subject. The creation of small poles in other places, as for example, a *museu da raia,* to portray the activity of smuggling, or the territorial unit of Rabagão, that will be dedicated to the subject of water. The central nucleus of the ecomuseum will be in the headquarters of the municipality, from the restoration of the castle towers and of some houses. Another of the emblematic creations of the ecomuseum will be the so-called Casa do Habitat. We are talking about a set of the ancient and most representative houses of the municipality that are going to be restored. A technical structure of information will be created that will also function as a kind of training school in the area of heritage preservation. But this investment "will only make sense if it gathers the population involvement and contributes to the local economy," said Fernando Rodrigues, to conclude that this is a project that has to "move people." The dynamization and spreading of these ideas is being undertaken by a team created to carry out the project. (in *Diário de Trás-os-Montes,* 22-06-2001)

We have to emphasize that the ecomuseum is a political, social, and economical instrument. Following the thesis of Mary Bouquet (2001:1) the museum "boom" was related to the objectivization and the politicization of culture. Before that, it was the Frenchman Hugues de Varine (1993:393) who propagated in Rivière the thesis that the ecomuseum was a political instrument for the people. The political dimension is verified in its origin, in an initiative of the Town Hall,[5] which commissioned a study from the company Quaternaire Portugal (Pérez Babo, 2001), who employed Hugues de Varine as external consultant. This strategy of giving a scientific view to the project will be present throughout the implementation process. This study is going to be carried out by local technicians in a realistic and pragmatic form, since they are the implementers of the proposal and they are the ones with expertise on the local context.

Economic factors were also taken into account at the beginning of the project, along with social and political dimensions. The constant concern of the politician to know "How much does it cost?" leads to a constant search for partners, mainly Galician, in order to secure European[6] funds. Economic benefits are also intimately associated with a strategy of tourist development, for which the ecomuseum represents an attraction or icon for tourists and hikers. It is true that tourism has some quantitative importance but it is much more important from the qualitative point of view and its contribution to employment and the diversification of the local economy. Tourism is more and more connected to activities such as fishing, hunting, paragliding, etc., but we cannot forget that part of the municipality of Montalegre is within the National Park of the Peneda-Gerês, a fundamental tourist area for the municipality (see Tables 10.5 and 10.6). Therefore, from this point of view the ecomuseum is considered a necessary tourist-cultural product for the social-economic development of the area.

In terms of social impacts, the ecomuseum must perform a very important social role if it is to mediate between the places, the visitors, the tourists, the school, the university, and the public authority. Based on this last perspective, the ecomuseum can be thought of as an instrument of symbolic reproduction of society (Iniesta, 1994:18) that produces cultural images (Pereiro Peréz and Vilar, 2002), which convey an ideological discourse of identities.

TABLE 10.5. Number of visitors to the tourism office of Montalegre, 1998 and 1999.

Visitor origin	Portugal	Spain	France	UK	Germany	Holland
1998	939	105	107	61	27	8
1999	1433	121	108	64	14	15

Source: Tourism Office of Montalegre.

TABLE 10.6. Tourism accommodation supply in Montalegre.

Accommodation	Establishments	Rooms	Approximate price/night
Hotels	1	42	55-89 euros
Inns and guest houses	2	34	45-90 euros
Boarding houses and residences	1	7	20-30 euros
Rural tourism	3	23	25-80 euros
Private houses	1	6	80 euros

Source: Own data.

The ecomuseum can be an instrument for or a project of the community that awakens and stimulates community participation. In the first case, the ecomuseum would follow the paradigm of cultural democratization (López de Ceballos and Salas Larrazábal, 1988:25) according to which the ecomuseum would supply the population with knowledge and know-how about a legitimate cultural legacy. It would be a museum of visitors, spectators, and consumers. It is what we call in Spain "cultural extension" and in Portugal "community extension." In the second case the paradigm of the definition is derived from cultural democracy (López de Ceballos and Salas Larrazábal, 1988:25); that is, the ecomuseum would work as an institution that involves the community as an active producer of its culture as well as of its cultural heritage. In this second paradigm, the ecomuseum belongs to the inhabitants, producers, and active and conscientious citizens of the region. Thus the ecomuseum would become an institution that would redistribute cultural power through anti-anomie and animation strategies.

THE FESTA DA MALHADA AND THE ROTA DOS ARTESÃOS: ECOMUSEUM, COMMUNITY, AND CULTURAL TOURISM

In the spring of 2002, after having successfully launched a proposal for contributing to the Ecomuseu do Barroso, we started to program our cooperation work. We were asked to cooperate in the organization of the festival Festa da Malhada in the village of Paredes do Rio (parish of Covelães) and to organize the Rota dos Artesãos (crafts route) on the same day as the festival, which was celebrating its second edition. The fieldwork in a village of nearly ninety inhabitants began during the month of July, and was based on key informants chosen by the community itself as representative of local expertise. Our work consisted, in the beginning, of gaining the confidence of the people of the village, so that soon we could produce reflexive memories of "traditional craft" knowledge: the weaver, basket maker, blacksmith, carpenter, mason, wooden shoemaker, baker, etc. With time, people, especially the most elderly, started to appreciate our work, and in a second phase we produced an audiovisual ethnography of the crafts, which constituted, without doubt, a great event for the people of the village, but it also served as an instrument of mediation and to reflect the application and return of the anthropologic knowledge produced. In this way, we tried to democratize the research and to deconstruct the cold and distant visions between subject and object to materialize a project of recovery of the value of the people and its knowledge as a main element of cultural heritage.

We must point out that the ritual process of staying overnight allowed us to overcome the initial distrust of the locals and also to surpass the "journalistic" and "neo-folklore" visions so typical as an interpretation of life in rural areas. After a time, people from the village of Paredes do Rio knew us better than they knew the engineers of the Parque Nacional da Peneda Gerês, which reveals the distance between subject-object of development practiced by some institutions (Escobar, 1995).

The Festa da Malhada and the Rota dos Artesãos were celebrated on August 10 and 11, 2002, under the organization of the Board of Covelães Parish and the Association of Paredes do Rio, together with the cooperation of the Parque Nacional da Peneda-Gerês and the Ecomuseu do Barroso. By participating in the festival, the locals harvested the crops and participated in the treshing of the rye; they celebrated their identity and interpreted their culture to friends and visitors. The village inhabitants conscientiously avoided the simple neo-folklore vision of the event, not dressing as in the old times but in modern clothes, defending their right to a worthy cultural change. In the two days of celebration we could observe and participate in the mowing, in the "carrada da messe," in the "emedar da messe," in the threshing, and in the rota dos artesãos. In these activities, the participation and the involvement of the community had already been intense for some weeks; strengthened even more by our fieldwork, which converted the traditional "objects of research" into subjects and agents of the inquiry process. At this point, we want to criticize the emptiness of concepts such as "participation" and "community involvement" that are often equated with the number of spectators or visitors (Herrero Prieto et al., 2001) and sometimes with the simple delivery of objects to the museum.

In the Rota dos Artesãos crafts objects were not thought of as artifacts to be seen and not touched in the passive, monotonous, and distant manner of a conventional museum (García Canclini, 1989:152); the locals and the visitors could participate in specific productive processes such as sawing or making overcoats of straw, in the original context of production. Also, in some cases the craft products, such as bread, straw overcoats, miniatures of wooden ploughs, etc. had been sold as decorative objects for private appropriation. This commercialization of old cultural products adapted for new markets creates new cycles of production and consumption that provide economic support to their producers. In addition, the consumer can connect the object to the person who produced it, and the context of production itself, without the need for intermediaries. In this way, the consumer understands better the meaning of the craft object, diminishing the fetishist way of seeing the object (Guidieri, 1997) and its decorative simulacrum (Baudrillard, 1981:15).

Far from the simple spontaneous creation of the people defined from a romantic vision that imagined pure communities, far also from being a simple process of conversion of memory into merchandise or displays for tourists, or consumers of exotic images (García Canclini, 1989), collective participation has been fundamental in the Festa da Malhada festival of the Ecomuseu do Barroso. We are conscious that the tourist-carrying capacity of a territory can be debilitated by the excess of programmed consumption, something that did not happen in the case of the festival, which promoted more fluid, intense, and rich communication between local people and visitors, who were invited to participate in work, the sharing of knowledge, food, and memories. We think that this factor is basic to encourage an alternative form of tourism, based on sociability and on the exchange of symmetrical experiences between host and guest (Smith, 1989), but also on the experience of a cultural practice re-created in its context by its protagonists. The ecomuseum becomes in this way a laboratory of meanings, sociabilities, and emotions, and not only a simple institution of management and administration of resources.

Through the involvement of the community, the ecomuseum has become a place of mediation and meeting between the young and old in the village, between residents and emigrants who return for their summer holidays, between people from the village and the city, between Portuguese and Galician people. Equally, this space of mediation serves to renew and to re-create the limits of the community, expressing also identity tensions with neighboring villages and populations.[7]

The involvement of the community also showed how the communities remember (Connerton, 1989): "It is very good that they remember the old things" (woman, about 80 years old, Sunday, 11-8-2002, participating in the threshing). This expresses well the idea that the ecomuseum can serve as a mnemonic-social instrument to aid in remembering collectively and also to recognize a debt toward the past. Thus, these activities promoted by the ecomuseum together with the communities are a way of supporting collective effort, and also they are a symbolic use of the memory that tries to create social cohesion. In this way, the heirs to the cultural heritage are involved in its maintenance.

In the third edition of the festival, in 2003, its meanings were strengthened: "Remembering traditions" (man, 80 years, 9-8-2003) and creating communitarian animation became its primary objectives. Celebrated in the summer, the festival served to strengthen the bonds of the community, not only of the residents, each time fewer and older, but also of the people who had emigrated to the Portuguese cities or to France. The festival also served to politically affirm the role of the autarchy and of the Parish Board toward the population of the village, their presence and ritual participation defining the political importance of these events, not only because they serve to remember traditions of the past, but also to remember the present, who governs and who wants to govern. The visitors and the tourists, among them a group of 50 Slovenian Boy Scouts, had a shared investment in the success of the event, and recognizing the visitors, their participation, involvement, and return, year after year, strengthens the value of the cultural activity. The tourists had the chance to make contact with the people of the village and their reinvented and re-created cultural practices. This is a cultural tourism practice that we teach to the visitors and that does not have a negative impact on the community because the local people control their own cultural resources. The major innovation in 2003 was the fact that the visitors had to pay for participating in the festival. This is another expression of the processes of mercantilization that culture is exposed to. So, for example, the idea of closing the village at weekends is being debated, so that the visitors would pay to see the work of the local artisans, who in reality are farmers.

CULTURAL HERITAGE, TOURISM, AND CROSS-BORDER DEVELOPMENT

The Ecomuseu do Barroso is a cultural tourism project that can only be understood in the context of the global politics of rural spaces, its cross-border context, and more concretely in its relations with Galiza. The museum cooperates occasionally with Galician as well as Portuguese universities, and even museums and other institutions on both sides of the border. The opportunities and needs for local financing motivate the launching of projects of transregional and transnational cooperation through European programs such as Interreg. The new European picture is, this way, changing the life of the people who live around the decreasingly national borders, rebuilding transnational and pan-European identities.

Beyond the international politics of development, the cosmopolitan vision of local development agents also regulates projects for disseminating our culture to tourists and their implementation. During our work with the Ecomuseu do Barroso, we had the chance to participate in cross-border activities with Portuguese and Galician technicians and politicians. This experience has helped us to think about the problems associated with the binomial tourism-culture. Here are some of them:

1. The first problem of cross-border cooperation is one of linguistic communication, which in the Portuguese and Galician case is reduced by linguistic proximity, the Galician language being closely related to Portuguese. The problems get more complicated when we are dealing with non-Galician Spanish technicians who ignore the linguistic codes of Galician-Portuguese, compelling the Galicians and Portuguese to undertake cultural translation for them. The Portuguese and the Galicians normally understand the Spanish much better than the Spanish understand the Galicians or the Portuguese.

2. The second problem that we observe is the lack of training and education in cultural tourism and heritage. This limits the projects a lot, because without the capacity to interpret the ways of life of communities, we can hardly help to improve their conditions of life.

3. The third observed problem is the creation of similar cultural products in neighboring municipalities, without any coordination of supply. There is a process of mimesis and uncritical imitation of neighboring examples. This leads to very similar, undifferentiated, and disorganized tourist-cultural offer. For example, in a cross-border proposal for the program Interreg III-A, the municipality of Muíños (Galiza) proposed renovating several ovens, exactly the same activity as the neighboring municipalities of Calvos de Randín (Galiza) and Montalegre (Portugal). In the same proposal, all the Galician municipalities wanted to create an ethnographic museum, as opposed to the Portuguese idea of an "ecomuseum." The four municipalities involved (Muíños, Calvos de Randín, Baltar, and Montalegre) intended to create belvederes, centers of tourist information, and parks.

4. The projects are normally conceived of in terms of infrastructure, but with little or no cultural programming. The result is the creation of facilities empty of content, poorly used, and without positive impacts on the local communities and tourists. People think that the simple architectural restoration of an old oven is sufficient to encourage tourists to visit it.

5. When we speak of cultural heritage, technicians tend to reduce it to the constructed heritage, reducing in this way the community's role as well as its needs: "We do not thank you for fixing the oven but for getting them a job" (development agent, about 40 years old, Montalegre, 7-10-2002).

In synthesis, cultural tourism appears in the cross-border context of Transmontano-Galego as a strategy of development to address the depopulation of rural areas and the difficult socioeconomic situation, problems shared by the two sides of the border, although they have different strategies for dealing with them. In the Portuguese case, the Ecomuseu do Barroso is a response to emigration—the abandonment of the countryside and the difficult terrain—that sees culture as a tool of integral development. The da Malhada festival in Paredes do Rio, in the context of the activities of the ecomuseum, represents an experience of contact and intercultural communication between the urban world and the rural world, toward which a debt is recognized.

In the present case we neither destroy the local cultures nor do we put the people in zoos; however, alternative forms of ethical and responsible cultural tourism are developed so that cultural and heritage resources are not seen exclusively as tourism resources. These resources are converted into products, but cannot be consumed the same way as other types of products, because they essentially consist of human experience and the active transmission of a lived culture.

NOTES

1. It is also relevant that the 1948 "Cambridge Conference on African Administration," sponsored by the "British Colonial Office," used the concept of "community development" instead of "mass education" for the first time. So the concept had a colonial root, and it was intimately connected to comunitarian education and social work with comunities. See Willigen, J. V. (1986:94). On the different theories of the development, see the syntheses by Monreal and Gimeno (1999) and Fernández de Larrinoa, K. (2000).

2. "A process of change in which the resources exploitation, the investments direction, the technological development orientation, and the institutional changes are consequent with the present and future needs" (WCED, 1987:9).

3. The communitarian organization appeared as a concept in 1955, emphasizing the notion of process. "The communitarian organization . . . is a process thanks to which a community can identify its needs or goals, it gives them an order of priority, adds trust in itself, and willing to work to satisfy those needs or goals, finds the internal and/or external resources to its achievement or satisfaction, acts toward those needs or those goals, and manifests attitudes and cooperation practices in the community" (Ross, 1955:40).

4. In 1971 a working lunch took place in Paris in which H. Varine, Riviere, and Berge Antoine-adviser of the environment minister Robert Poujade—were present. In September 1971, Robert Poujade enumerated the concept of the "ecomuseum" in the ninth ICOM conference. The concept is marked by initiatives in favor of the sustained development and in harmony with the environment:

- Ecological orientation
- Instrument for the popular participation
- Territorial regulation
- Population conscious awareness
- Situates objects in its context, preserves local skils and knowledge, educates, and makes people aware of the value of the cultural heritage

According to Lévi-Strauss, the origin of the ecomuseums goes back to the nineteenth century, to the universal exhibitions of 1867 and 1889. The fundamental concern was toward the daily reproduction and the ways of living. In the nineteenth century the main perspective was spatial (different human groups at the same time but in different places); nowadays the main concern is with time (different societies in the same space but at different times). Ecomuseums are therefore characterized by a number of features:

- Time is seen in its different dimensions: past, present, and future.
- An ecomuseum interprets the different spaces that make up a landscape.
- It should have a lab where historic and anthropological studies are made, but also specialist training and other functions.
- A conservation institute dedicated to the valorization of cultural and natural heritage.
- A scale in which the populations would participate in the resource and protection actions, teaching them to be aware to their problems and to participate actively in their resolution.
- It is very important to remember that word "ecomuseum" is only a word, since all the museums can develop programs of popular participation and contribute to the community development.

An ecomuseum is closely articulated with ethnological heritage.

See Riviére (1989).
    5. See www.espigueiro.pt/noticias.
    6. Since the implementation of the "Ecomuseu do Barroso," applications to the European Programme INTERREG have been prepared, one of them with the municipality of Sarria (Lugo-Galiza) subordinated to the theme of Tracks of Santiago de Compostela (See newspaper "El Progreso" de Lugo, 8-8-2002), another with Calvos de Randín, Muíños and Baltar (Ourense- Galiza), subordinated to the theme "Couto Mixto," a kind of Galician-Portuguese "Andorra" till the end of the nineteenth century. On this case see García Mañá (1988; 1996; 2000).

7. The name of the parish is Covelães, constituted by two villages, Paredes do Rio and Covelães, that compete with each other for the Parish Board. As a result of this identity tension, only a few people from Covelães have participated in the threshing in Paredes do Rio.

In the weekend that followed the threshing in Paredes do Rio (2002), in the parish of the villa another threshing was organized so that, according to one of the organizers, it would be much more "authentic" since it would follow more "traditional" patterns than those from Paredes do Rio on how to use traditional clothing. This is a social mimetic process very common in the invention and fabrication of traditions.

REFERENCES

Baudrillard, J. (1981/1972) *Para uma crítica da economia política do signo.* Lisboa: Edições 70.

Bouquet, M. (ed.) (2001) *Academic Anthropology and the Museum: Back to the Future.* Oxford: Berghahn Books.

Carretero Pérez, A. (1999) Museos etnográficos e imágenes de la cultura. In Aguilar Criado, E. (ed.) *Patrimonio Etnológico. Nuevas perspectivas de estudio.* Sevilla: IAPH Junta de Andalucía, pp. 94-109.

Connerton, P. (1989) *How Societies Remember.* Cambridge: Cambridge University Press.

Craik, J. (1997) The culture of tourism. In Rojek, C. and Urry, J. (eds) *Touring Cultures: Transformations of Travel and Theory.* London: Routledge, pp. 113-136.

Da Cruz, B. (2000) *A Loba.* Vigo: Xerais.

De Varine, H. (1993 /1989) La participación de la población. In Rivière, G. H. (ed.) *La museología. Curso de museología. Textos y testimonios.* Madrid: Akal, pp. 392-395.

Dias, N. (1997) *Roteiro de Museus. Lisboa e Vale do Tejo.* Lisboa: Olhapim Edições.

Dias, N. (2001) Does anthropology need museums? Teaching ethnographic museology in Portugal thirty years later. In Bouquet, M. (ed.) *Academic Anthropology and the Museum: Back to the Future.* Oxford: Berghahn Books, pp. 92-104.

Dias Guimarães, R. (2002) *O falar do Barroso.* Montalegre: Câmara Municipal.

Escobar, A. (1995) *Encountering Development.* Princeton: Princeton University Press.

Fernández de Larrinoa, K. (2000) *La cosecha pendiente. De la intervención económica a la infraestructura cultural y comunitaria en el medio rural.* Madrid: Los Libros de la Catarata.

García Canclini, N. (1989) *Las culturas populares en el capitalismo.* México: Nueva Imagen.

García Mañá, L. M. (1988) *La frontera hispano-lusa en la provincia de Ourense.* Ourense: Boletín Auriense-Museo Arqueológico de Ourense.

García Mañá, L. M. (1996) Apuntes sobre a evolución da fronteira Galego-Portuguesa. *Boletín do Instituto de Estudios Vigueses* 2, pp. 231-239.

García Mañá, L. M. (2000) *O Couto Mixto: Unha República Esquecida*. Vigo: Universidade de Vigo.

Guidieri, R. (1997/1992) *El museo y sus fetiches. Crónica de lo neutro y de la aureola*. Madrid: Tecnos.

Herrero Prieto, L. C., Terroso Cepeda, F., Figueira, J. J., and Odette Fernandes, P. (2001) Diagnóstico socioeconómico y valoración del turismo cultural de museos. In Nieto González, J. R., Serrano-Piedecasas Fernández, L. and Herrero Prieto, L. C. (eds) *El patrimonio histórico en el río Duero*. Zamora: Fundación Rei Afonso Henriques.

Iniesta I González, M. (1994) *Els gabinets del món. Antropología, museus i museologies*. Lleida: Pagès Editors.

Iniesta I González, M. (1999) Museos locales, patrimonios globales. In Aguilar Criado, E. (ed.) *Patrimonio Etnológico. Nuevas perspectivas de estudio*. Sevilla: IAPH Junta de Andalucía, pp. 110-129.

Jamin, J. (1993/1989) El museo de etnografía en 1930: la etnología como ciencia y como política. In Rivière, G. H. *La museología. Curso de museología. Textos y testimonios*. Madrid: Akal, pp. 161-170.

López de Ceballos, P. and Salas Larrazábal, M. (1988) *Formación de animadores y dinámicas de la animación*. Madrid: Popular.

Lourenço Fontes, A. (1992) *Etnografia Transmontana*. Vol. 1: Crenças e tradições do Barroso. Lisboa: Editorial Domingos Barreira.

Monreal, P. and Gimeno, J. C. (eds.) (1999) *La controversia del desarrollo. Críticas desde la antropología*. Madrid: Los Libros de la Catarata.

Pereiro Pérez, X. (2002) Turismo cultural: Leituras da antropologia. *Actas do I Congresso Internacional de Turismo Cultural*. Buenos Aires: NAYA.

Pereiro Pérez, X. (2003) Patrimonialização e transformação das identidades Culturais. In Portela, J. and Castro Caldas, J. (eds) *Portugal Chão*. Oeiras: Celta editora, pp. 231-247.

Pereiro Pérez, X. (2005) *Galegos de vila. Antropoloxía dun espazo rurbano*. Santiago de Compostela: Sotelo Blanco.

Pereiro Pérez, X. and Vilar Álvarez, M. (2002) Autoimágenes y heteroimágenes en los museos etnográficos gallegos. *Actas del IX Congreso de Antropología del Estado Español*. Barcelona: Federación de Asociaciones de Antropología del Estado Español.

Pérez Babo, E. (eds.) (2001) *Estudo de concepção e de programação do Ecomuseu do Barroso* (unpublished manuscript).

Rahnema, M. and Bawtree, V. (eds.) (1997) *The Post-Development Reader*. London: Zed Books.

Richards, G. (1996) *Cultural Tourism in Europe*. Wallingford: CAB International.

Richards, G. (2001) The development of cultural tourism in Europe. In Richards, G. (ed.): *Cultural Attractions and European Tourism*. Wallingford: CAB International, pp. 3-29.

Rivière, G. H. (1993/1989) *La museología. Curso de museología. Textos y testimonios*. Madrid: Akal, pp. 392-395.

Rocha, J. G. (ed.) (2001) *Barroso e suas Histórias de Vida*. Montalegre: Câmara Municial.

Ross, M. G. (1955) *Community Organization: Theory, Principles and Practice.* New York: Harper International.

Santos Dias, M. A. (2002) *Montalegre. Terras de Barroso.* Montalegre: Câmara Municipal de Montalegre.

Smith, V.L. (1989) *Hosts and Guests: The Anthropology of Tourism.* Philadelphia: University of Pennsylvania Press.

Sturtevant, W. (1969) Does Anthropology Need Museums? *Proceedings of the Biological Society of Washington* 82: 619-650.

Walsh, K. (1992) *The Representation of the Past: Museums and Heritage in the Post-modern World.* London: Routledge.

WCED (1987) *Our Common Future.* Oxford: Oxford University Press.

Willigen, J. V. (1986) *Applied Anthropology: An Introduction.* South Hadley: Bergin and Garvey Publishers.

Zeppel, H. and Hall, C.M. (1991) Selling art and history: Cultural heritage and tourism. *Journal of Tourism Studies* 2 (1): 29-45.

Chapter 11

Religious Tourism in Northern Portugal

Greg Richards
Carlos Fernandes

INTRODUCTION

Tourism related to religious sites and festivals, pilgrimage, or spirituality is a long-established and extremely important sector of the tourism market. For specific sites, such as the major pilgrimage sites of the major world religions, religious tourism may be the primary activity of a city or region. But religious sites provide an important underpinning to the basic tourism product even outside pilgrimage destinations, as cathedrals, churches, and monasteries often generate significant numbers of visitors, including those not traveling directly for religious purposes. One of the main challenges for religious tourism, however, reflects a basic problem of many traditional churches. The declining influence of many major religions in the daily lives of people means that the orientation toward religious sites or events may also change.

But perhaps paradoxically, the decline in traditional churchgoing in Europe in recent years has been paralleled in many cases by a growing interest in religion and religious travel. The reason for this seems simple: People are searching for meaning in their increasingly uncertain lives. Many people have not been able to find this through traditional forms of worship, so they are now taking to different forms of experience to find it. This includes the rediscovery of pilgrimage or journeys to sacred places.

Cultural Tourism: Global and Local Perspectives
© 2007 by The Haworth Press, Inc. All rights reserved.
doi:10.1300/5749_11

Like anything else in life, pilgrimage can be a routine experience, but in its most authentic expression it is thought to be a spiritually transforming journey. These journeys can involve extremely large numbers of people. There are also new forms of pilgrimage being developed alongside the traditional, ancient forms. This indicates that religious tourism is a far from simple concept. Before looking in more detail at the supply and demand for religious tourism in Northern Portugal, therefore, we will turn our attention briefly to the question of definition.

WHAT IS RELIGIOUS TOURISM?

In view of the fact that such journeys are obviously a combination of a religious experience and travel, it would be easy to characterize all visits to religious sites as religious tourism. But definitions of religious tourism based simply on a combination of "religion" and "tourism" are of little help in understanding the phenomenon. It is far more useful, for example, to try and understand what concepts such as "religion" or "pilgrimage" mean. In this way, one can also understand more closely what drives the tourist to travel.

Although it's not easy to define in simple terms, religion can best be described as a system of beliefs in a higher being that are held with great faith and commitment. There is a universal belief in a higher being in all religions, including those of Christian, Jewish, and Buddhist faiths.

> The religious sense is nothing more than man's [*sic*] original nature, by which he fully expresses himself by asking "ultimate" questions, searching for the final meaning of existence in all of its hidden facets and implications. (Giussani, 1997)

The fact that religion is so hard to define is one reason why religious tourism has had a relatively low profile in the past. Although people may be traveling for reasons related to religion or spirituality, such as a quest for meaning, they may not see this as being directly religious. These religious or spiritual travelers are therefore also not picked up by traditional tourism surveys, and much domestic religious tourism also goes unnoticed.

The number of tourists traveling purely for religious reasons is relatively small. Many studies conclude that spiritual motivations for engaging in pilgrimage outweigh religious ones. For example, even the pilgrims traveling to Santiago de Compostella do not all see themselves as traveling for religious reasons. Santos (2002) reports that the proportion of pilgrims indicating a religious motivation is about 50 percent, with perhaps a further 20 percent having a mixed "religious-cultural" motivation.

In addition, many of the trips usually seen as cultural tourism often involve a visit to a religious site. Data collected in France in 2002, for example, indicate that almost 40 percent of individual cultural tourists had visited a religious monument in the previous two years (AFIT, 2002). This rose to almost 50 percent for those traveling in tour groups (who also tend to be older on average). These people would not generally be seen as religious tourists, however, because their motivation for visiting a religious site is probably more cultural. This is also underlined in the relatively short visits paid by most cultural tourists to religious sites. Religious sites often have little to offer the casual visitor in terms of interpretation, animation, or other elements that could prolong the visit. This is perhaps not surprising in view of the pressure to maintain the authenticity of religious sites.

Another problem with quantifying the religious tourism "market" is that much religious tourism bypasses the traditional distribution channels of the tourism industry. Specialist religious travel companies cater to the needs of pilgrims, dealing directly with accommodation providers at the major pilgrimage sites. Because pilgrims have been seen as a market that is difficult to influence, they have also been overlooked in terms of tourism marketing, except in the case of major pilgrimage destinations. Not surprisingly, this relative lack of attention by the tourism industry has also led to a relative dearth of academic research in the area. This situation is now beginning to change as the significance of religious tourism is recognized in academic circles. The staging of the ATLAS Religious Tourism Expert Meeting in Fátima in April 2003 is a clear indication of this growing interest (Fernandes et al., 2004).

These problems indicate that a new approach is needed for defining and analyzing religious tourism, which gets away from the very narrow definitions used in official statistics.

It is clear that not all religious tourists are the same. This is also recognized in many academic studies of religious tourism, which often identify a continuum of motivations related to religious travel. Cohen (2001:14) discusses the distinction between "pilgrims" and "tourists," and points out that the simple dichotomy between the two is no longer tenable. He suggests that one needs to distinguish between domestic and foreign tourists, and that religious tourists form a separate category between pilgrims and tourists. In Cohen's study of the Chinese Vegetarian Festival in Phuket in Thailand, he characterizes pilgrims as those who are worshiping devotees of the gods for whom the festival is celebrated, while tourists are seen as "spectators who are attracted by the exotic character of some of the ritual events, but remain uninvolved, neither believing nor taking part in the ritual proceedings." Religious tourists, on the other hand, are those who come to observe but who will also occasionally engage in worship. The religious tourist in particular is in an ambivalent position, sometimes experiencing the festival as a spectacle, but also sometimes experiencing its transformatory effects.

This distinction between pilgrimage and tourism is one repeated by many other authors. For example, Murray and Graham (1997:514) define pilgrimage as "a religious phenomenon in which an individual or group sets forth on a journey to a particular cult location to seek the intercession of God and the saints of that place in an array of concerns." However, this definition of pilgrimage tends to ignore the importance of the journey in pilgrimage. For many pilgrims, traveling to the shrine may be just as important or even more important than the shrine itself. This is because pilgrimage is not just an external but also an internal journey. For other tourists, the shrine may be the only thing they are interested in, and many may see the shrine more as a cultural monument than a religious one. One of the additional complications may be that the transformation involved in undertaking a pilgrimage may change the type of tourism involved. A person starting out with purely cultural motives may become aware of an inner change as they travel, and may actually become pilgrims or religious tourists along the way (Haab, 1996).

Many authors also see religious tourism as a part of cultural tourism. Insofar as a religion is part of culture, this seems to make sense. Religious sites are also an important element of cultural tourism, so there is also a degree of overlap between the two. Petrillo (2003), for example, reports in the case of Italian sites that 93 percent of religious tourists report cultural motivations. Montaner Montejano (1996) also suggests a link to cultural tourism, with a continuum ranging from "pilgrims" to "believers" to "cultural tourists." A summary of some of the main dimensions of this continuum is given in Figure 11.1. As the boundaries between culture, religion, and spirituality continue to blur, it is likely that the context of "religious tourism" will change.

Smith (2003b:103) argues that there is a current trend toward spiritual tourism, "focusing on the quest for the enhancement of self through physical, mental, and creative activities." She sees many tourists rejecting the relatively hedonistic travel styles of the past and traveling in order to find meaning in other cultures, religions, and philosophies.

This review of studies of religious tourism indicates that the concept is far from clear. A number of different concepts may be grouped under the term "religious tourism" or may be closely related to it. These include pilgrimage, pilgrim-tourists, spiritual tourism, holistic tourism, cultural tourism, and creative tourism. The growing diversity of the concept of religious tourism also underlines the potential for future growth, particularly as traditional forms are replaced by new ones, often linked to the increasingly important role of spirituality in all spheres of life.

SPIRITUALITY AND THE QUEST FOR MEANING

The growth of spirituality has important implications for the development of religious tourism in the future. Spirituality has always

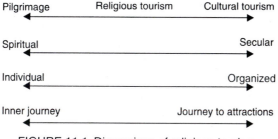

FIGURE 11.1. Dimensions of religious tourism.

been important in pilgrimage, but some analysts of religious tourism have now pointed to a shift away from traditional religious activities toward a much broader view of "spirituality" or "holistic" reasons for travel (Smith, 2003).

Pilgrims also seem to be increasingly seeking a spiritual rather than a religious experience. For example, Digance and Cusack (2002) note the growth of Christian and "new age pilgrimage" to Glastonbury in the United Kingdom. They estimate that the June pilgrimage attracts between 8,000, and 10,000 visitors to a town with a population of 8,000 during one weekend. The New Age movement has drawn on a wide range of influences, which include not just other religions such as shamanism or Buddhism, but particularly specific sites held to be sacred by prehistoric or indigenous peoples. The New Age movement therefore represents a more diverse approach to spirituality, which presents a challenge to traditional religions, but also opens up new perspectives, such as linking religious activity to appreciation of nature and landscape.

This shift toward more individualistic forms of activity and the addition of spiritual and holistic motivations to religious tourism has a number of implications. It indicates that the needs of the individual traveler must be considered more closely, and that small groups or custom-made tours will grow alongside "mass" forms of religious tourism. It suggests that people may be looking for different kinds of authenticity and for more contact with local people.

The basic reasons for this shift in the nature of tourism demand from traditional passive cultural tourism toward more active creative or spiritual tourism stem from broader social and cultural trends. One of the most important of these is the quest for meaning and the desire for personal development rather than materialistic possessions. As societies in Western Europe have become materially richer, so more people are able to concentrate on immaterial and spiritual matters. For example, Scitovsky (1976) has identified a shift away from "outer directed" consumption (materialistic consumption based on goods) to "inner directed" consumption (based on learning and development of self). People are no longer satisfied with passive experiences; they increasingly want to learn and be actively involved. In the case of religious attractions, this implies that visitors want to know more about the background of the site or event, but that they also want to be actively involved in the religious or spiritual life of the place they are visiting.

Essentially, the growing emphasis on the consumption of "inner-directed" experiences reflects the experience hunger of modern society. Stripped of the reassuring structures of modernity, such as the family, a job for life, and religion, people increasingly face an uncertain existence. Initially, the apparent freedom offered by the choice of experiences offered by the market may be seductive, but ultimately these separate, commoditized experiences are unsatisfying. This is when people begin to seek out narratives or explanations that can provide a holistic framework of understanding for the increasingly fragmented nature of human existence.

If one identifies this search for meaning as being central to religion and spirituality, it is probably also central to religious tourism. In order to harness this essential drive for cultural tourism development, however, it is important to analyze the nature of religious tourism demand and to identify those resources that are important as religious and cultural attractions. The following section therefore looks in more detail at current patterns of religious tourism demand and supply in general terms, prior to a more detailed analysis of the situation in Northern Portugal.

RELIGIOUS ATTRACTIONS—
SUPPLY AND DEMAND

The most widely quoted study of religious attractions is Nolan and Nolan's 1989 survey of religious tourism in Europe, which indicated that there were over 6,000 Catholic shrines in Western Europe, over half of which are dedicated to the Virgin Mary. Nolan and Nolan characterized the sites they studied as pilgrimage shrines, religious tourist attractions, or religious festivals. Real pilgrimage shrines may not be particularly popular, since some are visited purely by pilgrims. On the other hand, the major pilgrimage sites are very important in terms of attracting all types of visitors.

Jacowski et al. (2002) classify pilgrimage sites into different categories depending on their importance. They recognize global centers, which are the major Christian sites, based on history and tradition (Jerusalem, Rome, Athos), or the special nature of the sites (e.g.,

Fátima in Central Portugal); international centers, whose range does not exceed one continent; superregional centers, which are known outside their own region but which attract few foreign visitors (e.g., Braga in Northern Portugal) and regional centers (e.g., Peneda in the Alto Minho, Portugal).

Digance (2003) states:

> Indications are that pilgrimage is still as popular as ever, experiencing a marked resurgence around the globe over the last few decades. Long established shrines still continue to act as magnets for those in search of spiritual goals, and new ones, such as Medjugorje in Western Herzegovina in the former Yugoslavia (with its estimated 3,000 to 5,000 daily tourists) are also attracting the faithful from all parts of the globe.

This certainly seems to be reflected in the available figures for the numbers of pilgrims. Attix (1992) reported estimates of an annual total of 200 million pilgrims worldwide in 1992, of which a large proportion visited the major sites. More recent estimates produced in 2000 *(Documento de la Santa Sede sobre el Peregrinaje en 2000)* estimated an annual total of 220-250 million pilgrims, of whom 150 million are Christians. Assuming these figures are reliable, this indicates a growth in the pilgrimage tourism market of up to 25 percent in eight years, an annual increase of over 3 percent. This is significant, but still lags behind the growth in tourism as a whole. In Europe it is estimated that about thirty million Christians dedicate all or part of their holidays to pilgrimage. In Poland alone between five and seven million people are involved in pilgrimages every year, more than 15 percent of the population. Jacowski et al. (2002) estimate that there are about 300 million pilgrims who take part in journeys to supra-regional religious sites in Europe each year. Of these, they estimate that about fifty million are Christians traveling during their holidays. These journeys tend to be concentrated at twenty major sites.

Nolan and Nolan (1989) also point out that only 25 percent of cathedrals in Europe are pilgrimage destinations, so the potential of developing new pilgrimage streams is limited for most religious sites. Jacowski et al. (2002) relate the popularity of pilgrimage sites to the number of followers of a given religion (which means there is a large potential for major religions such as Catholicism), the geographical location of the site, available transport infrastructure, wealth, awareness, and pilgrimage tradition.

One major new product that has become important for some religious sites is the development of cultural routes and itineraries related to pilgrimage routes or religious sites. The most famous and perhaps most successful example is the route to Santiago de Compostela in Spain (see also Chapter 8). As Santos (2002) notes, religious motivations were by no means paramount in the revival of the Santiago route. He identifies a number of significant factors:

- A recovery of religious spirit related to uncertainty at the millennium
- Recovery of the European spirit
- Tourist strategy of Galicia
- Global events in Spain in 1992 (Barcelona Olympics, Seville Expo)

Murray and Graham (1997) illustrate how the Camino has become "a cultural resource" as well as a tourist attraction, being used by all four northern regions of Spain, through which it passes, as a means of tourism promotion. They also see the Camino as a prime example of "green tourism," since Compostellas (certificates given to pilgrims reaching Santiago) are only issued to those traveling either on foot or bicycle. However, the emphasis on physically traveling the route means that "pilgrims essentially qualify on the grounds of physical achievement rather than any necessarily spiritual motivation and are distinguished from secular tourists by their mode of travel" (p. 519).

The success of the Santiago route has spawned a range of other cultural routes based on religious themes or containing significant links to religious themes. Examples include the Baroque Route in France, the Via Francigena from Northern France to Rome, and the Monastic Influence Route across Europe, all of which are supported by the Council of Europe.

RELIGIOUS TOURISM IN PORTUGAL

In Portugal, most attention has been paid to a few major shrines and pilgrimage locations across the country. The prime example is

Fátima in Central Portugal, one of the most important pilgrimage destinations in the world. Research by Ambrósio (2001) indicates that Fátima has also developed rapidly as a major tourist destination, although the town itself remains relatively small. In 1931 Fátima had five hotels with fifty-five beds, but by 1997 there were thirty-one accommodation establishments with a total of 4,261 beds.

In the north region of Portugal, the development of individual local shrines has also been important in recent years. Pinto (2002), for example, has studied pilgrims visiting the shrine at Peneda. In interviews with pilgrims, he found that almost half of the participants in the Romaria da Peneda were aged over fifty. The vast majority of the pilgrims came from relatively low socioeconomic groups (agricultural workers or laborers), and only 5 percent had completed some form of higher education. About 23 percent of the pilgrims interviewed at Peneda had visited the shrine before in the last five years, but almost 30 percent of repeat visitors had not visited within the last 15 years. This indicates a fairly low level of repeat visitation. Over 80 percent of the pilgrims came from within the north region itself, the vast majority of these being drawn from the immediate area, and only 13 percent coming from Spain. This indicates a relatively low level of "tourism" at this shrine.

At the moment, therefore, it seems as if the potential for religious tourism in the north of the country is not being fully developed. This was the stimulus for the Chamber of Commerce of Braga and the Diocese of Braga to initiate a project titled *Religious Tourism As a Motor for Regional Development: The Potential for Religious Tourism in the Northern Region.* Co-funded by the ERDF Program (the EU Structural Funds), the project aimed to make more effective use of the local religious heritage, investigating how it can be integrated into the tourist market.

The main objectives of the research were as follows:

- To analyze the supply of and demand for religious tourism in the north of Portugal
- To create a database of religious tourism supply in the north of Portugal
- To present religious tourism development proposals for the north of Portugal

- To identify the international potential of religious tourism, in line with the promotion strategy already developed under the brand "Oporto and the north of Portugal," and in accordance with the strategies of the destinations that may be partners in commercial strategies

The data reported here concentrate in particular on tourism demand and the supply of religious tourism resources in the north of Portugal.

STUDY METHODOLOGY

In order to carry out the analysis, a mixture of primary and secondary research was employed, including surveys of visitors, travel industry intermediaries, and policymakers, and collection of secondary data on the supply of religious tourism attractions. By combining data on the demand for and the supply of religious tourism, the sites which have the greatest potential for religious tourism development can be identified.

One of the first steps in the research was to identify the "anchor-sites," or the key resources and localities around which the religious tourism product of the north of Portugal can be structured. The identification of these anchor-sites resulted from the analysis of a range of parameters that included not only the importance of the religious sites or events, but also visitor flows, the available services, the visibility of the resources and districts, as well as other indicators linked to tourist supply and demand in the north of Portugal. Conceptually speaking, the notion of anchor-site implies a degree of territorial specialization, which should create products that are more competitive in national and international markets. However, having identified the major anchor-sites for the region, a range of complementary facilities can then be identified that can strengthen the product as well as benefiting from the spin-off effects created by the anchor-sites.

The first step in the identification of the anchor-sites was to develop a "municipality spreadsheet" for each of the northern municipalities, with the aim of carrying out a detailed analysis of the region. The municipal level was chosen because it allows for a deeper and, at the same time, more even analysis of the development criteria. However, the municipality spreadsheet (see Figure 11.2) also included more lo-

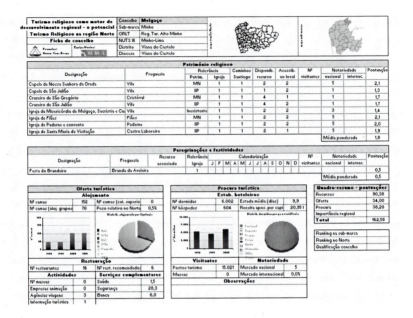

FIGURE 11.2. Example of a municipality spreadsheet used for the supply analysis.

cal information, namely the resources and important festivities of the municipalities. The spreadsheet therefore compiles local information (resources and religious festivities) with the municipal information (indicators of tourist supply and demand). Moreover, a third component was inserted, "regional importance," that implies the comparative analysis of the main locations in each subregion, identifying the more visible ones in a positive manner. As a result, each municipality can be positioned within the subregion and the region according to its classification as an anchor-site, the complementary of other products, and the potential for the development of the religious tourism product.

In order to measure the level of importance of each municipality, a number of criteria were established, and each group of criteria contributed a fixed proportion of the final score. The religious resources and festivities contributed 40 percent of the total score for the municipality, the tourism supply indicators 20 percent, the tourism demand indicators 20 percent, and the "regional importance" the remaining 20 percent of the final score. Finally, each major religious site or event in the municipality was given a further 5 percent, with the aim of giving maximum value to concentrations of resources and festivities of a religious character. The final "religious tourism potential" index that was calculated for each municipality could therefore add up to more than 100 percent for those areas with high potential and significant concentrations of religious heritage.

In order to find out more about existing demand for religious sites in northern Portugal, visitor surveys were also carried out at a range of sites in the region (see Table 11.1). A total of 1,001 questionnaire surveys were conducted at six religious sites in northern Portugal in the period July-September 2003. The questionnaire was designed to collect information on the motivation, religious orientation, behavior, expenditure, and activities of visitors to these sites. The survey sites were selected to provide a range of different sites in the four main regions in Northern Portugal.

The following section briefly describes the supply analysis, and this is followed by a description of the results of the visitor surveys.

RESULTS OF SUPPLY ANALYSIS

The supply analysis was designed to identify basic patterns of religious tourism potential in northern Portugal. This information con-

TABLE 11.1. Visitor survey sites and distribution of questionnaires.

Site	Location	No.	%
S. Bento	Terras de Bouro	240	24.0
I.S. Francisco	Porto	201	20.1
Bom Jesus	Braga	185	18.5
Sra. dos Remédios	Lamego	175	17.5
Igreja da Misericórdia	Chaves	164	16.4
Igreja Matriz	Chaves	36	3.6
Total		1001	100

tributed greatly to the definition of a strategy for the territorial structuring around the anchor-sites and the consequent presentation of proposals and recommendations for the development of religious tourism in the region. The synthesized maps (Figures 11.3-11.5) present the geographical distribution of the scores given to the existing religious tourism resources (heritage + festivities), as well as the tourism supply and demand. In terms of the analyzed heritage, the municipalities with the highest scores were the ones with the highest concentration of religious resources: Oporto scored 186.3 points; Guimarães 152.2; Braga 128.3; Vila do Conde 123.3; Ponte de Lima 119.3; and Lamego 114.7 (Figure 11.3).

As far as the tourism supply is concerned, the combination of the criteria corresponding to accommodation, restaurants, entertainment, and supplementary services generated a composite indicator of tourism supply, whose results can be seen in Figure 11.4.

The results of the supply analysis indicated that there was considerable potential for the development of religious tourism in a number of areas, particularly those with a combination of a rich supply of reli-

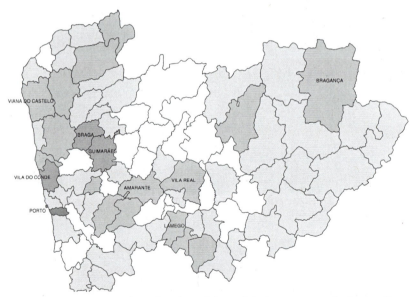

FIGURE 11.3. Anchor-sites: Scoring of the religious resources in the northern region. *Note:* Darker shades indicate higher scores.

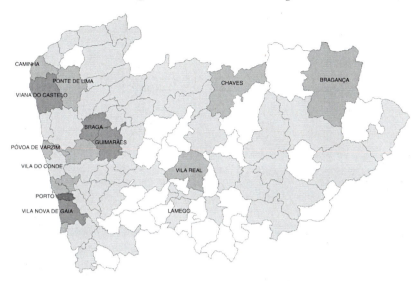

FIGURE 11.4. Anchor-sites: Composite scores for the tourist supply in the municipalities of the northern region. *Note:* Darker shades indicate higher scores.

FIGURE 11.5. Dynamics of religious tourism potential in the northern region. *Note:* Darker shades indicate higher scores.

gious heritage and existing tourism facilities. Oporto clearly has the highest potential, but other areas such as Braga and Lamego could also attract more religious tourism under the right circumstances. In order to assess the extent to which these areas can realize their potential, however, it is also important to consider the demand.

ANALYSIS OF VISITORS TO RELIGIOUS SITES

Just under 20 percent of the visitors interviewed were from the local area around the site (a radius of 50 km). A further 24 percent came from the north of Portugal region, 20 percent from another part of Portugal, and 38 percent from abroad. The largest group of foreign visitors came from France (13 percent of foreign tourists), largely because of the widespread out-migration from northern Portugal to France. The only other countries that contribute significant numbers to the visitor stream to religious monuments are Spain (9 percent) and Italy (3 percent), both Catholic countries where the religious culture is familiar. The level of foreign visitors surveyed at religious sites is lower than that for cultural sites in northern Portugal as whole (57 percent), as measured in surveys conducted in 2001 (Fernandes and Richards, 2002).

The age profile of the visitors was relatively old in comparison with cultural visitors in Europe as a whole (Richards, 2001). Over 55 percent of respondents were aged forty or older, compared with 47 percent of visitors to cultural attractions in northern Portugal as a whole (Fernandes and Sousa, 2002). The high average age is also reflected in the relatively low education level in the sample, with particularly Portuguese respondents over the age of forty tending to have completed either a primary or secondary education. Just over 41 percent of the sample had completed tertiary education, lower than in northern Portuguese attractions as a whole (53 percent). Women (52 percent) tended to slightly outnumber men (48 percent), which is not unusual for cultural sites in general.

Most of the sample considered themselves to be very religious (22 percent) or religious (44 percent), and only 13 percent of the sample considered themselves to be atheists. Of the religious believers, almost all indicated their faith as Catholic. This indicates a high level of concordance between the nature of the attraction being visited and the religious background of the visitors.

In terms of the type of holidays normally taken by the respondents, sun and beach holidays tended to be the most popular, followed by touring and cultural holidays. Other types of tourism, including religious tourism, were practiced by relatively small groups as their primary type of holiday. Religious tourism was far more popular as a second (8.4 percent) or third holiday type (12.4 percent) (see Table 11.2).

Motivation

The purpose of visit (see Table 11.3) most frequently mentioned was "holiday" in general, followed by a motivation to visit the religious attraction being surveyed (most important for domestic visitors) and, third, a general cultural visit. Pilgrimage accounted for just over 10 percent of responses. It is clear that the purpose of visit for most people is a fairly general one, usually comprising part of a holiday or a general cultural visit.

The most frequently mentioned motivation for visiting the site was to learn more about local culture, which was cited as being important or very important by 82 percent of respondents. Experiencing the atmosphere was the second most frequently mentioned motive (79 percent important), whereas motives more clearly related to religion and spirituality tended to be less important. Only 20 percent of the sample indicated that a spiritual experience was important in their decision to travel.

In terms of the type of experience (see Table 11.4) that people felt they actually had at the site, the most frequent response was that it was "interesting," followed by visiting the site in order to pray. By and large, it was the "cultural tourists" who were stimulated to visit because the site was interesting, whereas those with a religious motive were more likely to be going to pray. Very few people felt they had actually been transformed by the experience. This seems to indicate that at the survey sites at least, the link between religious tourism and spiritual transformation is rather weak.

TABLE 11.2. Tourists visiting religious sites by holiday type.

Holiday type (first or 1st option)	%
Sun and beach	43.8
Touring holiday	23.2
Cultural holiday	14.6
Rural tourism	5.8
Religious tourism	5.7
City trip	4.0
Health/sport	1.8
Mountain recreation	1.1
Total	100.0

TABLE 11.3. Motivation for visiting the survey area.

Motivation for visit	%
Holiday	42.1
To visit this attraction	31.7
Cultural visit	22.2
Visiting friends and relatives	18.1
Nature	11.8
Pilgrimage	10.3
Excursion	9.5
Shopping	5.6
Gastronomy	4
Visiting a spa	2.5
Business	1.3
Festival	1

Distinguishing the Religious Tourist

As outlined above, previous studies of religious tourism have tended to see it as a form of cultural tourism, very often with a continuum of motivations ranging from purely religious (or pilgrimage) to purely cultural.

TABLE 11.4. Type of experience during the visit.

Type of experience	%
It was an interesting experience	42.6
I went to pray	26.8
It was a cultural experience	26.0
It was an uninteresting experience	3.8
The experience transformed me	0.8

TABLE 11.5. Religious belief by type of tourist (%).

	Very religious	Relatively religious	Not very religious	Atheist
Cultural tourists	10.6	43.0	28.2	18.3
Religious tourists	51.8	46.4	1.8	
Total	22.2	43.9	20.7	13.1

TABLE 11. 6. Motive by tourist type (%).

	Motive cultural visit	Motive pilgrimage
Cultural tourists	55.4	2.3
Religious tourists	8.9	55.6
Total	43.3	16.0

The findings of this research seem to indicate considerable co-presence of religious and cultural tourists at the sites surveyed, but very little overlap between the two groups in terms of motivations, activities, or experience (see Tables 11.5 and 11.6). To look at the differences in more detail, the religious and cultural tourists were distinguished from one another through their responses to the questions on the type of holidays taken. Those indicating that religious holidays were their first choice were designated "religious tourists," and those choosing culture first were labeled "cultural tourists."

The cultural tourists were particularly likely to come from other regions of Portugal or from abroad, whereas religious tourists were

TABLE 11.7. Booking channels.

	% Respondents
All-inclusive package	12.4
Accommodation only booked via travel agent	7.6
Transport only booked via travel agent	6.3
Booked via Internet	3.8
Booked direct	31.0
No prior reservation	38.8
Total	100.0

TABLE 11.8. Accommodation use by tourist origin (%).

	Other location in Northern Portugal	Other region of Portugal	Abroad	Total
Own home	79	42	27	45
Hotel	8	27	34	25
Camp site	3	5	13	8
Private house	0	2	8	4
Visiting friends or relatives	7	17	9	10
Pousada	0	0	3	1
Self-catering	0	0	1	0
Youth hostel	0	0	0	0
Rural tourism accommodation	0	3	4	3
Other	2	5	3	3
Total	100	100	100	100

mainly Portuguese. The religious tourists were more likely to be women (55 percent), whereas the cultural tourists were evenly divided between males and females. Almost 70 percent of the cultural tourists had some form of higher education, compared with only 15 percent of the religious tourists. Not surprisingly, religious tourists

TABLE 11.9. Information sources for tourists.

Source	% respondents
Family and friends	45.8
Guidebook	43.4
Internet	28.6
Tourist information office	13.8
Tour operator brochures	11.2
Previous visit	9.9
Newspapers/magazine articles	6.0
Newspapers/magazine adverts	2.2
Radio/TV advertisements	1.1
Radio/TV programs	0.9
My church	0.2

TABLE 11.10. Tourist expenditure by holiday type.

Main holiday type	Average expenditure €
City break	795
Cultural holiday	680
Religious tourism	412
Touring	404
Sun and beach	390

tended to be far more religious, with over half saying they were "very religious," compared with just over 10 percent of cultural tourists.

Cultural tourists were also much more likely to see their visit as "cultural" than religious tourists, whereas religious tourists were more likely to see their visit as a form of pilgrimage. Even so, only just over half of the religious tourists indicated that their visit was a form of pilgrimage, which suggests that many religious tourists have broader motivations for visiting. This also seems to confirm that there are two distinct segments in the "religious tourism" population.

Travel Organization

One of the features of religious tourism noted in previous studies is the tendency for people to travel in large organized groups. The survey data indicate that the group size for religious tourists was over three times larger than for cultural tourists, and more likely to include children. In general, most of the visitors surveyed at the religious sites arrived independently, usually having made their own travel arrangements or with no prior bookings. Only 26 percent of respondents had booked some element of their journey via the travel industry (see Table 11.7).

The accommodation used by respondents was heavily influenced by visitor origin (see Table 11.8). Regional visitors tended to be traveling from home, as did a large proportion of tourists from other parts of Portugal. Foreign tourists tended to be staying in hotels more often, but over a quarter of foreign visitors were traveling from home. This underlines the importance of Portuguese migrants living in France, who have second homes in the area, as well as Spanish visitors in the total market.

In terms of sources of information (see Table 11.9), family and friends were most important, followed by guidebooks. Perhaps surprisingly, the Internet was ranked third in terms of importance. Closer analysis showed that the Internet was used mainly by younger secular visitors with a higher education qualification. Religious tourists did not use the Internet or guidebooks, and were far more likely than cultural tourists to have gained information from a previous visit. The level of Internet use is considerably higher than that recorded in surveys of cultural tourists in northern Portugal in 2001 (12.9 percent), but otherwise the use of information sources remains remarkably similar.

In terms of expenditure (see Table 11.10), the average total budget of the visitors was just over €500 per group. Not surprisingly, foreign tourists and tourists from other parts of Portugal spent much more than regional visitors. The average group spend by foreign tourists was €630, compared with just over €400 for tourists from the Norte region. Total expenditure was also strongly influenced by the type of holiday taken. "Sun and beach" tourists had the lowest average expenditure, but religious tourists also had relatively low total expenditure, basically because they tended to be domestic tourists. The highest levels of expenditure were recorded by those on city breaks and cultural holidays. This tends to indicate that the economic impact of religious tourism can be increased if more cultural tourists are attracted to visit religious sites.

CONCLUSIONS

The preliminary data presented in this chapter indicate the potential for religious tourism development in northern Portugal. Although development to date has been limited to a few major sites, the analysis shows that it should be possible to spread the development of religious tourism to more parts of the region. Particularly taking into account the potential for combining religious tourism with cultural and nature-based tourism, and the potential for developing "new age" or "spiritual" tourism, it should be possible to use the major anchor sites identified to stimulate regional development.

At present, however, there is a clear distinction between a more local religious tourism market, currently stimulated by pilgrimage motives, and a more globalized cultural tourism market. These two markets have very different motivations and different needs, as well as different patterns of activity in the destination. In many respects the local religious tourism market offers relatively little scope for further tourism development, particularly as the current generation of pilgrims ages and the enthusiasm for traditional religion wanes among young people. In developing new products and new markets, therefore, the religious tourism attractions of the region should think more seriously about the cultural tourism elements of current demand, and in particular the development of new products for emerging niches such as spiritual tourism.

Realizing this potential will clearly require a high level of intermunicipal cooperation, given the extent of the tourism regions identified. In addition, the importance of tourism supply factors identified in the research show the need for extensive collaboration between the public sector, which is responsible for policy and promotion, the church, which manages most of the sites, and the tourism sector, which provides the supporting facilities. This underlines the importance of networking in the future development of religious tourism in northern Portugal.

REFERENCES

AFIT (2002) *Etude des comportements des clienteles de visiteurs europeens sur les sites de patrimoine Francais.* Paris: AFIT.

Ambrósio, V. (2001) *Fátima: Território Especializado na Recepção de Turismo Religioso.* Lisbon: Instituto Nacional de Formação Turística.

Attix, S. A. (2002) New age-oriented special interest travel: An exploratory study. *Tourism Recreation Research* 27(2), 51-58.

Cohen, E. (2001) *The Chinese Vegetarian Festival in Phuket: Religion, Ethnicity and Tourism on a Southern Thai Island.* Bangkok: White Lotus.

Digance, J. (2003) Pilgrimage at contested sites. *Annals of Tourism Research* 30, 143-159.

Digance, J. and Cusack, C. (2002) Glastonbury: A tourist town for all seasons. In Dann, G. M. S. (ed) *The Tourist as a Metaphor of the Social World.* Wallingford: CAB International, pp. 263-280.

Fernandes, C., McGettigan, F. and Edwards, J. (2004) *Religious Tourism and Pilgrimage.* Arnhem: ATLAS.

Fernandes, C. and Sousa, L. (2000) (eds) *Turismo Cultural no Alto Minho: Um Estudo.* Viana do Castelo: Centro Cultural de Alto Minho, pp. 13-22.

Giussani, L. (1997) *The Religious Sense.* Montreal: McGill-Queen's University Press.

Haab, B. (1996) The Way as an inward journey: An anthropological enquiry into the spirituality of present-day pilgrims to Santiago. *Confraternity of St. James Bulletin,* 56, 16-32.

Jacowski, A., Ptaszycka-Jackoska, D., and Soljan, I. (2002) The world system of pilgrimage centres. *Turyzm,* 12(2), 51-63.

Montaner Montejano, J. (1996) *Estructura del mercado turístico.* Madrid: Síntesis.

Murray, M. and Graham, B. (1997) Exploring the dialectics of route-based tourism: The Camino de Santiago. *Tourism Management* 18(8), 513-524.

Nolan, M. and Nolan, S. (1989) *Christian Pilgrimage in Modern Western Europe.* Chapel Hill: The University of North Carolina Press.

Petrillo, C. S. (2003) Management of churches and religious sites: Some case studies from Italy. In Fernandes, C., McGettigan, F. and Edwards, J. (eds) *Religous Tourism and Pilgrimage.* Arnhem: ATLAS, pp. 71-86.

Pinto, J. (2002) Os Santos Esperam, Mas Não Perdoam: Un estudo sobre a romaria de Peneda. Unpublished manuscript.

Santos, X. M. (2002) Pilgrimage and tourism at Santiago de Compostela. *Tourism Recreation Research* 27, 41-53.

Scitovsky, T. (1976) *The Joyless Economy.* New York: Basic Books.

Smith, M. K. (2003) Holistic holidays: Tourism and the reconciliation of body, mind and spirit. *Tourism Recreation Research* 28(1), 103-108.

Chapter 12

Using Tourist Resources As Tools for Teaching and Creating Awareness of Heritage in a Local Community

Patricia de Camargo

INTRODUCTION

This chapter presents a preliminary description of two different pieces of research, the first in Curitiba in Brazil and the other in Las Palmas de Gran Canaria, Spain. The first was designed to test the efficiency of guided cultural routes as tools for teaching high school students to value their built heritage. The second is a much more ambitious project, which examines the role of intangible heritage and its potential use as a tool in schools, museums, and cultural institutions, aimed at making the local community revalue its identity. This should also stimulate greater participation in the formulation of cultural tourism policies directed at promoting sustainable, community-based development.

The keystone of sustainable development is the participation of the local community in the decision-making process, but for this participation to be used to the full, heritage awareness campaigns and educational and information programs must first be organized by and for the community, to enable them to formulate their sense of identity.

The Mediterranean Voices Project was formulated by the researchers Margaret Hart and Eugenio A. Rodríguez Cabrera.

This research is an attempt to offer potential ways of involving all the social stakeholders in a reevaluation of their heritage, and bringing them together to define common sustainable goals that will promote their continued well-being.

The research is based on the following theories and concepts: the theory of multiple intelligence, the concept of citizenship related to the consumption, and the theory of the culture of satisfaction.

We work on the basis of the theory of multiple intelligence, the basis of a new theory of learning developed by Howard Gardner (1993), together with the Zero Project at Harvard. Gardner did not believe that intelligence was monolithic and unidirectional, but

> the capacity to solve real-life problems; the capacity to create other problems to be solved; and the capacity to perform some kind of action or proportion some kind of service which can be valued by, and which will give added value, to one's own culture. (quoted in Campbell, 1990:21)

Gardner's theory emphasizes the multicultural nature of the human being and lists up to eight different kinds of intelligence: linguistic, logical-mathematical, spatial, kinaesthetic, musical, interpersonal, intrapersonal and naturalistic. Campbell (1990) defines these intelligences as "languages which all people speak, the extent of which is defined by the cultural framework in which the person is nurtured. These are tools for learning, solving problems, and being creative that all of us can use."

The new concepts of citizenship are related to consumption, which leads to a change of the spaces, and the space in which citizenship is established. This links with Galbraith's (1992) argument that we are facing the culture of satisfaction where the privileged do not think about the long-term, as they don't think long-term events can touch them, so concern about future generations is nonexistent. They just think about themselves. This generation does not deny the problem, but somehow delays its solution. How can we help them to understand the need for at least a middle-term perspective on their responsibility to future generations, without ignoring new social relations and the connection of the public to the private? How can we respect the various ways of learning about the world of each citizen, and so reach more people? How can we promote cultural tourism in areas where natural attractions are more valued by the local population? These questions were addressed during the research procedure.

CULTURAL ROUTES IN CURITIBA, PARANÁ, BRAZIL

Methodology

This practical piece of research was carried out in a network of private schools *(Organização Educativa Expoente)* in the city of Curitiba in Brazil, which is considered by many to be a model city and is used by many firms to launch new products and services. The aforementioned network of private schools produces and sells teaching materials to more than 450 schools in the whole of Brazil, accounting for some 130,000 students.

All of the students in the first and second cycles of Secondary Education in this network—that is, students between fourteen and sixteen years of age—answered the first questionnaire, which aimed to gauge their knowledge with respect to the built historic and cultural heritage in the city.

The data were analyzed and processed. One part of the sample (450 respondents) then took part in a tourist route known as the "Linha do Pinhão," where they visited twenty-two different spots chosen by the researcher. This route was designed in 1993 on the occasion of the celebrations for the Third Centenary of the city of Curitiba, Paraná, Brazil. During the visit, the students participated in activities created especially for the research project and based on the theory of multiple intelligences of Howard Gardner. Two weeks after the visit, the students who had taken part in the guided visit answered a second questionnaire, which gave feedback to the extent of the information acquired.

The students were not obliged to sign their questionnaires and were informed that they were participating in a research study and that they would not be given marks on the basis of the results, which indicates the trustworthy nature of the feedback.

ANALYSIS OF THE DATA OBTAINED
IN THE FIELD RESEARCH

Knowledge of the City

Figure 12.1 shows that most of the students had no knowledge of the history of their city (70 percent). The lack of previous knowledge meant that more historical detail had to be incorporated into the visit in order to cover the gap left in the educational curriculum, in that insufficient importance was attached to the history of the community.

We can also see that there was a lack of knowledge with respect to the city when the students were asked about the "Linha do Pinhão" (see Figure 12.2). Most of them did not know this cultural route, although a guidebook was published in 1996 that is still in circulation. Of the students who participated in the survey, 92 percent were un-

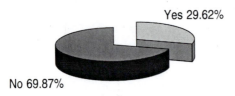

FIGURE 12.1. Knowledge of the history of the city.

aware of the existence of the Linha do Pinhão and even asked what kind of "line" it was without even making any associative link with built heritage or even their own city. Less than 8 percent of the students said that they were aware of the route, and even these students said after the visit that they only knew part of the route and that they were totally unaware of the historical background to the buildings and spaces that made up part of the route.

The route, Linha do Pinhão, did not appear in the first questionnaire as a tourist attraction to be recommended to people coming from other places to visit. After the visit, however, it did feature, showing that it had not done so beforehand due to total ignorance of its existence.

Although most of the students were unaware of the sights in the city, most of them (93 percent) considered that it would be interesting and fun to get to know them. This shows that the students have no prejudices with respect to this type of visit, that they have very little information, and that, therefore, they do not know how to access their heritage, their history, or their roots.

The absence of prejudices with respect to cultural visits is important in learning. The mere fact that the students move outside the school precinct represents an enormous opportunity for the more observant students to learn via application of their most highly developed form of intelligence. Thus, the student who has a highly developed visual intelligence will be able to better apply this intelligence in the contact with images in three dimensions. The naturalist will have a better opportunity to enter into harmony with the natural environment, the inter-personally developed will help their colleagues in an experience that facilitates exchange of ideas and contact, and so on.

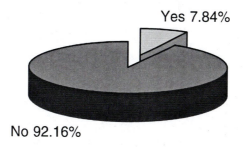

FIGURE 12.2. Knowledge of the Linha do Pinhão.

The Habit of Visiting Museums in the City

The extent to which students are unaware of the history of the city is high: Since, the museums tend to be repositories of history and they do not visit museums, they have had no contact with the history of the place. We can see that the portion of the pie chart regarding visits to the museum in Figure 12.3 is similar to those knowing something about the history of the city (Figure 12.1). Almost three-quarters of all students are not in the habit of visiting the city museums, and those who do, do so to complete homework tasks or on organized school trips.

Figure 12.3 shows the lack of knowledge of the students with respect to their heritage. The students do not enjoy their common heritage and do not visit museums except when they have to. The contact with the built heritage is not viewed as something pleasant or as a leisure activity.

Figure 12.4 is interesting because it shows that although the students know nothing of the history of the city and are not in the habit of visiting museums, most are interested in getting to know the museums.

The students have a latent interest in visiting museums despite the fact that this interest is not covered by the school or by the parents.

FIGURE 12.3. Do you visit museums in the city?

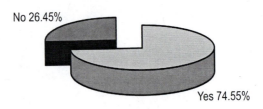

FIGURE 12.4. Interest in getting to know the city museums.

FIGURE 12.5. Belvedere.

Due to lack of relevant information, they do not follow through on their interest.

Learning

Two points can be analyzed here with respect to behavior: whether the students change their behavior and whether they acquire knowledge that they did not possess beforehand as a result of the cultural visit.

As far as knowledge is concerned, in the first questionnaire, the students answered questions with respect to historical figures and buildings and then were asked again about the same issues in the second questionnaire. Besides answering questions on the same subjects, in the second questionnaire they were also asked questions on the information given by the guide on the visit.

Before the visit, scarcely 5 percent of the students were familiar with the Belvedere (see Figue 12.5). After the visit, the proportion rose to over 80 percent. The route included a 25-minute visit to the Art Museum in Paraná, where they were told about the artists of Paraná who were responsible for initiating the movement known as *arte paranaense.* The ideal visit takes one hour and twenty minutes and so the visit was too hurried, which is reflected in the results of the questionnaire. However, there was still a significant increase in the number of students who recognized the names of the artists mentioned on the visit, showing that more directed and direct activities could produce better results.

Before the visit, only 7 percent of the students recognized Alfredo Andersen as the "father" of *arte paranaense.* After the visit, the percentage had risen to 32 percent of the students. Likewise, the sculptor Erbo Stenzel, who has works throughout the city, was only known to 3 percent of the students prior to their visit, compared with 34 percent afterward.

In the second questionnaire, there were also four questions relating to historical information received during the cultural visit. The students were offered a three-option multiple-choice formula. Over half the students answered the following questions correctly: for example, 54 percent said that the Igreja da Ordem was set up in 1737 and was, thus, the oldest church in the city. The Plaza Joao Candido is significant for many reasons, one of which is that the federal troops passed by there, which 73 percent of the students answered correctly. Thus, when history and built heritage are brought together, students are capable of making their own associations between text and image.

The paintings of Miguel Bakun are in the Art Museum, which was given a twenty-five-minute visit. Despite the short time devoted to the visit, 57 percent of the students answered correctly that he is considered to be the "Van Gogh" of art in Paraná. To answer this question, the students had to know how the artist painted in order to associate him with another artist from another time and place. It is difficult to establish associations and, thus, shows the learning potential to be harvested from a cultural visit.

After the visit, the students were asked if they had learned anything. Most of them (86 percent) said that they had participated actively.

Change in Behavior

Learning does not consist of merely amassing information but also involves acquiring new perspectives on the world, which allow us to assess and to modify our own behavior. Two questions were designed to analyze whether there was a change in the behavior of the students after their participation in the cultural visit.

One of the questions assessed the degree of interest in the protection of heritage after participating in the route, with four possible answers, as can be seen in Table 12.1.

This indicates that 60 percent of the students changed their views after the cultural visit, making a total of over 80 percent who believed that heritage preservation was of importance.

The next question was a repetition of a question formulated in the first questionnaire, which was: Would you be prepared to contribute toward this preservation, not necessarily with investments but by participating in campaigns or as a sponsor?

According to Figure 12.6, only 31 percent of the students were prepared to contribute toward preservation before the visit. After the visit, the figure rose to 64 percent. The students not only changed their perspective on heritage but also were prepared to change their behavior, by participating in preservation campaigns.

The students were no longer mere passive receptors of the city but became citizens, since this denomination can only be given to people who live in any given place, understand its importance, and fight to defend it. They are also aware that heritage preservation has to do with quality of life. The person who has no past has no future. Enjoying history contributes to the quality of life.

After the visit, the students acquired knowledge and changed their perspective on the city. The data presented show that the students learned content and developed skills thanks to the participation in the cultural visit, apart from reinforcing their identities as citizens.

TABLE 12.1. Interest in heritage protection.

Evaluation of interest in protection of heritage	%
Had no interest and the situation has not changed	8.12
Had no interest and now believe that it is important	35.14
Was interested and the visit changed nothing	24.32
Visit increased my interest even further	24.32

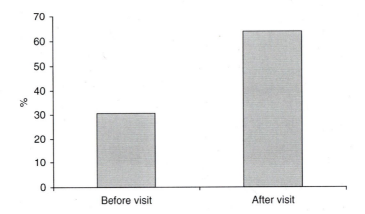

FIGURE 12.6. Willingness to contribute to preservation.

TABLE 12.2. Cultural attractions recommended for visitors.

Attraction	No. of recommendations
Jardim Botânico	261
Ópera de Arame	189
Parque Tanguá	181
Parque Barigui	157
Rua XV	89

Changes in Recommendations to Potential Tourists

After the visit, 70 percent of the students said that they would recommend the route to others, and 73 percent said that they would visit the route again with another person. This indicates that the students had learned something important and that they considered it worthwhile to have participated in the initiative.

Before the visit, the Linha do Pinhão was not mentioned by the students as being an attraction that they would recommend to somebody visiting Curitiba (see Table 12.2). After the visit, the Linha do Pinhão was mentioned directly and, indeed, became one of the most cited tourist attractions.

Apart from mentioning the Largo da Ordem, a place in the old town, the Linha do Pinhão, and other sites (the Museum of Religious Art, a Igreja do Rosario, a Igreja da Ordem, O Relógio das Flores, a Praça Joao Cândido, and the Art Museum), 68 percent of the students indicated the historic part of the city, their own routes, or some of the sites visited on the route, as opposed to 20 percent before the visit.

Table 12.3 shows the tourism attractions most quoted by the students before their visit coincide with the places most visited by tourists in Curitiba (see also Figure 12.7). This is not surprising, as the same research reveals that the tourists hear about these places through word of mouth, usually from friends or relatives, as shown in Table 12.4.

The engagement of the local community certainly would help in the promotion of cultural tourism as well as in the reduction of the high number of tourists in natural areas. It would also motivate a more equal distribution of this demand, also taking into consideration the increasing length of stay in the city.

Activity Journal

At the beginning of the visit, the students received an activity journal that they could use later as their own guidebook. The first activity was to describe one of the sites they had visited or to sketch it. Those

TABLE 12.3. Most frequently visited tourism attractions.

Tourism attraction visited	Mentions
Jardim Botânico	542
Opera de Arame	422
Parque Barigui	277
Parque Tanguá	219
Parques	156
Shopping	155
Santa Felicidade	123
Estaçao Plaza Show	120

Source: Paraná Turismo (2000).

Jardim Botânico

Ópera de Arame

Parque Tanguá

Rua XV

Parque Barigui

FIGURE 12.7. Some common tourism attractions.

TABLE 12.4. Sources of information used by first-time visitors to the city.

Information sources	Number
Friends/relative	240
Business	121
Television	38
Stopover	13
Congress/event	11

Source: Paraná Turismo (2000).

who wrote were advised after the visit on how to produce visual maps, which could be used to write more elaborately on the subject.

This option again is proposed by Gardner in that each activity offers multiple possibilities, since all students learn in different ways. Most of the students opted for linguistic activities (71 percent), but they used different ways of doing so. Despite the initial orientation, some students insisted on writing long texts, while others jotted down keywords and dates.

The students valued the experience positively, and 90 percent said it had been important for them to participate. The reaction of the students to the activity was better than expected. They gave positive feedback and said they had learned from their participation. Later feedback also gave the same results.

MEDITERRANEAN VOICES

Methodology

The second part of the research is designed to move forward and to take the process beyond the schools and outside the arena of formal education, by involving other social agents. The aim is to obtain the participation of museums, schools, and state-owned cultural institutions and to consult the local community, via a questionnaire, as to what they consider their identifying characteristics, that is, the buildings and customs they most identify with.

The aims of the research are much more broad, and new tools thus need to be designed to fit the needs of a learning process that promotes sustainability, while reinforcing creative capacity and community participation by boosting self-esteem.

The following research methods are proposed: analysis of the contents of the Web pages of museums and state-owned cultural institutions, monitoring of present educational packages and activities offered by the museums, participant observation in the teachers' training courses in Canarian content organized by the *Consejería de Educación, Cultura y Deportes,* questionnaires by age groups in the community designed to detect identifying characteristics. At the end of the period of analysis, a proposal will be made for an instrument that will be efficient in drawing the various social agents together in the pursuit of sustainability, by creating better citizens and making the locals into tourists of their own city.

The Mediterranean Voices Project

This research is being carried out within the framework of the project Mediterranean Voices, which is a EuroMed heritage II project, supported by the European Union. The EuroMed Program was set up on the initiative of the Euro-Mediterranean Forum at the Barcelona Conference in 1992.

The Mediterranean Voices project is a collaboration between London Metropolitan University and thirteen institutions in the Mediterranean region. The three-year project, which started in 2002, aims to analyze the living history of the historic centers of the participant cities. In each city a team of researchers and information technology specialists will record the experiences and memories of local residents. These oral histories cover a wide variety of themes, including the individual, the community, leisure, work, space, material objects, and culture.

After analysis, the recordings, photos, and documents are placed on the project Web site (www.med-voices.org). In addition, an exhibition will be held in each participating community to disseminate the results among local residents, as well as attract the attention of tourists and give them a new way of seeing the city.

According to one of its creators, the anthropologist Raoul Bianchi, the project aims to create a space for the expression of voices that for a variety of reasons are less often heard or are excluded from the monumental aspects of cultural heritage. Another participant, Meg Hart, sees the project aspiring to recuperate a world of memories and to introduce to new generations elements of their past that make sense of the present and indicate a path toward the future.

The focus of the research is cultural anthropology, deriving constructs of different experiences of and perspectives on intangible heritage by conducting interviews with the residents of the areas to be studied, the historic centers, and the cultural repositories, in Las Palmas de Gran Canaria, Vegueta, Triana, and the area known as the Riscos.

The empirical focus of the research, therefore, is on the intangible heritage of Vegueta and Triana and not on the built heritage, as such. The intangible is reflected in a whole range of patterns of sociability and local social interaction, such as photos, memorabilia, anecdotes, and tales of the past that can be elicited from the "informants" in interviews, using the technique of oral history. UNESCO defines "Intangible heritage" in the following way:

> The total range of manifestations of traditional folk or popular culture, that is, the collective work that emanates from any one culture, and which is based on its traditions. These traditions are passed on orally, or via activities, and are modified in time through a process of collective recreation. We can include oral traditions, customs, languages, music, dance, rituals, festivities, traditional medicine and remedies, culinary art, and all the skills relating to the material aspects of any culture, such as tools and habitat.

It is clear from this definition of intangible heritage that it cannot be "globalized" in the same way as tangible heritage, because it is embedded much deeper in the everyday lives of the people who inhabit a particular locality.

CONCLUSIONS

Education for tourism, both in the host destinations and the generating countries, would increase the quality of the experience for both, not only in the sense of greater enjoyment and a warmer reception being offered by the host but in fomenting interaction, making the host feel more a part of the whole process, and revaluing the local population as a repository of intangible heritage, the collective memory.

In times such as these, when individual development is considered to be more important than the communal good, the construction of a collective identity would help protect common areas where interaction is possible. Interpretation is a way of "playing" at learning, which entices people to open up new paths of research, to try new routes. The community must build the collective identity together and not have their identity externally imposed.

The heritage of a place is often misinterpreted by its own residents, who do not help in its maintenance or in its marketing, because there is a lack of previous knowledge and connection with this heritage; consequently, they are not able to enjoy it nor to appreciate it.

In order to avoid the idea of culture only belonging to the chosen few, we need to look for methods that will enable the citizens themselves to be the guides to their everyday lives and hope that, thus, they will reestablish their sense of "belonging" in a standardized, global virtual reality.

For this activity to be sustainable, it must be structured on a long-term, education-for-life basis. Through tourism and the personal learning experience proportioned by a sustainable community, living in harmony and dignity, we can offer a solution to the intolerance and xenophobia that affects our world.

Cultural attractions related to arts have an important universal function, which always recalls the collective unconscious. This implication related to cultural routes enables the students to become more sensitive, not just about their own place but also toward the world around them, building up not just citizens, but people who are able to establish a connection with different cultures, enjoying and respecting the cultures they visit.

REFERENCES

Camargo, H. L. (2002) *Patrimônio Histórico e Cultural*. São Paulo: Aleph.
Campbell, L., Campbell, C., and Dickinson, D. (1990) *Ensino e Aprendizagem por meio das inteligências Múltiplas*. Porto Alegre: Artmed.

Canclini, Nestor García (1995) *Consumidores y Ciudadanos: Conflictos multi-culturales de la globalización*. Mëxico: Grijalbo.

Galbraith, J.K. (1992) *La cultura de la satisfacción* (Third edition). Barcelona: Ariel, S.A.

Gardner, Howard (1993) *Arte, Mente y Cerebro: Una aproximación cognitiva a la creatividad*. Barcelona: Paidós.

Jafari, J. and Brent Ritchie, J.R. (1981) Towards a framework for tourism education: Problems and prospects. *Annals of Tourism Research* 8, 13-34.

Pires, Mário Jorge (2001) *Lazer e Turismo Cultural*. São Paulo: Manole.

Schumacher, E.F. (1987) *Lo pequeño es hermoso* (9th edn). Madrid: Hermann Blume.

Valls, J. (1992) *La imagen de marca de los países*. Barcelona: McGraw-Hill.

PART IV:
CULTURAL EVENTS
AND FESTIVALIZATION

Chapter 13

The Festivalization of Society
or the Socialization of Festivals?
The Case of Catalunya

Greg Richards

INTRODUCTION

As Camargo has pointed out in Chapter 12, in the "experience society" the basis of social relations is arguably shifting away from

This research has been supported by a Marie Curie Fellowship of the European Community program "Improving the Human Research Potential and the Socio-Economic Knowledge Base" under contract number HPMF-CT-2002-01842. Thanks are due to Nikolien van Isterdael for research assistance with the policymaker interviews, and to Marta Munté and Nuria Montmany of the Escuela Superior de Hostelería y Turismo Sant Ignasi for organizing fieldwork assistance for the surveys.

Cultural Tourism: Global and Local Perspectives
© 2007 by The Haworth Press, Inc. All rights reserved.
doi:10.1300/5749_13

collective modes of consumption and production and the maintenance of social bonds, toward the individualization of experience and
self-development. As Western societies increasingly begin to suffer
from "experience hunger," cultural tourism becomes a means of collecting individual experiences that can be used to create narratives
of the self or provide raw materials for distinction. In response to this
change, we may also be seeing the replacement of collective forms of
cultural provision (such as the subsidized provision of cultural facilities or the voluntary creation of cultural events) by a commoditized
symbolic production system that is designed to valorize the cultural
capital of places and events for consumption in the market.

One of the apparent effects of the positioning of culture as a symbolic good is its increasing employment as a tool for image-building,
employment creation, and economic boosterism. In this way, local
places and culture become products in the global marketplace. The
success of cities such as Rotterdam, Barcelona, and Sydney in using
events to reposition themselves in the global economy has stimulated
many others to follow suit. In fact, the success of Barcelona is now so
widely touted that analysts are beginning to refer to the "Barcelona
model." Barcelona is visited not only by an increasing number of leisure tourists, but also by a growing army of consultants, public officials, and academics, all intent on learning the secret of Barcelona's
success. Some look at the political structure (McNeil, 1999), some at
the creative resources of the city (Landry, 2000), and some at the
location and climatic advantages of Barcelona as a Mediterranean
metropolis (Montclús, 2000). While Catalan nationalism is often
cited as a major factor in stimulating the success of Barcelona (usually as an impetus to competition with Madrid), culture is often overlooked, and social factors attract little attention.

An even more interesting omission, in my view, is the lack of attention paid to cultural and other events in Catalunya. While the 1992
Barcelona Olympics are held up as a shining example of how to organize a major event and sell it on the global stage, most authors fail to
ask how this event articulates to other events in Catalunya. Were the
Olympics simply a one-off, a lucky fluke, a case of fortuitous timing,
or are more fundamental factors at play? This is a particularly important question in the light of the staging of the Universal Forum of Cultures in Barcelona in 2004. This major global event, which cost over

€300 million to stage, was supposed to follow on from the 1992 Olympics in boosting the image of Barcelona and contributing to urban development. This time, however, culture was central to the process.

In order to understand the global and local processes influencing cultural events in Catalunya, therefore, it is important to consider the context in which cultural events have been created in the past, and the relationship that these have to tourism. This chapter attempts to outline some of the reasons why Catalunya has been successful in the field of cultural tourism, paying particular attention to the cultural context in which it has developed.

CULTURAL EVENTS AND FESTIVALIZATION

The study of cultural events has in the past mainly centered around festivals. The term "festival" in English can be taken as a generic term derived from the Latin *festivitas,* which implies a social gathering for the purpose of celebration or thanksgiving (Waterman, 1998). Not surprisingly, this relatively general term has taken on a host of meanings over time (Schuster, 1995). Festivals may be arts events, community celebrations, or political or commercial events designed to promote a particular idea or specific products (such as the Festival of Britain in 1951). The word "festival" is also used to refer to events arranged around a single cultural product (such as the Cannes Film Festival) or a concentration of participatory activities, such as a children's festival. Although as Waterman suggests, the term "festival" usually has positive connotations, the widening meaning of the festival concept introduces more room for conflicting interpretations.

Much recent discussion of festivals in the social sciences has centered around the issue of whether festivals can either be considered to be "spectacles" or "rituals." Manning (1992:292) defined a spectacle as "a large-scale extravagant cultural production that is replete with striking visual imagery and dramatic action that is watched by a mass audience." Spectacles therefore are staged and basically nonparticipatory. Rituals, on the other hand, involve "the performance of more or less invariant sequences of formal acts and utterances not encoded by the performers" (Rappaport, 1992:250).

According to Handelman (1998), festivals often consist of both ritual and spectacle. The ritual elements are linked to transformation and rites of passage, and are geared toward the transformation of society. This is very clear in the original meaning of Carnival, which turned the social order on its head for a few days. On the other hand, spectacles are a more passive form of celebration, which hold up a mirror to society as it is. The existing social order remains unchallenged and unchanged. An additional aspect of change in modern festivals is that the focus of events is gradually becoming more external to the communities that produce them. Originally, festivals were largely produced and celebrated by local people, without any consideration of the outside world. In modern society festivals are increasingly aimed to attract tourists from outside the local community, to attract the attention of the media, and to develop an external audience as well as an internal one.

In Barcelona one can see this process to some extent with the major *festes* (Catalan for "fiesta" or "festival") in the city. For example, *La Mercè,* which is essentially Barcelona's main festival, has steadily added events and performance spaces to the program to satisfy the growing demand for spectacle. Recent years have seen the addition of elements predominantly related to relatively passive consumption, such as the *Festa al Cel,* an arial festival on the beach with kites and aeroplanes. The vast majority of events in the city, however, remain more related to "ritual" than to "spectacle." For most of the events the structure and content of the program changes little, and there is little attempt to develop spectacular elements to attract outsiders. Even relatively large events such as La Mercè retain many elements of "ritual," such as the processions of *gegants* (giant human figures) or *casteller* (human structures) performances.

In fact, as Waterman (1998:58) points out, dualistic classifications of festivals such as that between rituals and spectacles "do not provide enough substance to conceptualize the distinctions among festivals." In reality, each festival tends to include both of these elements to a greater or lesser degree. Some cultural events, such as Carnival in Rio, are more clearly oriented toward spectacle, but they still retain elements of ritual. Similarly, events such as the Sant Joan celebrations in Cuitadella in Menorca have a heavy ritual content, but have also taken on elements of spectacle over the years, such as an annual fireworks display. The relationship between ritual and spectacle may therefore change over time, and should be seen as a contested field of meaning rather than a simple dichotomy as suggested by Handelman.

Both rituals and spectacles involve particular configurations of time and space. As discrete events, the temporal dimension is of course important to both. However, the characteristics of a spectacle as a mass, nonparticipatory phenomenon tend to emphasize the role of space as a means of creating a spectacle, particularly given the emphasis on visual consumption. Rituals, on the other hand, more clearly involve a distinct temporal dimension, through the recurrence of specific acts and the frequent linkage of rituals to cyclical time. The differing emphasis given to temporal considerations (holding the event at a specific time) or spatial considerations (staging the event in a particular space) have changed over time, also promoting competition between the ritual and spectacular aspects of cultural events.

Many commentators have identified a shift away from the original ritual functions of festivals, toward an increasing spectacularization. This shift has been argued to produce a loss of meaning for local people, an increasing lack of interest in the cultural and ritual aspects of the events, and growing commoditization (e.g., Greenwood, 1977). More recently, Ravenscroft and Matteucci (2003), in their analysis of the *San Fermin* fiesta in Pamplona, argued that the fiesta represents a carnivalesque reversal of the everyday, which is deployed to maintain rather than challenge social order. The fiesta becomes a liminal space in which deviance is tolerated. The deviant practices of locals are also legitimized during the fiesta by the presence of tourists, who provide a convenient "cover" for such activity.

Festivals are also increasingly being used as a means of symbolic construction (Ruiz, 2000). In Jerez de la Fontera, a new *Fiesta de Otoño* was created in 1994 in order to improve the image of the city. The basic concept is to increase popularity and participation and to reflect the "essence" of Jerez. The event runs from September 23 to October 12, encasing existing celebrations, such as La Merced. It tries to synthesize traditional and modern culture and is aimed both at locals and tourists. But the model of participation in the Fiesta de Otoño is arguably passive. Citizens are reduced to the role of spectators in the festivalization process (see also Chapters 14 and 15).

Resisting Festivalization

Other authors, however, present a more nuanced view of the relationship between modernity, tradition, and cultural events. Costa (2002), in his analysis of *Las Fallas* of Valencia, however, argues that a strict dichotomy between tradition and modernity is not tenable for festivals such as Las Fallas, which create a "festive sociability" or a public sphere that is able to bridge the gap between tradition and modernity. Thus, festivals may be changed in modern societies, but they also have the power to change the experience of modern life and to create alternative views of modern rationality. In the case of Las Fallas, some commentators have even argued that the event has taken the place of civil society in Valencia (J. Sabate, personal communication, 2003).

Magliocco (2001:167) also sees the emergence of "festival reclamation," which is

> a phenomenon in which subjugated groups reclaim or reappropriate (re)presentations of them created by the dominant culture. Festival reclamation may entail the reappropriation or recreation of a separate festival as an exquisitely local celebration after a larger festival has become a tourist attraction. Thus when a town's primary festival no longer performs an identity narrative to which the population can subscribe, the community may choose to transform the festival through new activities, or to designate a new, separate festival to perform the identity with which the community identifies.

Schuster (2001:363) also has a more positive view of events, or "ephemera" as he terms them. Although many commentators argue that local events are usually appropriated by the media and commoditized for tourists, Schuster argues that although locally based events are subject to a wide range of influences and pressures, local resistance is much more resilient than many analysts suggest. "Ephemera, particularly signature ephemera, remain a particularly fruitful focus for detecting the distinctively local contribution to the image of a place."

The following sections examine the arguments surrounding the process of festivalization in the context of cultural events in Catalunya.

CULTURAL EVENTS IN CATALUNYA

One of the problems with applying models of festivalization derived from a north western European or American context to southern Europe is the fact that commodification of cultural events is a complex affair.

To start with, the engagement of the commercial sector in festes has a long history. In La Mercè in Barcelona, for example, there was widespread involvement of commercial "sponsors" at the beginning of the twentieth century. If anything, the relative role of the commercial sector has declined over time as the role of the public sector has grown, particularly since the restoration of democracy in the 1970s.

Even if fiestas in Spain have to attract commercial sponsors to help cover the cost of the increasingly spectacular events demanded by experience-hungry consumers, Schuster (2001:390) argues that this does not necessarily result in commoditization and alienation:

> In the end residents get involved in the most successful ephemera because they want to and they think their lives will be richer as a result. How else can one explain the growth of the traditional elements of citizen participation in, for example, Catalan festivals—the groups of *castellers* building human castles, the creation and display of each city's and each neighborhood's emblematic giants, the involvement of young people in groups of devils to present the *correfoc,* or the creation of floral carpets for the feast of Corpus Christi in Sitges?

Even in major events such as the Sitges Carnival, which is visited by hundreds of thousands of people (many of whom are foreign tourists), the people who are involved in the production of culture are largely unpaid—they participate for their own enjoyment and feeling of identity.

The vitality of cultural events at the grassroots level is confirmed by the quadrupling of festivals in Catalunya since 1976 (Cubeles and Fina, 1998), which indicates a growing willingness of people to participate. The range and number of events included in those festivals has also increased in recent years. Work by Crespi (2002) confirms that most of the "traditional" cultural events in Catalunya are in fact of very recent origin (see Table 13.1). In general, only processions for

TABLE 13.1. Origin of festes in Catalunya.

Type of event	Pre-1970	1970-1980	1980-1990	1990-2000
Setmana Santa (holy week) processions	64%	2%	21%	13%
Carnival	6%	31%	50%	13%
Pessebres Vivants	4%	14%	32%	49%
Medieval fairs			5%	95%

Source: Crespi (2002).

Setmana Santa (Easter Week) have existed since the Franco era. With the restoration of democracy there was a rapid recovery of traditional cultural events, particularly those taking place in the streets, such as Carnival. In the 1980s the *Pessebres Vivants* (re-creation of religious stories staged around Christmas) began to be resurrected. In the 1990s, however, there was a widespread emergence of "medieval fairs," which are not traditional events but have been created by local authorities largely to stimulate tourism and economic development. This indicates that the immediate post-Franco period saw a frenetic reclamation of traditional and popular culture, but that more recently this momentum has been harnessed by government for noncultural ends.

The basic reason for this relatively recent resurgence of tradition was the repression of the Franco regime. Under Franco, carnival was banned throughout Spain, and expressions of Catalan culture, such as s*ardanas* (traditional dances) were also restricted. As Prat and Contreras (undated:136) note, "the fundamental reason to explain the decline of our traditional customs in general and our festes in particular was the repression of Catalan culture under Franco."

Paradoxically, however, Franco's repression of cultural expression may ultimately have had the opposite effect. Deprived of normal channels of cultural, civic, and political expression, civil society in Catalunya built up extensive informal networks to keep the culture alive. Whereas in other places traditional culture was being eroded by the onslaught of modernity, in Catalunya it was conserved by being driven underground. This also ensured a dramatic resurgence of Catalan culture and in particular festival once democracy was restored.

Prat and Contreras (undated:114) comment: "the large numbers of participants at the Festes de la Mercè in recent years contrasts positively with the indifference to the celebrations organized by the Franquist administrations."

The picture in Catalunya seems to be reflected across Spain as a whole. As Pérez-Díaz (2003:467-468) comments:

> The importance of local fiestas has increased extraordinarily: the number of participants, the variety and range of activities, the amounts of money spent on them the last two decades have seen a proliferation of carnivals and fiestas that have been widely disseminated from their original locations.

The expansion of the number of festivals has been paralleled by an expansion in the number of traditional cultural associations and their range of activities. For example, Bargalló Valls (2000) indicates that the number of castellers groups increased almost tenfold between 1970 and 1998.

When looking at the motives for generating new festes, there is also a clear distinction in terms of the type of event. Stimulating Catalan culture is clearly the most important motivation overall, but for Carnival for example, secularization and democratization are more important (Crespi, 2002). In the case of medieval fairs in particular, economic development is the most important motivation (77 percent).

These data suggest a gradual shift in the role of cultural events, particularly in the sphere of reclaiming cultural rights but also in terms of generating economic benefits. An important question, however, is whether these changes have a relationship to tourism.

CULTURAL EVENTS AND TOURISM

One of the underpinnings of the commoditization argument is that cultural events have increasingly become oriented toward the needs of visitors or tourists rather than local residents. However, the extent to which this is true depends on the type of event being considered.

One could think about the festival system in Catalunya in terms of a hierarchy, from small-scale local events up to major national and international events. At the "apex" of this hierarchy are those festes that have been declared to be of "national interest," of which there are twenty-two in Catalunya. These include events such as *La Patum de Berga, la Dansa de la Mort* in Verges, *Les Festes de Santa Tecla* in Tarragona, and the *Festa Major de Gràcia* in Barcelona. On the next level of the hierarchy are the festes majors that are staged in almost every community in Catalunya. The cultural department of the Generalitat de Catalunya lists 1,014 such events. This figure matches closely the listing by Prat and Contreras (undated) of 1,153 festes majors in Catalunya.

But there are also far more local events that are not considered to be of interest to outsiders, and are therefore not listed in centralized sources. In Bages, for example, thirty-nine events are listed by the Generalitat, but Ballús (2000) lists 652 events for Bages alone, which indicates that the Generalitat list is just the tip of the iceberg. A similar situation exists in respect to events in El Priorat, which were studied by Paramon (1997) in 1994. He found that the total number of events was 440, compared with a current Generalitat listing of twenty-four events. A large proportion of these events were local festes majors (265 events), which are probably not considered worth listing by the Generalitat.

If the Generalitat list only contains about 6 percent of all festivals, as in the case of Bages and El Priorat, then the total number of festivals held in Catalunya could be as high as 17,000. However, other estimates tend to be more conservative. For example, the Generalitat (1998) mentions a total of 4,000 festes in Catalunya, although it gives no source for this figure.

Over 68 percent of festes listed by the Generalitat are concentrated in July, August, and September (see also Table 13.2). This is obviously advantageous in terms of guaranteeing good weather, but it creates a very crowded calendar of events in the summer, which is also the main tourist season. There is evidence that some municipalities create new events, or move existing ones in order to avoid competition with other festes during the main summer season (Pablo, 2000). This has also been linked to attempts to develop low-season activities to attract tourists (Crespi, 2002).

Festes are also actively marketed by local and national tourist boards. The guide *Cultural Events Catalonia 2002,* produced by the Catalan Tourist Board and the Generalitat's Department of Industry,

Commerce, and Tourism, listed a total of 403 events (see Table 13.3). These essentially represent the range of events at national level considered worthy of tourist attention by policymakers in the tourism arena. Of these events, sixteen were classified as being of "national interest" (of the twenty-two events so classified in Catalunya). Over

TABLE 13.2. Seasonal distribution of festes in Catalunya.

Month	No. of festes in Generalitat list, 2003	Prat and Contreras (undated) festes Majors
January	30	142
February	8	31
March	4	16
April	13	21
May	69	77
June	60	45
July	128	110
August	361	310
September	204	247
October	40	46
November	46	69
December	51	39
Total	1,014	1,153

TABLE 13.3. Events listed in *Cultural Events Catalonia 2002*.

Category	Number of events
Traditional and popular festivals	151
Gastronomy	75
Fairs	60
Music	50
Sport	21
Film	10
Dance	5
Circus	2

150 events were categorized as "traditional and popular festivals," with other large categories being "gastronomy," "fairs," and "music."

One sign that the tourism administration is trying to encourage a more even spread of events for tourism is the fact that the traditional festivals listed are spread throughout the year, with only a third being held between July and September.

The description of these events for tourists (in English) emphasizes aesthetic pleasure ("let yourself be carried away by your senses," p. 2), tradition ("a journey back to the old ways," p. 2), locality, and community. The traditional content of many of the festivals is also emphasized by the distribution of events through the year. There are particular concentrations around Easter and Christmas as well as the main summer festival period.

Tourism does therefore appear to be having an effect on the structure of the festa system in Catalunya, but the extent of change appears marginal. The vast majority of events remain small-scale, local affairs, relatively untouched by commoditization or tourism. To find more concrete evidence of change, one has to look more closely at specific events.

THE PROCESS OF "FESTIVALIZATION"

If one looks more closely at the history of Barcelona, for example, it can be seen that the city has a long history of developing cultural events for social, economic, and political reasons. Pablo (2000) argues that the Festa Major of Barcelona, La Mercè, was created as the Festa Major for Catalunya. The aims of staging such an event included providing rational recreation for the growing working classes of Barcelona, providing a showcase for new commercial products, and supporting both religious and political organizations.

Under Franco, the festa recuperated its religious heritage. The trappings of popular celebration were stripped away, and the crowds were kept at bay behind barriers watching well-ordered processions (Schuster, 1995). With democratization, festes became an important means of reclaiming public space. However, the space was filled not by an expansion of commercial activities, as has happened in many northern European cities. Jan Gehl (1996), for example, describes the process by which public space was reclaimed in Copenhagen through pedestrianization, but the vast majority of spaces created were given over to commercial use, such as pavement cafés. In Edinburgh, Howie (2000) also describes how festival spaces have become commodified, using the example of the Edinburgh Hogmany event, which began to restrict access to the city center on New Year's Eve.

Rather than festivalization, one might conceive of a "socialization" of festivals. Just as leisure in northern countries was rationalized during the nineteenth and twentieth centuries to contain or channel discontent and maximize economic and political spin-offs from popular culture, so fiestas in Spain and Catalunya have increasingly become tools of social integration.

As the Centre for the Promotion of Popular and Traditional Culture (undated) points out, "the socializing function also defines the festa. The festa opposes individualism and especially promotes community participation." This is reflected in the rhetoric that accompanies major festes in Catalunya. For example, the values espoused in the 2003 edition of La Mercè were "peace and civicism," and the event was used as the opening act of the "Forum Year," leading up to the Universal Forum of Cultures in 2004. Joan Clos, the Mayor of Barcelona, wrote in the 2003 edition of the program for La Mercè that the event is about occupying the streets, integration between diverse social groups, and a confirmation of collective spirit.

This indicates a high level of social goals for an event that might elsewhere be seen as a massive street party. The basic question, of course, is to what extent are these goals achieved? The rhetoric is at least very consistent among policymakers. Interviews with different policymakers and organizers of La Mercè, for example, revealed a consistent vision of the festa as a mechanism for promoting integration and social cohesion and stimulating people to participate in the social and cultural life of the city. The role of the voluntary sector in Barcelona and in La Mercè is underlined by the staging of a central "Display of Associations" in Plaça Catalunya. However, one of the interesting features of the event is also the extent to which the original concentration of activities in the center of the city (in order to increase accessibility and visibility) has been replaced by an effort to stage events in different parts of the city, to increase social cohesion.

Not everybody was totally positive about the effects, however, as some policymakers said that the attempts at integration led to parallel events being organized. Different population groups are attracted to different events, but there is little real mixing. For other respondents this is not necessarily a problem, because they view the fact that people have even visual contact with one another during the major events in La Mercè as positive. People can at least see that Barcelona is a diverse, multicultural city.

Most respondents were of the opinion that La Mercè had become more popular with tourists over the years. The fact that so many people are visiting Barcelona means that there are also many tourists around during the festival. However, as Pablo (2000) pointed out, during the Franco era La Mercè was actually more oriented toward tourism than it is now, with programs printed in several different languages. Even people who notice an increase in tourists do not necessarily find this a problem. One interviewee said that La Mercè had become an event for tourists, but because all the residents of Barcelona are also involved, this was no problem.

The general tone of the interviewees' assessment of La Mercè was that the festa had become a "metropolitan" event, with a wide scope of events for all the different groups in the city. However, the expansion of the festa does not necessarily imply a higher level of spectacle. For example, in the Festa al Cel, which with its airborne acrobatics is probably one of the most spectacular elements of La Mercè, one of the most important activities is actually teaching children how to make their own kites. And while the spectacle of the Festa al Cel was the biggest draw of the 2003 event with 400,000 spectators, the more reflexive and interactive Passaig de les Persones (with seminars, workshops, and children's activities) attracted many more participants (300,000) than the closing fireworks display at the base of Montjuic (175,000). (It should be noted, however, that there is considerable discussion surrounding the numbers of participants at these events; see www.contrastat.net.)

THE ROLE OF THE "LOCAL"

The critique of festivalization is usually built on two premises: First, that the level of commodification is increasing, and second, that the locus of control is shifting away from the civic and local toward the market and the global.

This, of course, raises the question of what is "local"? There is no time to go into the many contortions of this particular argument here, but suffice it to say that "local" is usually conflated with the residents of a geographically defined area. One problem, of course, is just how large or small that area should be. One might argue in the context of Barcelona that residents of Barcelona visiting a fiesta in Barcelona should be regarded as "locals." In reality, however, Barcelona is a big place, and for many residents of Barcelona the areas of the city outside their immediate surroundings are almost as foreign as Africa or Asia. In fact, even very close neighbors can be regarded with suspicion.

This process is evident in the Festa Major de Gràcia, for example, where the residents of one decorated street complained about interference from "outsiders." These outsiders were not foreign tourists, or even people from other parts of Barcelona, but rather people from the next street. This is an example of a high level of social capital, and particularly bonding capital, which makes events such as the Festa Major de Gràcia or La Mercè possible, but at the same time can become an exclusionary device if not managed properly.

As Crespi (2002) has argued, a certain degree of exclusion is actually necessary to maintain the fiesta. Without the anticipated "reward" of being a member of a select group, it would be much harder to mobilize large numbers of people to devote a large amount of time to creating and maintaining the fiesta.

For example, the street decorations alone for the 2003 Festa Major de Gràcia involved almost 300 people from twenty-two streets expending 22,350 hours of voluntary labor, not to mention a yearlong effort to collect the recycled materials to produce the decorations. This is equivalent to thirteen person years of labor, totally unpaid. This type of investment of time in the production of cultural events is not unusual. In Valencia the network of associations that participate in Las Fallas has over 200,000 members, or a quarter of the Valencian population. The participation in associations in Valencia is 22 percent of the population, nearly 20 percent higher than in Spain as a whole.

In the case of Catalunya, the bonding represented by the membership of and participation in associations is related strongly to the unity required to withstand the repression of the Franco regime. In the absence of support from public institutions of the Spanish state, Catalunya had to develop a dense network of associations to take over the provision of education, culture, and leisure. The need for self-reliance also produced a highly specific pattern of social capital. Catalunya has levels of interpersonal trust that are among the highest in world, matching those in the social-democratic states of Scandinavia and the Netherlands. This high level of bonding capital is not always matched by a high level of bridging capital, however. The level of institutional trust in Catalunya is among the lowest in Europe, largely due to a long history of mistrust of the institutions of the Spanish state.

The restoration of democracy did allow a rebuilding of bridging capital and institutional trust in some areas. The democratic municipalities in particular were placed at the forefront of efforts to reclaim public space and festivities that had been banned under Franco. The stimulation of cultural events therefore become a mechanism of restoring civic trust, as well as asserting identity and civic freedom. In the terminology of Pérez-Díaz (2003), the "uncivil" social capital of the Franco era was transformed into the "civil" social capital of the democratic era.

In this context, the reclamation of tradition and cultural celebrations became part of a civic project to rebuild social cohesion and to forge Catalan identity. Associations have remained very much at the forefront of cultural event production. Almost all of the cultural events in Catalunya are run by associations rather than by the municipalities. In Barcelona, of the traditional or popular cultural festivals, only La Mercè is managed by the local authority. The rest are run by local cultural associations, usually without any direct assistance for the public sector.

Where the public sector does play an important role, however, is in the provision of indirect support. In particular, the regulation of the use of public space allows the streets and open spaces to be used relatively frequently for events. This is also related to the question of democratization, and an attempt by the public sector to make people feel that the public space belongs to them. Local residents make good use of this opportunity, closing off streets with the sanction of the local authority to hold fiestas and other events with great regularity.

The grassroots approach to cultural production is also evident in the management of cultural events. While in most other places issues of safety have become paramount concerns for event organizers, in Catalunya there is still very much a "bottom-up" approach to safety.

Activities such as the *correfoc* (literally "fire-running") and *castells* can be dangerous, but strict safety guidelines would destroy their inherent character. The internalization and localization of safety at festes is underlined by the production of safety tips for visitors, which even for La Mercè are only written in Catalan.

This ability to produce culture "spontaneously" in public spaces is one of the most important factors contributing to the "atmosphere" of the city. In this way, the "local" becomes important in determining the cultural experience of the tourist, even if they have come to consume "national" or "global" culture.

THE ROLE OF THE "TOURIST"

From a tourism perspective, culture is an important motive for visiting Catalunya. However, the form of culture consumed by most visitors is very specific. Tourists tend to visit the major museums and monuments, particularly those concentrated in Barcelona.

Catalunya has been extremely successful in diversifying its tourism in recent years, managing to develop new markets alongside "traditional" sun, sea, and sand tourism, such as cultural tourism to Barcelona, conference tourism, and festival tourism. This development has been helped by the post-Franco renaissance of Catalan culture and identity, which has helped to position Catalunya as a destination in its own right, rather than simply the hinterland of the Costa Brava. Tourism promotion for Catalunya has also tried to emphasize the cultural differences between Catalunya and Spain and to establish Catalunya as a tourist "brand." This type of strategy mirrors that adopted by other autonomous communities in Spain (notably Galicia), but Catalunya seems to have been particularly successful in this respect. Catalunya now accounts for 26 percent of all tourism to Spain, making Catalunya the sixteenth largest tourism destination in the world.

The growth of tourism in Catalunya has also created tensions, however. In particular, Barcelona has emerged as the new engine of Catalan tourism. For example, tourism to Barcelona increased by 130 percent between 1990 and 2002, while tourism to the rest of Catalunya grew at about half this rate. There is little sign of this gap being closed, as tourism increased by 18 percent in Barcelona between

2000 and 2002, compared with 11 percent for Catalunya as a whole. This widening gap between the different regions of Catalunya, and particularly between Barcelona and the rest of the country, is a major problem for tourism planning and management.

Tourist attention seems to be steadily more fixated on the image of "hip" Barcelona, which has become the fourth most popular city break destination in Europe and now accounts for 30 percent of foreign tourism to Catalunya (Anton Clavé, 2002). This position is rapidly being reinforced by the growth of budget airlines, which delivered 25 percent of Barcelona's) foreign tourists in 2004. The coastal resorts also continue to attract large numbers of visitors, although the competition from other sun, sea, and sand destinations is growing. On the other hand, the interior of the country, which in many ways is the heartland of Catalan tradition and popular culture, receives just over 5 percent of all tourism. This pattern is reproduced in the cultural tourism products offered by foreign tour operators in Spain. Gomez et al. (2001) show that Catalunya hardly features as a destination for touring holidays in Spain, but Barcelona is the most popular "city only" destination, being offered by over 21 percent of tour operators.

Many tourists therefore probably remain unaware of the richness of Catalan culture beyond the major global icons such as Picasso, Dalí, Gaudí, and Miró, all of whom are also used to promote Spain abroad. The increasing separation of Barcelona from Catalunya is heightened by the concentration of the major icons in Barcelona (with the possible exception of Dalí, who attracts close to a million visitors a year to Figueres). Particularly for foreign tourists, the image of Catalunya as a country and destination in its own right is overshadowed by the dominant image of Barcelona as a "cultural capital" or by the Costa Brava as one of the Spanish "costas." As Anton Clavé (2002) points out, such images are difficult to change, even with the onset of new models of tourism. This fact has tended to hinder efforts to develop new cultural tourism products in the Catalan hinterland, particularly those based on traditional Catalan culture rather than the outposts of "global" culture, such as Figueres.

Catalan culture therefore remains an abstract concept for most tourists, and many visitors are probably not even aware they are in Catalunya. This is confirmed by numerous observations at Catalan festivals visited by tourists, which indicate that there is little understanding of the cultural phenomena they are consuming. Only when accompanied by "local" friends is there a reasonable chance that tourists will understand the full context of what they are seeing.

Even though many tourists are probably unaware of the details of the culture they are immersed in, there is little doubt that people perceive Catalunya and particularly Barcelona to be cultural places. A large part of the reason why tourists find Barcelona attractive is because of the lively street culture, which produces a specific "atmosphere" in the city. Atmosphere has been shown by the ATLAS research (Richards, 2001) to be an increasingly important part of the cultural tourism product, as people start suffering from "museum fatigue" or "monumental monotony." Very rarely, however, do tourists (or even academics) pause to consider where this atmosphere might stem from.

In the case of Barcelona (and probably other cities) there is a case for suggesting that atmosphere is strongly linked to the social capital present in a specific location. Social capital is not only the "glue" that holds people together, but it can also provide the link between different groups of people. This is the essential element that creates trust between people, and therefore also between locals and tourists. Arguably this trust is essential to the production of the trusting spaces necessary to creating a lively and livable atmosphere in any city, and it may be particularly vital for attracting tourists.

This is why a socialization approach to cultural events may be far more productive both in community development terms and in terms of cultural tourism. By developing events that help to build social capital, policymakers can help to develop a lively atmosphere in the city. This has been visible recently in Barcelona, where festes such as La Mercè and Santa Eulalia have been used to animate new spaces in the city that have been considered lacking in existing community bonds and linkages with people outside the community. The Raval, for example, has long been considered an undesirable area for outsiders, whether they be tourists or people from other parts of the city. This is now being changed slowly through the staging of events that attract people into the new spaces of the Raval, and particularly the Rambla de Raval, which has been carved out of an area of poor quality housing. The opening up of new spaces such as the Rambla de Raval is part of a wider urban development strategy given the name of "sponging" (*esponjament* in Catalan)—the idea being that "breathing holes" are punched into the urban fabric to make it more porous. In the case of the Rambla de Raval, that porosity has been further increased by developing cultural events, and now tourists are increasingly being tempted into the area.

A new atmosphere is being created, which at one level may resemble the gentrifying "pacification by cappucino" identified by Zukin (1995) in New York. In the case of the Raval, however, the gentrification is also being accompanied by an opening up of the area to tourists and people from other parts of the city, in a process that might be labeled "pacification by festa." The difference is that while in the case of New York the cappucino was a frothy byproduct of the gentrification process, in the Raval the festa has become an essential element of social capital generation, aimed at inclusion rather than exclusion. The events staged in the Rambla de Raval are not tourist spectacles, but are clearly aimed at local people, particularly children. There is also little sign of local resistance to the process of "socialization by festa," whereas the opposition to gentrification through property speculation (and particularly hotel construction) is clearly visible.

Research shows that the tourists as well as the residents both perceive that La Mercè is both a traditional event and a contemporary event—an arena in which tradition is "innovated" (Richards, 2004). One of the major sources of this innovation is the involvement of different cultural groups in the festa, as well as the inclusion of new spaces, which introduce a new dynamic into the event. This process also produces unexpected experiences—people "enjoy" the cultural product, even if they have become (knowingly or unknowingly) "accidental cultural tourists."

CONCLUSION

In Catalunya festivals are not generally staged for tourists, and neither are the vast majority of events commoditized in the way that has been described elsewhere. Cultural events are seen far more as a social tool, which is aimed at Catalan society itself. The presence of tourists is therefore seen at best as a happy accident, and at worst as a mild nuisance.

The important point about the socialization of festivals is that promotion of events is increasingly aimed at social, rather than economic goals. Even in the case of major festes such as La Mercè, the level of commercialization has declined in recent decades, as the role of the event has changed from a means of promoting commerce to a vehicle for socialization. The rhetoric of festes in Catalunya usually lacks the commercial overtones that are evident in many events in Northern Europe. Instead, the existence of such events is more often linked to political discussions, because the public sector has a crucial role in funding. Visitor numbers are inflated not so much to attract commercial sponsors, but to persuade local politicians to continue public funding (García, 1999). This has created a symbiotic system, in which politicians use festes as a backdrop for photo opportunities, and the festa provides the crowds which make their visit newsworthy.

Therefore festa culture is not aimed directly at tourists, but as Dodd (1999) has suggested in the case of cultural development in general, cultural tourism at festes is more a byproduct of locally oriented culture than a specific attempt to generate tourism. The fact that there are so many cultural events in Catalunya means that tourists almost inevitably encounter them, but the degree of specific cultural tourism to festes is low (particularly among international tourists).

In fact, one could argue that the position of festes in the cultural tourism product of Catalunya is a direct result of the distribution and form of social capital in Catalunya. Catalunya is rich in cultural events because of high levels of bonding capital, which in turn tends to exclude (or at least ignore) outsiders. This exclusion is also important for the maintenance of the festes themselves, since one of the main motivations for participation is exclusivity—access to spaces and/or status not available to people outside the group. This produces an interesting tension in the Catalan festa system, where particularly at major events the rhetoric of inclusion (La Mercè is for everyone) coexists with practices of exclusion (this is *our* festa).

The result of this tension seems to be that the Catalans are performing for themselves, rather than the tourists. High levels of bonding social capital allow them to ignore the presence of tourists while producing cultural products that are of interest for outsiders. In many cases there is also an indirect benefit from the presence of tourists in the form of increased attention for their cultural production. Greater numbers of visitors and/or media attention are also used as an argument to gain extra funding from sponsors or the public sector.

However, if events are divorced from their local context, there is no opportunity for bonding social capital to be brought into play—only economic and cultural capital are required. This is certainly the case with the 2004 Universal Forum of Cultures, which was a top-down "global" event devised as a follow-up to the 1992 Olympics. It is not surprising, therefore, that the event was beset by difficulties in organization and opposition from local groups. Whereas the Olympics succeeded in generating local pride and participation (even in the face of opposition), the Forum arguably failed to create a feeling of ownership among the people of Barcelona. More active forms of participation will need to be stimulated in order to animate "Europe's biggest square" in the post-Forum period.

REFERENCES

Anton Clavé, S. (2002) El model turístic de Catalunya enfront de les noves tendències de la demanda. *Revista de Geografia* 1: 119-129.

Ballús, Gloria (2000) *Guia de Festes del Bages*. Manresa: Centro d'Estudis del Bages.

Bargalló Valls, J. (2000) Manifestacions de cultura popular. La Festa. In Generalitat de Catalunya (1998) *Catalunya Dema: Jornades de debat octubre 1997-maig 1998*. Barcelona: Generalitat de Catalunya, pp. 657-661.

Centre for the Promotion of Popular and Traditional Culture (undated) *Fidelitzar el Turisme a Través de la Cultura Popular*. Barcelona.

Costa, Xavier (2002) Festive traditions in modernity: The public sphere of the festival of the "Fallas" in Valencia (Spain). *The Sociological Review* 50(4): 482-504.

Crespi, Monserrat (2002) L'activitat Festiva Popular en l'era de la Mundialització: el cas de Catalunya. PhD Thesis, University of Barcelona.

Cubeles, X. and Fina, X. (1998) *Culture in Catalonia*. Barcelona: Fundació Jaume Bofill.

Dodd, D. (1999) Barcelona, the making of a cultural City. In: Dodd, D. and van Hemel, A. (eds) *Planning Cultural Tourism in Europe: A Presentation of Case Studies and Theories*. Amsterdam: Boekman Foundation, pp. 53 -64.

García, Eva (1999) *La Feria de Abril de Catalunya*. MA Thesis in Public Management and Administration, University of Barcelona.

Gehl, J. and Gemzøe, L. (1996) *Public Spaces Public Life*. Copenhagen: Danish Architectural Press.

Generalitat de Catalunya (1998) *Catalunya Dema: Jornades de debat octubre 1997-maig 1998*. Barcelona: Generalitat de Catalunya.

Gomez, V. B, Lerema, A. H. and García, L. G. (2001) *Los viajes combinados de turismo cultural con destino Espana en los principales países emisore europeos.* Documento de Trabajo A 20013 Universidad de Alcalá, Escuela Universitaria de Turisme.

Greenwood, D. J. (1977) Culture by the Pound: An anthropological perspective on tourism and cultural commoditization. In Smith, V. L. (ed.) *Hosts and Guests: The Anthropology of Tourism.* Pennsylvania: University of Pennsylvania Press, pp. 129-138.

Handelman, D. (1998) *Models and Mirrors: Towards an Anthropology of Public Events.* New York: Berghahn Books.

Howie, F. (2000) Establishing the common ground: Tourism, ordinary places, grey-areas and environmental quality in Edinburgh, Scotland. In Richards, G. and Hall, D. (eds) *Tourism and Sustainable Community Development.* London: Routledge, pp. 101-118.

Landry, (2000) *The Creative City: A Toolkit for Urban Innovators.* London: Earthscan Publications.

Landry, C. and Bianchini, F. (1995) *The Creative City.* London: Demos.

Magliocco, S. (2001) Coordinates of power and performance festivals as sites of (re)presentation and reclamation in Sardinia. *Ethnologies* 23 (1): 167-188.

Manning, F. E. (1992) Spectacle. In Bauman, Richard (ed.) *Folklore, Cultural Performances, and Popular Entertainments.* Oxford: Oxford University Press, pp. 291-299.

McNeill, Donald (1999) *Urban Change and the European Left: Tales from the New Barcelona.* London: Routledge.

Monclús, Francisco Javier (2000) Barcelona's planning strategies: From 'Paris of the South' to the 'Capital of West Mediterranean.' *GeoJournal* 51: 57-63.

Pablo, Jordi (2000) *La Mercè Illustrada: Guia de la festa major de Barcelona.* Col.lecció El Mèdol - Guies, no. 7.

Paramon, C. C. (1997) Associacionisme ètnic al Baix llobregat. *Materials del Baix llobregat* 3: 111-121.

Pérez-Díaz, V. (2003) De la Guerra Civil a la Sociedad Civil: El capital social en España entre los años trienta y los años noventa del siglo XX. In Putnam, R. (ed.) *El Decline del Capital Social.* Barcelona: Galaxia Gutenburg, pp. 425-489.

Prat, J. and Contreras, J. (undated) *Les Festes Populars.* Barcelona: El Llar del Llibre.

Rappaport, Roy A. (1992) *Ritual.* In Bauman, R. (ed.) *Folklore, Cultural Performances and Popular Entertainments.* Oxford: Oxford University Press, pp. 249-260.

Ravenscroft, N. and Matteucci, X. (2003) The festival as carnivalesque: Social governance and control at Pamplona's San Fermin Fiesta. *Tourism, Culture & Communication* 4: 1-15.

Richards, G. (2001) El desarrollo del turismo cultural en Europa, *Estudios Turísticos* 150: 3-14.

Richards, G. (2004) Cultura popular, tradición y turismo en las festes de la Mercè de Barcelona. In Font, J. (ed.) *Casos de Turismo Cultural: De la planificación estratégica a la gestión del producto.* Barcelona: Ariel, pp. 287-306.

Ruiz, Esteban (2000) *Construccíon Simbólica de la Cuidad*. Madrid: Miño y Dávid.

Schuster, J. M. (1995) Two urban festivals: La Mercè and first night. *Planning Practice and Research* 10(2): 173-187.

Schuster, J. M. (2001) Ephemera, temporary urbanism and imaging. In L. J. Vale and S. B. Warner (eds) *Imaging the City—Continuing Struggles and New Directions*. New Brunswick: CUPR Books, pp. 361-396.

Waterman, S. (1998) Carnivals for élites? The cultural politics of arts festivals. *Progress in Human Geography* 22: 54-74.

Zukin, S. (1995) *The Cultures of Cities*. Oxford: Blackwell.

Chapter 14

Porto and Rotterdam
As European Capitals of Culture: Toward the Festivalization of Urban Cultural Policy

Erik Hitters

INTRODUCTION

Since 1985 a total of twenty-six cities have had the honor of being designated as European City or Capital of Culture. The event is becoming increasingly important for cities to celebrate their own unique cultural identity within the pluriform European Union. The designation as European Capital of Culture has become much sought-after. Rotterdam was, together with Porto, Cultural Capital of Europe in 2001. Like other port cities such as Glasgow and Antwerp, Rotterdam has tried to use the event as a means of repositioning itself as a cultural city. As Bianchini (1999) has pointed out, such "declining cities" have been using culture (and cultural events more specifically) increasingly as a means of city marketing in recent years. This means that the success of the event is often judged in terms of visitor numbers or spending, rather than in terms of the cultural content or longer-term image effects of the event. This interest marks the transition of the City/Capital of Culture from a low-key cultural festival into a major engine for urban redevelopment. This chapter argues that the cultural capital event has become a key factor in the festivalization of urban cultural policy in Europe.

Relatively few of the host cities have carried out evaluative research, and this means that the assessment of the event is usually based on assertion rather than fact. There is relatively little empirical research available on the effects of the Cultural Capital event for the city (Palmer/Rae, 2004). Has it generated a substantial increase in visitors and tourists to the city? How has it affected the cultural attractiveness of the city? Has the urban economy benefited? Will the city remain a "capital of culture" in the years to come? Until now, only partial answers to such questions from scattered research in individual cities are available. In particular, there has been little comparison of the different cities and events.

This chapter provides a review of research in the 2001 European Cultural Capitals Rotterdam (Netherlands) and Porto (Portugal). It consists of comparative qualitative data and survey data. The survey data focus in particular on the sociocultural visitor profile, their expenditure, and their image of the city. More details of the surveys can be found in Richards et al. (2002). Some 3,000 visitors were surveyed on these issues across a range of different types of cultural events during the year. The results allow an initial view of the economic, social, and cultural impacts of the event to be constructed. The qualitative research looks more specifically at the effects on the urban cultural infrastructure and the policy impacts of the event. It suggests that the staging of large cultural events has become a key strategy for urban areas in the twenty-first century. The question here is whether it is possible to assess the long-term effects of such an event.

THE FESTIVALIZATION
OF URBAN CULTURAL POLICY

The concept of festivalization is a fairly widely accepted phenomenon among analysts of urban policy and cultural trends (Häusserman and Siebel, 1993). In this chapter it refers to the increasing use of flagship festivals and large cultural events as a means to market major cities. Furthermore, I will argue that festivalization is not just limited to city marketing objectives but is becoming a new policy paradigm in the field of urban culture. This phenomenon can be linked to three major trends in urban cultural policy since the 1970s.

First, there was a general increase in competition between cities for the attention of tourists and other important stakeholders and consumers. As Richards and Wilson (2002) argue:

> Cities (or more usually city centers) have become stages for a continual stream of events which lead eventually to the "festivalization" of the city. Tourism, leisure, sport, and culture are no longer discrete elements of consumption to be enjoyed in their own specific arenas, but simply elements of what Ritzer (1999) terms the "means of consumption," which can be enjoyed in the street as much as in the opera house. The traditional barriers between different leisure forms, such as tourism, sport and culture, are disappearing. In such a climate, cultural events in particular have emerged as a means of improving the image of cities, adding life to the city streets and giving citizens renewed pride in their home city. Culture has also become an important means of attracting tourists from outside the city. This is an important point, since the economic benefits of staging cultural events can only really be captured if spending power is attracted from outside the city.

Second, festivalization can be linked to a crisis in the legitimation of public policies. Cultural policies aimed at the social distribution of culture have not had the desired effect of an increased participation of the lower socioeconomic strata in society. The welfare state's cultural policy suffered from a legitimation crisis. Research showed that cultural participation remained high among the upper and upper middle classes, but diminished among the middle to lower classes (Knulst, 1996). What is more, cultural participation of the new upper middle class audiences was hardly a result of public policy, but of the social dynamics of status rivalry and distinction (cf. Bourdieu, 1984). Cultural policy, then, was forced to shift its focus away from "high art," toward a much more inclusive definition of (popular) culture. The policy arena thus widened its scope to pop music, film, Web design, ethnic culture, entertainment, etc. And it searched for new means of distribution that were more accessible than the traditional theaters and museums. Consequently, festivals appeared to be the panacea.

The third trend in cultural policy is the increased budgetary pressure. Although budgets for cultural policy have remained fairly stable over the last years in most European countries, one can observe increasing pressure on those budgets. This can be tied to a general trend in public policy toward more accountability and measurable objectives (Hitters, 1996). For the field of cultural policy, this has proven to be a difficult task. The solution was often found not in looking for measurable objectives within the cultural field itself, but by stressing the external effects of cultural policies. Subsequently, investments in cultural provisions and even general cultural policies are relying more and more on positive interpretations of economic impact studies, tourism growth figures, and image and city marketing data.

TOWARD A TYPOLOGY
OF EUROPEAN CULTURAL CAPITALS

The Cultural Capital event was originally designed for cultural objectives, bringing together the unity and diversity of cultures in the European Union. As Corijn and Van Praet (1994) suggest in their history of Cultural Capitals, the event became a vehicle for political and socioeconomic aims, soon after its conception in 1984. The first cities organizing the event mainly staged cultural and artistic programs, such as Athens, Florence, Amsterdam, and Berlin. Most of these were fairly elitist and aimed at specialized audiences. Hardly anyone now remembers those events in these cities, whereas in Amsterdam and Paris most people presumably hardly noticed that their city was cultural capital.

A widely acknowledged turning point was Glasgow in 1990, which introduced a new model for Cultural Capitals, fusing art and culture with objectives of urban development and regeneration. Glasgow is by far the most successful of Cultural Capitals, serving as an archetype for all declining "second" cities in their efforts at enhancing their image and cultural identity. The city still benefits from the physical and image effects of the event. A third type was introduced by Antwerp in 1993. Here the event was aimed more broadly at the socioeconomic enhancement of the city. The objectives were to put Antwerp on the map as a tourist destination but also to strengthen the organizational infrastructure in the city for the cultural and tourism sector. Also, Antwerp is usually claimed to have been successful, although the effects have worn off over the years. This, then, suggests the typology of Cultural Capitals presented in Table 14.1.

In terms of budgets, one has to remark that a comparison of budgets is very risky, since many cities included not just the costs of the cultural program in the total budget, but in some cases also capital and infrastructure costs. This is particularly noticeable in the case of Thessaloniki, but infrastructure costs were also an important element in the budget of Porto 2001. Table 14.2 should therefore be read with prudence.

Neither of the two cities covered in this chapter fit neatly into one of these types. I would, however, suggest that Porto appears to be closer to the physical regeneration type, whereas Rotterdam fits more closely with the socioeconomic type. In both cities, however, sizeable parts of the program have been culturally elitist as well.

ROTTERDAM 2001: EUROPEAN CULTURAL CAPITAL

The Rotterdam Cultural Capital event in 2001 (R2001) had a very ambitious program, which eventually included 524 projects. The R2001 attracted a total of 2,250,000 visitors. This was a satisfactory attendance as far as the organizers were concerned, but less than the claimed attendance for some other Cultural Capital years. In 1996, for example, Copenhagen claimed a total of 7.5 million event visitors, and Antwerp claimed a total of 10 million visitors in 1993. One has to

TABLE 14.1. Typology of cultural capitals.

Cultural capital ideal type	Typical effects	Effects duration	Archetypal city
Cultural elitist model	Software, cultural program	Short-term	Berlin
Urban regeneration model	Hardware, physical infrastructure	Long-term	Glasgow
Socioeconomic model	Orgware, sociocultural infrastructure	Medium-term	Antwerp

TABLE 14.2. Budget of some European cities of culture/Cultural Capitals.

Year	City	Budget in million €
1985	Athens	27.2
1986	Florence	20.4
1987	Amsterdam	9.0
1988	Berlin	27.2
1989	Paris	0.6
1990	Glasgow	54.4
1991	Dublin	45.3
1992	Madrid	22.6
1993	Antwerp	40.8
1994	Lisbon	23.6
1995	Luxemburg	136.1
1996	Copenhagen	86.2
1997	Thessaloniki	285.8
1998	Stockholm	54.4
1999	Weimar	28.1
2001	Rotterdam	23.6
2001	Porto	100+

Source: Gemeente Rotterdam (2003).

be somewhat skeptical of these figures, since such estimates often include visitors to the city who had not actually attended any of the programmed events (Richards, 2000). A more realistic comparison may be the 3.5 million visitors to the Glasgow event in 1990, or the 2.2 million visitors who actually attended cultural capital events in Antwerp in 1993. Seen in this perspective, the total attendance was reasonable, but it was achieved by staging an ambitious program.

The R2001 projects were organized by a wide range of organizations, with varying degrees of involvement by R2001. Over 65 percent of the projects received a financial subsidy from R2001, while the rest received promotional and/or marketing support. This makes it difficult to assess the effects of the Cultural Capital event as a whole. For example, it cannot be established with any certainty what proportion of the projects in the program would have taken place without Rotterdam being designated European Cultural Capital. It is also difficult to establish how many of the visitors to events in the program came as a result of the marketing efforts of R2001 rather than the event organizers or the event venue. Because of this basic ambiguity about the extent to which R2001 itself had been instrumental in stimulating visitors to come to Rotterdam, we decided to take a very conservative approach to the estimation of its effects. In particular, it was decided to attribute visitor spending to R2001 only if it could be shown that visitors had come to the city specifically for the Cultural Capital program or to a specific event that they knew to be part of the program. In this way we can be more certain that there is a direct link between the marketing efforts of R2001 itself, visitors to the city, and their expenditure.

Methods

In order to help evaluate the extent to which R2001 was successful in achieving its aims, *Rotterdam Culturele Hoofdstad* (the event organizers) and the Rotterdam Development Corporation (OBR) asked the Arts and Culture Department of the ERASMUS University Rotterdam and the Association for Tourism and Leisure Education (ATLAS) to undertake visitor research. The main part of this study consisted of visitor surveys held at a number of events during 2001. The aim of these surveys was to establish a visitor profile for R2001 and to examine the motivations, activities, attitudes, and expenditure of people attending R2001 events. In addition to measuring the economic spin-off of the event, an important objective was to examine the image that visitors had of Rotterdam, and to evaluate whether R2001 had had any effect on that image. The long-term image effects of the event can only be measured over the next few years, but a short-term evaluation can be made by comparing the image R2001 visitors have of the city with measurements made by ATLAS in previous years in other locations. These surveys included questions about the image of different European cities as cultural destinations among cultural visitors in different European countries (Richards, 2001). The questionnaire used for the research was therefore largely based on the

TABLE 14.3. Rotterdam event typology: Share of events, visitors and survey respondents.

Orientation complexity	Local/national	International
Popular	57% Events 64% Visitors 35% Respondents	9% Events 7% Visitors 18% Respondents
High	21% Events 8% Visitors 15% Respondents	13% Events 21% Visitors 32% Respondents

ATLAS research, together with a number of questions on specific aspects of the Cultural Capital event in 2001.

In order to assess the profile of visitors to the event, a sample of events had to be selected for visitor surveys. In order to reflect the diversity of different events in the program, a number of events were selected on the basis of the type of cultural content and the type of visitors the event was aimed at. In terms of cultural content, the events can be classified along a continuum of "complexity" from high to popular culture. In terms of the visitor segments, the focus of the events can be identified as locally orientated, national, or international (see Table 14.3).

In order to examine the representativeness of the survey events, the profile of the events was compared with the total program of events. In the total program the majority of events were related to local/popular culture. However, the survey events were selected to generate a stratified random sample of visitors. In particular, it was felt important to achieve a reasonable sample of visitors from Rotterdam, the rest of the Netherlands, and abroad. Visitors were surveyed on exit from the event or attraction they were visiting. The majority of respondents were asked to fill in a self-completion questionnaire, but a large number of visitors were also interviewed by the survey team. A total of 2,153 completed questionnaires were collected from the survey events.

The Visitors

In terms of visitor origin, the weighted survey data indicate that about half of the visitors came from Rotterdam, with a further 12 percent from the neighboring region of Zuid Holland. Of the 40 percent of visitors who came from further afield, the majority of visitors were from the Netherlands, but the proportion of foreign visitors, at over 16 percent of the weighted total, was above the expectations of the organizers. This was due largely to the popularity of major international events. For example, the Hieronymus Bosch exhibition attracted a total of 220,000 visitors, 67 percent of them from abroad. Most visitors to Rotterdam had visited the city before. Almost half of the visitors indicated that they visited the city regularly. Even so, 22 percent of the respondents had never visited Rotterdam before, and among visitors who came specifically for R2001, the proportion of first-time visitors to the city is even higher—30 percent. It seems that R2001 was particularly effective in attracting new foreign visitors to the city. Almost two thirds of the foreign tourists interviewed had never been in Rotterdam before.

The majority of respondents were forty or older (55 percent). Visitors from Rotterdam were on average a bit younger, but even so almost 40 percent of the residents of Rotterdam were over forty. The visitors to R2001 as a whole were a little older than the average cultural visitor in Europe, where the ATLAS research indicated that 53 percent were over forty. Although the R2001 visitors were relatively old, the proportion of sixteen- to twenty-four-year-olds was still higher than in the population of Rotterdam as a whole. Just over 13 percent of the population of Rotterdam is aged between fifteen and twenty-four, while over 19 percent of our respondents were aged sixteen to twenty-four. For the age groups under thirty, the Rotterdam tourism monitor recorded 26 percent of visitors to Rotterdam in 2001, compared with 25 percent for our research. In terms of the type of event, younger visitors tended to be found at the locally oriented events, regardless of the cultural content. Older visitors on the other hand were found in high proportions at high cultural events, particularly those with an international orientation.

In comparison with the population as a whole, the visitors to R2001 were relatively highly educated. The proportion of visitors with a higher education was about 70 percent, compared with about 21 percent for the European population as a whole, and 23 percent of the Dutch population. A high proportion of highly educated visitors is to be expected at cultural events, and education level is consistently the best predictor of cultural participation. The majority of the respondents were working, either as employees or self-employed. The proportion of students recorded was lower than that in other ATLAS surveys (18 percent) in 2001, but the proportion of retired visitors was about the same.

The high educational level of the respondents is—not surprisingly—linked to high-level occupations and high incomes. Over 75 percent of the respondents indicated their profession fell into the top two classifications in the Dutch SBC (standard occupational classification) system, compared with 30 percent of the Dutch working population. An extremely high proportion of visitors indicated that they had an educational occupation or a job connected with culture. Almost half of the respondents indicated that their occupation was in some way connected with culture. Over 12 percent of those in employment indicated that they were teachers or lecturers, and a further 18 percent indicated they were students.

One of the aims of the R2001 event was to engage the whole population of the city in the event. In common with the other major cities in the Netherlands, Rotterdam has a significant proportion of residents who are first- or second-generation immigrants. In particular there are large populations of Moroccan or Turkish origin in Rotterdam. Ethnic origin was only monitored for the Dutch respondents to the survey, since the Dutch definition of foreign origin could not be easily applied to foreign tourists.

In total, about 19 percent of the Dutch respondents were born abroad, or had at least one parent born abroad. This is slightly higher than the proportion in the Dutch population (17 percent) but substantially lower than the proportion in the city of Rotterdam (55 percent). In particular, people from the "ethnic minorities" (e.g., Indonesia, Surinam, Turkey, Morocco) made up only 8 percent of the sample, and were therefore even less well represented than their share in the Rotterdam population (35 percent).

City Image and Festivalization

The image that visitors had of the city of Rotterdam was measured using a series of thirteen attributes (see Table 14.4). These attributes had already been used in previous image research on Rotterdam, providing the opportunity to compare the results. This, then, can provide

TABLE 14.4. Rotterdam 2001, image elements by visitor origin (% totally agree).

Image attribute of Rotterdam	Residents of Rotterdam	Residents of Zuid Holland	Other Dutch visitors	Foreign visitors	Total
Modern architecture	84.9	78.6	88.0	66.4	80.1
Water	79.9	83.8	89.1	68.5	79.6
Multicultural	83.1	81.3	85.3	60.2	77.5
Working city	84.2	79.7	81.3	57.0	76.3
International	74.4	77.5	84.3	61.8	73.7
Dynamic	66.3	70.9	75.4	44.9	63.7
Culture and art	64.0	65.3	71.3	38.1	59.0
Lots to discover	62.1	57.7	71.7	33.2	56.8
Events	65.8	60.4	65.8	26.2	55.7
Shopping	54.4	66.7	59.7	25.9	50.1
Nightlife	43.5	46.3	42.3	21.4	38.5
Cozy (gezelligheid)	38.5	41.1	32.2	13.0	31.1
Unsafe	20.5	19.1	21.4	8.4	17.7

us some insights as to the perception of Rotterdam as a city that is increasingly represented by an image of festivalization. In general, visitors tended to place cognitive attributes highest. The aspects of the city image that are most striking for visitors are the physical attributes of modern architecture and the water in the city, and the fact that the city has a highly multicultural population. Then come affective attributes, such as the concept of Rotterdam as a working city, its international orientation, and its dynamism. These elements of the image all stem from the function of Rotterdam as a major international port and a major industrial center. Culture and art are the highest rated of the activities that the city has to offer. This is followed by lots to discover and events, shopping and nightlife. Rotterdam is not really seen as a "cozy" *(gezellig)* city, apart from by the residents of Rotterdam. The majority of visitors do not feel that Rotterdam is unsafe, but the residents of Rotterdam feel more unsafe than visitors, perhaps because they are more aware of the crime that does take place. This indicates that festivalization, mainly represented in the affective attributes, appears not to be strongly associated with this city.

However, further analysis sheds a more nuanced light on the matter of festivalization. Some of the image attributes for Rotterdam are strongly correlated with one another and also with other aspects of the visitor experience. First, positive responses to the association of Rotterdam with events is most highly correlated with associations with "art and culture" and "lots to discover." Second, there is also a significant positive correlation ($r^2 = 0.484$) between the score given for the R2001 cultural program and the score for Rotterdam as a tourism destination. Third, the perception of Rotterdam as a city with lots of events was correlated with a high score for Rotterdam as a tourism destination. This points to a relatively successful outcome of a festivalization strategy aimed at attracting tourists to the city by staging flagship events, in this case the Cultural Capital. Apparently, the city as a cultural tourist destination benefits from this event when it is part of more general festivalization policy. Fourth, visitors below the age of thirty associate Rotterdam with events more often than visitors over thirty. These findings seem to point to a relative success of the festivalization policy of the city. Rotterdam as an event city is more highly appreciated by the young and culturally active part of the visitors to R2001, the same group that also rates the R2001 event as well as the city as a tourist destination higher than average.

Rotterdam was rated very highly as a tourist destination, with an average score of 7.5 on a 10-point scale. Residents of Rotterdam are more positive about their own city than visitors, probably due to a certain amount of local pride. Domestic tourists are also slightly more positive than the average, but foreign tourists were more critical. It is likely that Rotterdam suffers from a lack of typically "Dutch" monuments and attractions, and perhaps appeals less to foreign tourists than historical cities such as Amsterdam or the Hague. Not surprisingly, repeat visitors to the city are generally more positive than first-timers, probably because their expectations of the city are more realistic. In comparison with Porto, the other Cultural Capital for 2001, Rotterdam performed reasonably well. The general evaluation of Rotterdam is higher than for Porto. Also, the average score for the event visited on a scale from 1 through 10 was 7.1 for Porto and 7.5 for Rotterdam. The program for Porto was relatively poorly evaluated at 6.4 (R2001 6.9). In terms of the city as tourist destination, in addition, even the residents of Porto tended to be more critical about the city than the residents of Rotterdam.

The evaluation of the R2001 program as a whole was generally positive, although the score was lower than for the individual events in the program, probably because a large proportion of respondents were unable to give a score for the R2001 as a whole. This indicates that awareness of the program was relatively low, which probably had a negative effect on visitor evaluation, even for visitors who felt able to give a score. The low awareness of the program is probably related to its diversity. Because the theme "Rotterdam Is Many Cities" was designed to appeal to a wide variety of different groups, it would not be surprising if people were not aware of elements of the program that were not aimed at them. A further factor could be the marketing strategy, which placed the emphasis on devolved communications, with relatively little of the marketing budget being assigned to marketing the program as a whole. As one respondent remarked, "Apart from a few flags, you don't see much of R2001 in the city." Residents of Rotterdam also tended to be more negative about the program than visitors. In view of the fact that people traveling to Rotterdam have to make a greater investment in attending an event, there may be an element of cognitive dissonance in this difference. On the other hand, the expectations of the residents of Rotterdam may have been built up by the media prior to the event, and they may have been disappointed that the event was not more visible during the year itself. These findings point at the risk of such "aggressive" festivalization strategies, by raising expectations that become increasingly difficult to meet.

Conclusions

The most significant conclusions that can be drawn from our visitor surveys are summarized here:

1. Almost half the visitors to R2001 came from Rotterdam itself, but the event also generated more foreign tourism in the city in 2001.
2. The visitors tended to be above the age of forty, but young people between the ages of sixteen and twenty-four were also well represented.

3. Almost 70 percent of the visitors had a higher education and nearly three quarters had a high status occupation.
4. About 17 percent of the Dutch visitors to R2001 could be defined as being of foreign or ethnic origin according to official definitions. This is a reasonable reflection of the proportion of foreigners in the Dutch population as a whole, but lower than the proportion resident in Rotterdam.
5. R2001 attracted new visitors to the city. Over 22 percent of the visitor had not previously visited Rotterdam, and for visitors coming specifically for R2001 this rose to 30 percent.
6. The most important elements of the image of Rotterdam for visitors were the physical aspects of the city, particularly its modern architecture and water.
7. Culture and art are terms that suit Rotterdam according to almost 60 percent of the visitors.
8. Rotterdam as an event city is more highly appreciated by young and culturally active visitors.
9. Visitors had a high appreciation of Rotterdam as a tourist destination and were satisfied with the quality of the R2001 events they visited, but the R2001 program as a whole generated a lower level of satisfaction.

PORTO 2001: EUROPEAN CULTURAL CAPITAL

Porto is a city with a similar position to that of Rotterdam: the second city of Portugal and the industrial port city that has always stood in the shadow of the capital Lisbon. There is also a similar cultural rivalry between Porto and Lisbon as between Rotterdam and Amsterdam. The theme of the Porto 2001 Cultural Capital event was "Bridges to the Future." The aim of staging the Cultural Capital event in 2001 was not only to improve the cultural image of Porto, but also to achieve a number of more tangible improvements in terms of cultural programming, renovation of cultural infrastructures, urban and environmental renovation, and economic development and housing improvements.

Thus, Porto had a wider range of objectives than Rotterdam in 2001, which went far beyond the cultural field. Its budget was therefore much larger than that of Rotterdam, but since it included many improvements in physical infrastructure, it is hard to compare the two. Porto 2001 staged 452 events, which attracted a total of 1.25 million visits. The urban renovation program took up the bulk of the budget but also got a lot of media attention. In comparison to Rotterdam, the festivalization strategy seems to be only of limited importance for Porto.

The research was conducted in Porto by members of the Association for Tourism and Leisure Education (ATLAS) in Portugal: the Polytechnic Institute of Viana do Castelo and the Instituto de Assistentes e Interpretes in Porto. Visitor interviews were held in seventeen different locations in Porto between April 10 and June 13, 2001. A total of 525 completed Cultural Capital questionnaires were collected. These questionnaires were largely comparable with the questionnaires used in Rotterdam, with a mix of standard ATLAS questions and the same specific questions on aspects of the Cultural Capital event (see Richards et al., 2002). A further 141 standard ATLAS questionnaires were also collected in the city in 2001. The ATLAS questions included in the surveys provide not only the option of comparing the results with Rotterdam and other survey locations in 2001, but also with the previous ATLAS surveys conducted by the University of Porto in 1992.

The Visitors

The survey respondents in 2001 tended to be relatively young compared with cultural visitors in general, with over half the respondents being under thirty years of age. This pattern shows very little change over the past decade, with 52 percent of the 1992 ATLAS survey respondents also having been under thirty. Over 40 percent of the respondents had a higher education qualification, which is slightly higher than the Portuguese ATLAS surveys carried out in 2000 (39 percent) and also very high given the relatively young age of the sample. In comparison, only 10 percent of the Portuguese population between the ages of twenty-five and sixty-four had a higher education qualification in 1999. The majority of respondents had a high status profession, with over 60 percent being managers or professionals. Again, this is higher than the ATLAS 2001 figure for the rest of Europe (48 percent). About 30 percent of respondents indicated that their profession was connected with culture, which is lower than the previous Portuguese surveys (36 percent).

Almost 30 percent of the respondents lived or worked in Porto, with a further 46 percent being drawn from other regions of Portugal. The surrounding Norte region was the most common origin of visitors from other parts of the country (20 percent), but reasonable numbers of visitors came from the center (11 percent) and south of Portugal (12 percent). The remaining 24 percent of respondents came from abroad, with the United Kingdom, Spain, and France being the best-represented countries. In the ATLAS surveys conducted in Porto in 1992, only 65 percent of respondents were nonresident, which indicates an increase in visitors to the city over the long term. Just over 10 percent of the 1992 respondents came from abroad, which indicates a significant growth in foreign tourism in the last ten years.

In terms of cultural consumption in Porto, there was a high level of multiple-site visitation, particularly when compared with Rotterdam. This may be a result of the large proportion of visitors from outside the city who would tend to visit more than one site, and it may also be affected by the fact that interviews were conducted in the street. Whereas respondents in Rotterdam would not include the attraction they were interviewed at among their visits, the respondents in Porto would have included all sites visited in Porto. It seems that the Cultural Capital event generated considerable interest among Portuguese visitors from other parts of the country and foreign tourists. Residents of Porto were basically in the city center on business or shopping— the Cultural Capital was not very important as a motive for local people, not surprisingly.

City Image and Festivalization

Just as the theme of Porto 2001 suggests, the most obvious aspect of the image of Porto is the river (see Table 14.5), an image that is particularly strong for local residents. It is interesting to note that foreign visitors have a more positive image of Porto than visitors from other parts of Portugal in a few respects. They are slightly more likely to see Porto as a dynamic, international, multicultural city with an arts and cultural flavor than Portuguese respondents from outside Porto. This is unusual, as foreign visitors should have a weaker image of the city

TABLE 14.5. Porto 2001, image elements by visitor origin (% totally agree).

	Porto	Rest of Portugal	Foreign visitors
River	76.4	64.4	61.5
Shopping	63.8	58.1	40.0
Working city	58.4	37.8	18.9
Cozy	56.4	43.8	56.9
Nightlife	54.8	57.7	46.3
Dynamic	51.7	41.5	43.1
International	35.1	21.9	24.6
Events	32.4	30.1	24.4
Art and culture	32.2	37.9	43.8
Multicultural	27.2	20.6	29.0
Crime	16.8	13.0	5.7
Modern architecture	6.8	6.7	6.4
Unknown	1.3	4.2	7.9

than domestic tourists, which is certainly the case in Rotterdam. This suggests that Porto has been less successful in overcoming its domestic image as an industrial, provincial city than Rotterdam has. This may at least in part be due to the more muted effect of the Cultural Capital event.

In terms of activities the city has to offer, local residents tend to see Porto more as a shopping city than visitors do. This relates clearly to the fact that Porto residents are more likely to be visiting the center for shopping. Also, nightlife scores relatively well, whereas art and culture and events have a low score. Furthermore, the relatively weak score for Porto as an event city seems to indicate a very limited influence of the Cultural Capital event on the awareness of festivalization strategies.

One of the standard questions posed in the ATLAS surveys over the last few years concerns the attractiveness of a number of cities as cultural destinations. The ATLAS surveys provide a means of measuring the changing image of cities over time across Europe as a whole. When the results of the surveys in Porto itself are considered, Porto scored relatively highly as a cultural destination in comparison with other cities, which is not surprising. It was slightly surprising, however, that Rotterdam, the other Cultural Capital in 2001, scored higher than Porto among visitors. Porto residents in particular were proud of their own city, scoring it above Lisbon as a cultural destination. The strong links between Porto and the United Kingdom also seem to be underlined by the fact that Porto residents scored London better than Paris, while all other visitors placed Paris first. In general, however, Porto does not seem to have benefited from the Cultural Capital year in terms of its image outside the city. Its score actually fell in ATLAS surveys carried out in other cities in 2001, while that of Rotterdam rose. Perhaps surprisingly, local residents were significantly more critical about the events and the program than visitors from outside the city. Less surprising was the fact that visitors coming to Porto specifically for the Cultural Capital events were more enthusiastic about the Porto 2001 program than other visitors. As in Rotterdam, festivalization policies tend to raise the critical poise of the local residents.

Conclusions

The most significant conclusions that can be drawn from our surveys are summarized here:

1. There was little change in visitor profiles in Porto in 2001.
2. Visitors were generally managers or professionals, with 44 percent having a degree in higher education.
3. There are indications of a considerable increase in foreign tourism.
4. The physical characteristics of the city tended to dominate the image of visitors, especially the river.
5. Porto's image is poorly associated with events, pointing to a limited festivalization effect.
6. Foreign visitors had a relatively positive image of the city.
7. The 2001 event did not appear to improve the image of the city.

COMPARISON AND CONCLUSION

Both the Rotterdam and the Porto Cultural Capital events in 2001 had ambitious programs, which eventually included 524 projects in

Rotterdam and 452 in Porto. Rotterdam 2001 attracted a total of 2,250,000 visitors, almost twice as many as Porto, although this is not surprising given the relatively metropolitan nature of Rotterdam and neighboring cities. These were satisfactory figures as far as the organizers were concerned, but less than the claimed attendance for some other Cultural Capital years.

Both in Rotterdam and Porto, the surveys as well as the qualitative research that was conducted after the event suggest only limited lasting effects on the city. In both cities respondents and press coverage indicated that there was a lot of positive energy in the city in that year, proving that these "working" cities deserved a cultural image as well. In Porto, however, the urban renovation in 2001 received a lot of attention, but the increase in cultural audiences and city visits melted into the air in the following year. While in Rotterdam the cultural program was much more in focus, here, too, there were few lasting effects in cultural participation or cultural tourism. For example, Richards and Wilson (2004) show that tourism in Rotterdam rose by over 10 percent in 2001, only to fall back to pre-2001 levels in 2002.

Looking back at the typology of Cultural Capitals as presented above, a city such as Porto, mainly using the urban regeneration type, may well see more benefits from that. On the one hand, Porto has lasting effects with regard to cultural venues and infrastructure as well as a renovated "baixa," the inner city. On the other hand, the Cultural Capital event might well have served as a pretext to politically and socially legitimize the physical redevelopment. In Rotterdam, that closely resembles the socioeconomic model; the effects are less tangible. Some of the network infrastructure that was built up in 2001 is still effective, but for the most part the network vanished when the event's organizing corporation disappeared from the scene, taking along most of the human capital involved with it.

With respect to the question of festivalization, one can conclude that this appears to have had its influence in both Rotterdam and Porto, but that it is predominantly the case in Rotterdam. Both cities have used the event for broad urban development or economic and social objectives. The program in Rotterdam was very inclusive of popular culture and entertainment. The findings in Rotterdam point to a limited appreciation of festivalization strategies among the young and culturally active audiences. The cultural program in Porto was presumably more elitist, but the urban renovations benefited the entire city. However, both appear to suffer from narrowing of audience segments, with specific visitor profiles that can be tied to specific activities. One year after the event, both cities cut or redirected their cultural budgets. In that sense, the cultural sector is having a hard time proving its utility in a tougher economic climate. In both cities, festivalization seems to be a visible trend in cultural policy. Festivals, then, were used to generate change in the city, physical change in Porto, and social and cultural change in Rotterdam. The lack of structural follow-up in both cities indicates that we can observe a paradigmatic shift in cultural policy. The cultural *planning* paradigm is being slowly replaced by the paradigm of cultural *programming* of the city. The question then, is to what extent these cities can sustain their programming as cultural capitals in the years ahead.

REFERENCES

Bianchini, F. (1999) The relationship between cultural resources and tourism policies for cities and regions: Issues from European debates. In: Dodd, D. and van Hemel, A. (eds) *Planning Cultural Tourism in Europe: A Presentation of Case Studies and Theories*. Amsterdam: Boekman Foundation, 78-89.

Bourdieu, P. (1984) *Distinction: A Social Critique of the Judgement of Taste*. London: Routledge.

Corijn, E. and S. Van Praet (1994) *Antwerp 1993 in the Context of European Cultural Capitals: Art Policy as Politics*. Brussels: VUB.

Gemeente Rotterdam (2003) *Evaluatie Rotterdam Culturele Hoofdstad 2001*. Rotterdam: Bestuurdienst/Culturele zaken.

Häussermann, H. and W. Siebel (1993) *Festivalisierung der Stadtpolitik. Stadtentwicklung durch große Projekte*. Opladen: Leviathan Sonderheft 13.

Hitters, E. (1996) *Patronen van patronage. Mecenaat, protectoraat en markt in de kunstwereld*. Utrecht: Jan van Arkel.

Hitters, E. (2000) The social and political construction of a cultural capital: Rotterdam 2001. *International Journal of Cultural Policy* 6(2): 183-199.

Knulst, W.P. (1996) *De milde muze*. Utrecht: LOKV.

Palmer/Rae (2004) *European Cities and Capitals of Culture*. Brussels: Palmer/Rae Associates.

Richards, G. (2000) The European cultural capital event: Strategic weapon in the cultural arms race? *Cultural Policy* 6(2): 159-181.

Richards, G. (2001) *Cultural Attractions and European Tourism*. Wallingford: CAB International.

Richards G., E. Hitters, and C. Fernandes (2002) *Rotterdam and Porto: Cultural Capitals 2001: Visitor Research*. Arnhem: Atlas.

Richards, G. and J. Wilson (2002) The use of cultural events in city promotion: Rotterdam cultural capital of Europe 2001. Paper presented at *Events and Place Making: Building Destinations and Communities through Events,* Sydney, July 15-16, 2002.

Richards, G. and J. Wilson (2004) The impact of cultural events on city image: Rotterdam cultural capital of Europe 2001. *Urban Studies* 41(10): 1931-1951.

Ritzer, G. (1999) *Enchanting a Disenchanted World: Revolutionizing the Means of Consumption.* Thousand Oaks, CA: Pine Forge Press.

Chapter 15

Economic Impact
and Social Performance
of Cultural Macrofestivals

Luis César Herrero
José Ángel Sanz
María Devesa
Ana Bedate
María José del Barrio

CULTURE AS A TOOL
FOR ECONOMIC DEVELOPMENT
AND THE FESTIVALIZATION OF CITIES

The significance of the emergence of the "leisure society" lies not so much in the growth of leisure time, but in the fact that leisure has now become crucial in our hierarchy of values. We no longer work to live, we work to enjoy leisure. Leisure has changed from being characteristic of a small segment of the population (childhood and old age) to being a need for adults who have rejected the work ethic of twentieth-century industrial society to assume the prevailing hedonist ethics of our contemporary culture (Bourdieu, 1984; Harvey, 1990).

The growth in leisure consumption has also become a major engine for job creation through the boom in sports, the growth of tourism, the consumption of culture, and even some societal diseases like drug addiction. Tourism in particular has become a very important

Cultural Tourism: Global and Local Perspectives
© 2007 by The Haworth Press, Inc. All rights reserved.
doi:10.1300/5749_15

hallmark of contemporary society, and cultural tourism seems to have become one of the most relevant components of that sector (Richards, 1996; 2001). The growth of cultural tourism is, however, also related to new forms of cultural behavior in contemporary society. Culture, indeed, has changed from being an unusual leisure activity to being a basic need for many citizens; from being good for distraction to being a consumption routine; and from being a minority and elitist concern to being a mass market. What is particularly important about these social behaviors is that they are economically significant, insofar as people's leisure choices affect the demand for leisure goods and services, creating significant economic impacts and integrating leisure into the economy as a whole.

This process of the commoditization of leisure is considered by many to be a shocking idea, as if the economy and the market were capable by themselves of eliminating the essence of intelligence or beauty in the process of cultural creation; nevertheless, it constitutes a widespread phenomenon in current trends of cultural consumption, and it acts not only as an incentive for the preservation of cultural heritage, but also as a trigger to create new cultural products. This underlines the double role performed by culture nowadays: as a support of a society's collective memory and identification, on the one hand, and as a source of wealth and economic development on the other. The most emblematic example of this phenomenon may be, in fact, cultural tourism, since engaging in this kind of sightseeing turns culture (as an expression of people's identity, knowledge, and history) into merchandise, i.e., goods that can be demanded and consumed.

From this we could infer that culture is becoming more and more a factor of urban regeneration, and also more involved in interurban competition among those cities that see cultural tourism as a means to differentiate themselves and to attract new visitors and prospective residents. As noted by Hitters in Chapter 14, this trend has been particularly marked among declining industrial cities such as Glasgow and Bilbao, which needed to change their economic basis from production to service consumption and which have an urgent need to remodel their urban frameworks (Bianchini and Parkinson, 1993). However, this phenomenon has now become generalized to all urban areas, as signature architecture and new cultural attractions are utilized to create a more attractive image for tourists and residents alike.

Finally, we should emphasize the role played by culture in modern society as a tool for social cohesion. Culture is taking on this role because economics and politics have a limited capacity to resolve the major problems modern societies face, such as violence, exclusion, nationalist radicalism, religious fundamentalism, lack of solidarity, etc. If culture is understood as combining individual creativity and self-development and as being a fundamental basis for the establishment of a structure of values, it can contribute decisively to cohesion and society progress. Therefore, culture has shifted from being exclusively a realm of consumption and individual pleasure to representing a factor of economic development and social cohesion.

Major cultural festivals can therefore play a major role in attaining economic and social goals, since they can attract large audiences, help create new urban images, stimulate creativity, and build social cohesion. It is not surprising, therefore, that we are witnessing an amazing proliferation of cultural events in urban and rural environments in a process called *festivalization* (see Chapter 14). The European Capital of Culture event is probably the most refined example of the new trends of cultural tourism, where the prospects of changing the city go beyond the strictly cultural aims of the event itself. The initiative of the European Capital of Culture is mainly culturally rooted, since it was created as a means of boosting European identity through culture (European Commission, 1985), but it has gradually been reoriented toward generating externalities. In this new role, cultural tourism attracts spending and creates value; cultural facilities are developed to change cities both inwardly and outwardly, and the cultural program attempts to develop social identity and European cohesion.

As Hitters shows in Chapter 14, the starting point of the recent history of the European Capitals of Culture was probably the designation of Glasgow in 1990, which used its nomination to reverse urban decline, a model that has been copied and quoted over and over again. It is true that, nowadays, the designation of the European Capital of Culture constitutes an event of remarkable importance for the press and different institutions. First, the nomination makes headlines, at least on a national and European level, so that cities and countries compete for this designation, with the aim of confirming their cultural image and their position in the European urban system. Second, the organizational complexity of the event is becoming increasingly diverse and wide-ranging while attempting to produce significant medium- and long-term economic returns. Institutional formulas of management generally imply the joint participation of public- and private-sector organizations, a growing importance for business sponsorship, and increased civil society participation via voluntary service organizations (for more details see Richards, 2000, 2001).

In effect, the European Capitals of Culture can be considered as macrofestivals, since the main body of their cultural program is based on the performing arts and drama; nonetheless, they also include elements of cultural heritage, and the products of the cultural industries, especially in the activities of editing books and reproducing music and videos. Therefore, the European Capitals of Culture are very complex, since they consist of varied elements of supply and diverse cultural goods that demand different analytical approaches. Yet, there is another complexity to be taken into account in terms of economic impact, since the event involves not only the development of a concrete cultural program, but also wider economic development and urban marketing; so that along with the cultural organization itself, there is a need for new cultural facilities, urban redevelopment, tourist infrastructure, and communications in the city.

This research focuses on the economic impact of Salamanca 2002, the last European Capital of Culture nominated in Spain. It is based on the results of a survey of visitors to the cultural program, which also formed part of a wider study of the impact of the European Capitals of Culture carried out by the Association for Tourism and Leisure Education (ATLAS) (Richards et al., 2002; Herrero et al., 2003).

IMPACT STUDIES METHODOLOGY

Economic impact studies, also known as "effects methods," try to estimate the economic importance of the arts and analyze the activities and earning flows related to the existence of a concrete cultural activity (Martinello and Minnon, 1990). Although their definition can vary from case to case, the main goal of these studies is measuring the effects derived from the presence or existence of an activity or cultural organization in a concrete geographic area and over a specific period of time. It consists, in short, of presenting the major flows generated by cultural activity in the context of the local and/or regional economy (Greffe, 1990). The usual approach of this type of study is to estimate the size of the expenditure flows that give rise to the cultural sector and measure its overall impact. Nevertheless, they are not always limited to the earnings volume, but are complemented very often with the analysis of the employment created or the tax income generated (Heilbrun and Gray, 1993).

Impact studies are not especially complicated from a conceptual point of view, although they present numerous technical difficulties that demand the use of different sources of information, a survey of the cultural audience, and a detailed and careful analysis that avoids the tendency toward overestimation. The empirical applications of this methodology are wide, and in Spain we can mention the studies of Devesa et al. (2002) and Capaul (1988) on the cinema festivals of Valladolid and San Sebastian, respectively; and abroad, the studies of O'Hagan et al. (1989) on the Opera Festival of Wexford (Ireland) and the famous Edinburgh Festival study by the Scottish Tourist Board (1996). Also notable is the study of Van Puffelen (1987) on the economic impact of the cultural sector on the city of Amsterdam and that of Stanley et al. (1998) on the economic impact of two temporary exhibitions on Renoir and Barnes in Canada. More recently, there have been studies carried out by the Guggenheim Museum of Bilbao (2003) on its impact on the Basque Country's economy. Among the pioneering studies on this subject, it is worthwhile mentioning the study of the National Endowment for the Arts (1977) on the impact of artistic life in the city of Baltimore (United States) and the study carried out by the Port Authority of New York and New Jersey (1983) on the economic significance of the cultural sector in the metropolitan area of New York and New Jersey.

These studies of economic impact tend to adopt a common methodology, although there are some differences depending on the flows and agents under analysis. Hence, there are, generally speaking, three different types of measurable impacts or effects (Seaman, 2003): (1) the *direct expenses,* which correspond to the expenses carried out by the cultural activity or institution analyzed under different headings (wages, purchases, rents, implementation of programs, etc.) in the geographic area under study and in a concrete period of time; (2) the *indirect effects,* defined as expenses incurred by the audience as a consequence of the consumption of the concrete cultural good (ac-commodation, meals, transport, purchases, tickets, etc.); and (3) the *induced effects*, which are all those impacts that are not included in the previous categories and are spread out or expanded by the rest of the economic system, inside or outside the area under study.

The definition of this last category differs according to different studies: Some authors focus on the effects on the local, regional, or national economies, namely, on the multiplying effects on the economic system; others address more qualitative issues, such as the increase of the human capital of society, the improvement of the quality of life of citizens, or the appeal of new activities and jobs. These effects are much more difficult to measure, and for this reason, such studies are often only descriptive. In this research we will focus on the first of these approaches, that is, on the calculation of the economic effects in the short run of the cultural event of Salamanca 2002, using economic multipliers. In this sense, we can use the approach of the regional multiplier, through which concrete multipliers for a specific type of activity are constructed, or the input-output analysis, in which sectorial multipliers and general derivatives of the input-output tables (IOT) are used. For a more detailed description of this methodology and its application to tourism see Figuerola (2000, p. 160 ff). The latter will be the approach used in this research, so that we will be able to estimate the impact of the overall spending generated by Salamanca 2002, in both the regional and national economies.

The explicit application of the impact studies methodology to Salamanca 2002 as the European Capital of Culture demands a series of operative changes to adapt it to the peculiarity of a cultural event of this nature. The first one consists of the need to differentiate between those expenses exclusively related to the development of the cultural program of Salamanca 2002, which we will call generically *cultural spending,* and expenditure on new cultural facilities and tourist infrastructure, which we will call *spending on facilities and equipment.* A study oriented toward the estimation of the economic effects of a genuine cultural festival should consider exclusively expenditure on the cultural program, either through the cost of staging it or through visitor spending. Nevertheless, an event like the European Capital of Culture, especially over the last few years, also entails significant public investment in restoration and creation of new cultural equipment and

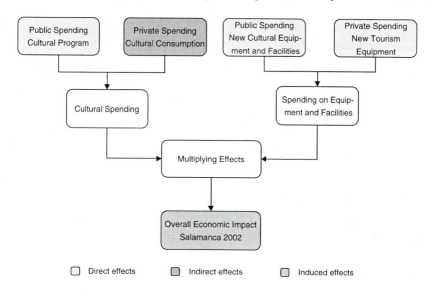

FIGURE 15.1. Model of economic impacts of Salamanca 2002.

tourist infrastructure. This has been the case of Salamanca 2002, so that the *cultural spending* and the *spending on equipment and facilities* are two items that need to be considered in the analysis of the economic impact of an event like this. For this reason, the distribution of direct, indirect, and induced expenses of the model of economic impact were applied to Salamanca 2002 as follows (see also Figure 15.1):

1. The *direct expenses* of the impact model include both the expenditure on equipment and facilities associated with the Salamanca 2002 event (cultural facilities and tourist infrastructure), as well as the public expenses derived from the development of the main cultural program implemented by the Salamanca 2002 Consortium.
2. The *indirect expenses* of the impact model refer to the expenditure by tourists and the audience at the different cultural events of the European Capital of Culture, which have been obtained through the basic survey of this research (Herrero et al., 2003).

3. Finally, the *induced effects,* created by direct and indirect expenditure, on the regional and national economies have been obtained through the input-output multipliers developed from the input-output tables of Castilla y León in 1995, the latest data available for the region. This information will be called *Overall Economic Impact of Salamanca 2002.*

In addition, we have included in the methodology and in the research study of Salamanca 2002 a new analysis of short-term and long-term effects, which we have called *institutional impact.* If analyzes various comparative indicators of economic impact *(output ratios),* total investment *(cost ratios),* and funding requirements *(funding ratios)* of the activities related to the cultural capital status. It is not, strictly speaking, an exhaustive study of institutional efficiency, but an indication of the social performance of Salamanca.

THE SOCIOECONOMIC IMPACT OF SALAMANCA 2002, EUROPEAN CAPITAL OF CULTURE

Direct Impact: Spending on Equipment and Facilities and Public Spending on Cultural Supply

The direct economic impact of Salamanca 2002 includes both the volume of investment in new cultural facilities and tourist facilities carried out in the city due to the event, as well as the public spending carried out in the implementation of the cultural program. Table 15.1 shows the cost of public investments in the restoration and/or the creation of cultural facilities for the events staged in Salamanca 2002. All the regional and public administrations, coordinated by the Salamanca City Council, as the holder of the designation of the European Capital of Culture, participated in the funding of these facilities. These facilities also constitute a long-term asset for the city in terms of its economic and cultural development. In this section we will only consider the overall investment figure (€46.5 million) as one of the components of the economic impact of Salamanca 2002 in the short and medium run.

TABLE 15.1. Spending on equipment and facilities in Salamanca 2002.

Spending on equipment and facilities	€
Santo Domingo exhibition room	2,585,182
Liceo theatre	7,875,156
Salamanca arts centre	9,124,307
Drama centre	12,797,147
Sánchez Paraíso multipurpose palace	14,177,236
Overall public spending new cultural facilities	46,559,030
Overall private spending* new touristic equipment	74,374,146
Overall spending on facilities and equipment	120,933,177

Source: Consorticio Salamanca, 2002.

*Estimated from the subsidy records of the agency for the Economic Development of Castilla y León.

Table 15.1 indicates the considerable private investment in modernizing and building new hotel facilities, so that the accommodation capacity of the city has doubled, especially in the higher accommodation categories. This response by the private sector is based not only on the boost of the European Capital of Culture, but also on the profits forecast in the medium run from Salamanca's positioning in the European and national hierarchies of cultural cities and venues. The figure for private investment (€74.3 million/$94.2 million) is, however, taken in this section as a direct factor of equipment and facilities that influence the economic impact of Salamanca 2002 in the short and medium run.

Finally, we will consider probably the most justified public expense within the group of direct effects of Salamanca 2002, namely expenditure on organizing the cultural program of the European Capital of Culture. These are included mainly in the cumulative budget of the Salamanca 2002 Consortium, as all of its expenses were allocated to organizing the cultural program of the European Capital of Culture in its broadest sense. It is worth noting that many other public and private agents contributed to the cultural program in 2002, such as the Caja Duero and the Universidad de Salamanca, but these have not been included in this analysis.

Table 15.2 shows this budget information in nominal terms, and it must be noted that in 2001 and especially in 2002 this includes Cultursa, a Public Limited Corporation whose sole shareholder is the Salamanca 2002 Consortium, created ad hoc to implement quickly the funding of the cultural events of 2002. For analytical purposes, in the calculation of the overall economic impact we have excluded the sale of tickets and goods of the Salamanca 2002 Consortium, in order to avoid duplications in the estimate of expenses, since these payments are already considered in the estimate of tourist cultural consumption, measured through audience surveys at the events of the European Capital of Culture. Thus, the overall public spending on the cultural supply of Salamanca 2003 amounts to €37.3 million ($47.3 million, a figure which will be considered as a direct element in the estimate of the overall economic impact of the European Capital of Culture.

TABLE 15.2. Annual and accumulated budget of Salamanca 2002 Consortium (€).

Year	2000	2001	2002*	Total
Expenses				
Staff	251,644	884,441	1,546,038	2,682,123
Cultural program	1,364,297	1,873,969	19,892,503	23,130,769
Equipment	412,294	444,042	4,021,324	4,877,660
Publicity and promotion	210,354	683,883	2,779,093	3,673,330
Other expenses	562,488	600,869	3,626,968	4,790,325
Overall expenses	2,801,077	4,487,204	31,865,926	39,154,207
Earnings				
Institutional funding	2,740,627	4,303.253	15,474,802	22,518,682
Private sponsorship and patronage	0	0	14,849,839	14,849,839
Other earnings (tickets, sales, etc.)	60,450	183,951	1,541,285	1,785,686
Overall earnings	2,801,077	4,487,204	31,865,926	39,154,207

Source: Consorticio Salamanca, 2002.

*Includes data from Salamanca 2002 Consortium and Cultursa.

Indirect Impact: Private Spending
in Cultural Consumption

The indirect effect is the overall spending on accommodation, transportation, meals, shopping, etc. made by visitors to the different events of the European Capital of Culture. The overall spending results from multiplying the spending per person by the overall number of visitors. This calculation is not simple, however, since there is a need to first solve certain methodological difficulties. The first is caused by not knowing the departure point of the members of the audience registered in the cultural program of Salamanca 2002; and, therefore, we cannot separate the payments made by the local audience and foreign tourists. In effect, we could exclude expenditure by locals, since for the inhabitants of the city attendance at the events of the European Capital of Culture would only involve a change in the components of their cultural consumption. However, in this research we will include spending by locals and visitors. We have done this for two reasons: first, because the program of Salamanca 2002 has an unusual nature and has probably prompted the local citizens to increase their cultural consumption; and second, since the main expenditure by the local audience will be on tickets—an item that, as we have already seen above, does not represent a large proportion of total spending on cultural events—we will not run the risk of producing a disproportionate overestimate.

Once this problem is solved, the estimation of the overall spending on cultural consumption of the events of Salamanca 2002 follows the sequence shown in Figure 15.2. The spending amount per visitor and event obtained from the sample of the survey (for more details see Herrero et al., 2003) is taken as a starting point and extended to the overall population of the audience of the European Capital of Culture, in proportion to the visits officially registered for each group of events. In the process of estimation there are two coefficients that will be applied to avoid overestimating the spending: a repetition coefficient, to avoid multiple visits of the same tourist; and a reduction coefficient, to ensure that the visit is mainly motivated by the European Capital of Culture event.

In calculating the number of persons that participated in Salamanca 2002, we know that a total of 1,927,440 tickets were sold (Consorcio

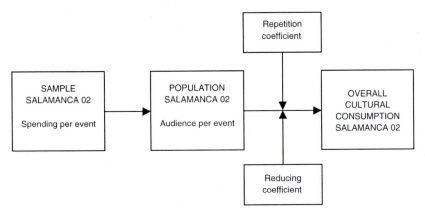

FIGURE15.2. Process of estimating the private spending on cultural consumption.

Salamanca 2002, 2003), but we do not know how many of those tickets were held by different people, which is key in estimating the overall indirect spending and avoiding duplicities in the spending per visitor. As we have already said, in order to calculate a more realistic figure for the number of participants in the European Capital of Culture in 2002, we have produced a *repetition coefficient,* by asking visitors if they had participated or intended to participate in any other event of the cultural program. Thus, we have considered that repeat visitors (72.06 percent) had attended at least two shows, reducing the total number of tickets proportionally. Nonetheless, in order to give a more precise figure, the reduction has been applied to the population in each of these six categories of events in which we have divided the cultural program. These data can be seen in Table 15.3.

We have considered, therefore, that a maximum of 1,204,314 different people participated in the events of Salamanca 2002, based on which we have been able to work out the estimates of the overall indirect spending, as shown in Table 15.4. Hence, the overall indirect spending measured through the cultural consumption of the audience of the European Capital of Culture slightly exceeds €368 million ($467 million).

Nevertheless, there is a final question: Can the €368 million be exclusively ascribed to the European Capital of Culture event? As we mentioned above, only those expenditures directly caused by the cultural event can be considered as real cultural expenditures, and there-

TABLE 15.3. Number of tickets sold and estimated visitor numbers, Salamanca 2002.

	Tickets	% Repeat visits	Estimated number of visitors*
Drama	62,295	66.67	41,529
Audiovisual presentations	18,557	70.00	12,062
Open city	731,075	80.95	435,172
Meetings, conferences, communications	12,272	60.00	8,590
Exhibitions	1,011,053	71.36	650,309
Music	92,192	77.10	56,652
Total	1,927,444		1,204,314

Source: Consorticio Salamanca, 2002 and own data.

*Calculated from total number of tickets sold, discounted for mulitple visits. As some individuals attended three or more cultural events, the calculation can be considered as a minimum repetition coefficient.

TABLE 15.4. Estimated indirect spending in Salamanca 2002.

	Average spending per visitor €	Estimated number of visitors	Overall spending €
Drama	79.38	41,529	3,296,572
Audiovisual presentations	90.12	12,062	1,087,027
Open city	485.50	435,172	211,276,006
Meetings, conferences, and communications	528.33	8,590	4,538,355
Exhibitions	194.81	650,309	126,686,696
Music	380.50	56,652	21,556,086
Total		1,204,314	368,440,742

Source: Own data.

fore it is necessary to ask visitors about their motivation. Hence, the research questionnaire included a question asking respondents to score their reasons for visiting Salamanca on a 1 to 5 scale, with the European Capital of Culture being one possible reason for attendance. We have taken 100 percent of the expenditure for those visitors who agreed that the Capital of Culture was a main reason for their visit. On the other hand, visitors who disagreed or totally disagreed with this statement (25.85 percent) had not visited Salamanca because it was European Capital of Culture, and their spending cannot be considered a direct consequence of the event (0 percent). For those that were neutral regarding the importance of the event in their motivation to visit (17.23 percent), we can consider as a hypothesis that 50 percent of their payments resulted from the event. Consequently, we can produce the following *reducing coefficient:*

$$RC = (0.5692 \times 1) + (0.1723 \times 0.50) + (0.2585 \times 0) = 0.6554$$

According to the estimates in this more realistic setting, only 65.54 percent of the spending of those surveyed can properly be assigned to the events of Salamanca 2002, so that the overall indirect effect would be €241.5 million ($306 million).

Induced Impact: Overall Economic Effect of Salamanca 2002

The induced effects can be defined as the impacts on the local, regional, and national economies derived from the direct and indirect effects of the cultural event—namely, the spending on equipment and facilities and the cultural spending of Salamanca 2002. The induced impact is estimated through the concept of the spending multiplier and we will use the input-output multiplier derived from the Input-Output Tables (IOT) of Castilla y León for 1995, distinguishing also the impact on the city of Salamanca and the Autonomous Community of Castilla y León from the impact on the rest of Spain. This is why we have calculated the internal multipliers—that is, those that estimate the economic effects on the region—and the overall multipliers of the system, which estimate the effect on Spain as a whole.

We should, however, clarify something before presenting the results. Although we have used the sectoral multiplier of the construction sector to estimate the spending on new cultural facilities and tourist infrastructure, since this spending deals mainly with the spending on equipment facilities and civil work, in the item concerning the cultural spending of Salamanca 2002 we have used a general multiplier for the service sector. This is because most of the expenditure considered here (either by the Salamanca Consortium or by visitors to the event) relates to services such as cultural production, advertising, accommodation, restaurants, etc.

Hence, on the one hand Table 15.5 shows the economic impact of the spending on equipment and facilities of Salamanca 2002, which accounts to €247.7 million ($314 million), from which 69.78 percent (€172.8 million) affects on the Autonomous Community of Castilla y León, 17.44 percent (€43.2 million) the rest of Spain, and 12.78 percent (€31.6 million) abroad. On the other hand, Table 15.6 shows the estimate of the economic impact of the cultural spending of Salamanca 2002, which amounts to €434.6 million ($551 million): 82.66 percent for Castilla y León (€359.2 million), 10.35 percent for the rest of Spain (€45 million), and 6.99 percent for the rest of the world (€30.4 million). This indicates that the economic impact of the cultural spending in the region is bigger than the spending on equipment and facilities, while the opposite situation is the case in the rest of Spain and the rest of the world (see Table 15.7).

TABLE 15.5. Economic impact of the spending on equipment and facilities in Salamanca 2002.

Overall investment in cultural and touristic infrastructures *(spending on equipment and facilities)*	€120,933,177
Regional sectorial multiplier*	1.42931128
National sectorial multiplier*	1.78647284
Overall sectorial multiplier*	2.04831274
Effect on Castilla y León	€172,851,154
Effect on the rest of Spain	€43,192,682
Effect on the rest of the world	€31,665,131
Overall economic effect	€247,708,967

Source: Own data and input-output tables of Castilla y León.

*Construction sector multiplier.

TABLE 15.6. Economic impact of cultural spending in Salamanca 2002.

	Realistic setting €
Direct effect	37,368,521
Indirect effect	241,476,062
Direct and indirect effects *(Cultural spending)*	278,844,583
Regional sectorial multiplier*	1.28841246
National sectorial multiplier*	1.44971000
Overall sectorial multiplier*	1.55869579
Effect on Castilla y León	359,266,835
Effect on the rest of Spain	44,976,945
Effect on the rest of the world	30,390,097
Overall economic effect	434,633,878

Source: Own data and Input-Output tables of Castilla y León.

*Service sector multiplier.

TABLE 15.7. Territorial distribution of the overall economic impact (%).

	On Castilla y León	On the rest of Spain	On the rest of the world	Total
Economic impact of spending on facilities and equipment	69.78	17.44	12.78	100.00
Economic impact of cultural spending	82.66	10.35	6.99	100.00
Total economic impact	77.98	12.92	9.10	100.00

In short, if we add the impact of cultural spending and spending on equipment and facilities, the European Capital of Culture event generated €532.1 million ($674 million) in Castilla y León, €88.16 million ($112 million) in the rest of Spain, and €62 million ($78.6 million) in the rest of the world; in other words, a distribution of 77.98 percent, 12.92 percent, and 9.10 percent respectively, whereas the overall economic effect on the country has been €682.3 million. The sectorial distribution of the overall economic impact is included in

TABLE 15.8. Sectorial distribution of the overall economic impact (%).

	On Castilla y León	On the rest of Spain	On the rest of the world	Total
Economic impact of spending on facilities and equipment	32.48	48.99	51.03	36.30
Economic impact of cultural spending	67.52	51.01	48.97	63.70
Total economic impact	100.00	100.00	100.00	100.00

Table 15.8, which also shows that 63.7 percent of the economic impact of Salamanca 2002 is related to the event itself, understood as a concrete cultural creation, and its associated consumption; whereas the rest, 36.3 percent, is related to the economic impact of the new cultural facilities and tourist facilities. Once again, if we consider only the overall economic effect of the European City of Culture in Castilla y León, the effect on the region's cultural spending is proportionally bigger than in the rest of the country, 67.52 percent compared to 51.01 percent, and lower than the impact of the spending on equipment and facilities (32.48 percent compared to 48.99 percent), which underlines the fact that the impact of cultural events on the local and regional economies is bigger than the spending on equipment, facilities, and civil work. Finally, the summary of these effects and their chronological evolution in the process of estimating the overall economic impact of Salamanca 2002 can be seen in Figure 15.3.

Institutional Impact

The institutional impact of this event concerns what we could call contributions from the Capital of Culture to society, producing an increment in general welfare. Measuring this involves two difficulties: first, the analytical complexity implied in an intangible value, and second, the impossibility of comparing it with other referents of the same nature. Thus, the analysis here does not represent a study of institutional efficiency but presents some indicators that, in a descrip-

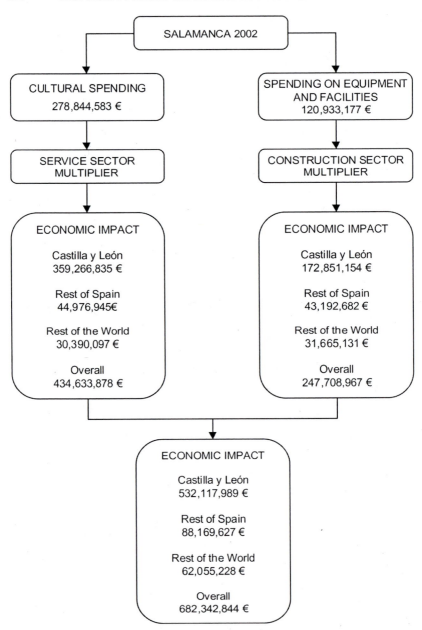

FIGURE 15.3. Estimate of the economic impact of Salamanca 2002—Main results.

tive way, approximate the performance of Salamanca 2002 as a social organization.

The first indicator comes from the study of the budgets of the Salamanca 2002 Consortium (see Table 15.2), where it can be seen that 60 percent of the expenses went to the Salamanca 2002 cultural program, compared to a quarter of the expenses devoted to equipment and buildings working expenses. Consortium publicity and promotional expenses represent 9.2 percent of the budget, even though this figure would be considerably higher if we were to also include expenses from sponsors and communication groups in the promotion of the logo and activities in the Capital of Culture Salamanca 2002. Such promotional expenditure totaled €360,607,263 ($461 million) (Consorcio Salamanca, 2002). Although this logically constitutes an extrabudgetary figure for the Consortium itself, it should be considered in this section as an extra publicity effort for the cultural event, as it doubtless contributed to attracting visitors and to strengthening the image of the city; therefore, they are implying a kind of social performance. Therefore, the private promotional expenditure was €187 ($237) per visitor and €327,527 ($415,387) per event.

Regarding the income for Salamanca 2002 Consortium (see Table 15.2), 57.5 percent came from public investment and 37.9 percent from the private sector over the whole period. However, this proportion is much more equal in the 2002 Capital of Culture year, when private sponsorship represented 46.6 percent of funding. Lastly, income from selling tickets and souvenirs from the Salamanca 2002 Consortium make up only 4.6 percent of funding, which reflects the fact that most of the events were free.

As far as the official cultural program of Salamanca 2002 is concerned (Table 15.9), the first issue that attracts our attention is the great concentration of events in the section Open City *(Ciudad Abierta)*—more than 70 percent of the total—which represents an explicit will to stage the Capital of Culture celebration as an all-year-round event that Salamanca citizens can also enjoy. Nevertheless, if we exclude this last event and focus on the cultural program, there is an even balance of disciplines—scenic arts, audiovisuals, music, exhibitions, and congresses—virtually 15 percent for each one. The visitor distribution is much more uneven, as the exhibitions section attracted 52 percent of the total visitors (84 percent if we exclude

TABLE 15.9. Results of the cultural programs Salamanca 2002.

Type of event	No. Events	%	No. Visitors	%	Visitors per event	Events per 1,000 visitors
Scenic Arts	52	4.7	62,295	3.2	1,198	0.83
Audiovisuals	65	5.9	18,557	1.0	285	3.50
Open City	789	71.7	731,075	37.9	927	1.08
Congresses	53	4.8	12,272	0.6	232	4.32
Exhibitions	46	4.2	1,011,053	52.5	21,979	0.05
Music	96	8.7	92,192	4.8	960	1.04
Total	1,101	100.0	1,927,444	100.0	1,751	0.57

Source: Consorcio Salamanca 2002.

TABLE 15.10. Cultural program of music and performing arts activities with an entry fee.

Type of event	Events	Functions	Visitors	Capacity	% Occupation	Visitors per function
Theater	38	95	46,184	53,621	86.13	486.15
Dance and circus	13	21	15,988	17,777	89.94	761.33
Classic music	50	53	29,711	33,161	89.60	560.58
Modern music	41	43	61,973	91,459	67.76	1,441.23
Total	142	212	153,856	196,018	78.49	725.74

Source: Consorcio Salamanca 2002.

Open City). This is basically due to the free nature of all the programmed exhibitions, but it is also motivated by the ease of consuming this type of cultural product. In the scenic arts and musical shows section, the most important element is the extremely high level of attendance to the different shows, which reached 90 percent of the seating capacity (see Table 15.10), which in turn represents a welcome and successful level of the programmed activities (cf. Herrero et al., 2003).

Finally, Tables 15.11 and 15.12 show some simple indicators that are constructed as a weighting of the number of visitors and number of events, according to some representative figures from short-term and half-term economic impact of Salamanca 2002 *(output indicators);* the cost of programs, spreading, and endowment of the Capital

TABLE 15.11. Institutional impact of Salamanca 2002: Visitor number indicators (figures in €).

Output indicators		Input indicators		Input/output ratios	Funding indicators	
Visitors per event	1,751	Promotional cost/visitor*	187		Public funding per visitor	12
Economic impact per visitor	225.5	Consortium cost/visitor	20	1,110.0%	Private funding per visitor	8
Equipment economic impact per visitor	128.5	Equipment cost per visitor	63	204.8%	Extra promotion per visitor	187
Total economic impact per visitor	354.0	Total cost per visitor	270	131.0%	Earned income per visitor	1

Source: Own data.

*Includes only promotional expenses of private agents.

TABLE 15.12. Institutional impact of Salamanca 2002: Event indicators.

Output indicators		Input indicators		Input/output ratios	Funding indicators	
Events per 2,000 visitors	1.14	Promotional cost per event*	€327,527		Public funding per event	€20,453
Economic impact per event	€394,762	Consortium cost per event*	€35,562	1,110.0%	Private funding per event	€13,488
Equipment economic impact per event	€224,985	Equipment cost per event*	€109,839	204.8%	Extra promotion per event	€327,527
Total economic impact per event	€619,748	Total cost per event*	€472,929	131.0%	Earned income per event	€1,622

Source: Own data.

*Includes only promotional expenses of private agents.

of Culture *(input indicators);* and the cultural event funding sources *(funding indicators).* The most significant results are first, that the average number of visitors per program event in Salamanca 2002 was 1,751 people. Secondly, the total economic impact of the Cultural Capital averaged €354 per visitor and €620,000 for each programmed event. If we compare these figures with the average of total cost per visitor and event—€270 and €472,000, respectively—we obtain a rate of extra wealth yield of 131 percent per unit. This result is even more important if we exclude the private sponsor expenses invested in the promotion of Salamanca 2002; thus, the cultural cost, strictly speaking (just Salamanca 2002 Consortium), is €20 per visitor, so that the cultural expense performance in terms of economic effects of this item would be 1,110 percent (Table 15.11). As far as tourist and cultural equipment investment are concerned, the expense per visitor is €63, while the economic impact of the spending on equipment and facilities is €128.5, that is to say, an extra 204.8 percent. If we look at Table 15.12, we can make identical comments regarding the percentages per event, which shows the performance of the activities carried out in terms of short-term and half-term economic impact.

In this way, the investment per visitor was €12 in public contributions, €8 from private sponsorship, only €1 by the Cultursa Consortium, and €187 as promotional investment by private sponsors. The figures in connection with the events are €20,453 of public funding per event, €13,488 of private sponsorship, and €1,622 of generated income. The private promotional expenses came to €327,527. Once again, the frequent private coparticipation in the funding of an event such as the Capital of Culture Salamanca 2002 becomes relevant.

CONCLUSIONS

Nowadays, culture plays a double role: on the one hand, it supports collective memory and social identification; and on the other hand, it is a source of income and economic activity. The most prominent example of this phenomenon is, no doubt, cultural tourism, in so far as *culture*, as a sign of identity, knowledge, and history, becomes a commodity, namely, a good that can be demanded and consumed. In this way, cultural tourism can become, first, a factor of economic development; and, second, a boost to the urban regeneration of cities, whose heritage recovery and new cultural facilities make them stand out from other areas and change their urban image to make it more appealing.

In this context, the most significant cultural example of this new trend is probably the European Capitals of Culture event, where the prospects of changing the city go beyond the cultural program. The event is mainly culturally rooted, but it has gradually been reoriented toward generating economic development. In this new role, cultural tourism attracts spending and creates value; and cultural attractions aim to change cities, both inwardly and outwardly.

Under the above considerations, in this chapter we have assessed the overall socioeconomic impact of the European Capitals of Culture, such as the city of Salamanca (Spain) in 2002, considering that their economic impact is not only a consequence of their cultural planning and visitors' spending, but also of an effort to invest in the city's equipment and facilities. Thus, the results of this research are salient insofar as they indicate, on the one hand, that cultural events constitute a remarkable source of wealth generation, according to the dimension of the overall economic impact of Salamanca 2002; and also because, on the other hand, it has been demonstrated that the effects of the strictly cultural expenditures are mostly concentrated locally and regionally, whereas the impact of expenditures on facilities are more widespread.

Although these figures indicate that cultural events and their associated tourism generate important economic flows for the regional and national economies, it is important to compare these impacts with the effects of different types of cultural investment. Being reasonably cautious with the comparison of different case studies and methodologies used, we can compare our results with the estimate of the economic impact of the cultural and tourism activities of the Guggenheim Museum of Bilbao, whose economic impact in 2002 amounted to €162.3 million ($205.7 million), or €816.7 million ($1035 million) if we accumulate its impact overits seven years of existence (Guggenheim Bilbao, 2003). As a result, taking only the impact of the strictly cultural spending of Salamanca 2002, its effect was 2.7 times greater than that generated by the Guggenheim Museum in the same year, or just over half the accumulated impact over seven years. This indicates that a *macrofestival* like Salamanca 2002 can be just as profitable in the short term as a new cultural facility such as the famous Bilbao Guggenheim Museum.

Last but not least, this chapter has also aimed to show that the economic impact models are reliable as a method for estimating those economic flows derived from a cultural event, confirming the need to pay strict attention to detail in the methodology, in order to avoid overestimation; and considering that the results are valid in the short and medium term. In other words, they are limited to the estimation of the impact of those expenditures derived from the celebration and development of the cultural event under analysis. Nonetheless, these figures can constitute the first step of a potential cost-benefit analysis of the investments made and, therefore, of the long-term impact of the cultural event.

REFERENCES

Benhamou, F. (1996) *L'économie de la culture*. Paris: Editions La Découverte.

Bianchini, F. and Parkinson, M. (1993) (eds) *Cultural Policy and Urban Regeneration. The West European Experience*. Manchester: Manchester University Press.

Blaug, M. (2001) Where are we now in cultural economics? *Journal of Economic Surveys* 15(2): 123-143.

Bordieu, P. (1984) *Distinction: A Social Critique of the Judgement of Taste*. London: Routledge.

Capaul, M. (1988) El impacto económico del Festival Internacional de Cine de San Sebastián. *Estudios Empresariales* 67: 47-54.

Consorcio Salamanca 2002 (2003) *Balance "Salamanca 2002, Ciudad Europea de la Cultura."* MIMEO, Salamanca.

Devesa, M., Herrero, L.C., Sanz, J.A. and Bedate, A. (2002) The economic impact of the Valladolid International Film Festival. Paper presented at the *Twentieth International Conference on Cultural Economics*, Rotterdam, The Netherlands.

Dziembowska, J. and Funck, R. (2000) Cultural activities as a location factor in European competition between regions: Concepts and some evidence. *Annals of Regional Science* 34: 1-12.

European Commission (1985) *Resolution of the Ministers Responsible for Cultural Affairs Concerning the Annual Event "European City of Culture."* Doc 7081/84, EC, Brussels.

Figuerola, M. (2000) *Introducción al estudio económico del turismo*. Madrid: Ed. Cívitas.

García, M.I., Fernández, Y. and Zofío, J.L. (2000) *La Industria de la Cultura y el Ocio en España*. Madrid: Fundación Autor.

Greffe, X. (1990) *La valeur économique du Patrimoine. La demande et l'offre de monuments*. Paris: Ed. Anthropos.

Guggenheim Bilbao (2003) *Impacto Económico de las actividades del Museo Guggenhein Bilbao en la economía del País Vasco en el año 2002.* MIMEO, Bilbao.

Hall, P. (2000) Creative cities and economic development. *Urban Studies* 37 (4): 639-649.

Harvey, D. (1990) *The Condition of Postmodernity: An Enquiry into the Origins of Cultural Change.* Oxford: Blackwell.

Heilbrun, J. and Gray, M. (1993) *The Economics of Art and Culture: An American Perspective.* Cambridge: Cambridge University Press.

Herrero, L.C. (2001) "Economía del Patrimonio Histórico." *Información Comercial Española* 792: 151-168.

Herrero, L.C. (2002) La Economía de la Cultura en España: Una Disciplina Incipiente. *Revista Asturiana de Economía* 23: 147-175.

Herrero, L.C., Sanz, J.A., Bedate, A., Devesa, M. and Barrio, M.J. del (2003) *Turismo cultural e impacto económico de Salamanca 2002, Ciudad Europea de la Cultura.* Valladolid: Departamento de Economía Aplicada, Universidad de Valladolid.

Hutter, M. and Rizzo, I. (1997) *Economics Perspectives on Cultural Heritage.* London: MacMillan Press.

Martinello, M. and Minnon, M. (1990) Les études d'impact: Objetifs et methods. In Wangermee, R. (ed) *Les malheurs d'Orphee. Culture et profit dans l'economie de la musique.* Brussels: Pierre Mardarga Editeurs, pp. 127-141.

National Endowment for the Arts (1977) *Economic impacts of the Arts and Cultural Institutions: A Model Assessment and Case Study in Baltimore.* NEA Research Division, Report 6, October, Washington.

O'Hagan, J., Barret, A. and Purdy, M. (1989) *The Economic and Social Contribution of the Wexford Opera Festival.* Dublin: Trinity College.

Port Authority of New York and New Jersey (1983) *The Arts As an Industry: Their Economic Importance to the New York and New Jersey Metropolitan Area.* New York.

Richards, G. (1996) *Cultural Tourism in Europe.* Wallingford: CAB International.

Richards, G. (2000) World culture and heritage and tourism. *Tourism Recreation Research* 25(1): 9-18.

Richards, G. (2001) El desarrollo del turismo cultural en Europa. *Estudios Turísticos* 150: 3-14.

Richards, G., Hitters, E. and Fernandes C. (2002) *Rotterdam and Porto: Cultural Capitals 2001: Visitor Research.* Arnhem: Atlas.

Scottish Tourist Board (1996) *Edinburgh Festivals Economic Study.* MIMEO, Edinburgh.

Seaman, B. (2003) Economic impact of the arts. In R. Towse (ed) *A Handbook of Cultural Economics*, pp. 224-231.

Smith, A. (1776) *Investigación de la naturaleza y causas de la riqueza de las naciones. Spanish edition of 1794, reproduced as a facsimile by the Consejería de Educación y Cultura de la Junta de Castilla y León, Valladolid.*

Stanley, D., Rogers, J., Smeltzer, S. and Perron, L. (1998) *Win, Place or Show: Gauging the Economic Success of the Renoir and Barnes Art Exhibits*. Quebec: Canadian Heritage.

Throsby, D. (1994) The production and consumption of the arts: A view of cultural economics. *Journal of Economic Literature* 32: 1-29.

Throsby, D. (2001) *Economics and Culture*. Cambridge: Cambridge University Press [Translation into Spanish: *Economía y Cultura*, Madrid: Cambridge University Press, 2001].

Towse, R. (Ed.) (1997) *Cultural Economics: The Arts, the Heritage and the Media Industries*, 2 vols. Cheltenham: Edward Elgar.

Van Puffelen, F. (1987) L'impact économique des arts á Amsterdam: méthodologie, résultats et questions. *Economie et Culture. 4ª Conference Internationale sur l'Économie de la Culture*. La Documentation Française, vol. IV.

Chapter 16

Conclusion: The Future of Cultural Tourism—Grounds for Pessimism or Optimism?

Greg Richards

The different contributions to this volume reflect not only a wide range of different disciplinary viewpoints and geographic locations, but also contrasting views on the potential for cultural tourism to contribute to local development in the face of globalization. In the view of some, local authenticity is rapidly being replaced by global pastiche, and local communities seem powerless to stop this process. According to others, local communities still have the power to create new and authentic forms of culture, which can satisfy the visitor as well as strengthen local identity. This division seems to mirror wider debates about the rise of "cultural pessimism," which Bennett (2001) argues is linked to environmental, moral, intellectual, and political narratives of decline in the "postmodern" world at the end of the twentieth century.

Whether one adopts a pessimistic or an optimistic view of cultural tourism depends to a large extent on one's position. There has tended to be a clear division, for example, between those involved in the cultural sector, who have largely been suspicious of the "Disneyfication" effects of tourism, and those linked to the tourism industry, who see the economic injections provided by tourists as saving, rather than degrading culture. However, there is growing evidence of a more so-

Cultural Tourism: Global and Local Perspectives
© 2007 by The Haworth Press, Inc. All rights reserved.
doi:10.1300/5749_16

phisticated approach in both the cultural and tourism sectors, which recognizes the need to prioritize cultural goals while accepting the necessity to keep cultures alive through development as well as preservation.

In his analysis of the relationship between culture and tourism, Eduard Delgado (2001:105) observed that "the new cultural tourism has to base itself, above all, on the offering experiences with three basic elements: diversity, interactivity, and context." The question of diversity in particular has clearly been at the forefront of debate in this volume, because much revolves around the question of how locations can use culture to create a sense of place. The "distinctiveness" of places was seen as important to this process, and was often seen as something to be preserved in the face of encroaching "placelessness." However, this discussion about diversity often ignored the other two crucial elements in Delgado's recipe. The "interactivity" he referred to was not technological, but a broader cultural concept: how to facilitate reflection and the exchange of opinion in a bidirectional manner. In this sense, distinction depends not just on physical spaces, but on the use of those spaces and the way in which people interact with one another in those spaces. This makes not just interaction important, but also the third element, context.

The issue of context is also touched upon by several of the authors, particularly in relation to authenticity and placelessness. Authenticity, as Schouten outlines in Chapter 2, is a much used and often abused concept in cultural tourism. The problem with much of the discussion surrounding authenticity is that people tend to look at sights or objects, while ignoring the context in which these sights are located. This is important, because if we ignore the local contexts in which global culture is consumed, we run the risk of seeing homogenization and placelessness where in fact there is increasing differentiation, distinctiveness, and attachment. This is evident in discussions of Augé's (1995) concept of "placelessness," which Melanie Smith links to globalization and homogenization of culture in Chapter 5. As Urry has recently pointed out in his review of the development of "new mobilities," the concept of placelessness as expressed by Augé is problematized by the emergence of new social and cultural relations, even in places of movement and transition.

An example of the contradictions that arose in the debate was the shopping mall. In Chapter 9, Jaume Franquesa and Marc Morell refer to the trend toward "malling" in urban areas, citing Crawford's (1992) work on malls in America. Crawford argued that shopping malls created an "alternative sense of community," which ultimately replaced "real" communities with structures controlled by commercial interests. However, this familiar example of cultural pessimism ignores the way in which the new contexts of commercial and popular culture also become sources of resistance and creativity. In the case of the shopping mall this more positive reading is exemplified by Kevin Smith's 1995 film *Mallrats,* which describes the everyday trials and tribulations of a group of teenagers whose spiritual home and point of reference is the local shopping mall. The mall is a space that many cultural critics have viewed as sterile, exclusionary, and inauthentic. However, Kevin Smith's characters show that even in such unlikely circumstances it is possible to create cultural optimism and a grassroots feeling of community, particularly as an act of resistance to the homogenizing forces of the mall. Such new relations between local and global, spaces and places, culture and everyday life become more complex in the rapidly changing, mobile landscape of (post)modernity.

The concept of dealing with mobilities rather than fixed cultural categories focuses attention on the constantly shifting cultural phenomena that are at the same time the object of tourism and the basis of the tourism culture itself. In terms of research on cultural tourism, perhaps we should be shifting our attention away from concepts of culture as a collection of "products" (museums, heritage centers, events) toward a more fluid concept of culture as process (links between production and consumption, processes of capital accumulation, identity formation, image creation). The emphasis on cultural flows as well as the "scapes" in which these take place (such as the homogeneous and heterogeneous spaces identified by Edensor, 1998) would help to deal more effectively with the de-differentiation of "high" and "popular" culture, increasing divergence between local, regional, and national cultures and the diversity of tourist consumption styles.

However, the growing de-differentiation evident in the cultural field as a whole is also posing specific problems for the study of cultural tourism. Richards (2001) has argued that "cultural tourism," in the sense of a clearly defined and coherent phenomenon, began to disappear at the moment of its identification. As soon as cultural tourism began to be analyzed as a separate field of consumption, so the diversity of the different cultural forms and tourism styles in this field also became more apparent, and cultural tourism itself began to dissipate.

The basic reason for this is that the definitional terms "culture" and "tourism" are both becoming overladen with meaning, to the extent that they become meaningless, or at least unusable as a means of discrimination. In the case of Barcelona, for example, the city has placed a great emphasis on the development of cultural tourism in recent years, with a view to attracting "quality tourists" and persuading visitors to stay longer and spend more. One of the indicators of the success of this strategy is the rising numbers of visitors to cultural attractions in the city, which increased their share from 48 percent to 58 percent of all attraction visits between 1994 and 2002 (Turisme de Barcelona, 2003). However, one of the fastest growing "cultural attractions" during this period was the museum of Barcelona FC, most of whose visitors actually come to see the football stadium. Is this a cultural attraction, a leisure attraction, or a form of sports tourism? In view of the fact that "Barca" is a cultural phenomenon in Catalunya, a strong case could be made for the stadium and its museum as cultural attractions. But the "cultural tourists" who visit the Nou Camp stadium are different from those visiting other museums in the city, or the architecture of Gaudí. They do not fit the classic profile of cultural tourists, and do not tend to see themselves as such. Not only can one debate the cultural position of such visitors, but their status as tourists is also not so secure. Many "tourists" visiting the stadium come with friends or family living in Barcelona, and many have already been to Barcelona many times. What is the difference between these "visitors" and the "residents" of Barcelona? Both seem to have very similar motivations, they often exhibit similar behavior as consumers of cultural attractions and events, and they experience similar problems.

This is a point also taken up by Jaume Franquesa and Marc Morell in Chapter 9. They argue that the distinctions between "locals" and "tourists" are disappearing, essentially because we are relating to leisure spaces as a form of consumption, rather than taking on specific roles as "citizens" or "hosts" or "guests." Such new relationships also problematize the role of "everyday" spaces. As Schouten points out in Chapter 2, the tourist industry has been basically concerned with selling dreams and escapism. But it is also evident that many people forsake the "dreams" offered by the tour operator to seek out exotic experiences in the everyday lives of others.

This is because the exotic, just like the "authentic," is in the eye of the observer. With creativity, the exotic can be manufactured from the mundane, and it is all too easy to reverse this process as well. Our ability to manufacture exoticism also problematizes the relationship between the distant and the exotic. Whereas Cohen (1979) postulated that the exotic should be found on the distant fringes of modern society, increasing ease of travel allows us to reach those places a lot more easily, and it allows some inhabitants of those places to travel to the tourist generating "center" as well. The communities that generate tourism are also becoming more and more diverse, and in consequence we know less and less about those in close proximity. At the same time a familiarization with the exotic is taking place through long-distance travel, the media, and the Internet. The exotic is no longer far away in geographical terms, but on our doorstep. In turn, the familiar greets us on the other side of the world in an air-conditioned hotel room, or fellow travelers from around the corner. This phenomenon is explored in a strip cartoon in *Ons Amsterdam,* a magazine about the history and culture of the Dutch city. In *A Tourist in His Own City* (van Driel and Blokker, 1997), an unemployed Amsterdammer decides to discover his native city, "with the inquisitiveness of a tourist, but with the knowledge and experience of a long-term resident." He dons a safari outfit, and begins "work" as a local tourist.

The introspective turn of tourism toward the local, the familiar, and the everyday is also a theme explored by Alain de Botton (2002) in *The Art of Travel.* The art of everyday tourism, it seems, is to view the everyday in new ways. The device employed by the protagonist of *A Tourist in His Own City* is to find new viewpoints from which he can gaze on the city. But the processes of globalization and localization are providing new conceptual viewpoints for tourists and locals all the time. By fragmenting and recombining spatial, cultural, and social structures, these processes provide us new platforms from which to survey the postmodern landscape of tourism. The new viewpoints also enable us to see links and connections that were previously less visible. For example, the "local" begins to see the newly emerging landscape of global tourism, not just in the local insertion of tourism spaces, but in the increasing diversity of the tourists themselves.

However, we should be cautious in fully accepting "postmodern" views of tourism. As Cohen (2004) points out, the voices of those who do not travel are often overlooked in the analysis of tourism. Staying at home may seem like an attractive option to those easily able to travel, because for them it is an option they can exercise. But for all those adopting new, flexible, and "postmodern" travel styles, there are even more people for whom "old-fashioned" modern modes of travel are attractive, enjoyable, and affordable. And Smith notes in Chapter 5, it is the elite who travel.

As Eduard Delgado (2001) rightly pointed out, it is not the physical space of cultural tourism that matters, so much as the interaction and human context of the space itself. Global culture is everywhere transformed by human action, and embedded in the local context. Local interaction and reflection can be utilized to creatively employ the raw materials of both global and local culture to make new cultural forms, sociabilities, and communities. These elements are at the heart of efforts to retain "placefulness" in tourism development (see Maitland, Chapter 6).

Such new cultural developments tend to become juxtaposed with existing cultural forms. As Schouten points out in Chapter 2, the feeling of loss that is usually associated with nostalgia not only signals the disappearance of the old, but it's usually triggered by the appearance of the new. Much of the "old" culture that we now lament was in fact created in the shock of the Industrial Revolution, in which placelessness was generated with as much vigor as it is today. However, human agency has over time turned the unfortunate new arrivals into much-desired means of attachment. In the United Kingdom, Victorian urban sprawl is lovingly restored and its emblems (such as iron lamp posts and railings) employed to provide "atmosphere" and sense of place in city centers. Similar trends are evident elsewhere; as Xerardo Pereiro Pérez points out in Chapter 10, communal ovens reminiscent of an older and poorer age are now being restored to attract tourists in Portugal.

The timescale of such nostalgia is also shortening, as the rise of township tourism in South Africa illustrates. As Pranill Ramchander shows in Chapter 3, township life may not be particularly attractive to those who have to live there, or to the tourists that visit, but there is a sense of rapidly passing history and looming nostalgia for cultural phenomena such as the shebeen. If Schouten is right, and a process of forgetting is what makes nostalgia possible, then contemporary attention spans must be falling as the supply of nostalgia grows.

A further point illustrated by the development of the shebeen is the widespread ability for endogenous culture to develop even under the most difficult circumstances. In some cases, the resilience of local culture will not only enable it to resist pressure to conform, but the process of suppression can also strengthen elements of local culture. External pressures may not only increase social and cultural cohesion, but also create a pent-up cultural energy that emerges once the source of pressure is removed. This is certainly evident in the emergence of the "Rainbow Nation" in South Africa (Chapter 4), but also in the case of regional and stateless cultures. The type of resurgence in local culture seen in Spain after the fall of Franco, for example, has been termed a process of "cultural isostasy" (Richards, 2004), implying the resurgence of culture following a long period of suppression. In such circumstances the cultural dynamism that emerges is often more vibrant than the original culture that people are seeking to re-create, leading to the reinvention and innovation of cultural forms.

As Patricia de Camargo shows in Chapter 12, cultural and heritage tourism can also be means for learning and exploring one's own environment, and hopefully awaken interest in other cultures, too. Research by ATLAS and the International Student Travel Confederation (Richards and Wilson, 2003) has underlined the importance of culture in the travel experiences of young people. Almost 80 percent of young travelers from eight different countries indicated that their appreciation and understanding of other cultures had increased as a result of their trip. Over half of the respondents also said that their understanding of their own culture had increased, indicating some degree of reflexivity about the relationship between host and guest cultures. These examples seem to give some grounds for a culturally optimistic approach to the future of cultural tourism.

However, what the evidence presented here also seems to indicate is that levels of optimism or pessimism depend heavily on the type of change we are analyzing. In many cases, the cultural pessimists look at changes in cultural products, bemoaning the loss of "authentic" culture, such as the Balinese carvings described by Schouten in Chapter 2. The cultural optimists, however, tend to look more often at process. Although the subject of carvings in Bali may have changed, the optimist can take heart in the fact that people are still using traditional techniques to produce them. The fact that changes in cultural products are usually more visible to the outside observer than cultural processes probably reinforces the trend toward cultural pessimism.

The perspectives presented in this volume underline the fact that the current field of cultural tourism is increasingly complex. Complexity is being added by the processes of globalization and localization, the rapidly changing cultural field, and the changes in the nature of tourism demand. It is for this reason that many of the contributions to this volume underline the need for new research perspectives and structures.

FUTURE RESEARCH DIRECTIONS

The ATLAS Cultural Tourism Research Group intends to take forward many of the new research initiatives suggested in this volume. Many potential lines of research have been discussed by the group, the most important of which are summarized in the following.

Spatial Implications

In the light of the impacts of "glocalization" on cultural tourism, there is a growing need to make links between the global and local, examining flows of people, culture, and finance across the different "scapes" utilized for cultural tourism. Some specific issues raised by group members included these:

- The spatial consequences of cultural tourism could be explored through the study of cultural quarters and "ethnoscapes."
- There is a need to pay more attention to the special circumstances prevailing in different areas of the world. In particular, there was a call to undertake specific research on cultural tourism in Africa, perhaps in conjunction with the ATLAS Africa group. Such studies could look at issues of globalization and localization, for example through the influence of former colonial links on current tourism patterns.

Understanding the Local

The "local" has always been privileged in narratives of authenticity. But as the debates in this volume have shown, what constitutes the local is still far from clear. This opens the way to a number of new areas of research:

- In the face of globalization, the local is remarkably persistent. Although cultural tourism is often accused of being a harbinger of modernization and the destruction of culture, homogenization still seems a long way off in most destinations. More attention needs to be paid to the structures and practices underpinning the local, and how these articulate with the tourist search for distinctiveness, difference, and novelty.
- The tourist perspective on cultural tourism, particularly in terms of allowing the tourists themselves to make their own interpretation of the meaning of their consumption.
- In what ways can cultural tourism add meaning to peoples' lives (both as "tourists" and "locals")?

Governance Issues

The complexity of cultural poses particular problems of governance, particularly in the relationships between the tourism and cultural sectors. What is the role of the private, the public sector, and the "third sector" in the future of cultural tourism?

There should be more attention paid to the planning systems within which cultural tourism functions (both from a cultural and a tourism perspective). The content/context dichotomy of the cultural tourism experience could be examined in terms of the embeddedness and institutional thickness of systems in different locations.

More evaluation of the outcomes of policy interventions is also needed. There is scope for the study of the qualitative and quantitative impacts of events and programs, such as the EU structural funds, in the field of cultural tourism.

The issue of the management of cultural tourism has been relatively under-researched in the past. More attention could be paid to the management of cultural tourism sites and the emerging networks of cultural tourism development and promotion, which join the public, private, and voluntary sectors.

More attention needs to be paid to the different categories of actors in the cultural tourism system—the tourists, residents, policymakers, suppliers, etc. At present we take the distinctions between these groups for granted, whereas these are often indistinct groups.

Research Methodologies

In the past, much research on cultural tourism has focused either on case studies or on quantitative surveys. There is therefore a need to create methodologies to link quantitative and qualitative data, as well as more qualitative observations of changes in the relationship between tourism, culture, and local communities, as suggested by Franquesa and Morell in Chapter 9.

Many of these areas of research will build on the previous research undertaken by the ATLAS Cultural Tourism Research Group, including the surveys undertaken in 2004 and 2006 (see Chapter 1). In the coming years we hope to be able to report further on the results of this initiative, as well as the research being undertaken by individual members of the network. Hopefully this work will contribute further to our understanding of cultural tourism at both local and global scales.

REFERENCES

Augé, M. (1995) *Non-Places: Introduction to an Anthropology of Supermodernity.* London: Verso.

Bennett, O. (2001) *Cultural Pessimism: Narratives of Decline in the Postmodern World.* Edinburgh: Edinburgh University Press.

Botton de, A. (2002) *The Art of Travel.* London: Hamish Hamilton.

Cohen, E. (1979) A Phenomenology of Touristic Experiences. *Sociology* 13: 179-200.

Cohen, E. (2004) Backpacking: Diversity and Change. In Richards, G. and Wilson, J. (eds.) *The Global Nomad: Backpacker Travel in Theory and Practice.* Clevedon: Channel View Publications, pp. 43-59.

Crawford, M. (1992) The World in a Shopping Mall. In Sorkin, M. (ed.), *Variations on a Theme Park.* New York: Hill and Way, pp. 3-30.

Delgado, E. (2001) L'art del turisme. In Belda, E. and Garcia, S. (eds.) *Turisme i Cultura.* Barcelona: Fundacio Interarts, pp. 101-108.

Driel, G. van and Blokker, B. (1997) Toerist in Eigen Stad. *Ons Amsterdam*, 49(5): 124-125.

Edensor, T. (1998) *Tourists at the Taj: Performance and Meaning at a Symbolic Site*. London: Routledge.

Richards, G. (1999) *Developing and Marketing Crafts Tourism*. Tilburg: ATLAS.

Richards, G. (2001) *Cultural Attractions and European Tourism*. Wallingford: CAB International.

Richards, G. (2004) Cultura popular, tradición y turismo en las festes de la Mercè de Barcelona. In Font, J. (ed.) *Casos de Turismo Cultural: De la planificación estratégica a la gestión del producto*. Barcelona: Ariel, pp. 287-306.

Richards, G. and Wilson, J. (2003) *Today's Youth Travelers: Tomorrow's Global Nomads?* Amsterdam: ISTC/ATLAS.

Turisme de Barcelona (2003) Tourism statistics 2003. www.barcelonaturisme.com. Visited June 29, 2004.

Index

THE HAWORTH HOSPITALITY PRESS®
Hospitality, Travel, and Tourism
K. S. Chon, PhD, Editor in Chief

THAILAND TOURISM by Arthur Asa Berger. (2007).

CULTURAL TOURISM: GLOBAL AND LOCAL PERSPECTIVES edited by Greg Richards. (2007). "An excellent collection of material that builds upon the editor's previous studies in the field as well as the work of ATLAS. Not only does the book reflect extremely well on the high quality of work that comes out of the ATLAS network on cultural tourism, but the work further reinforces Greg Richards' profile as a leader in the cultural tourism field." *C. Michael Hall, BA (Hons), MA, PhD, Professor, Department of Tourism, University of Otago*

GAY TOURISM: CULTURE AND CONTEXT by Gordon Waitt and Kevin Markwell. (2006). "This book provides an international overview of gay destinations and spaces. It addresses issues of how the tourism industry, in its search for the 'pink dollar,' yet again seeks to commodify and normalize experiences within commercial settings, and thus creates stereotypes that are not wholly satisfying for gay men. The authors are not afraid to court controversy by addressing gay issues in Islamic societies. In short, there is much in this book for tourism researchers unfamiliar with the social context of gay tourism. Such readers will emerge both better informed and with further questions to prompt their own thinking." *Chris Ryan, PhD, Professor of Tourism, University of Waikato Management School, New Zealand*

CASES IN SUSTAINABLE TOURISM: AN EXPERIENTIAL APPROACH TO MAKING DECISIONS edited by Irene M. Herremans. (2006). "As a tourism instructor and researcher, I recommend this textbook for both undergraduate and graduate students who wish to pursue their careers in parks, recreation, or tourism. The text is appropriate both for junior and senior tourism management classes and graduate classes. It is an excellent primer for understanding the fundamental concepts, issues, and real-world examples of sustainable tourism." *Hwan-Suk Chris Choi, PhD, Assistant Professor, School of Hospitality and Tourism Management, University of Guelph*

COMMUNITY DESTINATION MANAGEMENT IN DEVELOPING ECONOMIES edited by Walter Jamieson. (2006). "This book is a welcome and valuable addition to the destination management literature, focusing as it does on developing economies in the Asian context. It provides an unusually comprehensive and informative overview of critical issues in the field, effectively combining well-crafted discussions of key conceptual and methodological issues with carefully selected and well-presented case studies drawn from a number of contrasting Asian destinations." *Peter Hills, PhD, Professor and Director, The Centre of Urban Planning and Environmental Management, The University of Hong Kong*

MANAGING SUSTAINABLE TOURISM: A LEGACY FOR THE FUTURE by David L. Edgell Sr. (2006). "This comprehensive book on sustainable tourism should be required reading for everyone interested in tourism. The author is masterful in defining strategies and using case studies to explain best practices in generating long-term economic return on your tourism investment." *Kurtis M. Ruf, Partner, Ruf Strategic Solutions; Author,* Contemporary Database Marketing

CASINO INDUSTRY IN ASIA PACIFIC: DEVELOPMENT, OPERATION, AND IMPACT edited by Cathy H.C. Hsu. (2006). "This book is a must-read for anyone interested in the opportunities and challenges that the proliferation of casino gaming will bring to Asia in the early twenty-first century. The economic and social consequences of casino gaming in Asia may ultimately prove to be far more significant than those encountered in the West, and this book opens the door as to what those consequences might be." *William R. Eadington, PhD, Professor of Economics and Director, Institute for the Study of Gambling and Commercial Gaming, University of Nevada, Reno*

THE GROWTH STRATEGIES OF HOTEL CHAINS: BEST BUSINESS PRACTICES BY LEADING COMPANIES by Onofre Martorell Cunill. (2006). "Informative, well-written, and up-to-date. This is one title that I shall certainly be adding to my 'must-read' list for students this year." *Tom Baum, PhD, Professor of International Tourism and Hospitality Management, The Scottish Hotel School, The University of Strathclyde, Glasgow*

HANDBOOK FOR DISTANCE LEARNING IN TOURISM by Gary Williams. (2005). "This is an important book for a variety of audiences. As a resource for educational designers (and their managers) in particular, it is invaluable. The book is easy to read, and is full of practical information that can be logically applied in the design and development of flexible learning resources." *Louise Berg, MA, DipED, Lecturer in Education, Charles Sturt University, Australia*

VIETNAM TOURISM by Arthur Asa Berger. (2005). "Fresh and innovative.... Drawing upon Professor Berger's background and experience in cultural studies, this book offers an imaginative and personal portrayal of Vietnam as a tourism destination.... A very welcome addition to the field of destination studies." *Professor Brian King, PhD, Head, School of Hospitality, Tourism & Marketing, Victoria University, Australia*

TOURISM AND HOTEL DEVELOPMENT IN CHINA: FROM POLITICAL TO ECONOMIC SUCCESS by Hanqin Qiu Zhang, Ray Pine, and Terry Lam. (2005). "This is one of the most comprehensive books on China tourism and hotel development. It is one of the best textbooks for educators, students, practitioners, and investors who are interested in China tourism and hotel industry. Readers will experience vast, diversified, and past and current issues that affect every educator, student, practitioner, and investor in China tourism and hotel globally in an instant." *Hailin Qu, PhD, Full Professor and William E. Davis Distinguished Chair, School of Hotel & Restaurant Administration, Oklahoma State University*

THE TOURISM AND LEISURE INDUSTRY: SHAPING THE FUTURE edited by Klaus Weiermair and Christine Mathies. (2004). "If you need or want to know about the impact of globalization, the impact of technology, societal forces of change, the experience economy, adaptive technologies, environmental changes, or the new trend of slow tourism, you need this book. *The Tourism and Leisure Industry* contains a great mix of research and practical information." *Charles R. Goeldner, PhD, Professor Emeritus of Marketing and Tourism, Leeds School of Business, University of Colorado*

OCEAN TRAVEL AND CRUISING: A CULTURAL ANALYSIS by Arthur Asa Berger. (2004). "Dr. Berger presents an interdisciplinary discussion of the cruise industry for the thinking person. This is an enjoyable social psychology travel guide with a little business management thrown in. A great book for the curious to read a week before embarking on a first cruise or for the frequent cruiser to gain a broader insight into exactly what a cruise experience represents." *Carl Braunlich, DBA, Associate Professor, Department of Hospitality and Tourism Management, Purdue University, West Lafayette, Indiana*

STANDING THE HEAT: ENSURING CURRICULUM QUALITY IN CULINARY ARTS AND GASTRONOMY by Joseph A. Hegarty. (2003). "This text provides the genesis of a well-researched, thoughtful, rigorous, and sound theoretical framework for the enlargement and expansion of higher education programs in culinary arts and gastronomy." *John M. Antun, PhD, Founding Director, National Restaurant Institute, School of Hotel, Restaurant, and Tourism Management, University of South Carolina*

SEX AND TOURISM: JOURNEYS OF ROMANCE, LOVE, AND LUST edited by Thomas G. Bauer and Bob McKercher. (2003). "Anyone interested in or concerned about the impact of tourism on society and particularly in the developing world, should read this book. It explores a subject that has long remained ignored, almost a taboo area for many governments, institutions, and organizations. It demonstrates that the stereotyping of 'sex tourism' is too simple and travel and sex have many manifestations. The book follows its theme in an innovative and original way." *Carson L. Jenkins, PhD, Professor of International Tourism, University of Strathclyde, Glasgow, Scotland*

CONVENTION TOURISM: INTERNATIONAL RESEARCH AND INDUSTRY PERSPECTIVES edited by Karin Weber and Kye-Sung Chon. (2002). "This comprehensive book is truly global in its perspective. The text points out areas of needed research—a great starting point for graduate students, university faculty, and industry professionals alike. While the focus is mainly academic, there is a lot of meat for this burgeoning industry to chew on as well." *Patti J. Shock, CPCE, Professor and Department Chair, Tourism and Convention Administration, Harrah College of Hotel Administration, University of Nevada–Las Vegas*

CULTURAL TOURISM: THE PARTNERSHIP BETWEEN TOURISM AND CULTURAL HERITAGE MANAGEMENT by Bob McKercher and Hilary du Cros. (2002). "The book brings together concepts, perspectives, and practicalities that must be understood by both cultural heritage and tourism managers, and as such is a must-read for both." *Hisashi B. Sugaya, AICP, Former Chair, International Council of Monuments and Sites, International Scientific Committee on Cultural Tourism; Former Executive Director, Pacific Asia Travel Association Foundation, San Francisco, CA*

TOURISM IN THE ANTARCTIC: OPPORTUNITIES, CONSTRAINTS, AND FUTURE PROSPECTS by Thomas G. Bauer. (2001). "Thomas Bauer presents a wealth of detailed information on the challenges and opportunities facing tourism operators in this last great tourism frontier." *David Mercer, PhD, Associate Professor, School of Geography & Environmental Science, Monash University, Melbourne, Australia*

SERVICE QUALITY MANAGEMENT IN HOSPITALITY, TOURISM, AND LEISURE edited by Jay Kandampully, Connie Mok, and Beverley Sparks. (2001). "A must-read.... a treasure. . . . pulls together the work of scholars across the globe, giving you access to new ideas, international research, and industry examples from around the world." *John Bowen, Professor and Director of Graduate Studies, William F. Harrah College of Hotel Administration, University of Nevada, Las Vegas*

TOURISM IN SOUTHEAST ASIA: A NEW DIRECTION edited by K. S. (Kaye) Chon. (2000). "Presents a wide array of very topical discussions on the specific challenges facing the tourism industry in Southeast Asia. A great resource for both scholars and practitioners." *Dr. Hubert B. Van Hoof, Assistant Dean/Associate Professor, School of Hotel and Restaurant Management, Northern Arizona University*

THE PRACTICE OF GRADUATE RESEARCH IN HOSPITALITY AND TOURISM edited by K. S. Chon. (1999). "An excellent reference source for students pursuing graduate degrees in hospitality and tourism." *Connie Mok, PhD, CHE, Associate Professor, Conrad N. Hilton College of Hotel and Restaurant Management, University of Houston, Texas*

THE INTERNATIONAL HOSPITALITY MANAGEMENT BUSINESS: MANAGEMENT AND OPERATIONS by Larry Yu. (1999). "The abundant real-world examples and cases provided in the text enable readers to understand the most up-to-date developments in international hospitality business." *Zheng Gu, PhD, Associate Professor, College of Hotel Administration, University of Nevada, Las Vegas*

CONSUMER BEHAVIOR IN TRAVEL AND TOURISM by Abraham Pizam and Yoel Mansfeld. (1999). "A must for anyone who wants to take advantage of new global opportunities in this growing industry." *Bonnie J. Knutson, PhD, School of Hospitality Business, Michigan State University*

LEGALIZED CASINO GAMING IN THE UNITED STATES: THE ECONOMIC AND SOCIAL IMPACT edited by Cathy H. C. Hsu. (1999). "Brings a fresh new look at one of the areas in tourism that has not yet received careful and serious consideration in the past." *Muzaffer Uysal, PhD, Professor of Tourism Research, Virginia Polytechnic Institute and State University, Blacksburg*

HOSPITALITY MANAGEMENT EDUCATION edited by Clayton W. Barrows and Robert H. Bosselman. (1999). "Takes the mystery out of how hospitality management education programs function and serves as an excellent resource for individuals interested in pursuing the field." *Joe Perdue, CCM, CHE, Director, Executive Masters Program, College of Hotel Administration, University of Nevada, Las Vegas*

MARKETING YOUR CITY, U.S.A.: A GUIDE TO DEVELOPING A STRATEGIC TOURISM MARKETING PLAN by Ronald A. Nykiel and Elizabeth Jascolt. (1998). "An excellent guide for anyone involved in the planning and marketing of cities and regions. . . . A terrific job of synthesizing an otherwise complex procedure." *James C. Maken, PhD, Associate Professor, Babcock Graduate School of Management, Wake Forest University, Winston-Salem, North Carolina*

Order a copy of this book with this form or online at:
http://www.haworthpress.com/store/product.asp?sku=5749

CULTURAL TOURISM
Global and Local Perspectives

_____in hardbound at $69.95 (ISBN-13: 978-0-7890-3116-7; ISBN-10: 0-7890-3116-7)

_____in softbound at $34.95 (ISBN-13: 978-0-7890-3117-4; ISBN-10: 0-7890-3117-5)

340 pages plus index • Includes illustrations

Or order online and use special offer code HEC25 in the shopping cart.

COST OF BOOKS_____

POSTAGE & HANDLING_____
*(US: $4.00 for first book & $1.50
for each additional book)*
*(Outside US: $5.00 for first book
& $2.00 for each additional book)*

SUBTOTAL_____

IN CANADA: ADD 6% GST_____

STATE TAX_____
*(NJ, NY, OH, MN, CA, IL, IN, PA, & SD
residents, add appropriate local sales tax)*

FINAL TOTAL_____
*(If paying in Canadian funds,
convert using the current
exchange rate, UNESCO
coupons welcome)*

☐ **BILL ME LATER:** (Bill-me option is good on
US/Canada/Mexico orders only; not good to
jobbers, wholesalers, or subscription agencies.)

☐ Check here if billing address is different from
shipping address and attach purchase order and
billing address information.

Signature_____

☐ **PAYMENT ENCLOSED: $**_____

☐ **PLEASE CHARGE TO MY CREDIT CARD.**

☐ Visa ☐ MasterCard ☐ AmEx ☐ Discover
☐ Diner's Club ☐ Eurocard ☐ JCB

Account # _____

Exp. Date_____

Signature_____

Prices in US dollars and subject to change without notice.

NAME_____

INSTITUTION_____

ADDRESS_____

CITY_____

STATE/ZIP_____

COUNTRY_____ COUNTY (NY residents only)_____

TEL_____ FAX_____

E-MAIL_____

May we use your e-mail address for confirmations and other types of information? ☐ Yes ☐ No
We appreciate receiving your e-mail address and fax number. Haworth would like to e-mail or fax special
discount offers to you, as a preferred customer. **We will never share, rent, or exchange your e-mail address
or fax number.** We regard such actions as an invasion of your privacy.

Order From Your Local Bookstore or Directly From
The Haworth Press, Inc.

10 Alice Street, Binghamton, New York 13904-1580 • USA
TELEPHONE: 1-800-HAWORTH (1-800-429-6784) / Outside US/Canada: (607) 722-5857
FAX: 1-800-895-0582 / Outside US/Canada: (607) 771-0012
E-mail to: orders@haworthpress.com

For orders outside US and Canada, you may wish to order through your local
sales representative, distributor, or bookseller.
For information, see http://haworthpress.com/distributors

(Discounts are available for individual orders in US and Canada only, not booksellers/distributors.)

PLEASE PHOTOCOPY THIS FORM FOR YOUR PERSONAL USE.
http://www.HaworthPress.com   BOF06